# Lecture Notes in Computer Science 9555

Commenced Publication in 1973
Founding and Former Series Editors:
Gerhard Goos, Juris Hartmanis, and Jan van Leeuwen

More information about this series at http://www.springer.com/series/7412

Fay Huang · Akihiro Sugimoto (Eds.)

# Image and Video Technology – PSIVT 2015 Workshops

RV 2015, GPID 2013, VG 2015,
EO4AS 2015, MCBMIIA 2015, and VSWS 2015
Auckland, New Zealand, November 23–27, 2015
Revised Selected Papers

 Springer

*Editors*
Fay Huang
National Ilan University
Yi-Lan
Taiwan

Akihiro Sugimoto
National Institute of Informatics
Tokyo
Japan

ISSN 0302-9743         ISSN 1611-3349   (electronic)
Lecture Notes in Computer Science
ISBN 978-3-319-30284-3         ISBN 978-3-319-30285-0   (eBook)
DOI 10.1007/978-3-319-30285-0

Library of Congress Control Number: 2016931432

LNCS Sublibrary: SL6 – Image Processing, Computer Vision, Pattern Recognition, and Graphics

Printed on acid-free paper

This Springer imprint is published by SpringerNature
The registered company is Springer International Publishing AG Switzerland

# Preface

The 7th Pacific-Rim Symposium on Image and Video Technology (PSIVT 2015), held in Auckland, New Zealand, during November 23–27, 2015, was accompanied by a series of six high-quality workshops covering the full range of state-of-the-art research topics in image and video technology.

The workshops consisted of one full-day workshop and five half-day workshops and took place on November 23 and 24. Their topics diversely ranged from well-established areas to novel current trends: robot vision (RV 2015); 2D and 3D geometric properties from incomplete data (GPID 2015); vision meets graphics (VG 2015); passive and active electro-optical sensors for aerial and space imaging (EO4AS 2015); mathematical and computational methods in biomedical imaging and image analysis (MCBMIIA 2015); and video surveillance (VSWS 2015). Some of the workshops were a continuation of previous issues that were held in conjunction with PSIVT 2013 while some were newly organized. This means that PSIVTs have provided good opportunities for fostering research areas related to image and video technology.

The PSIVT 2015 workshop proceedings comprise a short introduction to each workshop and all workshop contributions were arranged by each of the workshop organizers. In total, 58 paper submissions were received (including dual submissions with the main conference) and sent out for double-blind peer review. Eventually, 29 presentations were selected by the individual workshop committee based on at least three reviews per submission, yielding an overall acceptance rate of 50 %. We thank everyone involved in the remarkable program – committees, reviewers, and authors – for their distinguished contributions.

We hope that you will enjoy reading these contributions, which may inspire your research.

November 2015

Fay Huang
Akihiro Sugimoto

# Workshop on 2D and 3D Geometric Properties from Incomplete Data (GPID 2015)

This workshop is organized under The 7th Pacific Rim Symposium on Video and Image Technology (PSIVT'15) held in Auckland in New Zealand in November 2015. It is a continuation of the previous PSIVT'13 workshop in Guanajuato in Mexico and chaired by R. Kozera, L. Noakes and A. Orłowski which in turn was a follow-up of the Workshop on Geometric Properties from Incomplete Data held in Schloss Dagstuhl, in Germany dated 2004 (chaired by R. Klette, R. Kozera, L. Noakes and J. Weickert).

Computer vision, image analysis and object identification involves different disciplines like mathematics, computer science, physics, biology, medicine and engineering. This workshop is designed to exercise such multidisciplinary nature of image and video analysis in the context of extracting geometrical properties and performing satisfactory classification of the observed objects coming from variety of sources like digital and biomedical images, biometrics, scanned paper documents (geodetic maps, paginated music notation, rigid body motion) as well as another 1D, 2D and 3D data. For such variety of data, different techniques for image segmentation (e.g. with interpolation or approximation), feature recognition, classification and geometrical analysis, numerical computation are of fundamental importance in a wide range of applications. Such fundamental areas in computer science dealing with different aspects of observations and measurements involve theoretical and practical aspects of objects identification and verification. High accuracy measurements of geometrical properties like trajectory and shape recovery, human gait and motion restoration, image processing and biometrics and other missing information are vital to the analysis of the hidden structure not fully transparent from various noisy or noiseless, often incomplete or ambiguous data. Symbolic aspects of computation involved are considered at different levels of generality of syntactic and semantic data structuring integrated within the framework of granular computing paradigm.

The research contribution is received from 12 countries. Each paper was peer-reviewed by three independent members of the Program Committee listed below.

We would like to thank all authors for their contribution, the Program Committee Members for the paper evaluation and most of all the PSIVT'15 Conference and Workshops Organizers for their constant support and help.

October 2015

Ryszard Kozera
Władysław Homenda
Lyle Noakes
Arkadiusz Orłowski
Khalid Saeed

# Organization

## Workshop Organizers

Ryszard Kozera (chair)    Warsaw University of Life Sciences - SGGW, Poland
Władysław Homenda    Warsaw University of Technology, Poland
Lyle Noakes    The University of Western Australia, Australia
Arkadiusz Orłowski    Warsaw University of Life Sciences - SGGW, Poland
Khalid Saeed    Białystok University of Technology, Poland

## Program Committee

Li Chen    University of the District of Columbia
Leszek Chmielewski    Warsaw University of Life Sciences - SGGW, Poland
Fay Huang    National Ilan University, Taiwan
Agnieszka Jastrzębska    Warsaw University of Technology, Poland
Jean-Luc Mari Felicja    University of Marseille
Okulicka–Dłużewska    Warsaw University of Technology, Poland
Andrzej Polański    Silesian University of Technology, Poland
Agnieszka Szczęsna    Silesian University of Technology, Poland
Andrzej Śluzek    Khalifa University of Science Technology
    and Research, The United Arabs Emirates

Konrad Wojciechowski    Silesian University of Technology, Poland
Simone Zappala    University of Vienna

# Workshop on Vision Meets Graphics (VG 2015)

These contributions were presented at the First Workshop on Vision meets Graphics (VG2015) in conjunction with the 7th Pacific Rim Symposium on Video and Image Technology (PSIVT 2015), held in Auckland, New Zealand on November 23rd, 2015.

Recent years have seen the convergence of computer graphics and computer vision. Image processing and computer vision techniques provide computer graphics with the means to create richer models and renderings than is practically possible when using purely synthetic models. Conversely, computer graphics can inform computer vision. For example, physical based models can act as priors to computer vision algorithms. We believe graphics and vision can be mutually beneficial. Computer graphics/computer vision convergence has many possible applications, such as augmented environments, videoconferencing, post-production of films, computer games, interactive TV, education and training, video-based consumer electronics and scientific imaging.

VG2015 received 8 full-paper submissions which underwent a double-blind review, with 5 reviewers per paper. A total of 4 papers were selected for the workshop, and are collected in these proceedings.

We were fortunate to have two invited speakers at the workshop, who have worked extensively in the convergence area of computer graphics and computer vision: Mark Sagar (Laboratory for Animate Technologies, Auckland Bioengineering Institute, University of Auckland) whose talk was on "Autonomous Facial Animation using models of embodied cognition" and David Mould (Graphics, Imaging and Games Lab, School of Computer Science, Carleton University). whose talk was on "Detail Preservation and Enhancement in Image Stylization". We would like to thank the invited speakers as well as all the members of the Programme Committee for their help in organising and running this event.

October 2015

Paul L. Rosin
Taehyun Rhee

# Organization

## Workshop Organizers

Paul L. Rosin                 Cardiff University, UK
Taehyun Rhee                  Victoria University of Wellington, New Zealand

## Program Committee

Kyungim Baek                  University of Hawaii, USA
Pierre Bénard                 University of Bordeaux, France
Mark Billinghurst             University of Canterbury, New Zealand
Nathan Carr                   Adobe Research, USA
Jongmoo Choi                  University of Southern California, USA
Soo-Mi Choi                   Sejong University, South Korea
Martin Constable              Nanyang Technological University
Grace Chu                     University of Maryland, College Park, USA
Patrice Delmas                The University of Auckland, New Zealand
Zhigang Deng                  University of Houston, USA
Neil Dodgson                  University of Cambridge, UK
Peter Hall                    University of Bath, UK
Junho Kim                     Kookmin University, South Korea
Young J. Kim                  Ewha Womans University, South Korea
Jan Eric Kyprianidis          TU Berlin, Germany
Yukun Lai                     Cardiff University, UK
Zohar Levi                    New York University, USA
Anthony Santella             Sloan-Kettering Institute, USA
Yeongho Seol                  Weta Digital, New Zealand
Yi-Zhe Song                   Queen Mary University, UK
Tinghuai Wang                 Nokia Research Center, Finland
Burkhard Wuensche             Auckland University, New Zealand
Seung-Hyun Yoon               Dongguk University, South Korea
Mingtian Zhao                 University of California, Los Angeles, USA

# Workshop on Robot Vision (RV 2015)

The workshop on Robot Vision (RV) was held in conjunction with the 2015 Pacific Rim Symposium on Video and Image Technology (PSIVT 2015), which was held in Auckland, New Zealand. The workshop was held on 23rd November 2015 at the same location. The contributions presented at this workshop are included in this volume.

This workshop provided an ideal venue for researchers to focus on issues specific to robot vision. The importance of robot vision as a research area is increasingly steadily, because of the many intelligent robots that are entering into peoples' lifes. Furthermore, vdVision is an extremely powerful sense as evidenced by humans and their miraculous power of visual perception. This coupled with the fact that vision systems are passive, low-power, and nowadays affordable makes robot vision an ideal sensor for intelligent robots. But many challenges remain before this dream will become reality. For example, a robot vision system should be able to drive an autonomous car and recognize the world around, but in reality we are still far away from developing such capable vision systems and autonomous cars use LIDAR sensors instead. In addition, robot vision provides challenges different from other computer vision problems, such as fusing vision data with LIDAR data, coordination of vision and motion, vision for drones, and machine learning applied to robot vision.

RV 2015 received contributions from 7 countries, registering a total of 9 papers submitted, out of which 6 were accepted for publication in these proceedings and for oral presentation. Each paper received between three to five reviews from the members of our Program Committee members, all experts in the area of robot vision. The reviewers provided detailed reviews, which allowed the authors to improve their papers. I believe the resulting program did not only include state of the art in robot vision research, but also some exciting new ideas for further developments and applications. In addition, the program included guidelines for robot vision practice that were hard-learned through years of experience.

The review process was carried out by our Program Committee composed of experts in their respective theme. Each paper received three to five reviews.

I owe thanks to Prof. Loulin Huang from the Auckland University of Technology, who worked tirelessly as organizer and local chair. Many thanks to my co-organizers Prof. Chia-Yen Chen from National University of Kaohsiung, Taiwan, and Prof. Young-Rae Ryoo from Mokpo National University, South Korea.

I would like to thank all reviewers for their hard work in guranteeing the quality of the workshop program and its associated publications.

Lastly, I would like to thank all the authors who submitted their research to this workshop. I am sure they had stimulating and fun time at the workshop.

October 2015                                                                Jacky Baltes
                                                      On behalf of the workshop organizers

# Organization

## Workshop Organizers

Jacky Baltes          University of Manitoba, Canada
Chia-Yen Chen         National University of Kaohsiung, Taiwan, R.O.C.
Loulin Huang          (Local Chair) University of Auckland, New Zealand
Young-Rae Ryoo        Mokpo National University, South Korea

## Program Committee

John Anderson         University of Manitoba, Canada
Youngchul Bae         Chonnam National University, South Korea
Chris Iverach-Brereton   University of Manitoba, Canada
J.H. Jeng             I-Shou University, Taiwan
Li-Wei Kang           National Yunlin University of Science and Technology,
                        Taiwan
Jan Kruse             Auckland University of Technology, New Zealand
Meng Cheng Lau        Universiti Kerbangsaan Malaysia, Malaysia
Youngho Lee           MNU U-VR Lab., South Korea
Guo-Shiang Lin        Da-Yeh University, Taiwan, R.O.C.
Wei-Yang Lin          National Chung Cheng University, Taiwan
Soroush Sadeghnejad   Amirkabir University of Technology, Iran
Gourab Sen Gupta      Massey University, New Zealand
Martin Stommel        Auckland University of Technology, New Zealand
Yang Wang             University of Manitoba, Canada
Chia-Hung Yeh         National Sun Yat-sen University, Taiwan

# MCBMIIA 2015: Abstracts of Invited Talks

24 November, 2015, Auckland, New Zealand

with conjunction to
7th Pacific Rim Symposium on Image and Video Technology (PSIVT)
23–27 November, 2015, Auckland, New Zealand

The Radon transform is the mathematical foundation for image reconstruction from projections. Mathematics provides non-invasive methods to measure human body and accurate algorithms to construct slice images of human body. The Radon transform was originally introduced in integral geometry in 1917. Although the transform had initially no relationship to image analysis, the connection between the Radon transform and the Fourier transform allows now us to design accurate and stable algorithms for image reconstruction from projections. Mathematics has, as a result, played a key role diagnosis in modern medicine. The image registration and higher-level segmentation of volumetric and spatiotemporal images are indispensable techniques for pre-processing of computer-aided diagnosis. In early pattern recognition, deformable shape matching was introduced as a two-dimensional extension of the dynamic warping of signals to character recognition. Three-dimensional registration problems are efficiently solved on GPU using modern numerical methods. Recently, there are tremendous progress in image acquisition techniques in multiple scales and multiple modalities. The large amounts of these image data are beyond hand craft works by experts and technicians. The employment of computer vision techniques that interpret spatiotemporal information from correction of low-dimensional information is a key solution to deal with such data in biology. The cell biologists realise that supports by automatic image processing systems allow them to discover new phenomena in cells, understand functionalities in the cell and behaviour of living cells. These are extension of stereology to dynamic microscopic images and videos. To totally care human, methodologies on computer vision that allow scientists to continually interpret biological functionalities from cells to organs are desired. The aim of this workshop is to prepare a discussion forum for researchers in computer vision and in biomedical imaging and image analysis to exchange new ideas and problems and to open new application fields in both fields. The forum will derive a bridge on these gaps from the viewpoints of mathematical and computational aspects in computer vision.

# Organization

## General Chair

Hidekata Hontani      Nagoya Institute of Technology, Japan

## Workshop Organizers

| | |
|---|---|
| Michael Cree | University of Waikato, New Zealand |
| Krim Hamid | North Carolina State University, USA |
| Atsushi Imiya | IMIT Chiba University, Japan |

## Program Committee

| | |
|---|---|
| Andreas Aplers | TUM, Germany |
| David Coeurjolly | CNRS, France |
| Michel Couprie | ESIEE Paris, France |
| Aasa Feragen | University of Copenhagen, Denmark |
| Hamid Gholamhosseini | Auckland University of Technology, New Zealand |
| Chun-Rong Huang | National Chung Hsing University, Taiwan |
| Xiaoyi Jiang | University of Münster, Germany |
| Yukiko Kenmochi | CNRS, France |
| Antonio M. López | UAB, Spain |
| Yoshitaka Masutani | Hiroshima City University, Japan |
| Kensaku Mori | Nagoya University, Japan |
| Yoshito Otake | Nara Institute of Science and Technology, Japan |
| Xue-Cheng Tai | University of Bergen, Norway |
| João Manuel R.S. Tavares | FEUP and INEGI, Portugal |
| Seiichi Uchida | Kyushu University, Japan |
| Martin Welk | UMIT, Austria |
| Burkhard Wuensche | University of Auckland, New Zealand |
| Otmar Scherzer | University of Vienna, Austria |
| Nataša Sladoje | University of Novi Sad, Serbia |

# Melanoma Image Processing and Analysis for Decision Support Systems

Hamid Gholamhosseini

School of Engineering, Auckland University of Technology
Private Bag 92006, Auckland 1142, New Zealand

Melanoma is the most aggressive form of skin cancer which is responsible for the majority of skin cancer related deaths. Image processing and analysis of melanoma images can result in (better) detection and early diagnosis and therefore reducing the mortality rate. Efficient pre-processing, image enhancement, segmentation, feature extraction and classification techniques have been developed to improve the performance of Computer Aided Diagnosis (CAD) of melanoma images. Border detection of lesions in melanoma images is important in improving the accuracy of CAD systems in detecting melanoma. We have developed a semi-automated algorithm to discriminate the foreground lesion from skin background by clicking on a small subset of the lesion. Implementing the image processing and analysis algorithms for CAD and decision support systems is computationally demanding. However, due to high inherent parallelism of such algorithms, systems with parallel processors could be useful for accelerating but they are energy intensive and costly. Special reconfigurable hardware such as Field-Programmable Gate Arrays (FPGAs) with powerful parallel processing feature can be used for achieving necessary performance of embedded systems with efficient utilization of hardware resources. In order to achieve acceleration of the image processing and analysis algorithms, we implement the most compute-intensive algorithms of the CAD and decision support systems onto FPGA for deploying as an embedded device. A hardware/software co-design approach was proposed for implementing Support Vector Machine (SVM) classifier for classifying melanoma images online. The hybrid Zynq platform was used for implementing the proposed classifier using High Level Synthesis design methodology. The implemented SVM classification system on Zynq demonstrated high performance with low resource utilization and power consumption, meeting several embedded systems constraints. Overall, the hardware implementation on FPGA could be extended in the future for other computationally demanding parts in the process, aiming to reach an efficient real-time decision support system for enhancing early detection of melanoma with high performance and low cost.

**Keywords**: Lesion segmentation • SVM • Melanoma • FPGA • Hardware implementation

# Segmentation of Organs with Atypical Shapes and/or Large Pathological Lesions from Medical Volumes

Akinobu Shimiz

Institute of Engineering, Tokyo University of Agriculture and Technology
2-24-16 Naka-cho, Koganei-shi, Tokyo, Japan 184-8588
simiz@cc.tuat.ac.jp

This study focuses on automated segmentation algorithms for an organ with an atypical shape and/or large pathological lesions. First, a sparse modeling based approach with lesion basis is presented for an organ with an atypical shape and large pathological lesions in a computed tomography (CT) volume. Second, a relaxed conditional statistical shape model (SSM) is presented to manage errors in conditions that involve an irregular shape of an organ and/or lesions. A sequentially graph cuts based segmentation algorithm with the relaxed conditional SSM is presented to show the effectiveness of such an SSM in segmentation. Third, algorithms for developing the SSMs and segmentation algorithms for postmortem imaging, in which the CT values and shapes of organs were significantly changed due to postmortem changes, are presented. Finally, future directions for segmentation in medical imaging will be presented with recent progresses of our research group, which include multi-shape graph cuts and fusion between an SSM and graph cuts.

**Keywords**: Segmentation • CT volume • Atypical shape • Pathological lesion • Postmortem imaging • Statistical shape model • Graph cuts

## References

1. Umetsu, S., Shimizu, A., Watanabe, H., Kobatake, H., Nawano, S.: An automated segmentation algorithm for CT volumes of livers with atypical shapes and large pathological lesions. IEICE Trans. Inf. Syst. **97**(4), 951–963 (2014)
2. Tomoshige, S., Oost, E., Shimizu, A., Watanabe, H., Nawano, S.: A conditional statistical shape model with integrated error estimation of the conditions; application to liver segmentation in non-contrast CT images. Med. Image Anal. **18**(1), 130–143 (2014)
3. Saito, A., Shimizu, A., Watanabe, H., Yamamoto, S., Nawano, S., Kobatake, H.: Statistical shape model of a liver for autopsy imaging. Int. J. Comput. Assist. Radiol. Surg. **9**(2), 269–281 (2014)
4. Nakagomi, K., Shimizu, A., Kobatake, H., Yakami, M., Fujimoto, K., Togashi, K.: Multi-shape graph cuts with neighbor prior constraints and its application to lung segmentation from a chest CT volume. Med. Image Anal. **17**(1), 62–77 (2013)
5. Patent Cooperation Treaty: PCT/JP2015/073277, Japanese patent application 2014-169911
6. http://www.tuat.ac.jp/∼simizlab/

# Higher-Order Graph Cuts and Medical Image Segmentation

Hiroshi Ishikawa

Department of Computer Science and Engineering, Waseda University
JST CREST Tokyo, Japan

Energy minimization is regularly used for medical image segmentation. Higher-order energies are perhaps not as common, but are nevertheless being used increasingly often. Whereas the common first- order (pairwise) potential can directly model only the relationship between pairs of pixels, the higher-order potential can model more complex and useful relationships between more than two variables. For instance, sets of pixels, chosen according to the shape to be segmented, can be encouraged to be entirely in one segment or the other by higher-order terms. In this talk, I will describe methods for minimizing higher-order energies using graph cuts as well as some real-world examples of their applications in medical image segmentation that have been deployed in commercial medical imaging software.

**Keywords**: Higher-order energy • Segmentation • Graph cuts • Markov random fields • MRF • Graphical model

## References

1. Ishikawa, H.: Transformation of general binary MRF minimization to the first order case. IEEE Trans. Pattern Anal. Mach. Intell. **33**(6), 1234–1249 (2011)
2. Kitamura, Y., Li, Y., Ito, W., Ishikawa, H.: Coronary lumen and plaque segmentation from CTA using higher-order shape prior. In: Golland, P., Hata, N., Barillot, C., Hornegger, J., Howe, R. (eds.) MICCAI 2014. LNCS, vol. 8673, pp. 339–347. Springer, Heidelberg (2014)
3. Kitamura, Y., Li, Y., Ito, W., Ishikawa, H.: Data-dependent higher-order clique selection for artery-vein segmentation by energy minimization. Int. J. Comput. Vision, in press (2015). doi: 10.1007/s11263-015-0856-3
4. Kohli, P., Ladický, L., Torr, P.H.S.: Robust higher order potentials for enforcing label consistency. Int. J. Comput. Vision **82**, 302–324 (2009)

This work was supported in part by JSPS Grant-in-Aid for Scientific Research on Innovative Areas (Multidisciplinary Computational Anatomy) JSPS KAKENHI Grant Number 26108003.

# Realistic 3D Cell Modelling for FEM Simulation

John Rugis

University of Auckland, Auckland, New Zealand
j.rugis@auckland.ac.nz
http://www.cs.auckland.ac.nz/~john-rugis/

We describe the latest results from an interdisciplinary project that encompasses a range of activities targeting anatomical data based structural modelling of individual salivary cell clusters, solution of cellular calcium dynamics function in full 3D simulations and interactive visualization of resultant calcium waves. Real biological samples were digitized using fluorescent markers and confocal microscopy. A set of image slices was used as the basis for a full 3D graphics model reconstruction of one cluster of cells. This anatomically correct model was used in turn as the basis for the creation of a 3D tetrahedral mesh suitable for finite element simulations. The same underlying 3D graphics mesh was used in the animated visualization of the calcium concentration simulation time series results. This work was conducted in collaboration with James Sneyd and Shawn Means from the Department of Mathematics at the University of Auckland and with David Yule from the School of Medicine and Dentistry at the University of Rochester.

**Acknowledgements.** This workshop was supported by the "Multidisciplinary Computational Anatomy and Its Application to Highly Intelligent Diagnosis and Therapy" projects funded by a Grant-in-Aid for Scientific Research on Innovative Areas from MEXT, Japan, Nagoya Institute of Technology, Japan and Institute of Management and Information Technologies, Chiba University, Japan.

# Passive and Active Electro-Optical Sensors for Aerial and Space Imaging (EO4AS 2015)

This volume presents the paper of the Workshop on Passive and Active Electro-Optical Sensors for Aerial & Space Imaging (EO4AS). These contributions were presented in conjunction with the 7th Pacific Rim Symposium on Video and Image Technology (PSIVT 2015), held in Auckland, New Zealand, on November 24th, 2015 and is supported by International Society of Photogrammetry and Remote Sensing (ISPRS) and Deutsche Gesellschaft für Photogrammetrie, Fernerkundung und Geoinformation (DGPF). Each paper was assigned to three independent referees and carefully revised.

The topics of the workshop covered new and improved methods, techniques, and applications of (electro-optical) sensors on airborne and space-born platforms.

Over the last half century there is a drastic development in air and space-borne platforms and active/passive electro-optical sensor. New optical sensors for observations of the Earth surface, oceans and the atmosphere provide a wide range of solutions for various applications. The aim is the acquisition of information about objects, structures, or phenomenon on the earth.

The huge amount of data, provided by these sensors, represents a new challenge regarding developments of processing, storage and evaluation techniques.

The aim of this workshop was to bring together engineers and scientists from academia, industry and government to exchange results and ideas for future applications of electro-optical remote sensing.

We would like to thank our authors for their efforts in their publications. We would like to thank the program committee members for providing very useful and detailed comments. We are also thankful to the sponsors: Humboldt-Innovation and Berlin Space Technology. In addition, we thank the work of local organizers PSIVT 2015 for their support.

November 2015

Ralf Reulke
John Robertson

# Organization

## Workshop Organizer

Ralf Reulke      Humboldt-Universität zu Berlin, Germany

## Local Chair

John Robertson      Auckland University of Technology, Auckland, New Zealand

## Program Committee

| | |
|---|---|
| Andreas Brunn | Black Bridge AG, Germany |
| Byron, Smiley | Skybox, USA |
| Clive Fraser | University of Melbourne, Australia |
| Uwe Knauer | Fraunhofer IFF, Germany |
| Stephan Nebiker | FHNW Muttenz, Switzerland |
| Peter Reinartz | DLR, Oberpfaffenhofen, Germany |
| Tom Segert | Berlin Space Technology, Berlin, Germany |
| Mark R. Shortis | RMIT Melbourne, Australia |

# PSIVT15 Workshop on Video Surveillance (VSWS 2015)

These contributions have been presented at the First Workshop on Video Surveillance (VSWS2015), held in conjunction with the 7th Pacific Rim Symposium on Video and Image Technology (PSIVT 2015), in Auckland, New Zealand, on November 24, 2015.

Surveillance can function both as a deterrent to help prevent crime as well as an investigative tool to aid us in identifying the actors and causes of incidents. Surveillance systems record multi-modal evidence and help carry out intelligent analytics to obtain a multi-perspective understanding. It can also alert security staff about security breaches, potentially dangerous events and hazardous situations. These security related events are captured in the content of surveillance video as low-level semantic signals, which bridges the gap between the physical world and the semantic cyberspace. If a picture is worth more than a thousand words, an event is perhaps worth thousands of pictures. Thus, the multi-modal surveillance content can convey invaluable security-related information. Without proper automated means of analyzing this information, it is extremely hard to manually process this big surveillance data for detecting events of interest.

VSWS2015 sought high-quality papers, which utilize the knowledge from computer vision, machine learning, pattern recognition, image and video mining, and artificial intelligence to deal with events in surveillance. We are indeed pleased that VSWS2015 received contributions from 5 countries, registering a total of 12 papers submitted, out of which 6 were accepted for publication in these proceedings and for oral presentation. The rigorous review process was diligently carried out by our Program Committee composed of experts in their respective theme. Each paper was peer-reviewed by three reviewers.

This workshop would never have been such a success without the efforts of many people. We are especially indebted to our authors for putting their efforts into their papers. We would like to thank the Program Committee members, who generously spent their precious time in providing quite useful and detailed comments, offering authors an excellent opportunity to improve their work presented in this workshop and their future research. Additionally, we appreciate the tremendous work done by the local organizers of PSIVT2015 for their support.

We hope you will find this collection of high quality research works very useful and interesting.

November 2015

Wei Qi Yan
Pradeep K. Atrey
Mohan S. Kankanhalli

# Organization

## Workshop Organizers

Wei Qi Yan              Auckland University of Technology, New Zealand
Pradeep K. Atrey        State University of New York at Albany, USA
Mohan S. Kankanhalli    National University of Singapore, Singapore

## Program Committee

Pradeep K. Atrey        State University of New York at Albany, USA
Boris Bačić             Auckland University of Technology, New Zealand
Feng Liu                Chinese Academy of Sciences, China
Manoranjan Paul         Charles Sturt University, Australia
Xin-Wen Wu              Griffith University, Australia
Wei Qi Yan              Auckland University of Technology, New Zealand
Xinguo Yu               Central China Normal University, China
Yong Zhao               Shenzhen Graduate School, Peking University, China

# Contents

**Robot Vision (RV 2015)**

**Mathematical and Computational Methods in Biomedical Imaging
and Image Analysis (MCBMIIA 2015)**

## Passive and Active Electro-Optical Sensors for Aerial and Space Imaging (EO4AS 2015)

## Video Surveillance (VSWS 2015)

# 2D and 3D Geometric Properties from Incomplete Data (GPID 2015)

# Optimal Knots Selection
# for Sparse Reduced Data

Ryszard Kozera[1](✉) and Lyle Noakes[2]

[1] Faculty of Applied Mathematics and Informatics,
Warsaw University of Life Sciences-SGGW, Nowoursynowska Street 159,
02-776 Warsaw, Poland
ryszard.kozera@gmail.com

[2] School of Mathematics and Statistics, The University of Western Australia,
35 stirling Highway, Crawley, Perth, WA 6009, Australia
lyle.noakes@uwa.edu.au

**Abstract.** We discuss an interpolation scheme (based on optimization) to fit a given ordered sample of reduced data $Q_m$ in arbitrary Euclidean space. Here the corresponding knots are not given and need to be first somehow guessed. This is accomplished by solving an appropriate optimization problem, where the missing knots minimize the cost function measuring the *total squared norm of acceleration* of the interpolant (here a natural spline). The initial infinite dimensional optimization (set to minimize an acceleration within the class of admissible curves) is reduced to the finite dimensional problem, for which the unknown optimal interpolation knots are to be found. The latter introduces a highly non-linear optimization task, both difficult for theoretical analysis and in derivation of computationally feasible optimization scheme (in particular handling medium and large number of data points). The experiments to compare the interpolants based either on optimal knots or on the so-called cumulative chords are performed for 2D and 3D data. The problem of interpolating or approximating reduced data is applicable in computer vision (image segmentation), in computer graphics (curve modeling in computer aided geometrical design) or in engineering and physics (trajectory modeling).

**Keywords:** Reduced sparse data · Interpolation · Knots selection

## 1 Introduction

The problem of fitting data points in Euclidean space $E^m$ is a classical problem for which there exist many different interpolation or approximation techniques (see e.g. [1–6]). Most classical interpolation schemes assume a given sequence of ordered data $\mathcal{M} = \{x_0, x_1, \ldots, x_n\}$ (where $x_i \in E^m$) together with the corresponding set of ordered interpolation knots $\{t_i\}_{i=0}^{n}$ (*parametric interpolation on non-reduced data*). The problem of data fitting and modeling gets more complicated while dealing with the *reduced data* i.e. when only $\mathcal{M}$ is available (termed as *non-parametric interpolation*). Here, for a given fitting scheme, different choices

© Springer International Publishing Switzerland 2016
F. Huang and A. Sugimoto (Eds.): PSIVT 2015 Workshops, LNCS 9555, pp. 3–14, 2016.
DOI: 10.1007/978-3-319-30285-0_1

of ordered interpolation knots $\{\hat{t}_i\}_{i=0}^{n}$ render different curves. An early work on this topic can be found in [7] which was later extended among all in [8–19], where various quantitative criteria (often for special $m = 2, 3$) are introduced to measure the appropriateness of particular choice of $\{\hat{t}_i\}_{i=0}^{n}$ (e.g. convergence rate for dense data $\mathcal{M}$ derived from the unknown curve). A more recent work in which different parameterization of the unknown knots are discussed, including the so-called *cumulative chord parameterization*

$$\hat{t}_i = 0, \qquad \hat{t}_{i+1} = \hat{t}_i + \|q_{i+1} - q_i\|, \tag{1}$$

can be found e.g. in [5], [20–26]. The analysis of convergence rates to the unknown curve $\gamma : [0, T] \to E^m$ and its length $d(\gamma)$ (based on different parameterizations and dense samplings) is also recently studied among all in [27–40].

In this paper we introduce a special criterion of choosing the unknown knots (applicable not only to dense but also to sparse data) minimizing the mean squared of norm of the second derivative of the interpolating curve. An initial infinite dimensional optimization problem (see Lemma 1) is reduced to the corresponding finite dimensional one (set to determine the unknown knots). The latter constitutes a constrained highly non-linear optimization task (knots must be ordered) difficult for the theoretical analysis and computationally sensitive to the increase of interpolation points while standard optimization techniques are invoked. An alternative (not analyzed in this paper) is a computationally feasible optimization scheme called *Leap-Frog* (see [41–44]) which is here adapted to compute the suboptimal knots for ordered data in arbitrary Euclidean space $E^m$. The performance of the *Leap-Frog Algorithm* is illustrated on 2D and 3D reduced data $\mathcal{M}$ (i.e. for $m = 2, 3$) and subsequently compared with the multi-dimensional analogue of *Secant Method* (see e.g. [2] or [46]). The initial guess is chosen according to cumulative chords (1).

The proposed scheme for knots selection is applicable, in data fitting and curve modeling (e.g. computer graphics and computer vision), in approximation and interpolation (e.g. in trajectory planning, image segmentation, data compression) as well as in many other engineering and physics problems (robotics or particle trajectory estimation). Specific applications for fitting sparse (and dense) reduced data $\mathcal{M}$ in $E^m$ can be found e.g. in [5,6] or [47].

## 2   Problem Formulation

Assume that *ordered (by indexing) data points* $\mathcal{M} = \{x_0, x_1, x_2, \ldots, x_n\}$ are given (here $x_i \in E^m$ and $x_i \neq x_{i+1}$, for $i = 0, 1, \ldots, n$ with $n \geq 2$). Such $\mathcal{M}$ is called *admissible data*. Define now a class (denoted by $\mathscr{I}_T$) of *admissible curves* $\gamma$ as piecewise $C^2$ curves $\gamma : [0, T] \to E^m$ (where $0 < T < \infty$ is fixed) interpolating $\mathcal{M}$ with the ordered *free unknown knots* $\{t_i\}_{i=0}^{n}$ satisfying $\gamma(t_i) = x_i$ (here $t_i < t_{i+1}, t_0 = 0$ and $t_n = T$). More specifically, we assume that any choice of ordered interpolation knots $\{t_i\}_{i=0}^{n}$ yields a curve $\gamma \in C^1([0, T])$ such that it extends over sub-segment $[t_i, t_{i+1}]$ (for each $i = 0, 1, \ldots, n - 1$) to $\gamma \in C^2([t_i, t_{i+1}])$ - i.e. $\gamma$ is $C^2$ except of being $C^1$ only at interpolation knots $\{t_i\}_{i=0}^{n}$. The reason why we do not confine our analysis within a more natural class of $\gamma \in C^2([t_0, t_n])$ is justified by the subsequent choice of computational scheme (called herein *Leap-Frog* - see [42]) which effectively deals with the optimization problem (3). This scheme is designed to iteratively produce the a sequence of curves $\gamma_{LF}^k \in \mathscr{I}_T$ generically positioned outside of the class $C^2([t_0, t_n])$ (i.e. $\gamma_{LF}^k \notin C^2([t_0, t_n])$). However, the computed optimum by Leap-Frog belongs to the tighter class of functions in $C^2([t_0, t_n])$ - see [41,48].

We look for *an optimal* $\gamma_{opt} \in \mathscr{I}_T$ minimizing the following functional:

$$\mathscr{I}_T(\gamma) = \sum_{i=0}^{n-1} \int_{t_i}^{t_{i+1}} \|\ddot{\gamma}(t)\|^2 dt , \tag{2}$$

i.e. satisfying

$$\mathscr{I}_T(\gamma_{opt}) = \min_{\gamma \in \mathscr{I}_T} \mathscr{I}_T(\gamma) . \tag{3}$$

For future needs define also $\mathscr{I}_T^i$ as the $i$-th *segment energy*:

$$\mathscr{I}_T^i(\gamma) = \int_{t_i}^{t_{i+1}} \|\ddot{\gamma}(t)\|^2 dt , \tag{4}$$

obviously satisfying the inequality $\mathscr{I}_T^i(\gamma) \leq \mathscr{I}_T(\gamma)$. Note that for each function $\gamma \in \mathscr{I}_T$ the corresponding sequence of unknown interpolation knots $\{t_i\}_{i=0}^n$ (with $t_0$ and $t_n = T$ fixed) satisfies with $n - 1$ internal components the following:

$$\Omega_{t_0}^T = \{(t_1, t_2, \ldots, t_{n-1}) \in \mathbb{R}^{n-1} : t_0 < t_1 < t_2 < \ldots < t_{n-1} < t_n = T\}. \tag{5}$$

Evidently (3) defines an infinite dimensional optimization task (considered over $\mathscr{I}_T$) not invariant with respect to an arbitrary $C^2$ class re-parameterization $\phi : [0, T] \to [0, \tilde{T}]$ (with $\tilde{T} > 0$).

*Remark 1.* Note that if we confine reparametrizations' class to the affine ones i.e. $\phi(t) = t\tilde{T}/T$ (with $\phi^{-1}(s) = sT/\tilde{T}$) then as $\phi^{-1}(s) = t$, $\phi^{-1'} \equiv T/\tilde{T}$ and $\phi^{-1''} \equiv 0$, formula (2) reads for $\tilde{\gamma}(s) = (\gamma \circ \phi^{-1})(s)$ (upon using integration by substitution) as:

$$\mathscr{I}_{\tilde{T}}(\tilde{\gamma}) = \frac{T^3}{\tilde{T}^3} \sum_{i=0}^{n-1} \int_{\tilde{t}_i}^{\tilde{t}_{i+1}} \phi^{-1'}(s) \|(\ddot{\gamma} \circ \phi^{-1})(s)\|^2 ds = \frac{T^3}{\tilde{T}^3} \sum_{i=0}^{n-1} \int_{t_i}^{t_{i+1}} \|\ddot{\gamma}(t)\|^2 dt$$

$$= \frac{T^3}{\tilde{T}^3} \mathscr{I}_T(\gamma) . \tag{6}$$

Thus a curve $\gamma_{opt} \in \mathscr{I}_T$ is optimal to $\mathscr{I}_T$ if and only if a corresponding $\tilde{\gamma}_{opt} \in \mathscr{I}_{\tilde{T}}$ is optimal for $\mathscr{I}_{\tilde{T}}$. Therefore we can effectively assume $t_n = T$ to be arbitrary. Similar argument can be applied to $t_0 = 0$ (we set $\phi(t) = t - t_0$ if the latter does not hold). $\qquad \square$

In the anticipation of the forthcoming materials we briefly re-introduce different families of *piecewise cubics* interpolating data points $\mathcal{M}$ (see also [10, Chap.IV]) subject to various boundary conditions. In addition, in the remark to follow we also formulate the specific energy formulation (a special case of (2)) for the family of the so-called natural splines.

*Remark 2.* First recall that *a cubic spline interpolant* $\gamma_{\mathcal{T}}^{C_i} = \gamma_{\mathcal{T}}^{C}|_{[t_i, t_{i+1}]}$, for given temporarily fixed interpolation knots $\mathcal{T} = (t_0, t_1, \ldots, t_{n-1}, t_n)$ (here the knots $\{t_n\}_{i=0}^{n}$ are admissible) is defined as

$$\gamma_{\mathcal{T}}^{C_i}(t) = c_{1,i} + c_{2,i}(t - t_i) + c_{3,i}(t - t_i)^2 + c_{4,i}(t - t_i)^3, \tag{7}$$

to satisfy (for $i = 0, 1, 2, \ldots, n - 1$; $c_{j,i} \in \mathbb{R}^m$, where $j = 1, 2, 3, 4$)

$$\gamma_{\mathcal{T}}^{C_i}(t_{i+k}) = x_{i+k}, \quad \dot{\gamma}_{\mathcal{T}}^{C_i}(t_{i+k}) = v_{i+k}, \quad k = 0, 1$$

with the velocities $v_0, v_1, v_2, \ldots, v_{n-1}, v_n \in \mathbb{R}^m$ assumed to be temporarily free parameters (*if unknown*). The coefficients $c_{j,i}$ (with $\Delta t_i = t_{i+1} - t_i$) are defined as follows:

$$
\begin{aligned}
c_{1,i} &= x_i, \\
c_{2,i} &= v_i, \\
c_{4,i} &= \frac{v_i + v_{i+1} - 2\frac{x_{i+1} - x_i}{\Delta t_i}}{(\Delta t_i)^2}, \\
c_{3,i} &= \frac{\frac{(x_{i+1} - x_i)}{\Delta t_i} - v_i}{\Delta t_i} - c_{4,i}\Delta t_i.
\end{aligned}
\tag{8}
$$

The latter comes from (7) and Newton's formula (see e.g. [4, Chap. 1])

$$
\begin{aligned}
\gamma_{\mathcal{T}}^{C_i}(t) &= \gamma_{\mathcal{T}}^{C_i}(t_i) + \gamma_{\mathcal{T}}^{C_i}[t_i, t_i](t - t_i) + \gamma_{\mathcal{T}}^{C_i}[t_i, t_i, t_{i+1}](t - t_i)^2 \\
&\quad + \gamma_{\mathcal{T}}^{C_i}[t_i, t_i, t_{i+1}, t_{i+1}](t - t_i)^2(t - t_{i+1}) .
\end{aligned}
$$

combined with $c_{1,i} = \gamma_{\mathcal{T}}^{C_i}(t_i)$, $c_{2,i} = \dot{\gamma}_{\mathcal{T}}^{C_i}(t_i)$, $c_{3,i} = \ddot{\gamma}_{\mathcal{T}}^{C_i}(t_i)/2$, and $c_{4,i} = \gamma_{\mathcal{T}}^{C_i'''}(t_i)/6$. Adding $n - 1$ constraints enforcing continuity of second derivatives of $\gamma_{\mathcal{T}}^{C}$ at $x_1, x_2, \ldots, x_{n-1}$ i.e. for $i = 1, 2, \ldots, n - 1$ $\ddot{\gamma}_{\mathcal{T}}^{C_{i-1}}(t_i) = \ddot{\gamma}_{\mathcal{T}}^{C_i}(t_i)$ leads (upon using (7) and (8)) to the $m$ tridiagonal linear systems (strictly diagonally dominant) of $n - 1$ equations in $n + 1$ vector unknowns representing velocities at $\mathcal{M}$ i.e. $v_0, v_1, v_2, \ldots, v_{n-1}, v_n \in \mathbb{R}^m$:

$$
\begin{aligned}
v_{i-1}\Delta t_i + 2v_i(\Delta t_{i-1} + \Delta t_i) + v_{i+1}\Delta t_{i-1} &= b_i, \\
b_i = 3\left(\Delta t_i \frac{x_i - x_{i-1}}{\Delta t_{i-1}} + \Delta t_{i-1} \frac{x_{i+1} - x_i}{\Delta t_i}\right).
\end{aligned}
\tag{9}
$$

The terminal velocities $v_0$ and $v_n$ (*if unknown*) can be calculated from the conditions $\ddot{\gamma}_{\mathcal{T}}^{C}(0) = \ddot{\gamma}_{\mathcal{T}}^{C}(T_c) = \mathbf{0}$ combined with (8) (this yields *a natural cubic spline interpolant* $\gamma_{\mathcal{T}}^{NS}$ - a special $\gamma_{\mathcal{T}}^{C}$) which supplements (9) with two missing linear equations:

$$2v_0 + v_1 = 3\frac{x_1 - x_0}{\Delta t_0} \quad, \quad v_{n-1} + 2v_n = 3\frac{x_n - x_{n-1}}{\Delta t_{n-1}}. \tag{10}$$

The resulting $m$ linear systems, each of size $(n + 1) \times (n + 1)$, (based on (9) and (10)) as strictly row diagonally dominant result in one vector solution $v_0, v_1, v_2, \ldots, v_{n-1}, v_n$ (solved e.g. by Gauss elimination without pivoting - see [4, Chap.4]), which when fed into (8) determines explicitly *a natural cubic spline* $\gamma_{\mathcal{T}}^{NS}$ (with fixed $\mathcal{T}$).

Combining (2) with (7) results in (*in fact it is also true for any spline $\gamma_{\mathcal{T}}^{C}$ provided the respective velocities $\{v_i\}_{i=0}^{n}$ are somhow prescribed - e.g. also for a Hermite or a complete spline [4, Chap. 4]*):

$$\mathcal{J}_T(\gamma_{\mathcal{T}}^{NS}) = \sum_{i=0}^{n-1} \int_{t_i}^{t_{i+1}} \|\ddot{\gamma}_{\mathcal{T}}^{NS_i}(t)\|^2 dt$$

$$= \sum_{i=0}^{n-1} \int_{t_i}^{t_{i+1}} \langle 2c_{3,i} + 6c_{4,i}(t - t_i) | 2c_{3,i} + 6c_{4,i}(t - t_i) \rangle dt$$

$$= 4\sum_{i=0}^{n-1} (\|c_{3,i}\|^2 \Delta t_i + 3\|c_{4,i}\|^2(\Delta t_i)^3 + 3\langle c_{3,i} | c_{4,i} \rangle(\Delta t_i)^2).$$

Upon introducing $c_{5,i} = c_{3,i} + c_{4,i}\Delta t_i$ the latter reduces into:

$$\mathcal{J}_T(\gamma_{\mathcal{T}}^{NS}) = 4\sum_{i=0}^{n-1} (\Delta t_i \|c_{5,i}\|^2 + (\Delta t_i)^3 \|c_{4,i}\|^2 + \langle c_{5,i} | c_{4,i} \rangle(\Delta t_i)^2). \tag{11}$$

By (8) we also have $c_{5,i} = ((x_{i+1} - x_i)/(\Delta t_i)^2) - (v_i/\Delta t_i)$ and thus

$$\Delta t_i \|c_{5,i}\|^2 = \frac{\|x_{i+1} - x_i\|^2}{(\Delta t_i)^3} + \frac{\|v_i\|^2}{\Delta t_i} - 2\frac{\langle x_{i+1} - x_i | v_i \rangle}{(\Delta t_i)^2},$$

$$(\Delta t_i)^3 \|c_{4,i}\|^2 = \frac{\|v_i + v_{i+1}\|^2}{\Delta t_i} + \frac{4\|x_{i+1} - x_i\|^2}{(\Delta t_i)^3} - \frac{4\langle v_{i+1} + v_i | x_{i+1} - x_i \rangle}{(\Delta t_i)^2},$$

$$\langle c_{5,i} | c_{4,i} \rangle(\Delta t_i)^2 = \frac{\langle x_{i+1} - x_i | v_i + v_{i+1} \rangle}{(\Delta t_i)^2} - \frac{2\|x_{i+1} - x_i\|^2}{(\Delta t_i)^3} - \frac{\|v_i\|^2}{\Delta t_i} - \frac{\langle v_i | v_{i+1} \rangle}{\Delta t_i}$$

$$+ \frac{2\langle v_i | x_{i+1} - x_i \rangle}{(\Delta t_i)^2}$$

which when passed to (11) yields finally

$$\mathcal{J}_T(\gamma_{\mathcal{T}}^{NS}) = 4\sum_{i=0}^{n-1} \Big( \frac{-1}{(\Delta t_i)^3} (-3\|x_{i+1} - x_i\|^2 + 3\langle v_i + v_{i+1} | x_{i+1} - x_i \rangle \Delta t_i$$

$$- (\|v_i\|^2 + \|v_{i+1}\|^2 + \langle v_i | v_{i+1} \rangle)(\Delta t_i)^2 \Big). \tag{12}$$

Clearly for a given data points $\mathcal{M}$ and each strictly increasing sequence of fixed knots $\{t_i\}_{i=0}^n$ the *natural spline* $\gamma_{\mathcal{T}}^{NS}$ exists and is unique. Note also that (12) (in contrast with each curve $\gamma_{\mathcal{T}}^{C_i}$ itself) involves only two vector coefficients $c_{3,i}$ and $c_{4,i}$ appearing in (7).

Once we vary the knots $\{t_i\}_{i=0}^n$ (subject to $t_0 < t_1 < t_2 < \ldots < t_{n-1} < t_n = T$ with $t_n = T$ and $t_0$ fixed) the corresponding space of such natural splines $\gamma^{NS}$ (denoted here by $\mathcal{I}^{NS}$) evidently satisfies $\mathcal{I}^{NS} \subset \mathcal{I}_T \cap C^2([0, T_c])$ (also $\gamma^{NS}$ is $C^\infty([t_i, t_{i+1}])$ for each $i = 0, 1, \ldots, n-1$ - we omit subscript $\mathcal{T}$ to emphasize that internal knots may vary).

If now we minimize (2) only over a class of natural splines $\mathcal{I}^{NS} \subset \mathcal{I}_T$ (such thinning of (2) and (3) to (12) is justified later in Lemma 1) then

$$\mathcal{I}_T(\gamma_{opt}^{NS}) = \min_{\gamma^{NS} \in \mathcal{I}^{NS}} \mathcal{I}_T(\gamma^{NS}) \tag{13}$$

reduces into finding optimal parameters for (13) $(t_1^{opt}, t_2^{opt}, \ldots, t_{n-1}^{opt})$ (here terminal knots $t_n = T$ and $t_0$ are constant) within the family of natural splines $\mathcal{I}^{NS}$, subject to the constraint $t_0 < t_1^{opt} < t_2^{opt} < \ldots < t_{n-1}^{opt} < t_n = T$. As we mentioned there is a one-to-one correspondence between natural spline $\gamma^{NS}$ and the interpolation knots. Consequently (13) can be reformulated (see also (5)) upon introduction $\hat{\mathcal{T}} = (t_1, t_2, \ldots, t_{n-1})$ into the following minimization problem in $\hat{\mathcal{T}}$:

$$\mathcal{I}_T(\gamma_{opt}^{NS}) = \min_{\hat{\mathcal{T}} \in \Omega_{t_0}^T} \mathcal{I}_T^F(t_1, t_2, \ldots, t_{n-1})$$

$$= \min_{\hat{\mathcal{T}} \in \Omega_{t_0}^T} \sum_{i=0}^{n-1} \int_{t_i}^{t_{i+1}} \|\ddot{\gamma}^{NS}(s)\|^2 ds$$

$$= \min_{\hat{\mathcal{T}} \in \Omega_{t_0}^{T_c}} 4 \sum_{i=0}^{n-1} \Big( \frac{-1}{(\Delta t_i)^3}(-3\|x_{i+1} - x_i\|^2 + 3\langle v_i + v_{i+1}|x_{i+1} - x_i\rangle \Delta t_i$$

$$-(\|v_i\|^2 + \|v_{i+1}\|^2 + \langle v_i|v_{i+1}\rangle)(\Delta t_i)^2 \Big). \tag{14}$$

Thus *an implicit* formula (12) yields, upon feeding $v_i$ from (9) and (10), the *explicit non-linear expression* for $\mathcal{I}_T^F$ (see (14)) ready for minimization over $\mathcal{I}^{NS}$ with respect to free variables $(t_1, t_2, \ldots, t_{n-1}) \in \Omega_{t_0}^T$. Note that the value of the energy $\mathcal{I}_T^F(\hat{\mathcal{T}})$ is always finite for each $\hat{\mathcal{T}} \in \Omega_{t_0}^T$ since $\gamma_{\mathcal{T}}^{NS} \in C^2$ and therefore $\|\ddot{\gamma}_{\mathcal{T}}^{NS}\|$ is continuous over a compact set $[t_0, t_n]$ (as $t_n = T < +\infty$).

The class of natural splines $\mathcal{I}^{NS}$ is invoked here since one can reduce (3) to the same optimization confined merely to the subclass of natural splines $\mathcal{I}^{NS} \subset \mathcal{I}_T$ (see [10, 41, 48]). In fact by [41] the following holds (for arbitrary fixed knots $t_0 < t_n = T$):

**Lemma 1.** *For a given admissible data points $\mathscr{M}$ in arbitrary Euclidean space $E^m$ the subclass of natural splines $\mathscr{I}^{NS} \subset \mathscr{I}_T$ satisfies*

$$\min_{\gamma \in \mathscr{I}_T} \mathscr{J}_T(\gamma) = \min_{\gamma^{NS} \in \mathscr{I}^{NS}} \mathscr{J}_T(\gamma^{NS}). \tag{15}$$

In the next section we test the optimization problem (15) (converted into (12) or (14)) on some 2D and 3D data.

## 3   Numerical Experiments

Experiments are performed with *Mathematica Package*. We compare now the performance of *Leap-Frog* (see [41]) with the *Secant Method* applied to (12) (as justified by (15)). The experiments are conducted only for sparse reduced data points $\mathscr{M}$ in $E^{2,3}$. They represent special cases of all admissible sparse reduced data in arbitrary $E^m$. The initial guesses are based on cumulative chords (1).

The first example deals with reduced data $\mathscr{M}$ in $E^2$ (i.e. for $m = 2$).

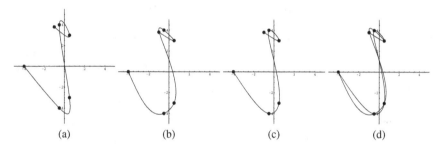

(a)                    (b)                    (c)                    (d)

**Fig. 1.** Natural splines interpolating data points $\mathscr{M}_{2D1}$ (a) $\gamma^{NS}_{\mathscr{T}_{uni}}$ with uniform knots $\mathscr{T}_{uni}$, (b) $\gamma^{NS}_{\mathscr{T}_c}$ with cumulative chords $\mathscr{T}_c$, (c) $\gamma^{NS}_{\mathscr{T}^{LF}_{opt}}$ with optimal knots $\mathscr{T}^{LF}_{opt} = \mathscr{T}^{SM}_{opt}$ (thus $\gamma^{NS}_{\mathscr{T}^{LF}_{opt}} = \gamma^{NS}_{\mathscr{T}^{SM}_{opt}}$) (d) $\gamma^{NS}_{\mathscr{T}_{opt}}$ and $\gamma^{NS}_{\mathscr{T}_c}$ plotted together.

*Example 1.* Consider for $n = 5$ the following 2D reduced data points (see dotted points in Fig. 1):

$$\mathscr{M}_{2D1} = \{(-4, 0), (-0.5, -4), (0.5, -3), (-0.5, 4), (0.5, 3), (-1, 3.8)\}.$$

A blind guess of uniform interpolation knots yields (rescaled to $T_c = \hat{T}_n$ - see (1)):

$$\mathscr{T}_{uni} = \{0, 3.38291, 6.76583, 10.1487, 13.5317, 16.9146\}$$

and the initial guess based on cumulative chord $\mathscr{T}_c = (t_0, \hat{\mathscr{T}}_c, T_c)$ (i.e. based on the geometry of the layout of the data) renders:

$$\mathscr{T}_c = \{0, 5.31507, 6.72929, 13.8004, 15.2146, 16.9146\}.$$

The natural splines $\gamma_{\mathcal{T}_{uni}}^{NS}$ (based on $\mathcal{T}_{uni} = (0, \hat{\mathcal{T}}_{uni}, 16.9146))$ and $\gamma_{\mathcal{T}_c}^{NS}$ (based on $\mathcal{T}_c$) yield the energies $\mathcal{J}_{\mathcal{T}_c}^F(\hat{\mathcal{T}}_{uni}) = 7.18796 < \mathcal{J}_{\mathcal{T}_c}^F(\hat{\mathcal{T}}_c) = 7.8536$. Both interpolants $\gamma_{\mathcal{T}_{uni}}^{NS}$ and $\gamma_{\mathcal{T}_c}^{NS}$ are shown in Fig. 1a and b, respectively. The *Secant Method* yields (for (12)) the optimal knots (augmented by terminal times $t_0 = 0$ and $t_5 = T_c$)

$$\mathcal{T}_{opt}^{SM} = \{0, 3.67209, 5.62892, 11.435, 14.5491, 16.9146\}$$

with the optimal energy $\mathcal{J}_{\mathcal{T}_c}^F(\hat{\mathcal{T}}_{opt}^{SM}) = 4.25388$. The *execution time* amounts to $T^{SM} = 7.037922sec$. The resulting curve $\gamma_{\mathcal{T}_{opt}^{SM}}^{NS}$ is plotted in Fig. 1c. Note that for each free variable *Secant Method* uses here two initial numbers $t_i^c \pm 0.5$. The *Leap-Frog Algorithm* decreases the initial energy $\mathcal{J}_{\mathcal{T}_c}^F(\hat{\mathcal{T}}_c)$ upon 42 iterations to $\mathcal{J}_{\mathcal{T}_c}^F(\hat{\mathcal{T}}_{opt}^{SM})$ (i.e. as for *Secant Method*) with optimal values satisfying $\mathcal{T}_{opt}^{LF} = \mathcal{T}_{opt}^{SM}$, up to the 6th decimal place - this is the iteration bound). The respective *execution time* $T^{LF} = 3.333620sec < T^{SM}$. The 0th, 1st, 10th, 20th, 30th and 42nd iterations *Leap-Frog* decrease the energy $\mathcal{J}_{\mathcal{T}_c}^F(\hat{\mathcal{T}}_c)$ to:

$$\{7.8536, 4.93366, 4.25839, 4.25389, 4.25388, 4.25388\}$$

with only the first two iterations contributing to major energy decrease (and hence the corrections of the initial guess for knots taken as $\mathcal{T}_c$). The resulting natural spline $\gamma_{\mathcal{T}_{opt}^{LF}}^{NS}$ (clearly the same as $\gamma_{\mathcal{T}_{opt}^{SM}}^{NS}$ yielded by *Secant Method*) based on $\mathcal{T}_{opt}^{LF}$ is shown in Fig. 1c and also visually compared with $\gamma_{\mathcal{T}_c}^{NS}$ in Fig. 1d. Note that if *Leap-Frog* iteration bound condition is changed e.g. to make current *Leap-Frog* energy equal to $\mathcal{J}_{\mathcal{T}_c}^F(\mathcal{T}_c^{SM})$ (say up to 5th decimal place) then only 22 iterations are needed here with shorter execution time $T_E^{LF} = 2.270440$ *sec* and with optimal knots

$$\mathcal{T}_{opt}^{LF_E} = \{0, 3.67502, 5.63183, 11.436814.5498, 16.9146\}.$$

We miss out now a bit on precise estimation of the optimal knots but we speed up the *Leap-Frog* execution time by obtaining almost the same interpolating curve as the optimal one (as $\mathcal{T}_{opt}^{LF_E} \approx \mathcal{T}_{opt}^{SM}$). The other iteration a posteriori stopping criteria can also be considered which even further accelerate *Leap-Frog* performance at almost no cost in difference between computed curve an optimal curve.                                                                              □

We pass now to an example of reduced data in $E^3$ (i.e. with $m = 3$).

*Example 2.* Consider for $n = 5$ the following 3D reduced data points (see dotted points in Fig. 2):

$$\mathcal{M}_{3D1} = \{(0,0,0), (-0.5,0,-4), (0.5,0,-4), (-0.5,0,4), (0.5,0,4), (-1,0,3.8)\}.$$

The uniform interpolation knots read (rescaled to $T_c = \hat{t}_n$ - see (1)) as:

$$\mathcal{T}_{uni} = \{0, 3.12133, 6.24266, 9.364, 12.4853, 15.6067\}$$

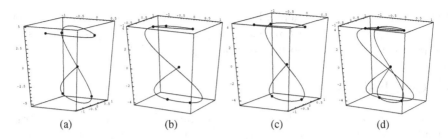

(a)                    (b)                    (c)                    (d)

**Fig. 2.** Natural splines interpolating data points $\mathscr{M}_{3D1}$ (a) $\gamma^{NS}_{\mathscr{T}_{uni}}$ with uniform knots $\mathscr{T}_{uni}$, (b) $\gamma^{NS}_{\mathscr{T}_c}$ with cumulative chords $\mathscr{T}_c$, (c) $\gamma^{NS}_{\mathscr{T}^{LF}_{opt}}$ with optimal knots $\mathscr{T}^{LF}_{opt} = \mathscr{T}^{SM}_{opt}$ (thus $\gamma^{NS}_{\mathscr{T}^{LF}_{opt}} = \gamma^{NS}_{\mathscr{T}^{SM}_{opt}}$) (d) $\gamma^{NS}_{\mathscr{T}^{LF}_{opt}}$ and $\gamma^{NS}_{\mathscr{T}_c}$ plotted together.

and the initial guess based on cumulative chord $\mathscr{T}_c$ is here:

$$\mathscr{T}_c = \{0, 4.03113, 5.03113, 13.0934, 14.0934, 15.6067\}.$$

The natural splines $\gamma^{NS}_{\mathscr{T}_{uni}}$ (based on $\mathscr{T}_{uni}$) and $\gamma^{NS}_{\mathscr{T}_c}$ (based on $\mathscr{T}_c$) yield the following energies $\mathscr{J}^F_{\mathscr{T}_c}(\hat{\mathscr{T}}_{uni}) = 10.145 > \mathscr{J}^F_{\mathscr{T}_c}(\hat{\mathscr{T}}_c) = 9.45031$. Again, both interpolants $\gamma^{NS}_{\mathscr{T}_{uni}}$ and $\gamma^{NS}_{\mathscr{T}_{uni}}$ are presented in Fig. 2a,b, respectively.

The *Secant Method* yields (for (12)) the optimal knots (augmented by terminal times $t_0 = 0$ and $t_5 = T_c$)

$$\mathscr{T}^{SM}_{opt} = \{0, 2.91851, 5.12399, 11.1964, 13.507, 15.6067\}$$

with the optimal energy $\mathscr{J}^F_{\mathscr{T}_c}(\mathscr{T}^{SM}_{opt}) = 4.65476$. The *execution time* amounts to $T^{SM} = 6.783365sec$. The resulting curve $\gamma^{NS}_{\mathscr{T}^{SM}_{opt}}$ is plotted in Fig. 2c. Note that for each free variable *Secant Method* uses here two initial numbers $t^c_i \pm 0.1$. *Leap-Frog* decreases the initial energy to $\mathscr{J}^F_{\mathscr{T}_c}(\hat{\mathscr{T}}^{LF}_{opt}) = \mathscr{J}^F_{\mathscr{T}_c}(\mathscr{T}^{SM}_{opt})$ (as for the *Secant Method*) with the iteration stopping conditions $\mathscr{T}^{LF}_{opt} = \mathscr{T}^{SM}_{opt}$ (up to 6th decimal point) upon 38 iterations. The respective *execution time* amounts to $T^{LF} = 3.757498 < T^{SM}$. The 0th (i.e. $\mathscr{J}^F_{\mathscr{T}_c}(\hat{\mathscr{T}}_c)$), 1st, 2nd, 10th, 13th, and 36th iterations *Leap-Frog* decrease the energy to:

$$\{9.45031, 5.30697, 4.83704, 4.65485, 4.65476, 4.65476\}$$

with again only the first three iterations contributing to major correction of the initial guess knots $\mathscr{T}_c$. The resulting natural spline $\gamma^{NS}_{\mathscr{T}^{LF}_{opt}}$ (clearly the same as $\gamma^{NS}_{\mathscr{T}^{SM}_{opt}}$ yielded by *Secant Method*) based on $\mathscr{T}^{LF}_{opt}$ is shown in Fig. 2c and also visually compared with $\gamma^{NS}_{\mathscr{T}_c}$ in Fig. 2d. Again if *Leap-Frog* iteration bound condition is changed e.g. to make current *Leap-Frog* energy equal to $\mathscr{J}^F_{\mathscr{T}_c}(\mathscr{T}^{SM}_c)$ (say up to 5th decimal place) then only 13 iterations are needed here with shorter execution time $T^{LF}_E = 1.878057 < T^{SM}$ and optimal knots

$$\mathscr{T}^{LF_E}_{opt} = \{0, 2.92093, 5.12632, 11.1981, 13.5079, 15.6067\}.$$

As previously, we miss out here a bit on precise estimation of the optimal knots but we accelerate the *Leap-Frog* execution time by obtaining almost the same interpolating curve as the optimal one (as $\mathcal{T}_{opt}^{LF_E} \approx \mathcal{T}_{opt}^{SM}$).                    □

## 4  Conclusions

In this paper we discussed the method of fitting reduced data $\mathcal{M}$ in arbitrary Euclidean space $E^m$ with natural splines $\gamma_{\mathcal{T}}^{NS}$ based on finding the best unknown knots $(t_1^{opt}, t_2^{opt}, \ldots, t_{n-1}^{opt})$ (and thus the best natural spline) to minimize the total mean of squared norm of acceleration of the interpolant. The original optimization problem (2) derived in a wider class of piecewise-$C^2$ class interpolants is reduced to the class of natural splines $\gamma_{\mathcal{T}}^{NS}$ - see Lemma 1. This in turn reformulates into the finite-dimensional constrained optimization task (14) in $(t_1, t_2, \ldots, t_{n-1})$-variables, subject to the satisfaction of the inequalities $t_0 < t_1 < t_2, < \ldots < t_{n-1} < t_n$. Two computational schemes are deployed to test the quality of the computed interpolants - i.e. Leap-Frog and Secant Method. They both do not rely on large size matrix inversion during the computational procedure. For sparse reduced data $\mathcal{M}$ our optimization set-up together with applied numerical schemes offer a feasible choice (supplemented with computational tools) of approximating the unknown interpolation knots $\{t_i\}_{i=0}^n \approx \{\hat{t}_i^{opt}\}_{i=0}^n$. Future work will include the theoretical analysis of the nature of (14) and convergence of tested iterative schemes to its local (global) minima (minimum).

Some recent related work on fitting reduced data $\mathcal{M}$ in $E^{2,3}$ can also be found in [49,50].

## References

1. Bézier, P.E.: Numerical Control: Mathematics and Applications. John Wiley, New York (1972)
2. Davis, P.J.: Interpolation and Approximation. Dover Pub. Inc., New York (1975)
3. Farin, G.: Curves and Surfaces for Computer Aided Geometric Design. Academic Press, San Diego (1993)
4. de Boor, C.: A Practical Guide to Spline. Springer-Verlag, New York (1985)
5. Kvasov, B.I.: Methods of Shape-Preserving Spline Approximation. World Scientific, Singapore (2000)
6. Piegl, L., Tiller, W.: The NURBS Book. Springer-Verlag, Heidelberg (1997)
7. Epstein, M.P.: On the influence of parameterization in parametric interpolation. SIAM J. Numer. Anal. **13**, 261–268 (1976)
8. Barsky, B.A., DeRose, T.D.: Geometric continuity of parametric curves: three equivalent characterizations. IEEE. Comp. Graph. Appl. **9**(6), 60–68 (1989)
9. Boehm, E., Farin, G., Kahmann, J.: A survey of curve and surface methods in CAGD. Comp. Aided Geom. Design **1**(1), 1–60 (1988)
10. de Boor, C., Höllig, K., Sabin, M.: High accuracy geometric Hermite interpolation. Comp. Aided Geom. Design **4**(4), 269–278 (1987)
11. Hoschek, J.: Intrinsic parametrization for approximation. Comp. Aided Geom. Design **5**(1), 27–31 (1988)

12. Lachance, M.A., Schwartz, A.J.: Four point parabolic interpolation. Comp. Aided Geom. Design **8**, 143–149 (1991)
13. Lee, E.T.Y.: Corners, cusps, and parameterization: variations on a theorem of Epstein. SIAM J. Numer. Anal. **29**, 553–565 (1992)
14. Lee, E.T.Y.: Choosing nodes in parametric curve interpolation. Comp. Aided Geom. Design **21**, 363–370 (1989)
15. Marin, S.P.: An approach to data parameterization in parametric cubic spline interpolation problems. J. Approx. Theory **41**, 64–86 (1984)
16. Nielson, G.M., Foley, T.A.: A survey of applications of an affine invariant norm. In: Lyche, T., Schumaker, L.L. (eds.) Math. Methods Comp. Aided Geom. Design. pp. 445–467. Academic Press, New York (1989)
17. Schaback, R.: Interpolation in $\mathbb{R}^2$ by piecewise quadratic visually $C^2$ Bézier polynomials. Comp. Aided Geom. Design **6**, 219–233 (1989)
18. Sederberg, T.W., Zhao, J., Zundel, A.K.: Approximate parametrization of algebraic curves. In: Strasser, W., Seidel, H.P. (eds.) Theory and Practice in Geometric Modelling, pp. 33–54. Springer-Verlag, Heidelberg (1989)
19. Taubin, T.: Estimation of planar curves, surfaces, and non-planar space curves defined by implicit equations with applications to edge and range image segmentation. IEEE Trans. Patt. Mach. Intell. **13**(11), 1115–1138 (1991)
20. Kocić, L.M., Simoncinelli, A.C., Della, V.B.: Blending parameterization of polynomial and spline interpolants. Facta Univ. (NIŠ) Ser. Math. Inf. **5**, 95–107 (1990)
21. Mørken, K., Scherer, K.: A general framework for high-accuracy parametric interpolation. Math. Comput. **66**(217), 237–260 (1997)
22. Noakes, L., Kozera, R.: Cumulative chords piecewise-quadratics and piecewise-cubics. In: Klette, R., Kozera, R., Noakes, L., Weickert, J. (eds.) Geometric Properties from Incomplete Data. Computational Imaging and Vision, vol. 31, pp. 59–75. Springer, The Netherlands (2006)
23. Kozera, R., Noakes, L.: Piecewise-quadratics and exponential parameterizations for reduced data. Appl. Maths Comput. **221**, 620–638 (2013)
24. Farouki, R.T.: Optimal parameterizations. Comp. Aided Geom. Design **14**(2), 153–168 (1997)
25. Rababah, A.: High order approximation methods for curves. Comp. Aided Geom. Des. **12**, 89–102 (1995)
26. Schaback, R.: Optimal geometric Hermite interpolation of curves. In: Dæhlen, M., Lyche, T., Schumaker, L. (eds.) Mathematical Methods for Curves and Surfaces II, pp. 1–12. Vanderbilt University Press, Nashville (1998)
27. Floater, M.S.: Point-based methods for estimating the length of a parametric curve. J. Comput. Appl. Maths **196**(2), 512–522 (2006)
28. Floater, M.S.: Chordal cubic spline interpolation is fourth order accurate. IMA J. Numer. Anal. **26**, 25–33 (2006)
29. Kozera, R.: Cumulative chord piecewise-quartics for length and curve estimation. In: Petkov, N., Westenberg, M.A. (eds.) CAIP 2003. LNCS, vol. 2756, pp. 697–705. Springer, Heidelberg (2003)
30. Kozera, R.: Asymptotics for length and trajectory from cumulative chord piecewise-quartics. Fundam. Inf. **61**(3–4), 267–283 (2004)
31. Kozera, R.: Curve modelling via interpolation based on multidimensional reduced data. Stud. Inf. **25**(4B–61), 1–140 (2004)
32. Kozera, R., Noakes, L.: $C^1$ interpolation with cumulative chord cubics. Fundam. Inf. **61**(3–4), 285–301 (2004)

33. Kozera, R., Noakes, L., Klette, R.: External versus internal parameterizations for lengths of curves with nonuniform samplings. In: Asano, T., Klette, R., Ronse, C. (eds.) Geometry, Morphology, and Computational Imaging. LNCS, vol. 2616, pp. 403–418. Springer, Heidelberg (2003)

34. Kozera, R., Noakes, L.: Smooth interpolation with cumulative chord cubics. In: Wojciechowski, B., Smółka, B., Paulus, H., Kozera, R., Skarbek, W., Noakes, L. (eds.) ICCVG 2004. Computational Imaging and Vision, vol. 32, pp. 87–94. Springer, The Netherlands (2006)

35. Noakes, L., Kozera, R.: More-or-less uniform sampling and lengths of curves. Quar. Appl. Maths **61**(3), 475–484 (2003)

36. Noakes, L., Kozera, R.: Interpolating sporadic data. In: Heyden, A., Sparr, G., Nielsen, M., Johansen, P. (eds.) ECCV 2002, Part II. LNCS, vol. 2351, pp. 613–625. Springer, Heidelberg (2002)

37. Noakes, L., Kozera, R., Klette, R.: Length estimation for curves with $\varepsilon$-uniform sampling. In: Skarbek, W. (ed.) CAIP 2001. LNCS, vol. 2124, pp. 518–526. Springer, Heidelberg (2001)

38. Noakes, L., Kozera, R., Klette, R.: Length estimation for curves with different samplings. In: Bertrand, G., Imiya, A., Klette, R. (eds.) Digital and Image Geometry. LNCS, vol. 2243, pp. 339–351. Springer, Heidelberg (2002)

39. Noakes, L., Kozera, R.: Cumulative chords and piecewise-quadratics. In: Wojciechowski, K. (ed.) ICCVG 2002. Association for Image Processing Poland, vol. II, pp. 589–595. Silesian University of Technology Gliwice Poland, Institute of Theoretical and Applied Informatics, PAS, Gliwice, Poland (2002)

40. Vincent, S., Forsey, D.: Fast and accurate parametric curve length computation. J. Graphics Tools **6**(4), 29–40 (2002)

41. Kozera, R., Noakes, L.: Fitting data via optimal interpolation knots. To be submitted

42. Noakes, L.: A Global algorithm for geodesics. J. Math. Austral. Soc. Ser. A **64**, 37–50 (1999)

43. Noakes, L., Kozera, R.: Nonlinearities and noise reduction in 3-source photometric stereo. J. Math. Imag. Vision **18**(3), 119–127 (2003)

44. Noakes, L., Kozera, R.: 2D Leap-Frog Algorithm for optimal surface reconstruction. In: Latecki, M.J. (ed.) SPIE 1999. Vision Geometry VIII vol. 3811, pp. 317–328. Society of Industrial and Applied Mathematics, Bellingham, Washington. (1999)

45. Noakes, L., Kozera, R.: Denoising images: non-linear Leap-Frog for shape and light-source recovery. In: Asano, T., Klette, R., Ronse, C. (eds.) Geometry, Morphology, and Computational Imaging. LNCS, vol. 2616, pp. 419–436. Springer, Heidelberg (2003)

46. Boyd, S., Vandenberghe, L.: Convex Optimization. Cambridge University Press, Cambridge (2004)

47. Janik, M., Kozera, R., Kozioł, P.: Reduced data for curve modeling - applications in graphics, computer vision and physics. Adv. Sci. Tech. **7**(18), 28–35 (2013)

48. Noakes, L., Kozera, R.: Optimal natural splines with free knots. To be submitted

49. Kuznetsov, E.B., Yakimovich, A.Y.: The best parameterization for parametric interpolation. J. Comp. Appl. Maths **191**, 239–245 (2006)

50. Shalashilin, V.I., Kuznetsov, E.B.: Parametric Continuation and Optimal Parameterization in Applied Mathematics and Mechanics. Kluver Academic Publishers, Boston, Dordrecht, London (2003)

# Moving Cast Shadow Detection Using Joint Color and Texture Features with Neighboring Information

Bingshu Wang[1], Wenqian Zhu[1], Yong Zhao[1(✉)], and Yongjun Zhang[2]

[1] School of Electronic and Computer Engineering,
Shenzhen Graduate School of Peking University, Shenzhen, China
{wangbingshu,zhuwenqian}@sz.pku.edu.cn, zhaoyong@pkusz.edu.cn
[2] College of Computer Science and Technology, Guizhou University, Guiyang, China
zyj6667@126.com

**Abstract.** Moving cast shadow detection is an important technique that increases the rate of accuracy in object detection. In this paper, we introduce a moving cast shadow detection method that is based on the assumption that the shadow regions are darker than the corresponding background regions and maintain the same chromaticity and texture. The proposed algorithm includes two main stages. The first is to detect candidate shadows by spectral ratio at pixel-level. The other is to extract shadows by jointly using three components of HSV chromaticity, improved local ternary pattern and the gradient for each pixel. Each color or texture component makes use of a pixel's neighboring information and comprises a single result. Three such detected results are combined to determine whether a pixel belongs to a shadow. Experimental results show that the method outperforms some state-of-the-art algorithms on a benchmark dataset of indoor and outdoor scene sequences.

**Keywords:** Moving cast shadow · HSV chromaticity · Improved local ternary pattern · Gradient · Neighboring information

## 1 Introduction

Moving object detection is core to a wide variety of visual surveillance applications including perimeter protection, content-based object indices, and behavior analysis. Accurate detection of moving objects is a constant task of image processing. Moving cast shadows—integral to this requirement—are frequently misclassified as moving objects because they share both the similar motion properties and background discrimination with objects. Such erroneous misclassification may affect geometrical properties and trigger distortion of real objects, encumbering effective processing of subsequent vision algorithms such as recognition and tracking. In addition, a shadow cast onto an object may increase the probability of that object being obscured. A moving cast shadow is generated by light source occlusion by an opaque object, making the shadow darker

© Springer International Publishing Switzerland 2016
F. Huang and A. Sugimoto (Eds.): PSIVT 2015 Workshops, LNCS 9555, pp. 15–25, 2016.
DOI: 10.1007/978-3-319-30285-0_2

than its respective covered background while retaining similar color and texture. A shadow is always coupled with the object that cast it and its motion behavior is similar to that object [1].

Diverse shadow detection methods [2–6], such as chromaticity-based methods and texture-based methods, have been proposed in recent years to address multiple moving cast shadow scenarios. Some evaluation metrics, such as shadow detection rate and shadow discrimination rate, have also materialized to evaluate shadow detection methods [1]. In addition, a suite of benchmark test datasets, including indoor and outdoor sequences, has also emerged [7].

The principle contribution of this paper is improvement of shadow detection rate by using a novel approach. Statistical data for shadows demonstrates insignificant change in the color inter-component ratio of shadow pixel point and respect to background pixel point. This results in the detection of all shadows with a modicum of misclassified objects. Following apprehension of candidate shadows, color consistency and texture invariance—including HSV color, improved local ternary pattern and gradient information— are taken into account and undergo rigorous development. Coupled with neighboring information utilization, pixel-level analysis for candidate shadows is performed. Experimental results validate the efficiency of this method and confirm that it outperforms some existing state-of-the-art methods.

In the following section, related works involving several state-of-the-art methods will be discussed. After that, Sect. 3 provides details relevant to the current method's procedure with joint color and texture features. Section 4 then shows the qualitative and quantitative results. The conclusion will be presented in Sect. 5.

## 2    Related Works

In the past decades many shadow detection algorithms are proposed and classified as different taxonomies. A two-layer classification is given in [1]. The first layer includes two parts: statistical and deterministic. The statistical class can be subdivided into parametric and non-parametric methods and the deterministic class is further divided into model-based methods and non-model based methods. Deterministic non-model based approach shows the best results for a general-purpose shadow detection by using the HSV color space.

Spectral, spatial and temporal domains are the source of features in methods. Each domain can be subdivided into many algorithms by features which are reckoned as a better taxonomy [3]. Intensity, chromaticity and physical properties belong to spectral domain. Geometry and texture are parts of spatial features. Chromaticity method [8], geometry method [9], physical method [10], small region (SR) texture-based method [11] and large region (LR) texture-based method [12] are common and basic methods. Chromaticity method is based on the assumption that shadow regions are darker but keep the chromaticity, for instance, HSV-based chromaticity method. Geometry method assumes that each blob consists of object and shadow and makes a distinction. Physical method models the appearance of shadow pixels and some methods try to establish an attenuation model. There are many texture-based methods such as SR and LR. SR considers more about the region-level correlation while LR adopts a method that distinguishes a blob whether it belongs to a shadow. Each method makes use of single property, which may achieve a good result in special scene. The proposed method comprehensively takes chromaticity and texture into account in order to adjust to various scenes.

The main difference between proposed method and the existing methods is that we use two color spaces (RGB and HSV) and combine three shadow detectors: HSV detector, improved local ternary pattern detector and gradient detector simultaneously. The existing methods utilize one or two cues for moving cast shadow detection. Due to the multiple features are utilized, robustness is improved. Experimental results in Sect. 4 show that our method's better performance.

There is a dominant strategy including two steps for moving cast shadow detection. The first step is to extract the candidate regions that contains all the possible shadows, and the second step is to achieve an accurate detection and discrimination. The principle is how to narrow the range of candidate shadows and keep real shadows as much as possible. Our method adopts the strategy, which has been proved efficient for outperforming five methods under the comparison of the standard evaluation dataset.

# 3    Shadow Detector Method

This paper puts forward to a framework for shadow detection. Two color spaces including RGB and HSV are employed. From the viewpoint of effectiveness, detection result of two color spaces is better than that of one color space. For each pixel, as long as the values of its three channels are lower than those of its background pixel simultaneously, it can be regarded as a candidate shadow pixel. So all real shadow pixels cannot be lost.

Meanwhile, some objects even noise that meet the standard will also be included. Then the detector based on HSV color space can build on the precedent work. Two kinds of texture features are also utilized to extract accurate shadows from candidate shadows and each of which is operated at pixel-level with the consideration of neighboring information. This method principle is shown in Fig. 1 and the objects in the framework are defined as follows:

- Frame, Foreground and Background represent current image, detected foreground image and background image respectively in sequences. Detected foreground image includes the moving objects and moving cast shadows.
- S1 is the candidate shadows detected by spectral ratio of RGB color space in the subsequent Sect. 3.1
- S2, S3 and S4 are the shadow detection results by using HSV detector, improved local ternary pattern (ILTP) detector and gradient detector respectively.
- S5 is the union result of S2, S3 and S4 though a voting process.

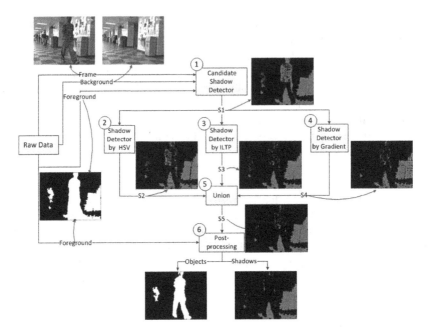

**Fig. 1.** Flowchart of shadow detection with joint color and texture information.

As shown in Fig. 1, the proposed shadow detection method consists of the following six steps.

1. Obtain the candidate shadows S1 from raw data.
2. Use HSV detector to detect shadows and gain S2 from S1.
3. Use ILTP detector to detect shadows and gain S3 from S1.
4. Use gradient detector to detect shadows and gain S4 from S1.
5. Obtain the union shadows S5 from S2, S3 and S4.
6. Use Foreground (from raw data) and S5 to generate the final Objects image and Shadows image.

These six steps are detailed in the following sections.

### 3.1    Candidate Shadow Detector by Spectral Ratio

The paper shares the typical assumption that the shadow region is darker than corresponding background, which helps to gain the preliminary candidate shadows. For each pixel, as long as all the channels' values (RGB) are lower than those of corresponding background pixel, it can be treated as a coarse candidate shadow pixel. Inevitably, some objects' or noisy pixels may be included. Experiments on benchmark images validate an assumption that the shadow pixel's ratio between the components of RGB color space does not change significantly

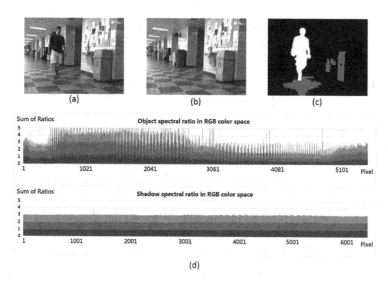

**Fig. 2.** Object-background spectral ratio and Shadow-background spectral ratio in RGB color space. Image (a) is current frame, (b) is the background image, (c) is the ground truth image, (d) is the statistic spectral ratio for all the object pixels and shadow pixels derived from (c). In (c) white pixels belong to object class while gray pixels belong to shadow class (Color figure online).

when comparing to its background pixel at the same position (see Fig. 2.). This can be applied to detect candidate shadows.

$$\Psi_r = \frac{F_b/F_g}{B_b/B_g}, \Psi_g = \frac{F_b/F_r}{B_b/B_r}, \Psi_b = \frac{F_g/F_r}{B_g/B_r}. \tag{1}$$

$$BGR\_Candidate\_Shadow = \begin{cases} 1 & if\ |\Psi_i - \mu| < \lambda\ \ i \in \{b,g,r\} \\ 0 & otherwise \end{cases}. \tag{2}$$

Here $F_i$ $(i \in \{r,g,b\})$ and $B_i$ represent color component of current frame pixel and background pixel, while $\Psi_i$ is spectral ratio and close to one in shadow regions but not necessarily in object regions. Shadows can be distinguished from objects by using Eq. (2). In shadow regions $\Psi_i$ value changes little while in object regions it has a wide range of values. The parameter $\mu$ is a reference value that revolves one around and $\lambda$ is a smaller value (less than 0.2).

## 3.2 Shadow Detector by HSV Color Space

Many shadow detection methods are based on HSV color space because the color space enhances the discrimination between objects and shadows [13]. It consists of two parts: color chromaticity and color brightness. We choose color chromaticity with ignore of the brightness condition due to the use in the pre-selection stage, otherwise it will be repetitive.

$$HSV\_Shadow = \begin{cases} 1 & if \quad \dfrac{\sum\limits_{i=1}^{n} |F_i^h - B_i^h|}{n} < \tau_h \wedge \dfrac{\sum\limits_{i=1}^{n} (F_i^s - B_i^s)}{n} < \tau_s \ . \\ 0 & otherwise \end{cases} \qquad (3)$$

The parameters $(\tau_s , \tau_h)$ represent the empirical thresholds varying from different scenes. Single pixel is isolated and opt to be a bit more arbitrary. When its neighboring information is made use of, the interference caused by uncertain factors such as sudden light changing tends to be reduced. The average difference value of a small region that centered in current pixel (see Eq. (3)) is calculated and used to determine whether current pixel belongs to a shadow class or not.

### 3.3   Shadow Detector by ILTP

Local binary pattern (LBP) was first introduced as an excellent means to describe local gray-level structure. However, LBP is easily affected by noise especially in the neighborhood-uniform regions. Tan modified LBP and proposed local ternary pattern (LTP) [14]. The difference between LBP and LTP is just from 2-valued to 3-valued codes, which improve the resistance and robustness to noise in many scenes.

$$\nu\,(x, i_c, t) = \begin{cases} 1, & x \geq i_c + t \\ 0, & |x - i_c| < t \ . \\ -1, & x \leq i_c - t \end{cases} \qquad (4)$$

A local neighborhood around each pixel is taken by LTP operator in gray image. The way of LTP code is given in Eq. (4), and $x$ represents the pixel that around centered pixel $i_c$ and $t$ indicates the tolerance to noise.

The LTP operator compares neighboring pixels with centered pixel but ignores the potential information between the neighboring pixels. Actually, the addition of comparison information of neighboring pixels can enhance the integrity of local texture pattern. The ILTP encoding procedure is illustrated in Fig. 3 that considers $3 \times 3$ neighborhoods. For one pixel, it is coded with 12-value in single channel. One way to enrich more information of ILTP is to take all the three channels of RGB color space into account.

Here, we denote $C(F_i(x))$ as the code-value for one pixel of current frame with $i$-th neighboring pixel and $C(B_i(x))$ as code-value of corresponding background pixel. The similarity between them is represented by $x(i)$. It will be assigned to one if $C(F_i(x))$ shares same value with $C(B_i(x))$ , otherwise zero. We denote $n$ as the sum of neighboring pixels and $\delta$ as the similarity between the current pixel and background pixel at the same position.

$$ILTP\_Shadow = \begin{cases} 1 & if \ \sum\limits_{i=1}^{n} x(i)/n > \delta \\ 0 & otherwise \end{cases} \ . \qquad (5)$$

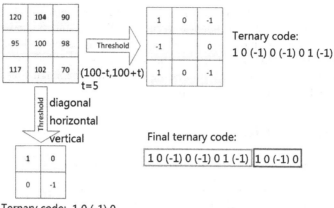

**Fig. 3.** Improved local ternary pattern for shadow detection.

## 3.4 Shadow Detector by Gradient

LR method places more importance on gradient information [12]. Like that, $\nabla_y$ is denoted as the vertical gradient (difference intensity between pixel in previous row and the pixel in next row) and $\nabla_x$ as the horizontal gradient (difference intensity between pixel in previous column and the pixel in next column). Meanwhile, $\nabla_i$ and $\theta_i$ are defined as gradient magnitude and direction respectively.

$$\nabla_i = \sqrt{\nabla_x^2 + \nabla_y^2}\,,\ \theta_i = \arctan\left(\frac{\nabla_y}{\nabla_x}\right). \tag{6}$$

$$Gradient\_Shadow = \begin{cases} 1\ if\ \dfrac{\sum\limits_{i=1}^{n}\sum\limits_{j\in\{b,g,r\}}\left|F(\nabla_i^j)-B(\nabla_i^j)\right|}{n} < \phi_m\ \wedge \\[2ex] \quad\ \dfrac{\sum\limits_{i=1}^{n}\sum\limits_{j\in\{b,g,r\}}\left|F(\theta_i^j)-B(\theta_i^j)\right|}{n} < \phi_d \\[2ex] 0\ otherwise \end{cases} \tag{7}$$

Specially, $\phi_m$ and $\phi_d$ are defined as deciding thresholds of gradient magnitude difference and direction difference respectively. The neighborhood pixels are exploited to help construct the gradient texture. This is a small region centered to current pixel. The gradient magnitude and direction in each pixel's small region in the foreground are associated with the corresponding pixel's small region in the background. Eq. (7) shows the detailed description of the gradient difference and direction difference simultaneously between the current frame and the corresponding background frame.

## 3.5 Union and Post-processing

A simple and typically voting mechanism is proposed to decide whether one pixel belongs to shadow class, which is similar with the best-of-three-games.

For each pixel, it will be regarded as a shadow pixel if there are at least more than 2 (including 2) detected shadow results in S2, S3 and S4. So the union shadow S5 will be obtained, and then post-processing is needed for the sake of achieving a preferable object image and shadow image. The post-processing includes open/close morphology processing and filling for small holes. Finally, the shadow will be segmented properly.

## 4 Experimental Results

### 4.1 Benchmark Sequences and Evaluation Metrics

The benchmark sequences were introduced in [1,15] and six typical scenes and sequences [7] were chosen, which consisted of indoor and outdoor scenes with different shadow detection challenges and the ground truth sequences were segmented manually.

$$\eta = \frac{TP_S}{TP_S + FN_S} , \xi = \frac{TP_F}{TP_F + FN_F}. \tag{8}$$

$$F\text{-}measure = \frac{2\eta\xi}{\eta + \xi}. \tag{9}$$

Shadow detection ($\eta$) and shadow discrimination rate ($\xi$) are two metrics (Eq. (8)) widely used to evaluate the performance of shadow detection methods. The comprehensive and cogent evaluate metric is denoted as *F-measure* (Eq. (9)). We denote $TP_S$ and $FN_S$ as the true positive and false negative pixels of detected shadows, $TP_F$ and $FN_F$ as the true positive and false negative pixels of detected objects.

### 4.2 Qualitative and Quantitative Results

Qualitative results on six sequences are given in Fig. 4 with the straightforward detected shadows and objects. Considering the different scenes, we set two groups of parameters: $\tau_s = 28, \tau_h = 40, \delta = 0.5, \phi_m = 15, \phi_d = 1.2$ and $\tau_s = 20, \tau_h = 40, \delta = 0.55, \phi_m = 15, \phi_d = 1.1$ for indoor scenes and outdoor scenes. The parameters are empirical and a systematic method to generate them needs to be invested in future. Specially, the *Campus* scene uses parameters for indoor scenes due to its weak shadow.

As a whole, the proposed method shows good performance comparing with other five methods: chromaticity method [8], geometry method [9], physical method [10], SR method [11] and LR method [12]. Quantitative results are presented in Table 1 with six kinds of sequences. Outdoor scenes such as *Highway1* and *Highway2* are challenging because of the very less chromaticity and texture information. It is inevitable that some points are easily misclassified as shadows especially at the objects' edges. It is easy to cause the occurrence of false positives by the air disturbance of edges, which results in the thinner detected objects.

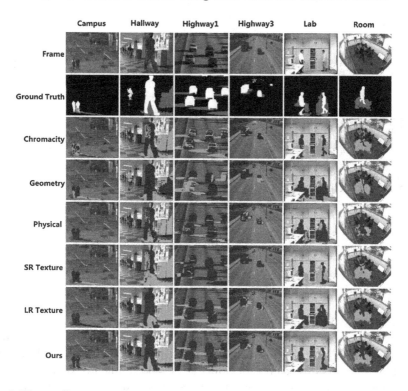

**Fig. 4.** The qualitative results of shadow detection. The green regions are the shadows and the blue regions are the objects (Color figure online).

**Table 1.** The $\eta$ measure evaluation of six methods.

| Methods | Campus | Hallway | Highway1 | Hallway3 | Lab | Room |
|---|---|---|---|---|---|---|
| Chromaticity | 0.5386 | 0.9356 | 0.7601 | 0.4508 | 0.9949 | 0.9662 |
| Geography | 0.6085 | 0.4866 | 0.6616 | 0.4273 | 0.4533 | 0.5477 |
| Physical | 0.459 | 0.5608 | 0.4247 | 0.3628 | 0.2428 | 0.5802 |
| SR | 0.5537 | 0.9609 | 0.1692 | 0.0577 | 0.8151 | 0.9338 |
| LR | 0.5039 | 0.9508 | 0.6046 | 0.3808 | 0.876 | 0.818 |
| Ours | 0.7359 | 0.9562 | 0.6857 | 0.4192 | 0.9109 | 0.9411 |

It can be found out that Fig. 5 shows the advantages of the proposed method. Results of indoor scenes are better than outdoor scenes due to the abundant chromaticity and texture information provided.

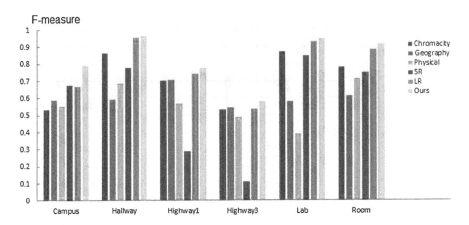

**Fig. 5.** The comparison of shadow detection results with $\theta$ metric by six methods.

## 5   Conclusion

This paper presents a novel method for moving cast shadow detection by using color and texture information. The innovative contribution is that we combine color information with texture features: two color spaces including RGB and HSV and two kinds of textures including ILTP and gradient. We adopt a two-step strategy for shadow detection: the first step is to detect candidate shadows and the second is to extract real shadows on the basis of first step. The pixel's spectral ratio is fit for efficient candidate shadow detection, and experiments validate it.

For all three detectors of HSV, ILTP and Gradient, neighboring information are utilized to supplement and classify pixel points of candidate shadows. Then a simple voting strategy is adopted to obtain a comprehensive shadow result. Experimental results on both indoor and outdoor scenarios show that our method gains a higher shadow detection rate. For all the tested sequences our method is average 4% larger than LR method at *F-measure* evaluation metric. Specially, the *F-measure* result of campus scene is significant, which is about 12% larger than any compared method. However, the challenges such as hard-shadows exist. Further research under strong light condition needs to be done, especially in outdoor scenes. In addition, an automatic mechanism of obtaining robust and systematical parameters could be invested in the next work.

## References

1. Prati, A., Mikic, I., Trivedi, M.M., Cucchiara, R.: Detecting moving shadows: algorithms and evaluation. J. IEEE Trans. Pattern Analy. Mach. Intell. **25**(7), 918–923 (2003)
2. Al-Najdawi, N., Bez, H.E., Singhai, J., Edirisinghe, E.A.: A Survey of cast shadow detection algorithms. J. Pattern Recogn. Lett. **33**(6), 752–764 (2012)

3. Sanin, A., Sanderson, C., Lovell, B.C.: Shadow detection: a survey and comparative evaluation of recent methods. J. Pattern Recogn. **45**(4), 1684–1695 (2012)
4. Jiang, K., Li, A.H., Cui, Z.G., Wang, T., Su, Y.Z.: Adaptive shadow detection using global texture and sampling deduction. J. IET Comput. Vis. **7**(2), 115–122 (2013)
5. Zhang, W., Fang, Z.Z., Yang, X.K., Wu, Q.M.J.: Moving cast shadows detection using ratio edge. J. IEEE Trans. Multimedia **9**(6), 1202–1214 (2007)
6. Qin, R., Liao, S.C., Lei, Z., Li, S.Z.: Moving cast shadow removal based on local descriptors. In: IEEE 20th International Conference on Pattern Recognition, pp. 1377–1380. IEEE Press, New York (2010)
7. The Test Sequences and Ground Truth. http://arma.sourceforge.net/shadows/
8. Cucchiara, R., Grana, C., Piccardi, M., Prati, A.: Detecting moving objects, ghosts, and shadows in video streams. J. IEEE Trans. Pattern Anal. Mach. Intell. **25**(10), 1337–1342 (2003)
9. Hsieh, J.W., Hu, W.F., Chang, C.J., Chen, Y.S.: Shadow elimination for effective moving object detection by gaussian shadow modeling. J. Image Vis. Comput. **21**(3), 505–516 (2003)
10. Huang, J.B., Chen, C.S.: Moving cast shadow detection using physics-based features. In: 2009 IEEE Conference Computer on Vision and Pattern Recognition, pp. 2310–2317. IEEE Press, New York (2009)
11. Leone, A., Distante, C., Buccolieri, F.: Shadow detection for moving objects based on texture analysis. J. Pattern Recogn. **40**(4), 1222–1233 (2007)
12. Sanin, A., Sanderson, C., Lovell, B.C.: Improved shadow removal for robust person tracking in surveillance scenarios. In: IEEE 20th International Conference on Pattern Recognition, pp. 141–144. IEEE Press, New York (2010)
13. Cucchiara, R., Grana, C., Piccardi, M., Prati, A., Sirotti, S.: Improving shadow suppression in moving object detection with HSV color information. In: 2001 IEEE Conference on Intelligent Transportation Systems, pp. 334–339. IEEE Press, New York (2001)
14. Tan, X., Triggs, B.: Enhanced local texture feature sets for face recognition under difficult lighting conditions. J. IEEE Trans. Image Process. **19**(6), 1635–1650 (2010)
15. Martel-Brisson, N., Zaccarin, A.: Kernel-based learning of cast shadows from a physical model of light sources and surfaces for low-level segmentation. In: 2010 IEEE Conference on Computer Vision and Pattern Recognition, pp. 1–8. IEEE Press, New York (2010)

# Detection of Surface Defects of Type 'orange skin' in Furniture Elements with Conventional Image Processing Methods

Leszek J. Chmielewski[1]([✉]), Arkadiusz Orłowski[1], Katarzyna Śmietańska[2],
Jarosław Górski[2], Krzysztof Krajewski[2], Maciej Janowicz[1],
Jacek Wilkowski[2], and Krystyna Kietlińska[1]

[1] Faculty of Applied Informatics and Mathematics (WZIM),
Warsaw University of Life Sciences (SGGW), ul. Nowoursynowska 159,
02-775 Warsaw, Poland
leszek_chmielewski@sggw.pl
[2] Faculty of Wood Technology (WTD),
Warsaw University of Life Sciences (SGGW), ul. Nowoursynowska 159,
02-775 Warsaw, Poland
katarzyna_laszewicz@sggw.pl
http://www.wzim.sggw.pl, http://www.wtd.sggw.pl

**Abstract.** An attempt was made to differentiate between surfaces of furniture elements having the *orange skin* defect and those free from it. As the detectors, the directional derivative of the image intensity along the dominating light direction and the modulus of the image intensity gradient were used. The detectors were tested on series of images with the small and large light incident angles. In case of both detectors, there existed sufficiently wide ranges of thresholds for which both sensitivity and specificity were 100 % for all the 19 images tested. The ranges of thresholds were wider for the light closer to tangential, and for the detector using the gradient modulus, than for the other cases. The optimum scale of the detectors was found different for each light conditions.

**Keywords:** Defect detection · Quality inspection · Furniture elements · Orange skin · Directional derivative · Gradient modulus · Image intensity

## 1 Introduction

Quality inspection is a vital element in furniture manufacturing. In this type of production the dimensions and shape accuracy [1,2] are equally important as the aesthetic aspect related to the visual appearance of the elements. To our best knowledge there are very little or virtually no reports on the quality inspection in furniture industry with the use of image processing methods. We have tried to demonstrate the applicability of these methods to some basic measurement tasks in our previous study [3] in which we have analyzed the images taken with a 3D scanner. In that study we have found that one of the common defects

F. Huang and A. Sugimoto (Eds.): PSIVT 2015 Workshops, LNCS 9555, pp. 26–37, 2016.
DOI: 10.1007/978-3-319-30285-0_3

is at the border or outside the range of applicability of the measurement technique considered. This was the surface defect called *orange skin* which can emerge in the painted surfaces. In this paper we shall demonstrate that *orange skin* can be successfully detected with the conventional 2D image processing methods.

As we have mentioned in [3], the status in the domain of furniture elements quality control is much different from that in the timber industry, where image-based analysis of structural and anatomical defects is a well developed technology with broad literature (see the reviews [4,5]).

The remainder of this paper is organized as follows. In the next Section the defect to be considered and its images will be presented. In Sect. 3 the method of detection of the defect will be described. In Sect. 4 we shall outline the way in which we shall assess the proposed method. The results of the assessment will be shown and discussed in Sect. 5. Finally, we shall conclude the paper in Sect. 6.

## 2   Defects and Images

*Orange skin* is a defect of finishing the surface with lacquer which manifests itself with uneven structure of the hardened surface. The reasons for this defect can be insufficient quantity or bad quality of dilutent, excessive temperature difference between the lacquer and the surface, bad pressure or distance of spraying, excessive air circulation during spraying or drying, and insufficient air humidity. The analyzed surfaces are flat and covered with lacquer, so the defect can be safely treated as the only reason for surface unevenness. Therefore, the considered surface of a furniture element has been divided into only two classes: the *orange skin* called also simply *skin* and the *good surface* called also *good*.

A number of typical furniture elements containing flat surfaces belonging to the two classes have been imaged with a typical, good quality color camera, at a moderate resolution of 2.5 M pixels (1288 × 1936 pix). Two light conditions were used, with light falling onto the object surface at a smaller angle (nearly tangentially) – conditions *light1*, and at a larger angle – conditions *light2*, to check for the influence of this angle on the contrast of the defect. Examples of images with the defective surface taken in light conditions *light1* and *light2* are shown in Fig. 1. An example of *Good surface* for *light2* can be seen in Fig. 2g1.

In Fig. 2 it has been shown how the images were prepared for testing the method. For each image, two more images were prepared by manually marking some parts of their surfaces. In the *mask image*, the part of the surface to be subject to analysis was marked with white color. In this way, these parts of the images were excluded which did not belong to the furniture element, and which did not belong to the planar surface where the defect could appear. In the *color image*, the regions belonging to the white mask in which the *orange skin* did not appear were marked by the green color, and the regions in which the *skin* appeared – with the red color. The characteristics of the *orange skin* defect is such that it appears in the large part or whole surface of the element, or it does not appear at all. Therefore, there were no objects with both *skin* and *good* surfaces. The numbers of images in the two sets are shown in Table 1.

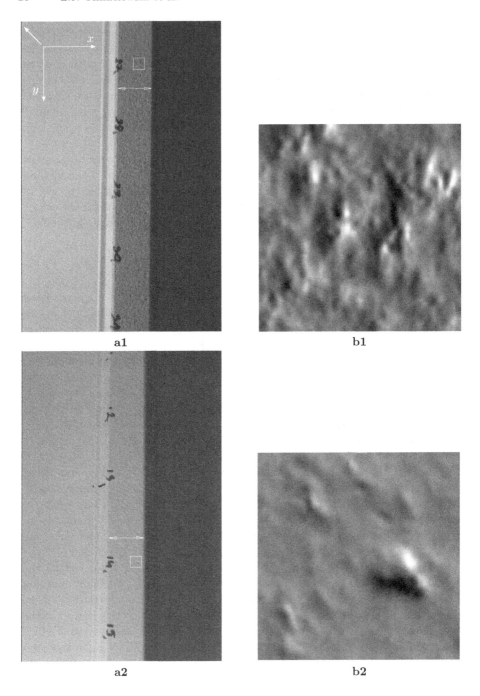

a1

b1

a2

b2

**Fig. 1.** Example of images with the *orange skin* surface defect made in light conditions: (**1**) *light1*, (**2**) *light2*. (**a**) Source image, dimensions 1288 × 1936 pixels; arrow corresponds to 12 mm ≡ 205 pixels. (**b**) Detail marked in the corresponding figure **a** with a square, dimensions 70 × 70 pixels, contrast enhanced. Coordinate system is shown displaced.

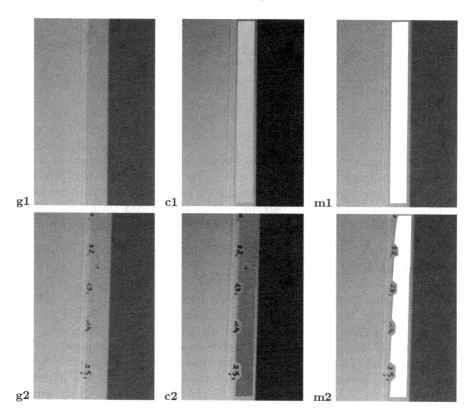

**Fig. 2.** Example subsets of test images for conditions *light2* for one of the elements with (**1**) class *good surface* (*good*) and one with (**2**) class *orange skin* (*skin*). (**g**) Grey image – the source; (**c**) color image with pixels belonging to the classes marked with colors: green for *good* and red for *skin*; (**m**) mask image with pixels belonging to the considered surface of the objects marked with white. Hand-written marks excluded (Color figure online).

## 3   Method

In tangential light the *orange skin* manifests itself with inhomogeneity of brightness, while the *good surface* is homogeneous, so it can be argued that a good method to distinguish between such two surfaces should be chosen from the textural measures (see e.g. [6]). However, in this introductory study we have decided to test the simpler method and to use the derivative operation. We have chosen the numerical approximation of the derivative combined with the Gaussian function filtering as proposed in classical literature [7] and later used extensively (e.g. [8]). This formulation makes it possible to take into account the scale at which we observe the differentiation result. This well known operation resolves itself to the convolution of the image intensity function with the functions shaped like that in Fig. 3. The parameter $\sigma$ of the Gaussian function will be further referred to as the *scale parameter* or simply *scale*.

**Table 1.** Numbers of test images in the two sets used.

| Set | No. with good surface | No. with orange skin | Total |
|-----|----------------------|---------------------|-------|
| light1 | 5 | 4 | 9 |
| light2 | 3 | 7 | 10 |
| Total | 8 | 11 | 19 |

We shall use two versions of the detector: the *directional* one calculated as the derivative of the image intensity function along the direction of the light, and the *nondirectional* one found as the modulus of the gradient of the image intensity function. The output from the detector will be thresholded with threshold $T$. Pixels with the output exceeding the threshold will be treated as defective.

## 4   Methodology of Verification

The object to be detected is the *orange skin* defect, and the remaining surface is the *good surface*. If one pixel is considered, then the true positive (TP) result is to properly classify the *skin* pixel, and the true negative (TN) result – to properly classify the *good* pixel. The erroneous classifications, false positive (FP) and false negative (FN) ones, are defined in a classical way. The detector would work well if the threshold were set so that the number of errors is minimal. However, there is no need that every single pixel is classified properly, but it would be still perfect if there are at least some true positive detections in each defective furniture element, and no false positive detections in any of the good elements. In more detail, if at least some defective pixels were detected in every defective element, the method would exhibit no *false negative* errors and it would be perfectly *sensitive*. If no defective pixels were detected in good elements, the method would exhibit no *false positive* errors and would be perfectly *specific*. If such a single threshold could be set for all the tested objects, the method could be considered good. The method would be acceptable also if there were some errors of the said types, but their numbers were small.

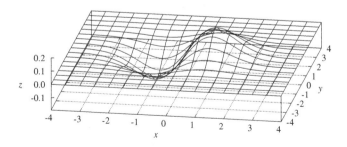

**Fig. 3.** Mask for the derivative with respect to $x$, for $\sigma = 1$.

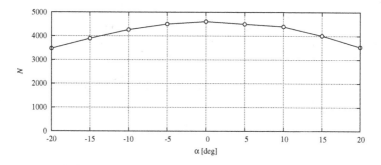

**Fig. 4.** Numbers of detections of *orange skin* regions with the directional detector at threshold $T = 300$, scale $\sigma = 2.0$, in the set *light2* for angles around the actual light direction $\alpha = 0°$.

Typically the relation of the sensitivity and specificity of a detector is displayed in ROC curves (cf. [9]). This is possible if the *ground truth* data are available. In the case of the classification of pixels, this is possible if the defective and good pixels can be univocally marked in the test images. In Fig. 1 one can see that this would be difficult for the *skin* defect, because its symptoms are sparsely displaced all over the surface of the furniture element. So, we shall use another way of displaying the results. We shall count the numbers of pixels with true positive (TP) detections of *skin* and false positive (FP) detections of *good* erroneously classified as *skin*. For this purpose, the pixels marked with colors, like in Fig. 2c1 and c2, will be used. We shall see if it is possible to find a threshold for which the number of true positive *skin* detections is over zero in every image containing a defective object, and simultaneously the number of false positive detections in images containing a good object is small or zero.

A limited set of images can by no means be treated as complete. However, due to that all the available images, without selection, were considered, and in each of them as many pixels were marked for tests as reasonable, the tests can be considered as a sufficient demonstration of the viability of the method.

## 5   Results and Discussion

### 5.1   Light Conditions 1

We shall start the analysis from the image set for light conditions *light1* because it seems that this set will constitute an easier problem to solve for the tested method due tu that the defect is easier to be seen in tangential light.

To use the directional detector it is necessary to set the angle at which the derivative will be calculated. In Fig. 4 it can be seen that the sensitivity of the detector to angle is not large. Therefore, the choice of the angle is not critical to the results. The light direction in the conditions *light1* was $0°$.

The graphs as described in the previous section for the series of test images are shown in Fig. 5. The graphs were obtained with the two detectors:

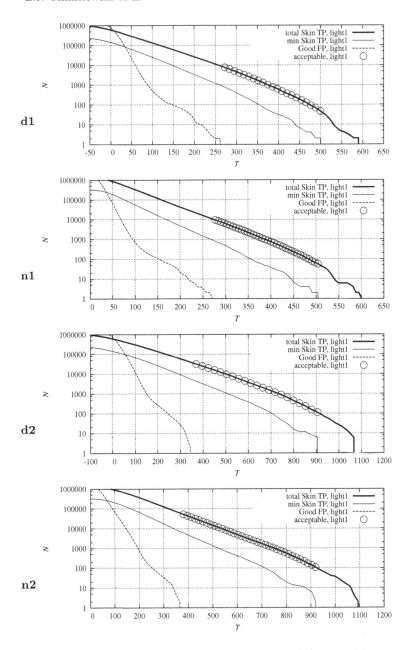

**Fig. 5.** Numbers of pixels above the threshold $T$ in images of objects with *orange skin* and good objects, for conditions *light1*, detected with: (**d**) the directional detector, and (**n**) the non-directional detector, and for two scales: (**1**) $\sigma = 2.0$, and (**2**) $\sigma = 3.0$. Total numbers of properly detected defects at thresholds for which no false detections in good objects occurred are marked with circles. *min Skin TP* is the number of *skin* pixels in the image in which this number was the smallest. Vertical scale is logarithmic so zero is not displayed.

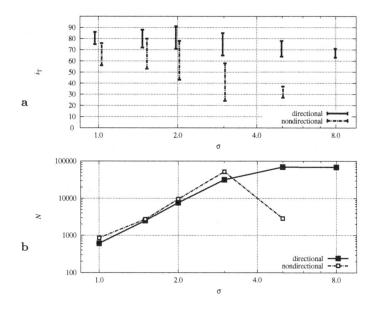

**Fig. 6.** Aggregated results for conditions *light1*: (**a**) bounds for the useful thresholds: the *lower* and the *upper threshold* (their indexes $i_T$): (**b**) total number $N$ of *skin* true positives at the lower threshold, for scales $\sigma \in \{1.5, 2.0, 3.0, 5.0, 8.0\}$. In Fig. a the results for directional and nondirectional detectors are displaced from their respective scales for better visibility. In Fig. b there are no results of the nondirectional filter for $\sigma = 8.0$ because the range of acceptable thresholds was empty.

the directional and the nondirectional one, as described in Sect. 3. The results for 100 thresholds spanning uniformly the whole range of outputs received from the detectors for all the images in the set were calculated. Only the significant parts of these results are shown.

As the threshold goes up, the numbers of detections decreases. The most interesting elements to notice are the threshold at which the number of false positives becomes zero, called the *lower threshold*, and the threshold at which the number of true positives in the image in which it is the smallest becomes zero, called the *upper threshold*. If the upper threshold is larger than the lower one, then there is a range of thresholds for which the detector works with perfect sensitivity and specificity, as far as the test images are considered. Such ranges are shown in Fig. 6. Absolute values of thresholds greatly depend on scale, so the indexes $i_T$ of the thresholds in the set of 100 thresholds, $i_T = 0, 1, \ldots, 99$, for a given series, are used, to put the graphs into a common scale.

In this Figure also the numbers of pixels found as true positives, for the given scales, is plotted. The width of the range of acceptable thresholds as well as this number of true positives can be treated as the quality measures of the detector.

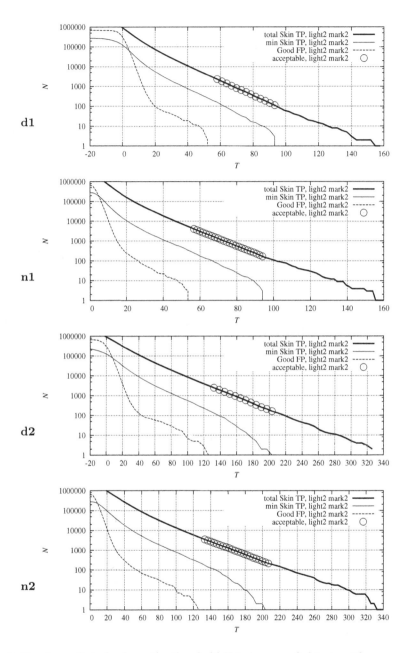

**Fig. 7.** Numbers of pixels above the threshold $T$ in images of objects with *orange skin* and good objects, for light conditions *light2*, detected with: (**d**) the directional detector, and (**n**) the non-directional detector, and for two scales: (**1**) $\sigma = 1.0$, and (**2**) $\sigma = 1.5$. Vertical scale is logarithmic so zero is not displayed. Total numbers of properly detected defects at thresholds for which no false detections in good objects occurred are marked with circles.

The range of acceptable thresholds is larger for the nondirectional detector, and is the largest for $\sigma = 2$ and 3. This is why the graphs in Fig. 5 were plotted for these particular scales. The thresholds can easily be set so that the outputs of the detectors perfectly fits the classification of the furniture elements tested.

The ranges of useful thresholds tend to have a maximum at some scale. For example, in Fig. 5a it is the largest for the nondirectional detector, for the scale $\sigma = 3$ and it is $\langle 24, 58 \rangle$ which corresponds to not less than $41 \pm 40\,\%$. It is important to check which scale is the most appropriate for the calculations. In any case, the scale should be matched to the resolution of the image.

The number of true positives grows with scale, but not in all the cases: in Fig. 6 it decreases between $\sigma = 3$ and 5. This suggests that the number of detection goes down as the scale of the detector moves away from the optimum.

## 5.2    Light Conditions 2

For light conditions *light2* the respective graphs are shown in Fig. 7. Also in this case it can be seen that there exist wide ranges of useful thresholds for all examples considered. These ranges are slightly wider for the non-directional detector than for the directional one, and wider for the scales $\sigma = 1.0$ and 1.5 than for the other scales (Fig. 8). The ranges of acceptable thresholds for *light2*

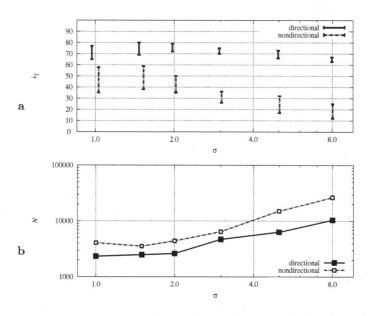

**Fig. 8.** Aggregated results for conditions *light2*: (**a**) bounds for the useful thresholds: the *lower* and the *upper threshold* (their indexes $i_T$); (**b**) total number $N$ of *skin* true positives at the lower threshold, for scales $\sigma \in \{1.5, 2.0, 3.0, 5.0, 8.0\}$. In Fig. **a** the results for directional and nondirectional detectors moved slightly to the left and right from their respective scales, for better visibility.

are more narrow than in the case of *light1*. This could have been expected, as the images are now less contrasted. However, it is still possible to set such a threshold so that *all* the examples can be properly recognized, and that this threshold does not have to be set very precisely. For example, for the nondirectional detector it is the largest for the scale $\sigma = 1$ and it is $\langle 35, 58 \rangle$ which corresponds to not less than $46 \pm 23\%$. At $\sigma = 1.5$ setting the threshold to $T = 165$ would give no false positives in any good object, and over 1000 pixels of defects detected in all bad objects (at minimum, 38 bad pixels in an image. The threshold could be safely changed by at least $\pm 10$, which is at least $\pm 6\%$.

The results for both light conditions can be considered as very good, since they provide for both sensitivity and specificity equal to one in all the examples.

An example of results for the image with *orange skin* of Fig. 2g2 is shown in Fig. 9. The three thresholds were chosen from the optimum range, seen in Fig. 7n2, so that the number of false detections of *good* pixels as *skin* in any test image was zero (only pixels belonging to white as well as color masks were counted). The number of pixels truly found as defective is safely large, at least for the two lower thresholds.

The simple convolution is a quick operation, but its time grows with $\sigma^2$. Therefore, it is profitable that good results can be obtained for small $\sigma$.

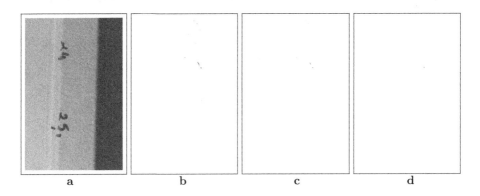

    a                      b                      c                      d

**Fig. 9.** Example results of detection of pixels from class *skin* (marked in black) in the lower half of image from Fig. 2g1 for scale 1.5, nondirectional detector, at different thresholds $T$: (**b**) 140, (**c**) 165 and (**d**) 190.

## 6   Conclusion

Images of furniture elements having the *orange skin* surface defect were considered. As the detectors of the defective surfaces two simple image processing operations were used. The first one was the directional derivative of the image intensity along the light direction. The second one was the modulus of the image intensity gradient. Both detectors performed well enough to consider the method perfectly sensitive and perfectly specific for the tested 19 images, of which 11 contained the defect and 8 did not. This was observed for both the lighting with a light close to tangential to the surface and the light with a smaller incident angle. For the tangential light the range of acceptable thresholds was wider. The results depend on the scale at which the derivatives were taken, but it is easy to find an optimum scale. The nondirectional detector using the modulus of the gradient occurred to preform better than the directional one, so the method does not have to be trimmed according to the light direction.

The results obtained so far indicate that the defect of type *orange skin* can be easily detected even with not very advanced image processing methods.

# References

1. Laszewicz, K., Górski, J.: Control charts as a tool for the management of dimensional accuracy of mechanical wood processing (in Russian). Ann. Wars. Univ. Life Sci.-SGGW, For. Wood Technol. **65**, 88–92 (2008)
2. Laszewicz, K., Górski, J., Wilkowski, J.: Long-term accuracy of MDF milling process-development of adaptive control system corresponding to progression of tool wear. Eur. J. Wood Wood Prod. **71**(3), 383–385 (2013)
3. Chmielewski, L.J., et al.: Defect detection in furniture elements with the Hough transform applied to 3D data. In: Burduk, R., Jackowski, K., Kurzyński, M., et al. (eds.) Proceedings of 9th International Conference Computer Recognition Systems CORES 2015. Advances in Intelligent Systems and Computing, vol. 403, pp. 631–640. Springer, Heidelberg (2015). doi:10.1007/978-3-319-26227-7_59
4. Bucur, V.: Techniques for high resolution imaging of wood structure: a review. Meas. Sci. Technol. **14**(12), R91 (2003)
5. Longuetaud, F., Mothe, F., et al.: Automatic knot detection and measurements from X-ray CT images of wood: a review and validation of an improved algorithm on softwood samples. Comput. Electron. Agric. **85**, 77–89 (2012)
6. Ilea, D.E., Whelan, P.F.: Image segmentation based on the integration of colour-texture descriptors - a review. Pattern Recogn. **44**(1011), 2479–2501 (2011)
7. Marr, D., Hildreth, E.: Theory of edge detection. Proc. Roy. Soc. B **207**, 187–217 (1980)
8. Lindeberg, T.: Edge detection and ridge detection with automatic scale selection. Int. J. Comput. Vis. **30**(2), 117–156 (1998)
9. Lusted, L.: Signal detectability and medical decision-making. Sci. **171**(3977), 1217–1219 (1971). doi:10.1007/978-3-662-07807-5

# Measuring Convexity via Convex Polygons

Paul L. Rosin[1($\boxtimes$)] and Joviša Žunić[2]

[1] School of Computer Science and Informatics, Cardiff University, Cardiff, UK
Paul.Rosin@cs.cf.ac.uk
[2] Mathematical Institute, Serbian Academy of Sciences and Arts, Belgrade, Serbia
jovisa_zunic@mi.sanu.ac.rs

**Abstract.** This paper describes a general approach to compute a family of convexity measures. Inspired by the use of geometric primitives (such as circles) which are often fitted to shapes to approximate them, we use convex polygons for this task. Convex polygons can be generated in many ways, and several are demonstrated here. These polygons are scaled and translated to ensure that they fit the input shape and produce a meaningful convexity measure. Subsequently, a convexity measure can be computed based on the degree of overlap between the two shapes.

**Keywords:** Shape measure · Convexity · Classification

## 1 Introduction

Shape is a characteristic of objects that is useful in both biological perception and computer vision, and many different shape characteristics exist, e.g. linearity circularity convexity, ellipticity, elongation, compactness, linearity, sigmoidality, tortuosity, etc. While there also exist many approaches to measure these various characteristics, several approaches are commonly used across a range of shape characteristics. For instance, shapes which can be described by parametric models can be fitted to the object, and the fitting error used to quantify the membership of the object to that class of shape. An example is shown in Fig. 1b in which a circle has been fitted to minimise the squared Euclidean errors of the data points. Such an approach is attractive, since the fitted model presents the ideal instance of the model most similar to the data, and therefore the errors fairly represent deviations from the shape characteristic [1]. Another popular approach for simple geometric models is to quantify the error with respect to the circumscribed or inscribed model, see Fig. 1c and d.

Convexity is a commonly used shape characteristic, and many convexity measures have been developed (e.g. [2–10]). Since it is not straightforward to determine what general convex geometric model is appropriate to fit in the least squared sense to the data, the dominant approach is to use instead the convex hull, as shown in Fig. 2a and c. This could be considered the analogue of the circumscribed circle presented in Fig. 1b. The convex skull (i.e. the largest convex polygon contained with the object) can also be used to measure convexity [8] – see Fig. 2b and d, but is rarely used due to the high cost of computing it

© Springer International Publishing Switzerland 2016
F. Huang and A. Sugimoto (Eds.): PSIVT 2015 Workshops, LNCS 9555, pp. 38–47, 2016.
DOI: 10.1007/978-3-319-30285-0_4

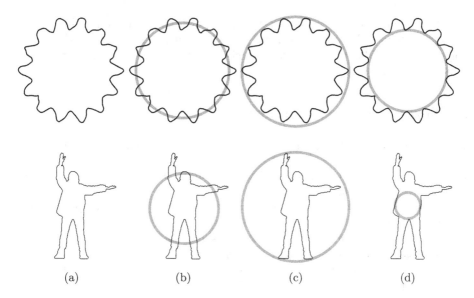

**Fig. 1.** Various approaches to fitting circles to data. (a) input shape (b) least squares fit of circle to data points (c) circumscribed circle (d) inscribed circle.

(i.e. $O(n^7)$, see [11]), which is in contrast to the convex hull, for which efficient algorithms exist. However, a disadvantage is that for shapes not close to an instance of the perfect model, the circumscribed/inscribed model of the convex hull does not provide a representative instance of the model, and therefore errors with respect to this model will not accurately reflect the shape characteristic.

As an alternative to the convex hull, Rosin and Mumford [8] described two symmetric convexity measures that were based on a "robustified" version of the convex hull, which was defined as the convex polygon that maximised its overlap with the input polygon. It can be seen in Fig. 3a that this polygon neither circumscribes or inscribes the input shape, and for the circle example it is rather

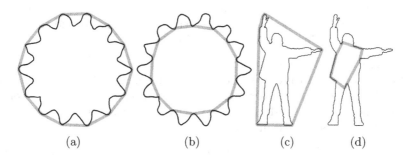

**Fig. 2.** Two approaches to fitting convex polygons to data. (a) & (c) convex hull (b) & (d) convex skull.

similar to the fitted circle in Fig. 1b. In this paper we present several alternative approaches which also produce convex polygons that partially overlap the input polygon (see Fig. 3b–f). Again, for the circle example they are similar to the fitted circle in Fig. 1b.

## 2   New Convexity Measures

The basic approach taken in this paper to compute a convexity measure is:

1. generate a convex polygon based on the input shape; several options are presented in this paper;
2. transform the convex polygon so that it corresponds as best as possible to the input shape; in this paper we have applied a scaling such that the areas of the input and convex polygons are the same, and have also translated the polygons to maximise their area of overlap;
3. compute a convexity measure; in this paper we have used the ratio of the area of overlap to the area of the input polygon.

We now describe the alternative approaches we have taken to step 1:

**Convex Hull** – $C_A^S$: A natural and efficient way to compute a convex polygon is to use the convex hull, see Fig. 2a and c.

**Smoothing** – $C_B$: It is known that if a curve is smoothed using the geometric heat flow equation it becomes more and more circular, eventually shrinking to a circular point in finite time [12]. We iteratively apply smoothing to the input shape until the result becomes convex, see Fig. 3c. Since the data has been heavily smoothed it is sufficient to test for convexity in a simple manner by checking, for a counterclockwise ordered curve, that at each vertex the sign of its subtended angle is positive. Alternatively more sophisticated methods (e.g. estimating curvature by fitting splines [13]) could be employed.

**Polygonal Simplification** – $C_Y$: There are many algorithms available. We use an optimal dynamic programming approach [14] applied to a subsampled version of the contour, which is reasonably efficient and robust. This provides a polyline containing $n$ line segments, and a binary search is applied to find the convex polygon with the maximum value of $n$, see Fig. 3d.

**Convexification** – $C_F$: The polygonal convexification process was described by Paul Erdös [15,16], and involves reflecting a polygon's concavities about their corresponding edges in the convex hull. Iterating this process results in a convex polygon, which has previously been used to measure convexity [17]. Two such convexified polygons are shown in Fig. 3e.

**Convexification with Flipturn**– $C_{FT}$: A modification of the above scheme, in which the concavities are reflected about the complete edge of the convex hull on which the concavity is located, and also have the order of their vertices reversed (an "extended flipturn") was also considered, see Fig. 3f.

**Fig. 3.** Some alternative approaches to fitting convex polygons to data. (a) Rosin and Mumford (b) rescaled convex hull (c) smoothed input polygon (d) polygonal simplification of the input polygon (e) convexification (f) convexification using extended flipturns.

For those methods that generate a convex polygon by enlarging the input shape (such as the convex hull or convexification) the rescaling applied in step 2 provides a balance between protrusion and intrusion irregularities. This is not otherwise present in the most common convexity measures area(S)/area(CH(S)) and perimeter(CH(S))/perimeter(S), which are therefore much more sensitive to protrusions than to intrusions.

For highly concave shapes there may be a large difference in areas between the original shape and its convex hull. Consequently, when the convex hull is shrunk to match the original shape's area there is the possibility that it will not intersect the original shape, leading to a measured convexity value of zero. Since it is undesirable for the convexity measure to produce zero (as shapes are assumed to have non-zero area) the shrunk convex hull is translated to ensure an overlap with the original shape. Although it would be possible to use more general transformations (e.g. rotation, affine with area preservation, etc.), if the convex hull example is considered then translation is the minimal transformation that produces a sensible convexity measure. That is, no non-zero area shape should produce a measured convexity equal to 0. It is generally most appropriate to use the simplest solution that is effective.

The translation parameters are determined using Powell's method [18]. To ensure that the estimation process converges even in situations where there is no intersection between the shrunk convex hull and the original shape, the convex hull is shrunk gradually (10 steps have been found to be sufficient for all our data). Optimisation of the translation parameters is then interleaved with iterations of shrinking. The effectiveness of the optimisation is demonstrated in Fig. 4.

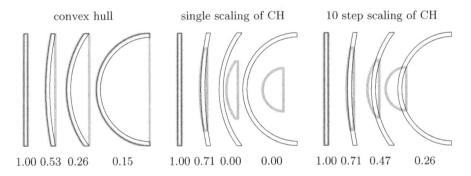

**Fig. 4.** Convex hull based convexity measure. Four shapes with increased bending are shown, as well as their convex hulls or rescaled convex hulls. Underneath each shape is shown its measured convexity value.

## 3    Experimental Results

In this section we provide several experiments in order to illustrate the behaviour and effectiveness of the new convexity measures proposed in this paper.

### 3.1    Lesions

The first experiment is to classify 40 lesions as either benign or malignant melanomas. The lesions have been rated by 14 dermatologists from a four point scale according to their probability of being a melanoma. Lee *et al.* [19] presented this data, and introduced an "overall irregularity index" which they showed provided a Spearman rank correlation of 0.88 against the mean expert rating. Previously we found that convexity measures also performed well on this task. The standard area based convex hull convexity measure $C_A$ had a similar correlation value of 0.888, while both Rosin and Mumford's [8] convex hull based measures $C_P$ and $C_Q$ achieved the high correlation value of 0.958.

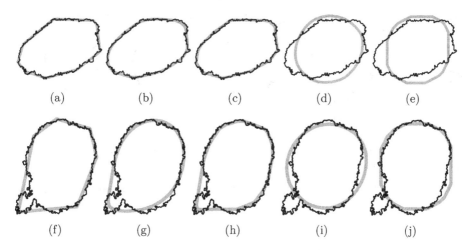

**Fig. 5.** Lesions rated by experts as having a low (top row) and high (bottom row) probability of being a melanoma. The convex polygons corresponding to $C_Y$, $C_B$, $C_A^S$, $C_F$ and $C_{FT}$ are overlaid.

**Table 1.** Spearman rank correlation of the proposed convexity measures against the mean expert rating of the probability of a lesion being a melanoma.

| $C_Y$ | $C_B$ | $C_A^S$ | $C_F$ | $C_{FT}$ |
|-------|-------|---------|-------|----------|
| 0.938 | 0.933 | 0.933 | 0.446 | 0.299 |

Figure 5 shows two lesions overlaid with the convex polygons. As Table 1 shows, most of the new convexity measures proposed in this paper also outperform the overall irregularity index, and come close to the high correlation value achieved by Rosin and Mumford's $C_P$ and $C_Q$ measures.

## 3.2   Greebles

Next, we replicate an experiment from Rosin and Mumford [8] in which they computed convexity for a set of 1137 polygons containing a variety of shapes

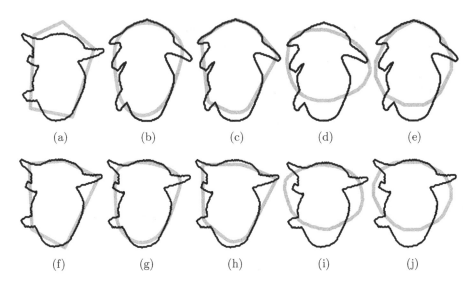

**Fig. 6.** Two examples of greebles; top row: female, bottom row: male. The convex polygons corresponding to $C_Y$, $C_B$, $C_A^S$, $C_F$ and $C_{FT}$ are overlaid.

**Table 2.** Convexity measures applied to 1137 polygons and ranked left to right by the standard deviation of the greeble ranks.

| $C_Q$ | $C_P$ | $C_B$ | $C_Y$ | $C_S$ | $C_A$ | $C_A^S$ | $C_J$ | $C_F$ | $C_{FT}$ | $C_L$ |
|---|---|---|---|---|---|---|---|---|---|---|
| 68.9 | 69.0 | 69.6 | 73.3 | 78.7 | 89.3 | 92.20 | 96.5 | 101.28 | 103.70 | 113.6 |

as well as 53 "greebles". The latter are synthetic test objects used as stimuli in psychological tests, and are shapes that have a qualitatively similar appearance with some minor variations in their four protrusions; two examples are shown in Fig. 6. The convexity measures are compared by ordering the full set of 1137 polygons according to each of the convexity measures. The standard deviation of the greeble ranks is computed, and low values indicate the effectiveness of a measure since it implies that the measure is stable and consistent across minor variations in shape. Results are shown in Table 2, and it can be seen that several of the new convexity measures (in particular $C_B$) are essentially as effective as the convexity measures based on the robust convex hull and the convex skull (i.e. $C_P$ and $C_Q$) [8].

### 3.3 Diatoms

This experiment uses the data from the ADIAC project. 808 contours were taken from images of diatoms (unicellular algae) which come from 38 taxa (classes) that were manually determined by an expert. Not only the boundary contours, but also each diatom's ornamentation, which consists of zero or more (mainly open) curve sections in the interior, are available – see Fig. 7. Previously we have classified this data using several convexity measures both alone and in combination with the following set of descriptors [10]: circularity, ellipticity, rectangularity, triangularity [20] aspect ratio, compactness, convexity, eccentricity, the first four rotation, translation, and scale moment invariants, four rotation, translation, and scale moment invariants [21], the first three affine moment invariants [22]. This experiment has been rerun using a nearest neighbour classifier with Mahalanobis distances and leave-one-out cross validation rather than oblique decision trees (as in [10]), and the new (improved) classification accuracies are shown in the top half of Table 3. The lower half of Table 3 shows the results of classification using the convexity measures proposed in this paper. It can be seen that the performance of the two sets of convexity measures is similar: while any individual convexity measure has a low classification rate, it is significantly boosted when combined with the (single) interior convexity measure, and is even more substantially increased when the 14 general shape descriptors are added. A further improvement is achieved by combining the general shape descriptors with the interior based convexity measure $C_J(I)$ and the new boundary based convexity measure $C_{FT}$ to obtain 91.58 %.

It is interesting to note that although the various convexity measures are nominally measuring the same shape characteristic, in fact they are capturing different aspects of convexity. Therefore when used together the different

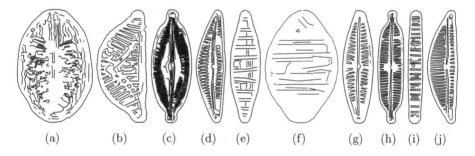

**Fig. 7.** Outer boundary and interior contours of examples of diatoms from different taxa.

**Table 3.** Classification percentage accuracies for 808 diatoms with 38 classes using convexity plus additional general shape measures.

|  | $C_A$ | $C_L$ | $C_J(B)$ | $C_J(I)$ | $C_J(B)$ & $C_J(I)$ |
|---|---|---|---|---|---|
| Convexity | 16.83 | 11.26 | 16.83 | 21.41 | 45.17 |
| Convexity and other features | 87.75 | 86.88 | 87.75 | 90.59 | 90.47 |

|  | $C_Y$ | $C_B$ | $C_A^S$ | $C_F$ | $C_{FT}$ |
|---|---|---|---|---|---|
| Convexity | 20.79 | 17.95 | 21.04 | 17.33 | 13.00 |
| Convexity and $C_J(I)$ | 47.52 | 47.40 | 45.54 | 45.67 | 40.22 |
| Convexity and other features | 88.61 | 87.75 | 87.75 | 85.77 | 87.25 |

convexity measures provide independent information that enables their combination to outperform any individual convexity measure. The convexity measures
previously tested in Žunić and Rosin [10], namely $C_A$, $C_L$, $C_J(B)$ and $C_J(I)$,
when combined provide 62.13 % accuracy, a three-fold increase on the individual
convexity measures. If both the old and new convexity measures are combined,[1]
namely $C_L$, $C_J(B)$, $C_J(I)$, $C_Y$, $C_B$, $C_A^S$, $C_F$ and $C_{FT}$ then the classification rate
increases to 77.48 %.

## 4   Conclusions

In this paper we have described a new approach to compute a family of convexity
measures. The procedure involves (1) generating a convex polygon, (2) fitting
the convex polygon to the input shape by applying a scaling and translation, and
(3) computing the convexity measure based on the input shape and the convex
polygon.

Several specific instances of this approach were demonstrated using the convex hull, smoothing, convexification, etc., to generate the convex polygon, while
for the convexity measure we used the ratio of the area of overlap of the two
shapes to the area of the input polygon. Moreover, many additional possibilities
exist for each of these two steps, which further expands the number of convexity
measures that can be generated.

The resulting convexity measures have the desirable properties that only
convex shapes have measured convexities equal to 1, and that no non-zero area
shape should produce a measured convexity equal to 0.

Experiments showed that the proposed convexity measures are effective for
classification, and that multiple convexity measures can be combined with each
other and with non-convexity measures to improve classification rates.

**Acknowledgement.** This work is partially supported by the Ministry of Science of
the Republic of Serbia, projects OI174008/III044006.

## References

1. Neal, F., Russ, J.: Measuring Shape. Taylor & Francis, Boca Raton (2012)
2. Boxer, L.: Computing deviations from convexity in polygons. Pattern Recogn. Lett.
   **14**, 163–167 (1993)
3. Corcoran, P., Mooney, P., Winstanley, A.C.: A convexity measure for open and
   closed contours. In: Proceedings of British Machine Vision Conference, pp. 1–11
   (2011)
4. Kakarala, R.: Testing for convexity with Fourier descriptors. Electron. Lett. **34**,
   1392–1393 (1998)
5. Martin, R., Rosin, P.: Turning shape decision problems into measures. Int. J. Shape
   Model. **10**, 83–113 (2004)

---

[1] Including $C_A$ with all the other convexity measures caused a small drop in accuracy
to 76.61 %.

6. Pao, H., Geiger, D., Rubin, N.: Measuring convexity for figure/ground separation. In: International Conference on Computer Vision, pp. 948–955 (1999)
7. Rahtu, E., Salo, M., Heikkilä, J.: A new convexity measure based on a probabilistic interpretation of images. IEEE Trans. Pattern Anal. Mach. Intell. **28**, 1501–1512 (2006)
8. Rosin, P., Mumford, C.: A symmetric convexity measure. Comput. Vis. Image Underst. **103**, 101–111 (2006)
9. Stern, H.: Polygonal entropy: a convexity measure. Pattern Recogn. Lett. **10**, 229–235 (1989)
10. Žunić, J., Rosin, P.: A new convexity measurement for polygons. IEEE Trans. Pattern Anal. Mach. Intell. **26**, 923–934 (2004)
11. Chang, J., Yap, C.: A polynomial solution for the potato-peeling problem. Discrete Comput. Geom. **1**, 155–182 (1986)
12. Grayson, M.: The heat equation shrinks embedded plane curves to round points. J. Differ. Geom. **26**, 285–314 (1987)
13. Kozera, R., Noakes, L.: Smooth interpolation with cumulative chord cubics. Comput. Vis. Graph. **32**, 87–94 (2006)
14. Perez, J., Vidal, E.: Optimum polygonal approximation of digitized curves. Pattern Recogn. Lett. **15**, 743–750 (1994)
15. Aichholzer, O., Cortés, C., Demaine, E., Dujmović, V., Erickson, J., Meijer, H., Overmars, M., Palop, B., Ramaswami, S., Toussaint, G.: Flipturning polygons. Discrete Computational Geom. **28**, 231–253 (2002)
16. Erdös, P.: Problem number 3763. Amer. Math. Monthly **42**, 627 (1935)
17. Rosin, P.: Classification of pathological shapes using convexity measures. Pattern Recogn. Lett. **30**, 570–578 (2009)
18. Press, W., Flannery, B., Teukolsky, S., Vettering, W.: Numerical Recipes in C. Cambridge University Press, Cambridge (1990)
19. Lee, T., McLean, D., Atkins, M.: Irregularity index: a new border irregularity measure for cutaneous lesions. Med. Image Anal. **7**, 47–64 (2003)
20. Rosin, P.: Measuring shape: Ellipticity, rectangularity, and triangularity. Mach. Vis. Appl. **14**, 172–184 (2003)
21. Sonka, M., Hlavac, V., Boyle, R.: Image Processing, Analysis, and Machine Vision. Thomson-Engineering, Toronto (2007)
22. Flusser, J., Suk, T.: Pattern recognition by affine moment invariants. Pattern Recogn. **26**, 167–174 (1993)

# Iris Segmentation Using Geodesic Active Contours and GrabCut

Sandipan Banerjee[1]([⊠]) and Domingo Mery[2]

[1] Department of Computer Science and Engineering, University of Notre Dame,
Notre Dame, USA
sbanerj1@nd.edu
[2] Department of Computer Science, Pontifica Universidad Catolica de Chile,
Santiago, Chile

**Abstract.** Iris segmentation is an important step in iris recognition as inaccurate segmentation often leads to faulty recognition. We propose an unsupervised, intensity based iris segmentation algorithm in this paper. The algorithm is fully automatic and can work for varied levels of occlusion, illumination and different shapes of the iris. A near central point inside the pupil is first detected using intensity based profiling of the eye image. Using that point as the center, we estimate the outer contour of the iris and the contour of the pupil using geodesic active contours, an iterative energy minimization algorithm based on the gradient of intensities. The iris region is then segmented out using both these estimations by applying an automatic version of GrabCut, an energy minimization algorithm from the graph cut family, representing the image as a Markov random field. The final result is refined using an ellipse-fitting algorithm based on the geometry of the GrabCut segmentation. To test our method, experiments were performed on 600 near infra-red eye images from the GFI database. The following features of the iris image are estimated: center and radius of the pupil and the iris. In order to evaluate the performance, we compare the features obtained by our method and the segmentation modules of three popular iris recognition systems with manual segmentation (ground truth). The results show that the proposed method performs as good as, in many cases better, when compared with these systems.

## 1 Introduction

Biometric features have become very popular in person identification and are being frequently used at present in defense, private organizations and government bodies. While fingerprints are still the most prevalent biometric feature, iris texture has come forth as a major player as well since the last decade or so. Its rising popularity can be gauged by the fact that iris texture information is being stored along with fingerprint of over 1 billion Indian citizens for the UIDAI project [1]. Many commercial iris recognition software has become available in the market as well. For any iris recognition system to work however, it is essential that the iris is first segmented out correctly from the eye images. But the quality

© Springer International Publishing Switzerland 2016
F. Huang and A. Sugimoto (Eds.): PSIVT 2015 Workshops, LNCS 9555, pp. 48–60, 2016.
DOI: 10.1007/978-3-319-30285-0_5

**Fig. 1.** Some near infra-red eye images with varying levels of illumination, occlusion and iris shape.

of the segmentation can be drastically affected by heavy occlusion, casting of shadows, non-uniform illumination and varying shape of the iris. Examples of near infra-red (IR) eye images with varying illumination, occlusion and iris size can be seen in Fig. 1. Therefore, having an efficient algorithm which can segment the iris in a near-perfect manner in all such cases is crucial.

Recognition based on iris texture came under the spotlight through John Daugman's research, where he used geometric features to segment out the iris by fitting a circle around it [2,3]. The relatively older iris segmentation algorithms, [4,5] being two of the popular ones, are also based on the eye geometry and work well only with images where a circular fit is possible. Consequently, noisy results are obtained from images consisting of high level of occlusion, shadows and non-circular iris shape. Some of the recent papers on the topic [7–10], which investigate iris segmentation from degraded images in visible wavelength and from distantly acquired face images, all use modern image segmentation techniques to eliminate such cases. Geodesic active contours (GAC) [6] is one such segmentation algorithm used for iris segmentation [11]. It uses intensity gradient in images to iteratively evolve an initial curve and fit it around the contour of an object via energy minimization.

The application of the concept of graph cuts in the area of image segmentation was first proposed in [13]. The image is modeled as a Markov random field and an objective function is minimized to segment the object. Histogram of the intensity of few hard-labeled foreground and background pixels marked by the user is used to categorize unlabeled pixels and minimize the objective function in a one-shot manner. Graph cuts have gained much popularity in image segmentation and have been used extensively since then [14,15]. The GrabCut algorithm was proposed to further fine-tune this technique by reducing user interaction [12]. The user draws a rectangular box around the object to specify pixels as sure background (pixels outside the box) and unlabeled pixels (inside the box). A Gaussian mixture model (GMM) is used, instead of a histogram, to categorize pixels in the box by learning parameters based on their intensity in an iterative fashion to get the segmentation. The user can additionally mark pixels inside the box as sure foreground or background to refine the segmentation (like the user marking process in graph cut). Pundlik *et al.* have discussed the use of graph cuts for iris segmentation in [16]. First, the eye image is labeled into eyelash and non-eyelash pixels using texture information with graph cuts, then they segment out the iris region from the non-eyelash pixels.

Our work uses both the GAC model and GrabCut for iris segmentation. A near central point inside the pupil is located by profiling the intensity of the near IR eye image. An initial estimation of the outer contour of the iris (the limbic boundary) and the contour of the pupil is localized by running GAC twice from the point found inside the pupil. The coordinates of the rectangular box (around the iris) and user marks (hard-labels) for sure foreground (iris) and background (pupil) pixels inside it, are computed fully automatically from these estimates without any user effort and are drawn in the image. The iris region is then segmented out from this image by running GrabCut. The segmentation is further refined by fitting an ellipse around the iris and the pupil. The contribution of our approach is twofold. First, we have developed a new robust and automatic algorithm based on GAC and GrabCut which gives an optimal iris segmentation in an iterative manner, instead of a single-shot learning approach. The robustness of our approach is comparable to that of the segmentation modules of three popular iris recognition systems (IrisBEE, VeriEye and MIRLIN). Second, the full code of our method written in Python is available for researchers to use in their own studies[1]. We have described the different steps of the algorithm, experiments and results in more detail in the following sections.

## 2   Proposed Method

Our method can be broadly broken down into the following steps: (a) pre-processing, (b) contour estimation using GAC, (c) iris segmentation using Grab-Cut and (d) a post-processing step for refinement of the segmentation using ellipse fitting. The mask with the elliptical outlines of the iris and the pupil is placed on the original image to get the final segmentation. The different steps are schematically represented in Fig. 2.

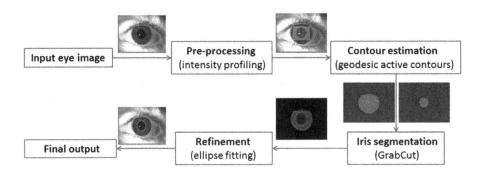

**Fig. 2.** Different steps of the algorithm. Intermediate images show input and output.

---

[1] https://github.com/sbanerj1/IrisSeg.

## 2.1   Pre-processing: Intensity Based Profiling

The goal of the pre-processing step is to locate a central-ish point inside the pupil of the eye image. The image is first divided into three equal parts area-wise in both horizontal and vertical directions. The intersecting region at the center of the image is chosen for profiling since the pupil is generally located in the vicinity of the central region of the eye. Profiling lines are passed in this region, 5 pixels apart in both horizontal and vertical directions, capturing the intensity of each pixel they pass through. The $x$ and $y$ coordinates of all pixels which are within a threshold (set at 20 for our experiments) to the minimum pixel intensity, $i.e.$, the darkest pixel in the region, are stored. We get a near central point $(c_x, c_y)$ in the pupil by computing the mean of the $x$ and $y$ coordinates of all such $dark$ pixels (for a total of $n$ pixels):

$$c_x = \frac{1}{n} \sum_{i=1}^{n} x_i, c_y = \frac{1}{n} \sum_{i=1}^{n} y_i \qquad (1)$$

Let $maxH$ and $maxV$ be the length (in pixels) of the longest profiling line containing $dark$ pixels in horizontal and vertical directions respectively. We store the length (in pixels) of the longest line between the two, denoted as $maxL$, as shown below:

$$maxL = \begin{cases} maxH, \text{if } maxH > maxV \\ maxV, \text{otherwise} \end{cases} \qquad (2)$$

So $maxL$ is the length of the longest profiling line containing $dark$ pixels across both directions. Figure 3 shows an example of profiling lines for a near IR eye image in our database. The coordinates of the central point $(c_x, c_y)$ and the value of $maxL$ are both used in contour estimation in the next step.

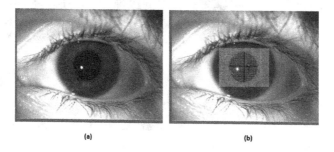

(a)                                        (b)

**Fig. 3.** (a) original eye image. (b) profiling lines are shown in white, dark pixels in green, longest lines containing dark pixels are shown in red and blue for horizontal and vertical directions respectively (Color figure online).

## 2.2  Contour Estimation: Geodesic Active Contours

Contour evolution methods are being used in computer vision research for years now, geodesic active contours (GAC) being a very prominent example. GAC tries to find a contour around the boundary of separation between two regions of the image, foreground (object) and background. This is done using the features of the content in the image (intensity, gradient). The method works by solving partial differential equations (PDE) for an embedding function which has the contour as its zero-levelset. It starts with an initial curve for detecting boundaries, denoted as $\gamma(t)$, where t is the parameter for the evolution step. Let $\psi$ be a function which captures the signed distance from the curve $\gamma(t)$. $|\psi(x, y)|$, for instance, specifies the distance of the point (x, y) from $\gamma(t)$.

The curve $\gamma(t)$ can be termed as a level set of $\psi$, where a level set is a set of points which have the same value of $\psi$. $\psi$ is called the embedding function of $\gamma(t)$ since it implicitly embeds the evolution of the curve. So if $\psi = 0$, *i.e.*, the zero-th level set, then we are on the curve $\gamma(t)$. This embedding function is evolved iteratively to get the contour of the object based on the intensity gradient and the morphological features of different regions in the image. But in most cases, the evolution of the curve does not stop at the boundary region because of varied intensity gradients along the edge. A geodesic term is introduced to stop curve evolution and ensure the curve is attracted towards the boundary regions in such cases, and hence the name. More details about the method can be found in [6,11].

For our work we have used the implementation[2] of morphological GAC, a variant of the traditional GAC model, which has been described in [17]. For an eye image, we run the GAC method twice with the near central point $(c_x, c_y)$ as its center (see (1)), first to detect the outer boundary of the iris and then for

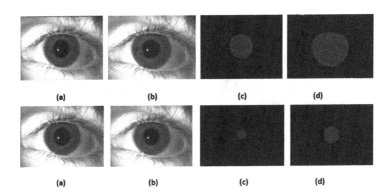

(a)          (b)          (c)          (d)

(a)          (b)          (c)          (d)

**Fig. 4.** Top: (a) initial iris contour (in red), (b) final contour after 120 iterations, (c) initial iris estimation, (d) final estimation. Bottom: (a) initial pupil contour (in red), (b) final contour after 50 iterations, (c) initial pupil estimation, (d) final estimation (Color figure online).

---

[2] https://github.com/pmneila/morphsnakes.

the pupillary boundary. In the first case the diameter of the initial curve is set a few pixels (60 for the set of images we used) more than $maxL$ (see (2)). For the pupil, the diameter is set as $0.6 \times maxL$. We set a hard limit on the number of iterations, 120 for the iris and 50 iterations for the pupil, before the evolution stops. The result of the GAC method for estimation of outer boundary of the iris and the pupil can be seen in Fig. 4. The contour estimations for both the iris and the pupil are stored and used for the iris segmentation process in the next step.

## 2.3    Iris Segmentation: GrabCut

The segmentation model proposed in [12] is based on the same idea of energy minimization in graph cuts [13]. But instead of an one shot learning approach using greyscale intensity histograms from the hard labeled foreground and background pixels in graph cuts, Gaussian mixture models (GMM) are used in Grab-Cut to learn parameters for the foreground and background based on the pixel intensities in color space. The process starts with the user drawing a box around the region of interest and hard labeling some sure foreground and background pixels. The image is then modeled into a weighted graph with each pixel corresponding to a node. Two additional nodes, the source and sink terminals representing the foreground and background respectively, are also introduced in the graph. Weights are assigned to each edge formed between neighboring pixels (called *n-links*) and between a node and the source or the sink terminal (*t-links*). The graph is then disconnected into two parts using min-cut [15]. Consequently, every unlabeled pixel in the box gets categorized as either foreground or background, *i.e.*, we get a segmentation. The process continues iteratively till convergence. However, the algorithm requires some user effort due to its semi-interactive nature.

We automate this box drawing and hard labeling process, using the contour estimations from GAC, so that no user effort is required. From the outer contour estimation of the iris, we locate the rightmost, leftmost, highest and lowest points on it. With the coordinates of these four points, the rectangular box around the iris is drawn on the image (after normalization, if necessary). The whole of the iris, pupil and some parts of the sclera, eyelids and eyelashes are usually inside this box. Similarly, we calculate four points in the four directions from the contour estimation of the pupillary boundary to get the location of a smaller rectangular box around the pupil. Since most pixels in the region between the two rectangular boxes belong to the iris, we label a few pixels in this region as sure-foreground, in six directions. Since the smaller box created from the pupil contour contains pixels mostly belonging to the pupil, some of them through the middle are marked as sure-background. The rectangular box and the hard label swipes generated from the contour estimations in Fig. 4 can be seen in Fig. 5(a). Again, this whole process is fully automatic and needs zero effort on the user's part.

The graph is then constructed from this image with the source and sink terminals (Fig. 5(b)). The weights of the t-links and n-links are computed as well. Applying min-cut iteratively on this graph gives the optimal segmentation.

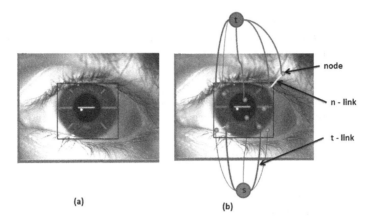

**Fig. 5.** (a) rectangular box containing iris, hard-labeled foreground pixels (in red), hard-labeled background pixels (in green), (b) graph formed from the image with n-links connecting nodes with neighborhood nodes and t-links connecting them with source (s) and sink (t) terminals (Color figure online).

For our set of eye images, 10 iterations generally produce a good segmentation. Most of the iris pixels are correctly labeled, as can be seen from Fig. 6(a). The pixels belonging to the sclera, specular highlights, eyelids and eyelashes are removed (labeled as background) as the GMM parameters are learned from the hard-labeled pixels outside the box.

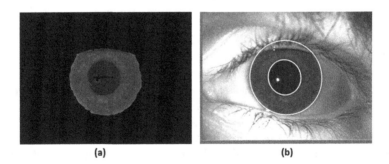

**Fig. 6.** (a) segmented iris after 10 iterations, (b) final segmentation after ellipse fitting.

## 2.4   Refinement: Ellipse Fitting

The segmented iris produced by GrabCut needs to be refined and its boundary fitted into the original eye image. To get a smooth curve from the segmentation, we use an ellipse fitting method[3] based on minimum squared error. The method

---

[3] http://opencv.sourcearchive.com/documentation/1.0.0-6/fitellipse_8py-source.
html.

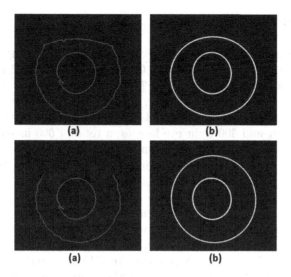

**Fig. 7.** Top: (a) original (closed) profile, (b) asymmetrical iris mask. Bottom: (a) open profile after removal of points in occluded region, (b) correct symmetrical iris mask.

tries to fit an ellipse to the set of points at the boundary region of the segmentation (the contour) which generates the minimum squared error. To do this, we first get a profile of the iris (and pupil) segmentation. This gives a closed set of points on the outer boundary of the iris (and pupil) where the ellipse is to be fit. Fitting two ellipses on to these boundary points should produce the refined iris and pupil mask.

However, occlusion due to eyelids or eyelashes can be detrimental to this ellipse fitting process. GrabCut only segments out the region of the iris which is visible, *i.e.*, has intensities similar to other iris pixels. So in case of occlusion, the profiling of the iris boundary segmented by GrabCut gives us a set of points which fit to the wrong ellipse. The symmetrical shape of the iris is lost in this case, as can be seen in Fig. 7 (top row). To fix this problem, we check the length (in pixels) of the upper and lower tip of the segmented iris from the pupil. If one is much smaller compared to the other, below $0.75 \times$ the larger distance for our set of images, then we conclude that part to be occluded (as the iris shape is symmetrical). In that case we remove all points in the occluded region (the smaller end from the pupil) from the profile of the iris. This produces an open set of points, with majority of the points in the curve still intact. Fitting the ellipse on to these set of points gives a much better and symmetric iris shape, as shown in Fig. 7 (bottom row). Any occlusion in the pupil boundary (quite rare) gets fixed automatically in the process. The elliptical iris and pupil outlines generated, are now applied on the original eye image. This gives us the final refined segmentation (Fig. 6(b)).

## 3    Experimental Results

In this section, we present the segmentation results obtained using the proposed method. The method was tested on the GFI database described in [18], which consists of 3000 images with both eyes of 750 males and 750 females. The images were taken with an LG 4000 sensor using near IR illumination and have a resolution of 480 (height) × 640 (width) pixels and 8-bit/pixel. For our experiments, we selected 300 left and 300 right eye images, a total of 600 images, randomly. The effectiveness of our method is shown in Fig. 8 for 25 left and 25 right eye images. It is clear, that it segments the iris correctly and is able to predict the occluded part of the iris after the ellipse fitting.

In order to evaluate the performance of our method, we tested our results against ground truth data (manual segmentation). To get a better understanding of the performance, the segmentation modules of three well known iris recognition systems were selected: IrisBEE (contour processing and Hough transform based method) [19], Neurotechnology's VeriEye SDK (active shape model based method) [20], and MIRLIN iris recognition SDK, currently owned by FotoNation [21], and their segmentation results were compared against the ground truth as well.

From all four methods (the three mentioned software and ours) and manual segmentation, we obtained two circles: one for the external boundary of the iris and the other for the pupillary boundary. From each circle, we measured the center and the radius. To get the circular radius for the iris segmented with our method, the average of the length of the two axes of the fitted ellipse was taken while the center was kept the same. We calculated the circular features for the ellipse fitted to the pupil similarly. The performance of all four methods were compared to manual segmentation by measuring the Euclidean distance between the centers ($x$ and $y$ coordinates) and the difference of the radius in pixels. Since the average size of the iris in these images was found to be 246 × 246 pixels, we normalized each difference given in pixels by dividing it by 246. The averages of all differences and distances for all methods with the ground truth was computed. The results from the comparison can be found in Table 1.

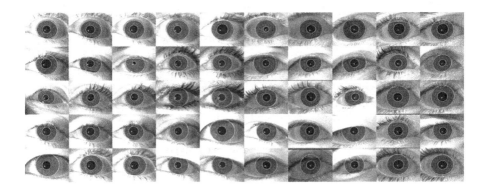

**Fig. 8.** Segmentation results for 25 left and 25 right eye images.

**Table 1.** Comparison with ground truth data

| Method | Pupil center | Pupil radius | Iris center | Iris radius |
|---|---|---|---|---|
| IrisBee | 0.55 % | 0.26 % | 1.63 % | 1.13 % |
| VeriEye | 0.51 % | 0.20 % | 1.52 % | 0.91 % |
| MIRLIN | 1.05 % | 0.58 % | 1.62 % | 0.69 % |
| Proposed Method | 0.49 % | 0.37 % | 1.87 % | 1.11 % |

We also extracted out the binary segmentation donut for each image for all the four methods and ground truth. We measured the precision and recall for each image by pixelwise comparison of the donuts for each method with that of the ground truth, as shown below:

$$Pr = TP/D, Re = TP/P \qquad (3)$$

where $Pr$ stands for precision and $Re$ stands for recall. $D$ and $P$ are the set of positive pixels ('1') in the method segmentation and manual segmentation donuts respectively. While the intersection of the positive pixel sets of the method and manual segmentation donuts is denoted as $TP$. We further calculated the accuracy of segmentation as:

$$Acc = (TP + TN)/(P + N) \qquad (4)$$

where $Acc$ stands for accuracy and $N$ is the set of negative pixels ('0') in the manual segmentation donut. The intersection of the negative pixel sets of the method and manual segmentation donuts is denoted as $TN$. The mean $Pr$, $Re$ and $Acc$ values are calculated over the 600 images for all the four methods and can be found in Table 2.

**Table 2.** Pixelwise comparison with ground truth data

| Method | Precision | Recall | Accuracy |
|---|---|---|---|
| IrisBee | 0.974 | 0.940 | 0.989 |
| VeriEye | 0.948 | 0.983 | 0.991 |
| MIRLIN | 0.948 | 0.975 | 0.990 |
| Proposed Method | 0.947 | 0.965 | 0.988 |

On analyzing the segmentation results of all four methods, it is found that the proposed method performs better than the other three methods in many cases, especially when there is occlusion due to eyelids or protruding eyelashes in the image. In Fig. 9, the faulty segmentation results for IrisBee, MIRLIN and VeriEye can be seen on the top row and segmentation results for the corresponding images with our method on the bottom row. It can be observed that our method does a better job in these cases, especially in detecting the pupil. Furthermore, we observe that IrisBee and especially VeriEye perform consistently over the whole span of the dataset, while MIRLIN's performance varies considerably with it having the highest standard deviation for the accuracy (*Acc*) metric among all the four methods.

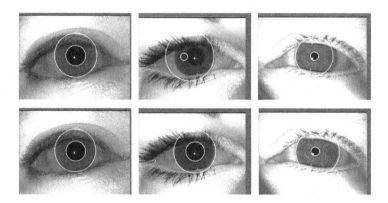

**Fig. 9.** Top: IrisBee, MIRLIN and VeriEye faulty segmentations respectively. Bottom: segmentation with proposed method.

In this regard, it is worth mentioning that our method fails to get a perfect segmentation in some of the images, usually because the intensity distribution around the eye in those images are quite similar to that of the iris. This can be attributed to high degree of occlusion by eyelashes and heavy make-up or the images being hazy (as in the right most two images in Fig. 1). As a result, optimal segmentation wasn't reached in 10 iterations of GrabCut for these images.

## 4    Conclusion

In this paper, we have presented a new algorithm which performs iris segmentation automatically in cases with less constrained conditions, including variability in levels of occlusion, illumination and different locations of the iris. The main contribution of our paper is that we have developed a new robust algorithm for iris segmentation based on geodesic active contours (GAC) and GrabCut. The robustness of our algorithm is due to four reasons: *(i)* a near central point inside the pupil is automatically detected using intensity based profiling of the eye image; *(ii)* using that point as the center, the contours of the iris and the pupil are estimated using GAC (an iterative energy minimization algorithm based on the gradient of intensities); *(iii)* the iris region is segmented using both these estimations by applying an automatic version of GrabCut (an energy minimization algorithm from the graph cut family, representing the image as a Markov random field); and *(iv)* the final result is refined using an ellipse-fitting method based on the geometry of the GrabCut segmentation.

In order to validate the proposed method, we tested it on 600 near IR iris images selected randomly from the GFI dataset. To evaluate its performance, we compare the segmentation results from our method to ground truth data. The differences in locations of the centers of the pupil and iris; and the radii of the pupil and iris were less than 2 %. We also obtain a 98.8 % accuracy when comparing segmentation donuts pixel-by-pixel with the ground truth. To better gauge the performance, we also compare the results with that of the segmentation modules of three other popular iris recognition systems (IrisBEE, VeriEye and MIRLIN) and found them to be very identical. Since the performance of our method is found to be similar to the performance of these recognition systems, we believe that the algorithm we developed could be used by other researchers in their own studies.

Our future work involves further improving the approach in two ways. The current implementation of our algorithm in Python takes about 7 s for running GrabCut and 18 s on average for running the morphological GAC operation twice on a Windows 7 machine with 4 GB of memory. Optimizing the code will definitely speed up the process. Adding an automatic eyelash-removal step in pre-processing could give a better contour estimation in fewer iterations of GAC and GrabCut, effectively saving time. We also plan on tuning the parameters of the code and trying different combinations of them, using different ellipse fitting methods to get an idea of how they affect the performance of the system.

**Acknowledgment.** The authors would like to thank Juan E. Tapia for providing the segmentation results from the recognition systems, Sujoy Biswas for directing us towards GrabCut and Patrick J. Flynn for improving the paper with his suggestions.

# References

1. UIDAI. https://uidai.gov.in/
2. Daugman, J.: High confidence visual recognition of persons by a test of statistical independence. IEEE Trans. Pattern Anal. Mach. Intell. **15**(11), 1148–1161 (1993)
3. Daugman, J.: Statistical richness of visual phase information: update on recognizing persons by iris patterns. Int. J. Comput. Vision **45**(1), 23–38 (2001)
4. Feng, X., Fang, C., Ding, X., Wu, Y.: Iris localization with dual coarse to fine strategy. In: Proceedings of the IAPR International Conference on Pattern Recognition, pp. 553–556 (2006)
5. He, Z., Tan, T., Sun, Z.: Iris localization via pulling and pushing. In: Proceedings of the IAPR International Conference on Pattern Recognition, pp. 366–369 (2006)
6. Caselles, V., Kimmel, R., Sapiro, G.: Geodesic active contours. In: Proceedings of the International Conference on Computer Vision, pp. 694–699 (1995)
7. Proenca, H.: Iris recognition: On the segmentation of degraded images acquired in the visible wavelength. IEEE Trans. Pattern Anal. Mach. Intell. **32**(8), 1502–1516 (2009)
8. Tan, T., He, Z., Sun, Z.: Efficient and robust segmentation of noisy iris images for non-cooperative iris recognition. Image Vis. Comput. **28**(2), 223–230 (2010)
9. Tan, C.W., Kumar, A.: Unified framework for automated iris segmentation using distantly acquired face images. IEEE Trans. Image Process. **21**(9), 4068–4079 (2012)

10. Tan, C.W., Kumar, A.: Towards online Iris and periocular recognition under relaxed imaging constraints. IEEE Trans. Image Process. **22**(10), 3751–3765 (2013)
11. Shah, S., Ross, A.: Iris segmentation using geodesic active contours. IEEE Trans. Inf. Forensics Secur. **4**(4), 824–836 (2009)
12. Rother, C., Kolmogorov, V., Blake, A.: GrabCut - interactive foreground extraction using iterated graph cuts. Proc. ACM SIGGRAPH **23**(3), 309–314 (2004)
13. Boykov, Y., Jolly, M.P.: Interactive graph cuts for optimal boundary & region segmentation of objects in N-D images. In: Proceedings of the International Conference on Computer Vision, pp. 105–112 (2001)
14. Boykov, Y., Veksler, O., Zabih, R.: Fast approximate energy minimization via graph cuts. IEEE Trans. Pattern Anal. Mach. Intell. **23**(11), 1222–1239 (2001)
15. Boykov, Y., Kolmogorov, V.: An experimental comparison of Min-cut/Max-flow algorithms for energy minimization in vision. IEEE Trans. Pattern Anal. Mach. Intell. **26**(9), 1124–1137 (2004)
16. Pundlik, S., Woodard, D., Birchfield, S.: Iris segmentation in non-ideal images using graph cuts. Image Vis. Comput. **28**(12), 1671–1681 (2010)
17. Marquez-Neila, P., Baumela, L., Alvarez, L.: A morphological approach to curvature-based evolution of curves and surfaces. IEEE Trans. Pattern Anal. Mach. Intell. **36**(10), 2–17 (2013)
18. Tapia, J., Perez, C., Bowyer, K.W.: Gender classification from iris images using fusion of uniform local binary patterns. In: Proceedings of the International Workshop on Soft Biometrics at ECCV, pp. 751–763 (2014)
19. Phillips, P.J., Bowyer, K.W., Flynn, P.J., Liu, X., Scruggs, W.T.: The Iris challenge evaluation 2005. In: Proceedings of the IEEE International Conference on Biometrics: Theory, Applications and Systems, pp. 1–8 (2008)
20. VeriEye SDK. https://www.neurotechnology.com/verieye.html
21. FotoNation. https://www.fotonation.com/

# Robust Segmentation of Aerial Image Data Recorded for Landscape Ecology Studies

Rafael Guillermo Gonzalez Acuña[1]([⊠]), Junli Tao[2], Daniel Breen[2],
Barbara Breen[2], Steve Pointing[2], Len Gillman[2], and Reinhard Klette[2]

[1] Centro de Investigaciones en Óptica, León, Guanajuato, Mexico
rafael@cio.mx
[2] Auckland University of Technology, Auckland, New Zealand

**Abstract.** Remote sensing from unmanned aerial vehicles provides an
opportunity to bridge the gap between fine scale ground-based measurements and broad scale observations from conventional aircraft and
satellites. The advantages of this approach include safe access to hazardous or difficult terrain and conditions, the ability to survey at specific times and spatial scales, and the increasingly affordable cost of
this technology. These benefits have led to a rapidly expanding range
of applications in natural resource management and research including
mapping of terrain, vegetation cover and condition, threatened species,
habitat and the impacts of agriculture, forestry, urbanisation and climate
change. The analysis of these often large datasets requires reliable segmentation and classification algorithms to efficiently process information
for use in landscape ecology and adaptive management. In this paper,
four segmentation methods are compared using images of native vegetation, introduced weeds and agriculture recorded from a quadcopter flown
over a warm temperate island (Waiheke Island, New Zealand), and also
images recorded from a fixed wing UAV in a polar desert (McMudro Dry
Valleys, Antarctica). We propose a post-processing method to improve
the segmentation performance of the algorithms and demonstrate how
this can contribute to improving research outcomes in natural resource
management, conservation and agriculture.

**Keywords:** Image segmentation · Aerial video data · UAV · Waiheke
Island · Antarctica · Performance evaluation · Segmentation measure

## 1 Introduction

*Unmanned aerial vehicles* (UAVs) were initially developed for military purposes
but their potential was quickly recognised for civilian applications. Examples
include [18] who proposes the use of UAVs for vineyard management based on
vegetation canopy reflectance, mapping of invasive weeds [17] to plan herbicide
applications, or using an infra-red camera to map the *crop water stress index*
(CWSI) to guide irrigation. [2,6] use UAVs to monitor soil erosion. [21] use aerial
data for quantifying tree height by reconstructing 3D clouds of points.

© Springer International Publishing Switzerland 2016
F. Huang and A. Sugimoto (Eds.): PSIVT 2015 Workshops, LNCS 9555, pp. 61–72, 2016.
DOI: 10.1007/978-3-319-30285-0_6

Vegetation classification is a an important source of information for conservation science, agriculture, forestry and planning. UAV technology provides an alternative to ground-based measurements and satellite data as a means of obtaining suitable imagery for vegetation classification. [19] uses $k$-means clustering to classify airborne laser scans from UAVs into two different forest regions. [7,9,15] also use UAV remote sensing to classify vegetation. [22] compares classification methods for data recorded from an UAV.

The basic intention of image segmentation is the partitioning of an image into connected regions of pixels defined by similar colour or texture. In general it is concluded in the papers cited above that segmentation-based classification methods outperform pixel-based classification methods. In this paper, we compare four segmentation algorithms using aerial data recorded with UAVs over a warm temperate island (Waiheke Island, New Zealand) or in a polar desert (McMudro Dry Valleys, Antarctica) [3]. Figure 1 shows a mosaic generated from individual frames of a video recorded in New Zealand.

The algorithms compared are *simple linear iterative algorithm* (SLIC) [1], a *Gaussian mixture model* (GMM) [13], a *hidden Markov model with expectation maximisation* (HMM-EM) [20], and a *mean-shift* (MS) algorithm [5]. We assess the performance of these algorithms in classifying native forest, agriculture and invasive weeds, and also dry valley habitats in Antarctica. However, as none of these methods performed well, we propose a post-processing technique to merge

**Fig. 1.** Native vegetation, exotic weed species and agricultural land on Waiheke Island, Auckland, New Zealand. Mosaic processed using Pix4Dmapper Pro 2.071 from Sony Action Cam images taken from a Blade QX350 quadcopter

and split output regions to improve the classification of the original segmentation algorithms.

The segmentation step (i.e. being only an initial step in a sequence of scene analysis procedures) aims at separating the scene into semantic regions, for instance, into lawn, forest, patches of gravel, or houses. We use a colour and texture similarity measure for post-processing.

The paper is structured as follows. Section 2 presents the segmentation methods and discusses the drawbacks for our image data. In Sect. 3, the proposed post-process is reported. A comparative performance analysis is given in Sect. 4. Section 5 concludes.

## 2  Segmentation Methods

The trials were conducted on images from Waiheke Island, New Zealand, recorded with a Sony Action Cam HDR100 camera mounted on a Blade QX350 version 3 quadcopter UAV, and from the Taylor Dry Valleys in Antarctica recorded from a fixed wing Skycam "Polarfox" with Sony Nex5 camera (Bollard-Breen et al. 2015). The images were initially segmented using the SLIC, GMM, HMM & EM, and MS algorithms. Each method has its merits and drawbacks for tackling different image segmentation tasks.

### 2.1  Tested Segmentation Methods

We briefly recall those segmentation methods later used in Sect. 4. Given an $N \times N$ image $I$ (for notational simplicity in this paper we assume square images), those four methods are applied to generate a *labelling* $f$ (i.e. the segmentation result) which assigns uniquely a segment number (i.e. the *label*) to each of the $N^2$ pixels.

**SLIC.** SLIC is a segmentation algorithm that segments images into "nearly convex" regions called *superpixels*. It uses a strategy similar to *k-means* but with some crucial modifications. Every cluster has a defined neighbourhood, and the algorithm is spatially constrained to only merge pixels if they are near the cluster. The size of the considered neighbourhood is proportional to the number $k$ of clusters in the image. This number $k$ is the only input parameter for the procedure.

The clustering distance depends on the $L^\star a^\star b^\star$ colour of the pixels and their $(x, y)$ coordinates. See [1,14] for details. Consider pixel $(x_i, y_i, L_i, a_i, b_i)$ and cluster centroid $(x_j, y_j, L_j, a_j, b_j)$. SLIC uses the following distance between both:

$$D_{SLIC} = \sqrt{d_c^2 + \frac{d_s^2}{S^2}\lambda^2}, \quad \text{where} \quad S = \sqrt{N/k} \tag{1}$$

$$d_c = \sqrt{(L_i - L_j)^2 + (a_i - a_j)^2 + (b_i - b_j)^2} \tag{2}$$

$$d_s = \sqrt{(x_i - x_j)^2 + (y_i - y_j)^2} \tag{3}$$

where $d_c$ is the color distance, $d_s$ the spatial distance, $S$ is the length of one side of a *cluster neighbourhood*, and $\lambda > 0$ is a weight constant. See [1].

**GMM.** GMM specifies a segmentation method based on a parametric model in which the probability density function of the levels in the image is a mixture of a number of different Gaussian density functions. The goal of GMM is to find the optimal thresholds that divide the probability density function of the image (i.e. the histogram of the given image) in $\kappa$ Gaussian density functions, where each Gaussian density function represents a region of the image. See [13]. The Gaussian density function has the following form:

$$\Pr(u|C_j) = \frac{1}{\sigma_j \sqrt{2\pi}} \cdot e^{-\frac{(u-\mu_j)^2}{2\sigma_j^2}} \tag{4}$$

where $\Pr(.|C_j)$ is the $j$th Gaussian density function for image values $u$; $\sigma_j^2$ is the standard deviation, and $\mu_j$ is mean value of this Gaussian density function.

**HMM & EM.** HMM & EM is an edge-prior preserving segmentation algorithm which can be used for obtaining accurate segmentation labels by using the maximum a posteriori (MAP) criterion. This algorithm uses an initially segmented image, which is obtained using GMM or $k$-means clustering with estimated parameters. See [20].

HMM & EM is defined for images $I = (\mathbf{u}_1, \ldots, \mathbf{u}_{N^2})$, drawn from an assumed distribution, where $N^2$ is the total number of pixels, and each $\mathbf{u}_i$ represents the values of the colours of a pixel, with $\mathbf{u}_i = [u_{iR}, u_{iG}, u_{iB}]^\top$. Let $L = \{l_1, \ldots, l_m\}$ be a set of possible labels, also drawn from an assumed distribution. See [20]. The goal of HMM & EM is to find a labeling $f^*$ (i.e. which maps all $N^2$ values uniquely into set $L$) which satisfies

$$f^* = \mathrm{argmax}_f \{\Pr(I|L, \Theta)\Pr(L)\} \tag{5}$$

where $\Theta = \{\theta_l : l \in L\}$ is a set of distribution parameters

$$\theta_l = \{(\mu_{l,1}\sigma_{l,1}, w_{l,1}), \ldots, (\mu_{l,g}\sigma_{l,g}, w_{l,g})\} \tag{6}$$

for $g$ Gaussian components, each having $\mu$ as mean value and $\sigma$ as standard deviation; $w$ is a weighting probability.

**MS:** MS is a variant of the steepest-ascent method to seek stationary peaks in a density function defined in a property space. Properties are values in the image (values directly available, such as colour values at pixels or coordinates, or values derived at pixels, such as local variance or gradient values). The algorithm is basically a density estimator. Discrete gradients are estimated in property space using a local weighting function (the *kernel*) for approximating derivatives. Let $r$ be the radius of the kernel function $K$, and $K'$ is the derivative of this kernel $K$.

The resulting steepest-ascent gradient defines the mean-shift vector, thus a new location in property space, where the procedure repeats, until the magnitude of the gradient is close to zero. The used density estimator has the following form:

$$E_K(\mathbf{u}) = \frac{c_k}{Mr^n} \sum_{i=1}^{M} K(\frac{1}{r^2}||\mathbf{u} - \mathbf{u}_i||_2^2) \tag{7}$$

The function is defined by kernel $K$ at property points or vectors $\mathbf{u}$ in an $n$-dimensional property space, $c_k$ is a normalization constant, $M$ is the number of property vectors $\mathbf{u}$. For time-efficiency reasons we use a simplified MS algorithm, basically without the second (delineation) step in [5].

## 2.2   Drawbacks of the Segmentation Methods

The above segmentation methods have some important drawbacks for the considered application, and we discuss those here. See Figs. 2 and 4.

**SLIC.** SLIC has two main problems, over-classifying a single relatively homogenous region into many different superpixels, and forming large superpixels that contain two or more regions inside. The latter mostly occurs with superpixels around the borders of the image, or where there are not enough superpixels to segment the image.

**GMM.** GMM tends to create many isolated pixels and many *islands* (i.e. connected regions of pixels that are surrounded by pixels of another region). Borders between regions are also not well defined, and the regions intercalate gradually.

**HMM & EM.** HMM & EM tends to classify images into nested regions where a segment is surrounded by a larger region, which in turn lies within another larger region. This pattern does not adequately describe the patterns present in studied vegetation or landscape images.

**MS.** In the mean-shift segmentation, the number of clusters depends on the image and creates a very large number of labels for segments belonging to the same semantic region. This can be avoided by a post-processing algorithm to join similar regions into single segments.

# 3   Proposed Post-processing

Given a label map $I^m$ generated by a segmentation method (i.e. representing a labelling function $f$ in form of an image), we propose post-processing to improve the segmentation performance of those methods by splitting segments, merging segments, and avoiding islands. In this section, we report the proposed post-process.

**Splitting Segments.** We introduce color similarity to decide whether to further split segments or not. In $I^m$, one segment may contain multiple regions, such as both grass and forest regions, which require further segmentation. We introduce color similarity for deciding further splitting segments or not. The splitting condition is formulated as follows:

$$\sigma_{color_i} < \tau_1 \tag{8}$$

$$\sigma_{color_i} = \sqrt{\sigma_{L_i}^2 + \sigma_{a_i}^2 + \sigma_{b_i}^2} \tag{9}$$

where $i$ denotes the $i$th segment, and $L$, $a$, and $b$ are the color components in the L*a*b* color space. $\sigma$ denotes the standard deviation. If the value of the standard deviation $\sigma_{color_i}$ is over the threshold $\tau_1$, the segment $i$ is further segmented using the SLIC method.

---

**Algorithm 1. Splitting segments**

---

1: **for** $i = 1$ to $N_{segments}$
2: $\sigma_{color_i} = \sqrt{\sigma_{L_i}^2 + \sigma_{a_i}^2 + \sigma_{b_i}^2}$
3: **if** $\sigma_{color_i} > \tau_1$
4: Apply SLIC to segment $i$
5: Update the labelling $f$ (or map $I^m$) and $N_{segments}$
6: **end if**
7: **end for**

---

**Merging Segments.** As a result of the original segmentation, or after performing further splitting, a region (e.g. grass) might be segmented into too many smaller segments. We use color similarity and a texture-based measure for merging segments. The Laplacian kernel calculates an approximate of second-order derivatives along horizontal and vertical directions in an image; we compute the Laplacian in luminosity images [8,10]. Due to changes in illumination, misclassifications may occur as the texture information is illumination independent.

The merging condition is defined as follows:

$$D_{ij} < \tau_2 \tag{10}$$

$$\mathcal{L}_{ij} < \tau_3 \tag{11}$$

$$D_{ij} = \sqrt{(L_i - L_j)^2 + (a_i - a_j)^2 + (b_i - b_j)^2} \tag{12}$$

$$\mathcal{L}_{ij} = |\mathcal{L}_i - \mathcal{L}_j| \tag{13}$$

where $L_i$ is the average value of luminosity of the segment $i$, $L_j$ is the average value of the luminosity of segment $j$, and $a_i$ and $a_j$ are the average values of the $a$ component of the segment $i$ and $j$, respectively, and $b_i$ and $b_j$ are the average values of the $b$ component of the segments $i$ and $j$, respectively. $\mathcal{L}_i$ and $\mathcal{L}_j$ are the average values of the Laplacian of segments $i$ or $j$, respectively. If the color similarity $D_{ij}$ or texture similarity $\mathcal{L}_{ij}$ is smaller than a threshold, the two segments $i$ and $j$ are merged into one segment.

**Algorithm 2. Merging segments**

1: **for** $i = 1$ to $N_{segments}$
2: **for** $j = 1$ to $N_{segments}$
3: **if** $i = j$
4: $D_{ij} = \sqrt{(L_i - L_j)^2 + (a_i - a_j)^2 + (b_i - b_j)^2}$
5: $\mathcal{L}_{ij} = |\mathcal{L}_i - \mathcal{L}_j|$
6: **if** $D_{ij} < \tau_2 || \mathcal{L}_{ij} < \tau_3$
7: Merge segment $i$ and segment $j$ into one
8: Update the labelling $f$ (or map $I^m$) and $N_{segments}$
9: **end if**
10: **end for**
11: **end for**

**Avoiding of Islands.** An island is a connected cluster of pixels that is surrounded by pixels of another segment. These islands complicate the interpretation of the resulting image, so we use a filter, sized $3 \times 3$, to remove small islands. If more than four adjacent pixels (using 8-adjacency) have the same segment label, and the label is different from the central pixel label, the central pixel label is changed to the majority label in the 8-neighborhood.

**Algorithm 3. Avoiding islands**

1: **for** i=2:size(Label image,1)-1
2: **for** j=2:size(Label image,2)-1
3: Take the 8-adjacent pixels that surround the current pixel: $f(i+1,j)$, $f(i-1,j)$, $f(i,j+1)$, $f(i,j-1)$, $f(i+1,j-1)$, $f(i-1,j+1)$, $f(i+1,j+1)$ and $f(i-1,j-1)$
4: Check their labels
5: Find $L_{maxfrequency}$, the label that occurs most frequently in the 8-neighborhood
6: **if** $L_{maxfrequency} > 4$ **do**
7: The current pixel is labelled by this most frequent label $f(i,j) = L_{maxfrequency}$
8: **end if**
9: **end for**
10: **end for**

## 4    Comparative Performance Analysis

The experiments are conducted on images recorded with a Sony NEX5N14Mp camera mounted on a Swampfox UAV. The test parameters for individual methods were set to $\tau_1 = 5.5$, $\tau_2 = 62$, and $\tau_3 = 2.3$ for the illustrated Waiheke video, and to $\tau_1 = 3.5$, $\tau_2 = 50$, and $\tau_3 = 0.2$ for the used Antarctica images.

The original segmentation results are shown in Fig. 2. The SLIC method generates similar-sized nearly rectangular segments and follows edges between grass and forest. GMM labels segments pixel-by-pixel which generates many small islands. The GMM segments follow outlines of interest better than SLIC segments. The HMM-EM method generates smooth multiple-layer segments and is sensitive to regions with different colours or texture. MS generates an enormous number of islands; the results of the applied MS algorithm appear to be too sensitive to value changes.

The segmentation results with the post-processing are shown in Fig. 3. The borders between grass and forest are improved significantly. The various color and texture regions within the forest are separated to a certain level. The post-processing parameters $\tau$ can be adjusted accordingly for different applications.

The results change with the thresholds used. Here we present results for thresholds that divide the used Waiheke images into forest and grass. However, the thresholds can also be adjusted to achieve a modified segmentation for different targets, for example for groups of trees.

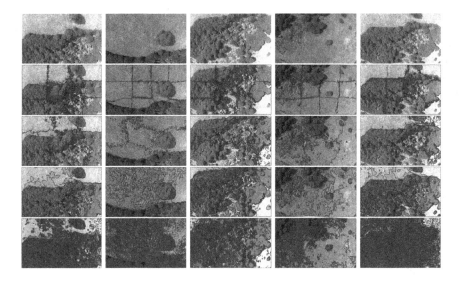

**Fig. 2.** Segmentation results of original segmentation methods. *Top* to *bottom*: input images, results by SLIC method, results by GMM method, results by HMM-EM method and results by MS method

Figure 4 shows results using the original segmentation techniques for two images from data base. In the first column are the images, the second column are the resulting images when SLIC is applied, the third column are the resulting GMM images, and in the last column are the images when HMM-EM is used.

In Fig. 5 we illustrate the effects of our post-process. The post-process helps to clean the results of the GMM (avoiding the islands). In the resulting GMM images, borders follow better the outlines of interest than SLIC. Also, in this case, the HMM-EM method generates smooth multiple-layer segments.

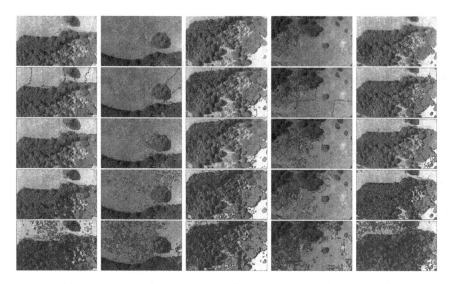

**Fig. 3.** Segmentation results after the proposed post-processing. *Top* to *bottom*: input images, results by SLIC method with post-processing, results by GMM method with post-processing, results by HMM-EM method with post-processing and results by MS method with post-processing

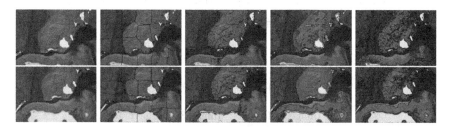

**Fig. 4.** Segmentation results of the Antarctica images with the original segmentation methods. *Left* to *right*: input images, results by SLIC method, results by GMM method, results by HMM-EM method and results by MS method

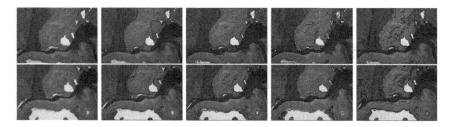

**Fig. 5.** Segmentation results of the Antarctica images when it is applied the proposed post-processing. *Left* to *right*: input images, results by SLIC method with post-processing, results by GMM method with post-processing, results by HMM-EM method with post-processing and results by MS method with post-processing

## 4.1   Quantitative Measurement

Let $\mathcal{S} = \{S_1, \ldots, S_{N_{segments}}\}$ be a segmentation result. We introduce a quantitative measure for $\mathcal{S}$. In this measure, segments with small standard colour deviation and larger areas are preferred. The measure is defined as follows:

$$\chi(\mathcal{S}) = \frac{1}{N_{segments}} \sum_{i=1}^{N_{segments}} \frac{A_i}{\sigma_{color_i}+1} \qquad (14)$$

where $i$ denotes segment $S_i$, $\sigma_{color_i}$ is the standard colour deviation in $S_i$, $N_{segments}$ is the total number of segments, and $A_i$ is the number of pixels in $S_i$, known to be a good estimator for the area of a region [11]. We identify a larger value of $\chi(\mathcal{S})$ with a *better* segmentation performance for the defined target. Results of this measure for the shown Waiheke images are listed in Tables 1 and 2. Results for the shown Antarctica images are in Table 3.

**Table 1.** Values $\chi(\mathcal{S})$ for the original Waiheke segmentation results

|         | Image 1 | Image 2 | Image 3 | Image 4 | Image 5 |
|---------|---------|---------|---------|---------|---------|
| SLIC    | 204.11  | 276.14  | 163.37  | 288.22  | 181.2   |
| GMM     | 296.78  | 390.23  | 241.49  | 391.55  | 261.91  |
| HM & EM | 202.41  | 249.78  | 203.62  | 351.72  | 205.23  |
| MS      | 72.87   | 64.21   | 85.75   | 82.63   | 42.98   |

**Table 2.** Values $\chi(\mathcal{S})$ for the post-processed Waiheke segmentation results

|         | Image 1 | Image 2 | Image 3 | Image 4 | Image 5 |
|---------|---------|---------|---------|---------|---------|
| SLIC    | 502.98  | 687.92  | 539.12  | 571.75  | 451.96  |
| GMM     | 905.78  | 980.01  | 638.01  | 624.22  | 582.71  |
| HM & EM | 695.18  | 602.08  | 489.18  | 493.94  | 367.85  |
| MS      | 133.51  | 128.45  | 166.78  | 242.45  | 143.89  |

**Table 3.** Values $\chi(\mathcal{S})$ for original and post-processed Antarctica segmentation results

|                              | SLIC   | GMM    | HM & EM | MS     |
|------------------------------|--------|--------|---------|--------|
| Image 6                      | 269.22 | 325.66 | 319.25  | 212.85 |
| Image 6, post-processed      | 397.18 | 368.78 | 450.31  | 464.58 |
| Image 7                      | 249.18 | 376.02 | 301.19  | 222.43 |
| Image 7, post-processed      | 361.21 | 565.47 | 569.49  | 465.22 |

# 5   Conclusions

This paper compared four segmentation methods on aerial data recorded with an UAV. Different methods have their own merits and drawbacks. SLIC generates similar sized segments. GMM produces isolated regions, and HMM & EM generates regions with smooth borders. MS produces an enormous number of isolated pixels, but the post process cleans the resulting images. We propose post-processing for splitting and merging segments. The parameter settings can be adjusted according to requirements of given applications. We also introduced a measure for evaluating segmentation results and illustrated the measure based on samples of video data recorded at a warm temperate island (Waiheke Island, New Zealand), and in a polar desert (McMudro Dry Valleys, Antarctica).

In conclusion of our extensive experiments, we consider a two-step procedure as being very attractive in our further studies: First, apply GMM and post-processing for having "clean" borders between regions of interest (possibly followed by spline approximation [4,12] for smoother borders). Second, apply SLIC only within each region provided by the first step for identifying ecologically important smaller segments.

**Acknowledgments.** Authors thank Dongwei Liu for experimental support.

# References

1. Achanta, R., Shaji, A., Smith, K., Lucchi, A., Fua, P., Süsstrunk, S.: SLIC superpixels compared to state-of-the-art superpixel methods. IEEE Trans. Pattern Anal. Mach. Intell. **34**, 2274–2282 (2012)
2. Bellvert, J., Zarco-Tejada, P.J., Girona, J., Fereres, E.: Mapping crop water stress index in a pinot-noir vineyard: comparing ground measurements with thermal remote sensing imagery from an unmanned aerial vehicle. Precis. Agric. **15**, 361–376 (2014)
3. Bollard-Breen, B., Brooks, J.D., Jones, M.R.L., Robertson, J., Betschart, S., Kung, O., Cary, S.C., Lee, C.K., Pointing, S.B.: Application of an unmanned aerial vehicle in spatial mapping of terrestrial biology and human disturbance in the McMurdo Dry Valleys, East Antarctica. Polar Biol. **38**, 573–578 (2015)
4. Boor, C.: A Practical Guide to Splines. Springer, New York (1978)
5. Comaniciu, Q., Meer, P.: Mean shift: a robust approach toward feature space analysis. IEEE Trans. Pattern Anal. Mach. Intell. **24**, 603–619 (2002)
6. d'Oleire-Oltmanns, S., Marzolff, I., Peter, K.D., Ries, J.B.: Unmanned aerial vehicle (UAV) for monitoring soil erosion in Morocco. Remote Sens. **4**, 3390–3416 (2012)
7. Dunford, R., Michel, K., Gagnage, M., Piégay, H., Trémelo, M.L.: Potential and constraints of unmanned aerial vehicle technology for the characterization of Mediterranean riparian forest. Int. J. Remote Sens. **30**, 4915–4935 (2009)
8. Gonzalez, R.C., Woods, R.E.: Digital Image Processing, 3rd edn. Prentice Hall, New York (2008)
9. Ishihama, F., Watabe, Y., Oguma, H.: Validation of a high resolution, remotely operated aerial remote sensing system for the identification of herbaceous plant species. Appl. Veg. Sci. **15**, 383–389 (2012)

10. Klette, R.: Concise Computer Vision. Springer, London (2014)
11. Klette, R., Rosenfeld, A.: Digital Geometry. Morgan Kaufmann, San Francisco (2004)
12. Kvasov, B.: Methods of Shape-Preserving Spline Approximation. World Scientific Pub, London (2000)
13. Lalit, G., Thotsapon, S.: Gaussian-mixture-based image segmentation algorithm. Pattern Recogn. **31**(3), 315–325 (1998)
14. MacQueen, J.B.: Some methods for classification and analysis of multivariate observations. In: Proceedings of Berkeley Symposium Mathematical Statistics Probability, pp. 281–297 (1967)
15. Mitchell, J.J., Glenn, N.F., Anderson, M.O., Hruska, R.C., Halford, A., Baun, C., Nydegger, N.: Unmanned aerial vehicle hyperspectral remote sensing for dryland vegetation monitoring, signal processing. In: Proceedings of Workshop Hyperspectral Image, pp. 1–10 (2012)
16. Otsu, N.: A threshold selection method from gray-level histograms. IEEE Trans. Syst. Man Cybern. **9**, 62–66 (1979)
17. Peña, J.M., Torres-Sánchez, J., de Castro, A.I., Kelly, M., López-Granados, F.: Weed mapping in early-season maize fields using object-based analysis of unmanned aerial vehicle (UAV) images. PLoS ONE **8**, e77151 (2013)
18. Primicerio, J., Di Gennaro, S.F., Fiorillo, E., Genesio, L., Lugato, E., Matese, A., Vaccari, F.P.: A flexible unmanned aerial vehicle for precision agriculture. Precis. Agric. **13**, 517–523 (2012)
19. Vehmas, M., Eerikäinen, K., Peuhkurinen, J., Packalén, P., Maltamo, M.: Airborne laser scanning for the site type identification of mature boreal forest stands. Remote Sens. **3**, 100–116 (2011)
20. Wang, Q.: HMRF-EM-image: Implementation of the hidden Markov random model and its expectation-maximization algorithm (2012). arxiv: 1207.3510 [cs.CV]
21. Zarco-Tejada, P.J., Diaz-Varela, R., Angileri, V., Loudjani, P.: Tree height quantification using very high resolution imagery acquired from an unmanned aerial vehicle (UAV) and automatic 3D photo-reconstruction methods. Eur. J. Agron. **55**, 89–99 (2014)
22. Zhang, Z.: Native vegetation classification using remote sensing techniques: A case study of dairy flat regrowth bush by using the AUT Unmanned Aerial Vehicle. Doctoral dissertation. University of Technology, Auckland (2014)

# Integrated Parallel 2D-Leap-Frog Algorithm for Noisy Three Image Photometric Stereo

Ryszard Kozera[1](✉), Felicja Okulicka-Dłużewska[2], and Lyle Noakes[3]

[1] Faculty of Applied Mathematics and Informatics,
Warsaw University of Life Sciences-SGGW, Nowoursynowska Street 159,
02-776 Warsaw, Poland
ryszard.kozera@gmail.com
[2] Faculty of Mathematics and Information Science,
Warsaw University of Technology, Koszykowa Street 75, 00-662 Warsaw, Poland
f.okulicka@mini.pw.edu.pl
[3] School of Mathematics and Statistics, The University of Western Australia,
35 Stirling Highway, Crawley, Perth, WA 6009, Australia
lyle.noakes@uwa.edu.au

**Abstract.** In this paper a feasible computational scheme for reconstructing a smooth Lambertian surface $S_L$ from noisy images is discussed. The noiseless case of Photometric Stereo relies on solving image irradiance equations. In fact, the entire shape recovery consists of gradient computation and gradient integration. The presence of added noise re-transforms the latter (depending on the adopted model) into a high-dimensional linear or non-linear optimization, solvable e.g. by a 2D-Leap-Frog. This algorithm resorts to the overlapping local image snapshot optimizations to reduce a large dimension of the original optimization task. Several practical steps to improve the feasibility of 2D-Leap-Frog are integrated in this work. Namely, an initial guess is obtained from a linear version of denoising Photometric Stereo. A non-integrable vector field estimating the normals to $S_L$ is rectified first to yield an initial guess $S_{L_a} \approx S_L$ for a non-linear 2D-Leap-Frog. Computationally, the integrability of non-integrable normals is enforced here by Conjugate Gradient which avoids numerous inversions of the large size matrices. In sequel, $S_{L_a}$ is fed through to the adjusted version of non-linear 2D-Leap-Frog. Such setting not only improves the recovery of $S_L$ (from $S_{L_a} \approx S_L$ to $\hat{S}_{L_a} \approx S_L$) but also it removes potential outliers (upon enforcing a continuity on $\hat{S}_{L_a}$) occurring in the previous version of 2D-Leap-Frog. In addition, a speed-up of shape reconstruction is achieved with parallelization of non-linear 2D-Leap-Frog applied to the modified cost function. The experiments are performed on images with different resolutions and varying number of kernels. Finally, the comparison tests between standard 2D-Leap-Frog (either linear or non-linear) and its improved outlier-free version are presented illustrating differences in the quality of the reconstructed surface.

**Keywords:** Noisy Photometric Stereo · 2D-Leap-Frog · Parallelization

© Springer International Publishing Switzerland 2016
F. Huang and A. Sugimoto (Eds.): PSIVT 2015 Workshops, LNCS 9555, pp. 73–87, 2016.
DOI: 10.1007/978-3-319-30285-0_7

# 1   Introduction

In a single image *shape-from-shading problem* one searches for a smooth ($C^1$ or $C^2$ class) surface $S$ obtained from its image $\Omega$ and illuminated by a "distant" light-source direction $p = (p_1, p_2, p_3)$ - here the light-source is positioned either at infinity or is located sufficiently far away. As shown in [1], the shape-from-shading problem is modeled by the corresponding *image irradiance equation*, which over $\Omega$ reads as:

$$R(n_1(x, y, z), n_2(x, y, z), n_3(x, y, z)) = E(x, y). \tag{1}$$

Here, the function $E : \Omega \to [0,1]$ measures the intensity of the light reflected from the surface $S$ while being illuminated from the direction $p$. left-hand side of (1) i.e. the mapping $R$ is called *a reflectance map*. The latter encapsulates the surface's light reflectance properties. It is controlled by the shape of $S$ and by the physical structure of the material covering $S$. Finally, the vector $n(x, y, z) = (n_1(x, y, z), n_2(x, y, z), n_3(x, y, z))$ represents the normal to $S$ at a given point $(x, y, z) \in S$. If additionally $S = graph(u)$ (here $u : \Omega \to \mathbb{R}$ is a smooth function) then $z = u(x, y)$ and $n(x, y, z)$ modulo sign reads as $n(x, y) = (u_x(x, y), u_y(x, y), -1)$. Consequently, the original image irradiance equation (1) reduces into $R(x, y) = E(x, y)$. Finding the exact formula for the reflectance map $R$ related to the specific materials coating $S$ constitutes a non-trivial task. A possible approach is to use a look-up table found with the aid of the so-called *calibration hemi-sphere* (see [1]). On the other hand, for certain materials the mapping $R$ can be determined (or closely approximated) by exploiting the respective laws of optics [1,2]. Indeed, if one deals with a particular class of *Lambertian surfaces* then $R$ is proportional to the $cos(\alpha)$, where $\alpha$ is the angle between the normal $n \perp S$ and light-source illumination direction $p$. Thus for the Lambertian surface $S_L$ the image irradiance equation (1) is reformulated into a well-known form [1]:

$$\frac{p_1 u_x(x, y) + p_2 u_y(x, y) - p_3}{\sqrt{p_1^2 + p_2^2 + p_3^2}\sqrt{u_x^2(x, y) + u_y^2(x, y) + 1}} = E(x, y). \tag{2}$$

Clearly one admits in (2) an arbitrary constant shift of $u$ and hence any vertical translation of $S_L$. Naturally this preserves the shape of $S_L$. However, as it turns out, (2) is still generically *ill-posed* [1,3–9]. There are different techniques relying on availability of extra information or based on thinning the class of admissible solutions to enforce either a partial or a full *well-posedness* of (2) - see e.g. [1,7,9,10]. One of the adopted feasible stances to disambiguate (2) is to illuminate $S_L$ consecutively from multiple linearly independent directions. Such approach imposes extra constraints on the reconstruction problem (2) and is called *Photometric Stereo* - see [1,7,9,10]. As well-known, three light-source Photometric Stereo is sufficient for a unique surface recovery (modulo its vertical shift $C$). The case of two light-source Photometric Stereo is more complicated as merely a generic uniqueness, modulo $u+C$, prevails (see [10–12]).

Consequently, its analogue of noisy model is more intricate and as such is omitted here. Though four (or more) light-sources yield also uniqueness, its noisy Photomoteric Stereo model (a natural extension of three images) becomes more robust as it tightens stronger a negative influence of noise on reconstructed $S_L$ (given more available data). In this paper we focus on three image Photometric Stereo. The reconstruction process is split into two explicit independent phases: *an algebraic* and *an analytical step*. First, the gradient $\nabla u$ is uniquely computed from the following system (here (2) is used with each light-source direction, respectively):

$$\frac{\langle n|p\rangle}{||n|| \cdot ||p||} = E_p(x,y), \quad \frac{\langle n|q\rangle}{||n|| \cdot ||q||} = E_q(x,y), \quad \frac{\langle n|r\rangle}{||n|| \cdot ||r||} = E_r(x,y), \quad (3)$$

over $\Omega = \Omega_1 \cap \Omega_2 \cap \Omega_3$ (see e.g. [1,10,13]) which yields a unique $\nabla u$ expressed explicitly in terms of $E_p$, $E_q$, $E_r$, $p$, $q$ and $r$. Both symbols $\langle \cdot | \cdot \rangle$ and $|| \cdot ||$ from above represent an Euclidean dot product and the corresponding norm in $\mathbb{R}^3$, respectively. The next step involves the verification of *the continuous integrability condition* (applied to computed $\nabla u$) $\int_{\gamma_c} u_x dx + u_y dy = 0$, which is to hold along each closed curve $\gamma_c \in C^1(\Omega)$ over simply-connected $\Omega$. The *integration formula* $u(x,y) = u(x_0, y_0) + \int_\gamma u_x dx + u_y dy$ gives $u \in C^1(\Omega)$ (modulo constant $C = u(x_0, y_0)$ taken as arbitrary) - see [14]. Here $\gamma \in C^1(\Omega)$ is an arbitrary curve joining any $(x,y) \in \Omega$ with a fixed $(x_0, y_0) \in \Omega$. Note that the above integrability condition is often replaced by $u_{xy} = u_{yx}$, if admissible class of $u \in C^1(\Omega)$ is trimmed to $C^2(\Omega)$. Real images $\hat{E}_p$, $\hat{E}_q$ and $\hat{E}_r$ are digitized forms of $E_p$, $E_q$ and $E_r$ as they are represented over pixels instead of being measured over each point $(x,y) \in \Omega$. In addition, an extra camera noise infiltrates such digitization process. Commonly in computer vision one admits a Gaussian noise added to all images with mean $\mu = 0$ and varying standard deviation $\sigma \in [0.01, 0.10]$. The linear approach to handle noisy Photometric Stereo relies on rectifying computed digitized *non-integrable vector field* $v = (v_1, v_2) \in \mathbb{R}^2$ (rendered from (3) with $\hat{E}_p$, $\hat{E}_q$ and $\hat{E}_r$ entered) to the unique closest integrable $\hat{v}$, which satisfies a digitized analogue of continuous integrability condition - see e.g. [15–17]. The majority of such schemes rely on solving the corresponding *linear discrete optimization task* which often depends on a large number of parameters representing image resolution. Such emerging challenging computational burden can be alleviated e.g. by applying *a linear 2D-Leap-Frog* or Conjugate Gradient (see [18–22]). Both schemes manage to deal with multiple inversions of large size matrices (see also [22,24,25]). However a linear rectification is based on statistical principle of maximum likelihood, which assumes a Gaussian noise to be generated at the level of computed $v$. This implicit assumption is clearly violated here. Indeed, in reality the Gaussian noise contaminating three input images loses its character once filtered through the solutions $(u_x, u_y)$ of (3) to yield $v$. As shown in [26] this fact is manifested by poorer shape reconstruction if either $\sigma \geq 0.05$ or normals $n \perp S_L$ vary too abruptly. In order to remove such discrepancy *a non-linear* digitized version of (2) is introduced (see e.g. [26]). More specifically, for a noisy image $\hat{E}_p$ (also for $\hat{E}_q$ and $\hat{E}_r$) with $N \times N$ pixel resolution, a central-difference derivative approximation reformulates (2) into *a non-linear discrete minimization problem* in $\hat{u} \in \mathbb{R}^{N^2-4}$:

$$
\mathscr{E}_p(\hat{u}) = \sum_{i,j=2}^{i,j=N-1} \left( \frac{p_1 \frac{\hat{u}_{i+1,j}-\hat{u}_{i-1,j}}{2\Delta x} + p_2 \frac{\hat{u}_{i,j+1}-\hat{u}_{i,j-1}}{2\Delta y} - p_3}{\|p\|\sqrt{\left(\frac{\hat{u}_{i+1,j}-\hat{u}_{i-1,j}}{2\Delta x}\right)^2 + \left(\frac{\hat{u}_{i,j+1}-\hat{u}_{i,j-1}}{2\Delta y}\right)^2 + 1}} - \hat{E}_p(i,j) \right)^2,
$$

(4)

where $\hat{E}_p(i,j)$ (and $\hat{u}_{i,j}$) stands for the value of $\hat{E}$ (or of $\hat{u}$) at $(i,j)$-pixel. To simplify further computation one also assumes $\Delta x = \Delta y = \Delta$ and $\Omega = [0,1] \times [0,1]$. We also use notation $\mathscr{E}_p^{ij}$ for each component of (4). Note that all boundary pixels $\in \partial\Omega$ are omitted in (4) since central-difference derivative approximation does not permit numerical estimates of $\nabla u$ over $\partial\Omega$. In addition, four $\Omega$ corner pixels are also excluded from $\hat{u}_{ij}$ due to the horizontal (vertical) nature of central-difference derivative approximation. Upon adding all three performance indices (see (4)) one defines a *a total performance index* (or a cost or energy function):

$$
\mathscr{E}(\hat{u}) = \mathscr{E}_p(\hat{u}) + \mathscr{E}_q(\hat{u}) + \mathscr{E}_r(\hat{u}),
$$

(5)

to be minimized with $\hat{u}_{opt} \in \mathbb{R}^{N^2-4}$. Each component of (5) over $(i,j)$-pixel is denoted here by $\mathscr{E}^{ij}$. The non-linearity of (5) impacts now even heavier on some optimization schemes like Newton's Method which (once applied to (5)) faces multiple inversions of large size matrices $D^2\mathscr{E} \in M_{(N^2-4)\times(N^2-4)}(\mathbb{R})$ (with $N$ big). One of feasible computational schemes to handle (5) is *a non-linear 2D-Leap-Frog* (see [26,27]) which likewise its linear counterpart decomposes (5) into multiple low dimension overlapping optimization tasks. To test the performance of non-linear 2D-Leap-Frog, the initial guess $\hat{u}_0$ in [26] is generated synthetically by perturbing ideal solution $u$ of (3) at centers of each image pixels with the respective Gaussian noise (this time $\sigma$ is large to substantially distort $u$). In case of real Photometric Stereo, the function $u$ is unknown and therefore the scheme for finding a good initial guess $\hat{u}_0$ requires some adjustment. In addition, though a non-linear 2D-Leap-Frog performs better than a linear model of denoising Photometric Stereo, the reconstructed surface $\hat{S}_{L_a}$ is contaminated by the outliers mainly occurring along $\partial\Omega$ (see [26]). A median filter in a post-reconstruction phase is applied to remove such outliers in [28,29]. However, the latter does not yield satisfactory results if either outliers are too big or are too close to each others. This is also addressed in this paper by incorporating a new outlier removal scheme directly into the reconstruction step. It is achieved by supplementing local costs functions (5) with extra measurement to enforce the continuity of $\hat{u}$ (which is to obeying both (5) and $C^0$ constraint). Finally, to speed up the computational process we implement modified 2D-Leap-Frog in parallel setting (unmodified parallel version was already tested in [23]). This paper integrates all important components of noisy Photometric Stereo summarized as:

1. Finding an initial guess $\hat{u}_0$ for non-linear optimization scheme. Conjugate Gradient is applied to the linear model of denoising Photometric Stereo [21].

2. Modification of (4) (into (6)) incorporating the continuity constraint to filter out the outliers from the reconstructed surface - see Subsect. 2.1. A non-linear 2D-Leap-Frog performing this task is applied in this paper - see Subsect. 2.2.
3. Parallelization of modified 2D-Leap-Frog used in step 2 (see Sects. 3 and 4).

## 2  Continuity Adjustment and Non-linear 2D-Leap-Frog

A detailed determination of a decent initial guess $\hat{u}_0$ with the aid of Conjugate Gradient is given in [21, 22] and as such is here omitted.

### 2.1  Continuity Enforcement

We enforce now the continuity constraint in (5) only along the boundary pixels of $\Omega$ (though it can be equally done over entire image). Focusing on such pixels accounts to the outliers' localization which predominantly occur along the boundary pixels (see [26]). The latter has a three-fold justification. *Firstly*, the image irradiance equation (3) are accounted in (5) only over internal image pixels due to the central-difference derivative approximations applied to $\nabla u$. *Secondly*, $C^1$ implies $C^0$ and thus internal pixels implicitly assume continuity (also in its discrete form). *Lastly*, 2D-Leap-Frog (linear or non-linear one - see [18, 26]) relies on freezing majority of variables and minimizing the corresponding performance index (e.g. (5)) over small number of free variables (which this time can be computationally handled e.g. by Newton's Method). The free variables represent $\hat{u}_{ij}$ over $(i, j)$-pixels which all belong to the selected $\Omega$-snapshot (either a square or a rectangle). The optimization process relies on varying unlocked variables (and thus snapshots) covering $\Omega$ in overlapping mode. Once a total snapshot coverage of $\Omega$ with no self repetitions is accomplished (consecutive or distributed mode is usually admitted) one iteration of 2D-Leap-Frog is completed. Generically, there are 9 types of local snapshot optimizations (see [18]) i.e.: *bottom-left, top-left, top-right, bottom-right corner snapshots and bottom-, left-, top-, right- boundary snapshots and finally the internal snapshot* (applied the most frequently). 2D-Leap-Frog adaptively and iteratively changes the unlocked value of $\hat{u}_{i,j}$ by including the $(i, j)$-pixel in neighbouring local snapshot optimizations during a single iteration. Noticeably, pixels in $\partial\Omega$ have in their proximity a scarcer number of adjacent overlapping snapshots (which size is also permitted to vary) as opposed to the internal ones. This impacts on the adaptivity quality of 2D-Leap-Frog over all boundary pixels. For $\delta_{i,j} = (\hat{u}_{i+1,j} - \hat{u}_{i,j})^2$ and $\rho_{i,j} = (\hat{u}_{i,j+1} - \hat{u}_{i,j})^2$ the forward-difference continuity correction over the left-boundary pixels is: $\mathscr{E}_L(\hat{u}) = \sum_{j=2}^{N-1} \delta_{1,j} + \sum_{i=2}^{N-2} \delta_{i,1}$. Similarly one defines $\mathscr{E}_T$, $\mathscr{E}_R$ and $\mathscr{E}_B$ over top-, right- and bottom- boundaries, respectively. Coupling the latter with (5) yields *a modified performance index function*:

$$\mathscr{E}_{C^0}(\hat{u}) = \mathscr{E}(\hat{u}) + \mathscr{E}_L(\hat{u}) + \mathscr{E}_T(\hat{u}) + \mathscr{E}_R(\hat{u}) + \mathscr{E}_B(\hat{u}). \tag{6}$$

The task is now to find $\hat{u}_{opt}$ which globally minimizes (6). The initial condition $\hat{u}_0$ is computed as indicated in Step 1 (see the closing of Sect. 1). A non-linear

2D-Leap-Frog to find a local minimum of (6) is used in this paper. As shown in [26] 2D-Leap-Frog converges to a critical point (usually a local minimum) for any smooth performance index function. In addition, an extra analysis in [26] formulates sufficient conditions under which a global minimum for $\mathscr{E}$ is reached. A similar analysis for $\mathscr{E}_{C^0}$ exceeds the scope of this paper and is omitted. Newton's Method is applied to all local optimizations with the first initial guess as the respective values from $\hat{u}_0$ over the first snapshot. During the $s$-iteration of 2D-Leap-Frog (and selection of $t$-snapshot) an initial guess is formed by these values of $u^{(s,t-1)} \in \mathbb{R}^{N^2-4}$ which correspond to the unlocked variables of $t$-snapshot optimization. Upon completing $t$-snapshot optimization we update $u^{(s,t-1)}$ to $u^{(s,t)} \in \mathbb{R}^{N^2-4}$ by feeding in $u^{(s,t-1)}$ all optimal values of unlocked pixels standing for $t$-snapshot minimization. The common overlap (e.g. for small size snapshots) involves either horizontal or vertical half-snapshot translations. The stopping condition for 2D-Leap-Frog amounts here to a cap on a prescribed number of iterations. Experiments show that the corresponding energy is substantially decreased only within the first 5–12 initial iterations. The subsequent steps diminish the energy marginally while still consuming considerable amount of time and memory access.

## 2.2  Local Snapshot Optimizations

We introduce now local performance indices over *internal, left-boundary and bottom-left corner snapshots*, respectively. The remaining 6 types of local optimizations are analogous. Note that over each snapshot the respective local performance index should be calculated over all $(k,l)$-pixels which energy $\mathscr{E}^{kl}$ is well-defined and depends on any unlocked $(i,j)$-pixel (here $\hat{u}_{ij}$ is relaxed to a free variable). Otherwise the total performance index $\mathscr{E}_{C^0}$ may increase despite decreasing inappropriately chosen local energy function. Indeed, for the wrongly omitted pixels the increase of energy may well exceed its trimming gained over all pixels contributing to the local performance index. The size of each snapshot can vary but it cannot cross over certain values (limited by selected local optimization scheme), as otherwise computational burden is too excessive. In this paper $6 \times 6$, $5 \times 6$ and $5 \times 5$ pixel-sizes for three types of snapshots are applied. The snapshot's size cannot be too small either to avoid too dense coverage of $\Omega$ by local optimizations (each depending on iterative numerical computations).

Over each snapshot's type *Mathematica FindMinimum* function is invoked with the default Newton's Method and default number of iterations.

*(a) Internal snapshot optimization:* is generically dealt by 2D-Leap-Frog. Recall that continuity constraint is left-out as generic snapshot $\Omega^g$ (here $6 \times 6$ mask shifted over $\Omega$) is isolated from $\partial\Omega$. The essential local variables in $\Omega^g$ (see Fig. 1a) are represented by either unlocked variables $\{v_1, v_2, v_3, v_4\}$ or locked variables $\{w_1, w_2, \ldots, w_{20}\}$ over the corresponding pixels. The rest of the blank pixels in Fig. 1a refer to locked pixels which do not contribute to the local

energy $\mathscr{E}^g$ depending here on free variables $v = (v_1, v_2, v_3, v_4)$ and defined over $\{v_1, v_2, v_3, v_4, w_1, w_2, \ldots, w_8\}$-pixels as:

$$\mathscr{E}^g(v) = \sum_{i=1}^{4} \mathscr{E}^g_{v_i} + \sum_{j=1}^{8} \mathscr{E}^g_{w_j}, \tag{7}$$

where (see (4) and Fig. 1a) e.g. $\mathscr{E}^g_{v_2} = \mathscr{E}^{gp}_{v_2} + \mathscr{E}^{gq}_{v_2} + \mathscr{E}^{gr}_{v_2}$ (at $v_2$-pixel) reads as:

$$\mathscr{E}^{gp}_{v_2} = \left( \frac{p_1 \frac{w_3 - v_1}{2\Delta} + p_2 \frac{v_4 - w_2}{2\Delta} - p_3}{\|p\| \sqrt{1 + \left(\frac{w_3 - v_1}{2\Delta}\right)^2 + \left(\frac{v_4 - w_2}{2\Delta}\right)^2}} - \hat{E}_p(i(v_2), j(v_2)) \right)^2, \tag{8}$$

with $\mathscr{E}^{gq}_{v_2}$ and $\mathscr{E}^{gr}_{v_2}$ computed similarly to (8) upon replacing $p$ with $q$ or $r$, accordingly. Here $(i(v_2), j(v_2))$ represents a center of a pixel in $\Omega$ which coincides with the $v_2$-pixel of $\Omega^g$ masking the respective image sub-domain during Leap-Frog $(s,t)$-iteration. The remaining 11 energies in (7) are analogously treated upon using (4), (8) and Fig. 1a. The current values of contributing locked variables in $\Omega^g$ are assigned to the corresponding updates of $\Omega$-pixels computed during $(s, t-1)$-iteration of 2D-Leap-Frog. The same procedure applies to the initial guess $(v_1^0, v_2^0, v_3^0, v_4^0)$ needed to minimize (7).

| | | $w_{16}$ | $w_{15}$ | | |
|---|---|---|---|---|---|
| | $w_{17}$ | $w_6$ | $w_5$ | $w_{14}$ | |
| $w_{18}$ | $w_7$ | $v_3$ | $v_4$ | $w_4$ | $w_{13}$ |
| $w_{19}$ | $w_8$ | $v_1$ | $v_2$ | $w_3$ | $w_{12}$ |
| | $w_{20}$ | $w_1$ | $w_2$ | $w_{11}$ | |
| | | $w_9$ | $w_{10}$ | | |

a)

| | | $w_{15}$ | $w_{14}$ | | |
|---|---|---|---|---|---|
| | $w_{16}$ | $w_6$ | $w_5$ | $w_{13}$ | |
| $v_4$ | $v_5$ | $v_6$ | $w_4$ | $w_{12}$ | |
| $v_1$ | $v_2$ | $v_3$ | $w_3$ | $w_{11}$ | |
| $w_7$ | $w_1$ | $w_2$ | $w_{10}$ | | |
| | $w_8$ | $w_9$ | | | |

b)

| | | $w_{10}$ | $w_9$ | | |
|---|---|---|---|---|---|
| $w_{11}$ | $w_4$ | $w_3$ | $w_8$ | | |
| $v_6$ | $v_7$ | $v_8$ | $w_2$ | $w_7$ | |
| $v_3$ | $v_4$ | $v_5$ | $w_1$ | $w_6$ | |
| $v_0$ | $v_1$ | $v_2$ | $w_5$ | | |

c)

**Fig. 1.** The main three types of snapshots for modified 2D-Leap-Frog.

*(b) Left-boundary snapshot optimization:* incorporates also the continuity constraint over $\Omega^{lb}$ (here $5 \times 6$ mask translated over $\Omega$). This time the essential local variables in $\Omega^{lb}$ (see Fig. 1b) are represented by either unlocked variables $\{v_1, v_2, \ldots, v_6\}$ or locked variables $\{w_1, w_2, \ldots, w_{16}\}$ over the corresponding pixels. Again the remaining blank pixels in Fig. 1b refer to locked pixels not participating in local energy $\mathscr{E}^{lb}$ depending here on free variables $v = (v_1, v_2, \ldots, v_6)$ and defined over $\{v_2, v_3, v_5, v_6, w_1, w_2, \ldots, w_6\}$-pixels (as far as discrete image irradiance equation (4) is concerned) and also incorporating forward-difference continuity over $\{v_1, v_4, w_7\}$-pixels as follows:

$$\mathscr{E}^{lb}(v) = \sum_{i=2, i\neq 4}^{6} \mathscr{E}^{lb}_{v_i} + \sum_{j=1}^{6} \mathscr{E}^{lb}_{w_j} + \mathscr{E}^{lb}_c, \tag{9}$$

where $\mathscr{E}_{v_i}^{lb}$ and $\mathscr{E}_{w_j}^{lb}$ are calculable similarly to (7) (see Fig. 1b) and $\mathscr{E}_c^{lb} = (v_2 - v_1)^2 + (v_5 - v_4)^2 + (v_4 - v_1)^2 + (w_{16} - v_4)^2 + (v_1 - w_7)^2$. Similarly, the current values of contributing locked variables in $\Omega^{lb}$ are the updates of $\Omega$-pixel values computed during $(s, t-1)$-iteration of 2D-Leap-Frog. A similar approach is used to determine the initial condition $(v_1^0, v_2^0, \ldots, v_6^0)$ needed to minimize (9). The remaining three cases of this type are treated analogously.

   *(c) Bottom-left corner optimization:* over $\Omega^{blc}$ (a $5 \times 5$ mask moved over $\Omega$) and its three analogues cover the neighbourhoods of four corners of $\Omega$. Recall that corner pixel values $u(1,1)$, $u(1,N)$, $u(N,1)$ and $u(N,N)$ are originally excluded thus admitting a digitized solution $\hat{u} \in \mathbb{R}^{N^2-4}$. These four missing values can be filled after termination of 2D-Leap-Frog by a straightforward 4-parameter linear optimization in fact enforcing the continuity of extended $\hat{u} \in \mathbb{R}^{N^2}$ at four corner pixels (see [26]). The alternative is to integrate the latter into each corner snapshot optimization which is adopted in this paper for modified 2D-Leap-Frog (thus from now on it is assumed that $\hat{u} \in \mathbb{R}^{N^2}$). Here the essential local variables in $\Omega^{blc}$ (see Fig. 1c) are represented by either unlocked variables $\{v_0, v_1, \ldots, v_8\}$ or locked variables $\{w_1, w_2, \ldots, w_{11}\}$ over the corresponding pixels. The omitted blank pixels in Fig. 1c refer to locked variables which do not contribute to local energy $\mathscr{E}^{blc}$ depending now on free variables $v = (v_0, v_1, \ldots, v_8)$ and defined over $\{v_4, v_5, v_7, v_8, w_1, w_2, w_3, w_4\}$-pixels (as far as discrete image irradiance equation (4) is concerned) and also including forward-difference continuity over $\{v_0, v_1, v_2, v_3, v_4, v_6\}$-pixels as follows:

$$\mathscr{E}^{blc}(v) = \sum_{i=4, i\neq 6}^{8} \mathscr{E}_{v_i}^{blc} + \sum_{j=1}^{4} \mathscr{E}_{w_j}^{blc} + \mathscr{E}_c^{blc}, \tag{10}$$

where again $\mathscr{E}_{v_i}^{blc}$ and $\mathscr{E}_{w_j}^{blc}$ are defined similarly to (7) (see also Fig. 1c) and $\mathscr{E}_c^{blc} = (v_4 - v_1)^2 + (v_5 - v_2)^2 + (v_2 - v_1)^2 + (w_5 - v_2)^2 + (v_4 - v_3)^3 + (v_7 - v_6)^2 + (v_6 - v_3)^2 + (w_{11} - v_6)^2 + (v_1 - v_0)^2 + (v_3 - v_0)^2$. The last two components in $\mathscr{E}_c^{blc}$ enforce the continuity of $\hat{u} \in \mathbb{R}^{N^2}$ at added $(1,1)$-pixel. Again the current values of contributing locked variables in $\Omega^{blc}$ are the updated values of $\Omega$-pixel computed during $(s, t-1)$-iteration of 2D-Leap-Frog. A similar approach applies here to determine an initial guess $(v_0^0, v_2^0, \ldots, v_8^0)$ needed to minimize (10). Again the remaining three cases of this type are treated analogously.

## 3   Parallelization of Modified 2D-Leap-Frog

The parallel version is implemented on the PC four core shared memory machine with the processor Intel Core, CPU 3.00 GHz, 4.00 GB RAM (by using *Mathematica 9.0* package). The parallel (2, 3 or 4)-kernels are launched by *Mathematica LaunchKernel[]* and *DistributeDefinitions[]* functions. For $k$ kernels used, the entire image $\Omega$ is divided into disjoint $k$-horizontal parts, i.e. $\Omega = \cup_{i=1}^{k} \Omega_i$ and $\Omega_i \cap \Omega_j = \emptyset$, for $i \neq j$ - see Fig. 2. Each $\Omega_i$ is swept out by one iteration of $i$-th kernel with (interchangeably first horizontally and then vertically) overlapping

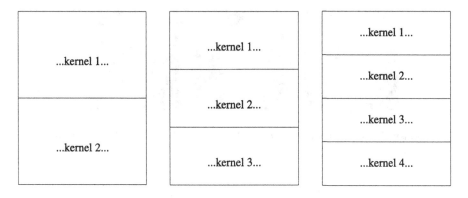

**Fig. 2.** Divisions of $\Omega$-grid in the parallel version of modified 2D-LF.

half-snapshots local optimizations. Next, border pixels along $\partial\Omega_i$ (or $\partial\Omega_{i+1}$) between two adjacent sub-regions $\Omega_i$ and $\Omega_{i+1}$ are updated by single horizontal run of 2D-LF procedure. Naturally, different "lines" of border pixels are covered in parallel. This terminates one iteration of parallel modified 2D-Leap-Frog (over $\Omega$). Note that the sequential 2D-Leap-Frog (which sweeps $\Omega$ with consecutive horizontal overlaps) varies from parallel 2D-Leap-Frog (border pixels between two adjacent sub-regions are performed at the end of each iteration). The latter may cause minor dissimilarities in reconstructed surfaces for sequential versus parallel ones or in parallel solutions computed with different number of kernels.

## 4   Numerical Experiments

Input images examined in this paper have $16 \times 16$, $32 \times 32$ or $64 \times 64$ pixel resolutions. To test the performance of 2D-Leap-Frog, we eliminate a potential non-conformity of the adopted exact Lambertian model assumed to be ingrained in real images, by considering exclusively synthetic Lambertian images $E_p$, $E_q$ and $E_r$. To secure the latter, all images are generated by substituting ideal $\nabla u$ (for which $S_L = graph(u)$) into (3). In sequel, the Gaussian noise is supplemented to $E_p$, $E_q$ and $E_r$ yielding the respective noisy images $\hat{E}_p$, $\hat{E}_q$ and $\hat{E}_r$ which in turn serve as input data. It is also implicitly assumed that the entire $\Omega = [0, 1] \times [0, 1]$. The case of $(x, y) \in \Omega$ for which $cos(\alpha) < 0$ (representing invisible part of $S_L$ - see (2)) is here artificially admitted in order to simplify the implementation of modified non-linear 2D-Leap-Frog. Still image irradiance equation (3) over invisible part of $S_L$ can be set-up and analyzed. Newton's Method is used for local snapshot optimizations (a default option in *Mathematica FindMinimum* function).

*Example 1.* Consider the Lambertian surface $S_{L_1} = graph(u_1)$, where function $u_1(x, y) = \frac{1}{16}(20f((x, y), w_1) - 15f((x, y), w_2) + 12f((x, y), w_3))$, with $w_1 = (\frac{3}{4}, \frac{1}{2})$, $w_2 = (\frac{1}{4}, \frac{1}{3})$, $w_3 = (\frac{1}{3}, \frac{4}{5})$ and $f(\tilde{v}_1, \tilde{v}_2) = e^{-100\|\tilde{v}_1 - \tilde{v}_2\|^2}$ for $\tilde{v}_1, \tilde{v}_2 \in \mathbb{R}^2$,

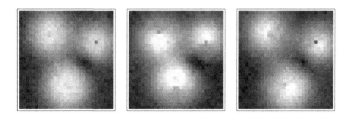

**Fig. 3.** Noisy digitized images $\hat{E}_p$, $\hat{E}_q$ and $\hat{E}_r$ for surface $S_{L_1}$ with Gaussian noise $\mathcal{N}(0.0, 0.05)$.

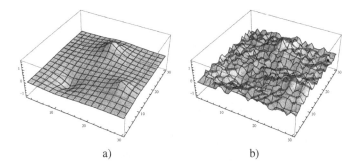

a)                    b)

**Fig. 4.** (a) Ideal $S_{L_1}$, (b) reconstructed $S_{L_{1a}}$ by using CG (with Gaussian noise $\mathcal{N}(0.0, 0.05)$).

is defined over $\Omega = [0,1] \times [0,1]$. The light-source directions are: $p = (0,0,-1)$, $q = (0, \frac{1}{3}, -\frac{1}{\sqrt{2}})$ and the third one is $r = (\frac{1}{\sqrt{7}}, 0, -\frac{1}{\sqrt{2}})$ The noiseless digitized images $E_p$, $E_q$ and $E_r$ of $S_{L_1}$ are contaminated with the Gaussian $\mathcal{N}(0.0, 0.05)$ noise to yield $\hat{E}_p$, $\hat{E}_q$ and $\hat{E}_r$ shown in Fig. 3. The ideal surface $S_{L_1}$ and the reconstructed surface $S_{L_{1a}}$ by Conjugate Gradient (abbreviated with CG - see [21]) are shown in Fig. 4 with $32 \times 32$ pixel image resolution. The latter forms an initial guess to the non-linear 2D-Leap-Frog (with 2D-LF shorthand notation). Figure 5 demonstrates two surfaces $\hat{S}_{L_{1a}}^o$ and $\hat{S}_{L_{1a}}^{not(o)}$ (and the difference between them) obtained without or with 2D-LF outlier removal modification (with 13 iterations). Next the parallel version of modified 2D-LF is tested (with 6 iterations). Figure 6 shows the reconstructed surfaces $\hat{S}_{L_{1a}}^{not(o)}$ using either 2, 3 or 4 kernels (for $32 \times 32$ image resolution). The respective *speed-ups* of the parallel modified 2D-LF for different image resolutions and for varying number of kernels are presented in Table 1a. Note that the speed-up can be greater than the number of created kernels. It is the result of the speed of the memory access. Each kernel operating in a parallel mode deals with updating smaller tables as compared with a single kernel performing a similar task on its own - thus a memory access is quicker. □

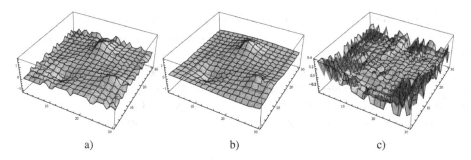

a)                    b)                    c)

**Fig. 5.** $S_{L_1}$ reconstructed by 2D-LF: (a) $\hat{S}^o_{L_1a}$ without, (b) $\hat{S}^{not(o)}_{L_1a}$ with outlier removal (with Gaussian noise $\mathcal{N}(0.0, 0.05)$), (c) the difference between $\hat{S}^{not(o)}_{L_1a}$ and $\hat{S}^o_{L_1a}$.

**Table 1.** Speed-ups in parallel modified 2D-LF Algorithm for $S_{L_1}$ and $S_{L_2}$.

| | a) Example 1 | | | | b) Example 2 | | | |
|---|---|---|---|---|---|---|---|---|
| Resolution | 1 kernel | 2 kernels | 3 kernels | 4 kernels | 1 kernel | 2 kernels | 3 kernels | 4 kernels |
| $16 \times 16$ | 1 | 1.5 | 1.5 | 1.6 | 1 | 1.2 | 1.3 | 1.2 |
| $32 \times 32$ | 1 | 2.0 | 2.3 | 2.8 | 1 | 2.2 | 2.7 | 2.9 |
| $64 \times 64$ | 1 | 2.4 | 3.0 | 3.6 | 1 | 2.0 | 2.6 | 3.4 |

*Example 2.* Let $S_{L_2} = graph(u_2)$, where $u_2(x,y) = (0.75 + \frac{1}{3} * (1 - tanh((x + y - 2)^2 + (x - y)^2 - \frac{25}{3}))$ is defined over $\Omega = [0,1] \times [0,1]$. The light-source directions are: $p = (0,0,-1)$, $q = (1 - \sqrt{3}, 0, -1 - \sqrt{3})/(2\sqrt{2}) = (-0.258819, 0.0, -0.965926)$ and the third one $r = (\frac{1}{2}\sin\frac{\pi}{24}, \frac{\sqrt{3}}{2}\sin\frac{\pi}{24}, -\cos\frac{\pi}{24}) = (0.0652631, 0.113039, -0.991445)$. The noiseless digitized images $E_p$, $E_q$ and $E_r$ of $S_2$ upon contaminated with Gaussian noise $\mathcal{N}(0.0, 0.05)$ yield the respective noisy images $\hat{E}_p$, $\hat{E}_q$ and $\hat{E}_r$ (see Fig. 7). Figure 8 illustrates the ideal surface $S_{L_2}$ and the reconstructed one $S_{L_2a}$ by CG Algorithm (with $32 \times 32$ image resolution). As previously $S_{L_2a}$ forms an

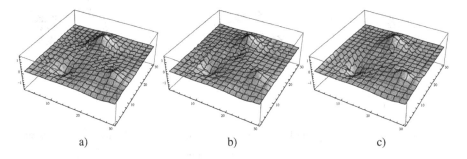

a)                    b)                    c)

**Fig. 6.** $S_{L_1}$ reconstructed by parallel modified 2D-LF using (a) 2, (b) 3 and (c) 4 kernels.

initial guess to the non-linear 2D-LF. Figure 9 illustrates the surfaces $\hat{S}^o_{L_{2a}}$ and $\hat{S}^{not(a)}_{L_{2a}}$ (and the difference between them) generated without or with 2D-LF outlier removal (with 13 iterations). Finally, the parallel version of modified 2D-LF (with 6 iterations) is exercised. Figure 10 illustrates the reconstructed surfaces $\hat{S}^{not(0)}_{L_{2a}}$ upon applying either 2, 3 or 4 kernels (for $32 \times 32$ image resolution). The resulting accelerations reached by parallel modified 2F-LF for different image resolutions and varying number of kernels are shown in Table 1b. □

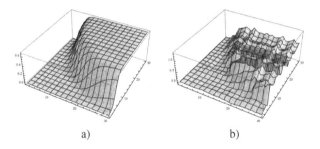

**Fig. 7.** Noisy digitized images $\hat{E}_p$, $\hat{E}_q$ and $\hat{E}_r$ for surface $S_{L_2}$ with Gaussian noise $\mathcal{N}(0.0, 0.05)$.

a)                                b)

**Fig. 8.** (a) Ideal $S_{L_2}$, (b) reconstructed $S_{L_{2a}}$ by CG (with Gaussian noise $\mathcal{N}(0.0, 0.05)$).

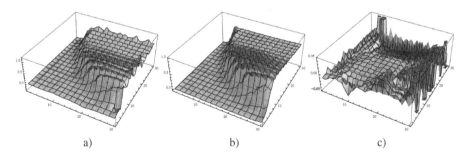

a)                        b)                        c)

**Fig. 9.** $S_{L_2}$ reconstructed by 2D-LF: (a) $\hat{S}^o_{L_{2a}}$ without, (b) $\hat{S}^{not(o)}_{L_{2a}}$ with outlier removal (with Gaussian noise $\mathcal{N}(0.0, 0.05)$), (c) the difference between $\hat{S}^{not(o)}_{L_{2a}}$ and $\hat{S}^o_{L_{2a}}$.

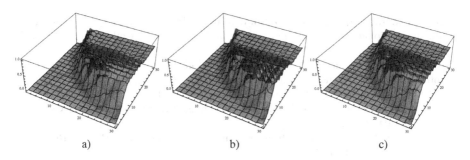

**Fig. 10.** $S_{L_2}$ reconstructed by parallel modified 2D-LF using a) 2, b) 3 and c) 4 kernels.

## 5    Conclusions

In this paper we propose an integrated feasible computational scheme i.e. *a modified non-linear 2D-Leap-Frog* (including its parallelization) to reconstruct the Lambertian surface from three light-source noisy Photometric Stereo images. The initial guess obtained from Conjugate Gradient (see [21]) and the continuity enforcement (obliterating the boundary outliers) combined with parallelization of 2D-Leap-Frog confirm to perform very satisfactory in all conducted experiments. Note that 2D-Leap-Frog is versatile as adaptable to *any optimization task depending on large number of variables* (see e.g. [30]). Future work includes genuine camera images with large image resolution, for which the size of each snapshot may vary and unshaded pixels are excluded (to yield $\Omega \subset [0,1] \times [0,1]$). The latter most likely requires a more powerful hardware amenable to parallel computation. Another potential investigation refers to two-source noisy Photometric Stereo (see [10–12]), where only generic uniqueness prevails and as such should be accounted in 2D-Leap-Frog. Finally, a similar analysis to [26] establishing sufficient conditions for *modified non-linear 2D-Leap-Frog to render a global minimum* of (6) would undeniably complement this work. More work on related topic can also be found in [31–33].

## References

1. Horn, B.K.P.: Robot Vis. McGraw-Hill, New York (1986)
2. Luneburg, R.K.: Mathematical Theory of Optics. University of California Press, Berkeley and Los Angeles (1964)
3. Kozera, R.: Uniqueness in shape from shading revisited. J. Math. Imag. Vision **7**, 123–138 (1997)
4. Horn, B.K.P., Brooks, M.J.: Shape from Shading. MIT Press, Cambridge (1989)
5. Kozera, R.: On complete integrals and uniqueness in shape from shading. Appl. Math. Comput. **73**(1), 1–37 (1995)
6. Brooks, M.J., Chojnacki, W., Kozera, R.: Impossible and ambiguous shading patterns. Int. J. Comput. Vis. **7**(2), 119–126 (1992)
7. Oliensis, J.: Uniqueness in shape from shading. Int. J. Comput. Vis. **6**(2), 75–104 (1991)

8. Brooks, M.J., Chojnacki, W., Kozera, R.: Circularly symmetrical eikonal equations and non-uniqueness in computer vision. J. Math. Anal. Appl. **165**(1), 192–215 (1992)

9. Brooks, M.J., Chojnacki, W.: Direct computation of shape-from-shading. In: 12th International Conference on Pattern Recognition, Jerusalem, Israel, pp. 114–119. IEEE Computer Society Press, Los Alamitos, CA (1994)

10. Kozera, R.: Existence and uniqueness in photometric stereo. Appl. Math. Comput. **44**(1), 1–104 (1991)

11. Kozera, R.: On shape recovery from two shading patterns. Int. J. Pattern Recognit. Artif. Intell. **6**(4), 673–698 (1992)

12. Onn, R., Bruckstein, A.: Uniqueness in shape from shading. Int. J. Comput. Vis. **5**(1), 105–113 (1990)

13. Woodham, R.J.: Photometric method for determining surface orientation from multiple images. Opt. Eng. **19**(1), 139–144 (1980)

14. Horn, B.K.P.: Height and gradient from shading. Int. J. Comput. Vis. **5**(1), 37–75 (1990)

15. Wei, T., Klette, R.: On depth recovery from gradient vector field. In: Bhattacharaya, B.B., et al. (eds.) Algorithms, Architectures and Information Systems Security, pp. 765–797. World Scientific Publishing Co., Pte. Ltd., Singapore (2009)

16. Simchony, T., Chellappa, R., Shao, M.: Direct analytical methods for solving poisson equations in computer vision problems. IEEE Trans. Pattern. Recognit. Mach. Intell. **12**(5), 435–446 (1990)

17. Frankot, R.T., Chellappa, R.: A method of enforcing integrability in shape from shading algorithms. IEEE Trans. Pattern. Recognit. Mach. Intell. **10**(4), 439–451 (1988)

18. Noakes, L., Kozera, R.: The 2-D Leap-Frog, noise and digitization. In: Bertrand, G., et al. (eds.) Digital and Image Geometry. LNCS, vol. 2243, pp. 352–364. Springer, Heidelberg (2001)

19. Noakes, L., Kozera, R.: The Lawn-Mowing Algorithm for noisy gradient vector fields. In: Latecki, L.J. (ed.) Vision Geometry VIII. Proceedings SPIE, vol. 3811, pp. 305–316. Denver, CO, USA (1999)

20. Noakes, L., Kozera, R.: The 2-D Leap-Frog Algorithm for optimal surface reconstruction. In: Latecki, L.J. (ed.) Vision Geometry VIII. Proceedings SPIE, vol. 3811, pp. 317–328. Denver, CO, USA (1999)

21. Kozera, R., Okulicka-Dłużewska, F.: Conjugate gradient in noisy photometric stereo. In: Chmielewski, L.J., Kozera, R., Shin, B.-S., Wojciechowski, K. (eds.) ICCVG 2014. LNCS, vol. 8671, pp. 338–346. Springer, Heidelberg (2014)

22. Saad, Y.: Iterative Methods for Sparse Linear Systems. SIAM, Philadelphia (2003)

23. Cameron, T., Kozera, R., Datta, A.: A parallel Leap-Frog Algorithm for 3-source photometric stereo. In: Wojciechowski, K., et al. (eds.) ICCVG 2004, pp. 95–102. Springer, Dordrecht (2006)

24. Hackbush, W.: Iterative Solution of Large Sparse Systems of Equations. Springer, New York (1994)

25. van der Vorst, H.A.: Iterative Krylov Methods for Large Linear Systems. Cambridge Monographs on Applied and Computational Mathematics. Cambridge University Press, Cambridge (2009)

26. Noakes, L., Kozera, R.: Nonlinearities and noise reduction in 3-source photometric stereo. J. Math. Imag. Vis. **18**(3), 119–127 (2003)
27. Noakes, L., Kozera, R.: Denoising images: non-linear Leap-Frog for shape and light-source recovery. In: Asano, T., Klette, R., Ronse, C. (eds.) Geometry, Morphology, and Computational Imaging. LNCS, vol. 2616, pp. 419–436. Springer, Heidelberg (2003)
28. Kozera, R., Tchórzewski, J.: Outlier removal in 2D Leap Frog Algorithm. In: Cortesi, A., Chaki, N., Saeed, K., Wierzchoń, S. (eds.) CISIM 2012. LNCS, vol. 7564, pp. 146–157. Springer, Heidelberg (2012)
29. Arce, G.R.: Non-Linear Signal Processing: A Statistical Approach. Wiley, New Jersey (2005)
30. Noakes, L.: A global algorithm for geodesics. J. Math. Austral. Soc. Ser. A **64**, 37–50 (1999)
31. Castelán, M., Hancock, E.R.: Imposing integrability in geometric shape-from-shading. In: Sanfeliu, A., Ruiz-Shulcloper, J. (eds.) CIARP 2003. LNCS, vol. 2905, pp. 196–203. Springer, Heidelberg (2003)
32. Hurt, N.E.: Mathematical methods in shape-from-shading: a review of recent results. Acta Appl. Math. **23**, 163–188 (1991)
33. Wöhler, C.: 3D Computer Vision: Efficient Methods and Applications. Springer-Verlag, Berlin Heideberg (2009)

# Heuristic Assessment of Parameters of the Local Ground Approximation from Terrestrial LIDAR Data

Marcin Bator, Leszek J. Chmielewski$^{(\boxtimes)}$, and Arkadiusz Orłowski

Faculty of Applied Informatics and Mathematics (WZIM),
Warsaw University of Life Sciences (SGGW), ul. Nowoursynowska 159,
02-775 Warsaw, Poland
{marcin_bator,leszek_chmielewski,arkadiusz_orlowski}@sggw.pl
http://www.wzim.sggw.pl

**Abstract.** The recently proposed quality measure is used to find the local ground approximation (LGA) from the data measured with the terrestrial laser scanning (TLS). The measure is the number of points in a thin layer located directly above the approximating surface. It can be optimized with the hill climbing algorithm. The method is robust against the data which can be treated as outliers from the ground model, so the TLS data have neither to be filtered nor segmented into those pertaining to the ground and to other objects (trees or lower vegetation). The results are compared with those obtained with the Hough transform-based method and assessed visually, with a positive result. If the ground does not depart too far from the assumed planar shape, the errors are small in relation to those obtained with other measurement modalities.

**Keywords:** Local ground approximation · LGA · Terrestrial laser scanning · TLS · Quality measure · Optimization · Digital terrain model · DTM

## 1 Introduction

Terrestrial laser scanning (TLS) is used in the research on automatic inventory control of forests. The data form a 3D cloud of points measured as reflections from objects, that is, the trees, other vegetation like bushes, the ground and any other objects which are present in the field of view of the scanner. The main target of the forest inventory is to calculate the volume of timber in the measured area. Classically, the inventory was made with the use of tree heights and the tree trunk diameters at the height of 1.3 m from the ground level, which is traditionally called the *breast height diameter*. Other measurements, like for example tree diameter at other heights, were also used. Needless to say, any trial of making the corresponding measurements automatically make it necessary to know the ground level at the foot of the tree.

© Springer International Publishing Switzerland 2016
F. Huang and A. Sugimoto (Eds.): PSIVT 2015 Workshops, LNCS 9555, pp. 88–97, 2016.
DOI: 10.1007/978-3-319-30285-0_8

The ground level has frequently been measured with conventional geodetic methods as well as with airborne laser scanning (ALS) giving rise to the digital terrain models (DTM) (for example [1,2]; a literature survey can be found in [3]). The use of TLS for building the DTM was a rare case. In [4] the least squares estimation and interpolation was used to enhance the DTM found from TLS and complemented with other data. In [5] a precise DTM was found from TLS and data measured with an unmanned aerial vehicle. One of the first reports on finding the DTM solely from TLS is [6]. In some publications on the forest measurements the terrain model is not mentioned, like in [7].

According to [8] the standard deviation of the error of the digital terrain model found from ALS measurements can be 0.6 m. In [6] where the TLS results for the ground location were compared to the ALS ones treated as the reference the root mean square deviation equal to 0.25 m was reported. Therefore, in some locations it can exceed these values. Using the measurements made locally with TLS should not only make it possible to obtain the forest inventory results from one measurement session, but could also reduce the errors.

Due to the masking of the distant objects by the nearer ones the terrestrial laser scanning can practically be used up to the distance of approximately 15 to 20 m [9]. These results were obtained for typical tree densities in the forest in Poland. Therefore, in our work, we shall use the term *local ground approximation* (LGA) rather than the DTM. This is because we shall not attempt to develop the model of the entire terrain in the measurement stand around one LIDAR scanner location, but to provide the proper reference for measuring the tree parameters from this location.

In our previous papers we have investigated the possibility of using the ground approximation by a planar surface. In [10] the plane parameters were found with a variant of the Hough transform called there the Variably Randomized Iterated Hierarchical Hough Transform (VRIHHT). In [11] a set of measures which can be used to estimate the quality of the ground models were proposed and tested. In both papers attention was paid to the robustness of the methods against the presence of outlaying values in the data, due to that from the point of view of the ground measures, all the measurements not pertaining to the ground, that is, belonging to the trees, bushes etc. can be treated as outliers. In this way, the ground approximation can be found from the raw data measured with the LIDAR, without any prior segmentation of filtering.

Methods other than the Hough transform described in [10] should be sought, due to that if the ground model is changed from the planar one to some more complex form, the HT can appear excessively time and memory consuming.

In this paper we shall test the viability of the quality measure, proposed in [11], as the sole optimization criterion in the process of finding the local ground approximation. This measure indicated as the most appropriate one for assessing the ground model was referred to in [11] as $Q_3^l$. This quality measure will be the only link binding the result with the domain of forest ground level calculation. The optimization method used will be the generic hill-climbing (HC) algorithm.

We shall keep in mind that the HC algorithm can stop in a local extremum. Therefore, the results obtained will be tested in two ways. First, the results will be visualized and will be assessed by human investigation. Second, the results will be compared to those obtained with another method described in [10], both in the visual way and by comparing the values of the quality measure achieved.

The remainder of this paper will be organized as follows. In Sect. 2 we shall first recall the ground approximation method and the measure of its quality, and then the optimization method with which this quality measure will be maximized. In Sect. 3 we shall present the method with which the viability of the method was tested, and the results of these tests. Finally, in Sect. 4 we shall sum up the conclusions which can be made as a result of the presented study.

## 2  Method

### 2.1  Local Ground Approximation and Quality Measure

According to [11], the ground will be approximated with a plane $\Pi$ in the coordinate system $Oxyz$ expressed by

$$A\,x + B\,y + C\,z + D = 0\,. \tag{1}$$

Denote an $i$-th measurement point by $P_i = P_i(x_i, y_i, z_i)$, $i = 1, \ldots, M$. Denote by $d(P_i, \Pi)$ the signed distance between this point and the plane $\Pi$:

$$d(P_i, \Pi) = \frac{A\,x_i + B\,y_i + C\,z_i + D}{\sqrt{A^2 + B^2 + C^2}}\,. \tag{2}$$

As the quality measure of the ground approximation (1) we shall use the measure $Q_3^l$ proposed in [11] as

$$Q_3^l(\Pi) = \sum_{i=1}^{M} N_3^l(P_i, \Pi)\,, \text{ where} \tag{3}$$

$$N_3^l(P_i, \Pi) = \begin{cases} 1 & \text{if } 0 \leq d(P_i, \Pi) < l\,, \\ 0 & \text{otherwise}\,. \end{cases} \tag{4}$$

Therefore, $Q_3^l$ is the number of measurement points inside a layer of height $l$ above the plane. Its maximization should yield a plane located just under the layer containing the largest number of points.

It can be noted that if $\Pi$ according to (1) is replaced with another approximating surface and (2) is redefined accordingly, the measure $Q_3^l$ can still be used in an unchanged form.

### 2.2  Optimization with the Hill Climbing Method

As it has been stated above, the measure $Q_3^l$ will be maximized to find the parameters of the LGA. The primary idea was to use the genetic algorithm (GA) as the optimization method. Genetic algorithms are a universal tool for global optimization, which always lead to good solutions irrespective of which assumptions, if any, can be made on the optimization criteria. Before using the GA, which is a very general method but can be time hungry, we have made a trial with the hill climbing (HC) method which is a simpler and also quicker tool. HC is one of the simplest heuristics working on complete solutions [12]. It can be schematically written down as Algorithm 1.

**Algorithm 1.** Hill climbing optimization

```
choose starting solution and set it as current solution
do
    assess current solution
    assess solutions for neighboring values of parameters
    if ( exists better neighboring solution )
        set best neighboring solution as current
while ( current solution is improved )
```

To assess the solution the measure $Q_3^l$ according to (3) with the parameter $l = 0.05$ m was used. As the starting solution the horizontal plane was chosen, displaced by 1.3 m below the zero point of the LIDAR scanner coordinate system center. It is a common practice to set the LIDAR so that its center is at the *breast height* above the ground. As the neighboring values for the parameters $A, B, C$ and $D$ the values differing by the step $s$ were used. The calculations were made for four constant values of $s$ equal to $0.1, 0.01, 0.001$ and $0.0001$ and for variable $s$ changed according to two strategies specified further. The initial value of $s$ was $0.1$. If a better neighbor can be found, the calculations are continued with the same step. Otherwise, the step is halved. Calculations stop if there is no better neighbor and $s \leq 0.0001$. Otherwise, the better neighbor is set as current. Then the first strategy *sg-return* was to return to the largest step $0.1$ and the second one *sg-continue* was to continue with the current step.

## 3   Testing the Method

### 3.1   Data

We have used all the data sets scanned in 2011 at 15 stands near Głuchów in the Grójec Forest District, Mazovian Voivodship (Central Poland), with the terrestrial LIDAR scanner FARO LS HE880. The sets will be referred to as G01-G15. A data set for each stand was collected from a single position of the scanner. The sets contained between 12 and 22 millions of measurement points belonging to the trees, bushes and grass, and the ground. The set G10 was excluded from this study due to that it contained data of a stand which departed very far from the planar model considered here (see [11] for details).

### 3.2   Results of the Tests

The drawback of the HC algorithm is that it can stop in a local extremum. By comparing the result with those found with HT it could be found whether this was the case. Tests made indicated that the HC method yielded larger values of the quality measure than those for the results of the HT, already assessed as acceptable in [10]. Further, to see whether the results achieved conform to the expectations, the results were visualized. For this, 0.01 m wide vertical slices were cut from the data along the horizontal axes $Ox$ and $Oy$ and shown with the measuring points contained inside and cuts through the planes approximating the ground. In this way, for each data set two images were obtained.

In Table 1 the results for 14 data sets, for the Hough transform (in the version with all data points) and for all the versions of the hill climbing optimization are shown: for variable step with two strategies and for constant step with four values.

**Table 1.** Results of optimization – achieved values of the measure $Q_3^l$ for the Hough transform (HT) with all the data taken into account (HT) and six variants of HC with $Q_3^l$ as the optimization criterion. Average number of iterations until stabilization for all data sets given in the second row. Best result for each data set, in the sense of maximum $Q_3^l$, typeset **bold**.

| Set | HT | HC with $Q_3^l$ | | | | | |
|---|---|---|---|---|---|---|---|
| | | *sg-return* | *sg-continue* | $s = 10^{-1}$ | $s = 10^{-2}$ | $s = 10^{-3}$ | $s = 10^{-4}$ |
| No. iter | | 78,90 | 22,43 | 2,30 | 15,77 | 149,30 | 1092,33 |
| G01 | 4302794 | **4639980** | **4639980** | 3842784 | 4578294 | 4639078 | 1396536 |
| G02 | 3041891 | **3359955** | **3359955** | 2795328 | 3324298 | 3359025 | 1463245 |
| G03 | 4871221 | 6433712 | **6433848** | 3222021 | 6389405 | 6432473 | 2801175 |
| G04 | 4955470 | **6454744** | **6454744** | 4306104 | 6434044 | 6452912 | 6454680 |
| G05 | 2622571 | **3053982** | 3053975 | 2270557 | 3047939 | 3053191 | 3052169 |
| G06 | 4474230 | 5296824 | 5296824 | 3133640 | 5161469 | **5297056** | 3383733 |
| G07 | 6759960 | **9006977** | **9006977** | 4677454 | 8981072 | 9005881 | 9006708 |
| G08 | 7113005 | 10132162 | 10132162 | 8615957 | 9405729 | 10127568 | **10132580** |
| G09 | 5243061 | **6532281** | **6532281** | 5667501 | 6433235 | 6529922 | 6531014 |
| G11 | 6229232 | **8998283** | **8998283** | 2747618 | 8735206 | 8996286 | 1583847 |
| G12 | 7717864 | 10635960 | 10635960 | 1647341 | 10582841 | 10635238 | **10636016** |
| G13 | 5705181 | **10112587** | **10112587** | 7129943 | 9662389 | 10110759 | 10112500 |
| G14 | 5146301 | 8417649 | 8417649 | 5998452 | 8161496 | 8413424 | **8417688** |
| G15 | 6247893 | **7987105** | **7987105** | 4028943 | 7850807 | 7983638 | 1099045 |

In most cases, the best results are obtained with the variable step strategy with returning to the large step (*sg-return*), as well as with the continuation with the small step (*sg-continue*). However, from these two strategies the continuation with the small step needs less iterations. In some cases the optimization with constant small steps yield better results, but the difference in the quality measure is relatively small. Therefore, the HC with the varying step, with the strategy *sg-continue*, can be finally chosen as the best one. The results obtained with the HT have significantly worse results in the terms of the achieved $Q_3^l$.

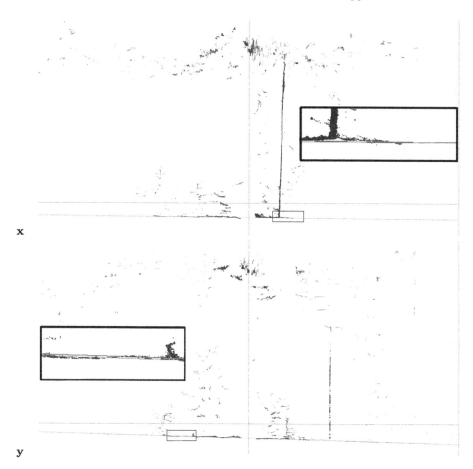

**Fig. 1.** Full views of results for data set G06: sections along (**x**) $Ox$; (**y**) $Oy$. Fragments in rectangles 5× enlarged, so a pixel corresponds to $0.1 \times 0.1$ m. See text for explanation of colors (Color figure online).

The results obtained with the best version of the HC, as chosen above, and two version of the HT will be shown in Figs. 1, 2 and 3. In Fig. 1 the overall layout of the data and results is shown and the details are enlarged to make it easier to see what is the range of the errors of the approximation and to show which parts of the images are important. In Figs. 2 and 3 only these significant parts are shown.

In Fig. 1 the actual dimensions of the imaged area are: width 40 m and height 20 m (17 m over the horizontal axis and 3 m below). In the remaining figures the width is the same, but a 3.14 m thick layers are cut from the most interesting parts of the images. The data points are marked with blue. The results of the HC method are marked with green. Two results of two versions of the HT differing by the fraction of data used in calculations are marked, accordingly: yellow for

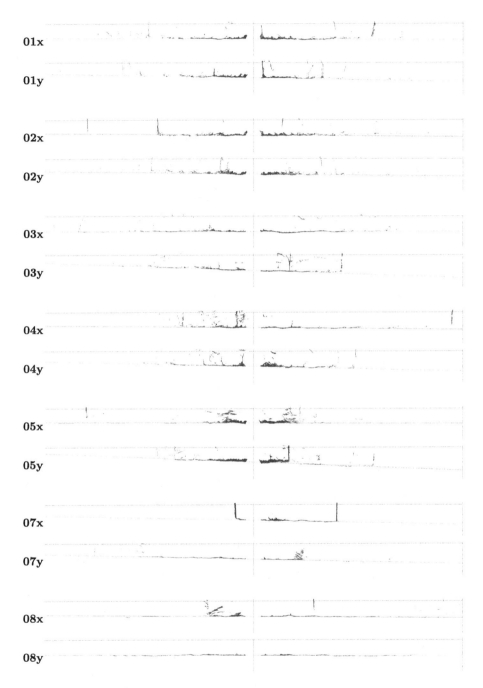

**Fig. 2.** Lower fragments of views of results for data sets G01-G05 and G07-G08. See text for explanation of colors (Color figure online).

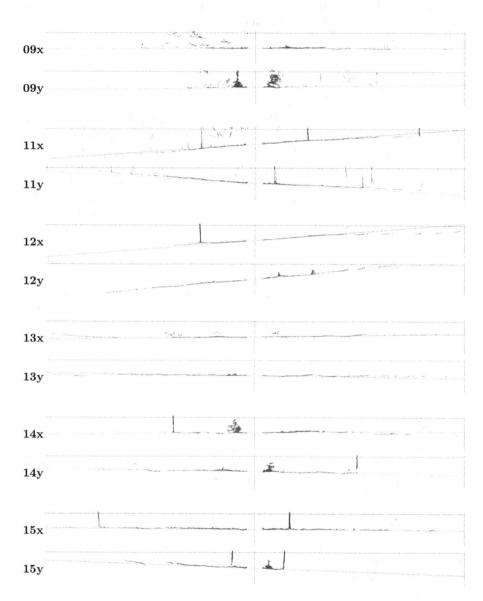

**Fig. 3.** Lower fragments of views of results for data sets G095 and G11-G15. Data set $G10$ was excluded due to the ground departed very much from planarity, so the approximation (1) was not appropriate. See text for explanation of colors (Color figure online).

all the data used in calculations, and red for a variable fraction equivalent to 0.01 of the data (see [10] for details; these two results can be the same or differ only slightly). Results of HC are drawn on top of those for HT.

### 3.3   Discussion and Results

The differences between the results obtained with the hill climbing according to the quality measure $Q_3^l$ and the Hough transform are not large. As a rule, the plane according to $Q_3^l$ is lower than that found with the HT. This conforms with the construction of $Q_3^l$ which promotes the location of the ground *below* the most dense cloud of the data, while HT finds the plane which passes *through* the dense data cloud. This observation is in favor of the results found with $Q_3^l$ and HC optimization, with respect to the results from the HT, although both results are usually close to each other. In visual inspection, both results conform to the expected location of the ground as a rule; obviously, they are slightly farther from the ground measurement points in cases where the ground departs from flatness, like for example in data sets G11-G13 and G15, but the differences are far less than 0.6 m referred in [8] and close to 0.25 m reported in [6]. Therefore, the planar approximation is acceptable for the plain terrains tested. As it could be expected, it fails for the regions where the ground level is uneven.

The results can be treated as satisfactory, within their range of applicability. The LGA – the local ground approximation – with the equation of a plane can be considered a sufficiently accurate ground model in the investigated application.

## 4   Conclusion

The possibility of finding the local approximation of the ground level, called here LGA, directly from the raw Terrestrial laser scanning data was investigated. The method used was the optimization method in which a quality measure recently proposed specially for the application of interest was used. The quality measure was the number of points contained in a layer of specified thickness located directly above the ground approximating surface. The thickness of the layer was 0.05 m. The measure does not limit the form of the LGA, but in this paper a planar model was used, which is admissible in plain regions. At present, the simple hill climbing algorithm was applied. In the considered application, the proposed quality measure proved to yield good results. Other more advanced optimization methods and local ground approximation functions will be investigated in future.

## References

1. Sithole, G., Vosselman, G.: Experimental comparison of filter algorithms for bare-Earth extraction from airborne laser scanning point clouds. ISPRS J. Photogrammetry Remote Sens. **59**(1–2), 85–101 (2004)

2. Srinivasan, S., Popescu, S., Eriksson, M., Sheridan, R., Ku, N.W.: Terrestrial laser scanning as an effective tool to retrieve tree level height, crown width, and stem diameter. Remote Sens. **7**(2), 1877–1896 (2015)
3. Stereńczak, K., Zasada, M., Brach, M.: The accuracy assessment of DTM generated from LIDAR data for forest area - a case study for Scots pine stands in Poland. Baltic For. **19**(2), 252–262 (2013)
4. Costantino, D., Angelini, M.: Production of DTM quality by TLS data. Int. J. Remote Sens. **46**, 80–103 (2013)
5. Eltner, A., Mulsow, C., Maas, H.G.: Quantitative measurement of soil erosion from TLS and UAV data. Int. Arch. Photogrammetry Remote Sens. Spat. Inf. Sci. **2**, 119–124 (2013)
6. Puttonen, E., Krooks, A., Kaartinen, H., Kaasalainen, S.: Ground level determination in forested environment with utilization of a scanner-centered terrestrial laser scanning configuration. IEEE Geosci. Remote Sens. Lett. **12**(3), 616–620 (2015)
7. Dassot, M., Colin, A., Santenoise, P., Fournier, M., Constant, T.: Terrestrial laser scanning for measuring the solid wood volume, including branches, of adult standing trees in the forest environment. Comput. Electron. Agric. **89**, 86–93 (2012)
8. Stereńczak, K., Kozak, J.: Evaluation of digital terrain models generated in forest conditions from airborne laser scanning data acquired in two seasons. Scand. J. For. Res. **26**(4), 374–384 (2011)
9. Zasada, M., Stereńczak, K., Dudek, W., Rybski, A.: Horizon visibility and accuracy of stocking determination on circular sample plots using automated remote measurement techniques. For. Ecol. Manage. **302**, 171–177 (2013)
10. Chmielewski, L.J., Orłowski, A.: Ground level recovery from terrestrial laser scanning data with the variably randomized iterated hierarchical hough transform. In: Azzopardi, G., Petkov, N., Yamagiwa, S. (eds.) CAIP 2015. LNCS, vol. 9256, pp. 630–641. Springer, Heidelberg (2015). doi:10.1007/978-3-319-23192-1_53
11. Bator, M., Chmielewski, L.J., Orłowski, A.: Where is the ground? quality measures for the planar digital terrain model in terrestrial laser scanning. In: Murino, V., Puppo, E. (eds.) ICIAP 2015. LNCS, vol. 9279, pp. 343–353. Springer, Heidelberg (2015). doi:10.1007/978-3-319-23231-7_31
12. Michalewicz, Z., Fogel, D.B.: How to Solve it: Modern Heuristics. Springer, Heidelberg (2013)

# A Parallel Implementation for Computing the Region-Adjacency-Tree of a Segmentation of a 2D Digital Image

Fernando Díaz-del-Río[1], Pedro Real[1($\boxtimes$)], and Darian Onchis[2]

[1] H.T.S. Informatics' Engineering, University of Seville, Seville, Spain
fdiaz@atc.us.es, real@us.es
[2] Faculty of Mathematics, University of Vienna, Vienna, Austria
darian.onchis@univie.ac.at

**Abstract.** A design and implementation of a parallel algorithm for computing the Region-Adjacency Tree of a given segmentation of a 2D digital image is given. The technique is based on a suitable distributed use of the algorithm for computing a Homological Spanning Forest (HSF) structure for each connected region of the segmentation and a classical geometric algorithm for determining inclusion between regions. The results show that this technique scales very well when executed in a multicore processor.

**Keywords:** Digital image · Segmentation · RAG · Parallel algorithm

## 1 Introduction

An important high level processing task in image understanding is to find a topological and structured description of the segmentation previously performed at low level processing, mostly independent of size and contrast characteristics of the extracted regions. The most usual representations are graph-based and the reasoning used in the region-node connectivity calculus involves two topological properties: adjacency and inclusion. The Region Adjacency Graph (RAG) [18–20] can be considered as the germ notion of all these models and it is composed of a set of nodes, one by region of the image, and there is an edge between two nodes if and only if the two corresponding regions are neighbors. Within the traditional context of square pixel-based 2-dimensional digital images, the most usual adjacency relationships between regions employed for the RAG are 4 or 8-neighborhoods. In order to exclusively highlight the ambient isotopic property "to be surrounded by" as adjacency relationship between regions or boundaries of regions, the notion of *Region-Adjacency Tree* (or RAG tree, for short) (also called *homotopy tree, inclusion tree* or *topological tree*) is created [6,20,21]. Restricted to binary 2D digital images, the RAG tree contains all the homotopy type information of the foreground object (black object) but the converse is, in general, not true [21]. Aside from image understanding applications [2],

© Springer International Publishing Switzerland 2016
F. Huang and A. Sugimoto (Eds.): PSIVT 2015 Workshops, LNCS 9555, pp. 98–109, 2016.
DOI: 10.1007/978-3-319-30285-0_9

RAG trees have encountered exploitation niches in geoinformatics, rendering, dermatoscopics image, biometrics,... [3,4].

Common operations for modifying RAGs are splitting and merging of regions. Most of the methods using these split-and-merge techniques are employed in "improving the quality of initial oversegmentations". Some split-and-merge RAG-based methods consider low-level information of the image for the region merging task [10,12,13,22]. Others take into account not only local knowledge of the image but also the extraction of "global" information about image models [1,8,9,23].

The contribution of this paper consists of the design and implementation of an parallel algorithm for computing the RAG of a given segmentation, based on a suitable distributed use of the algorithm for computing an HSF structure for each 4-connected region. The paper has the following sections. Section 2 is devoted to recall the machinery for computing the structures needed for HSF construction already given in [7]. Next, a parallel algorithm for constructing RAG starting from a HSF is showed in Sects. 3 and 4. Section 5 is devoted to show the advantages of our parallel implementation and to present the scalability results, and finally the conclusions are summarized.

## 2    About HSF Framework for RAG Tree Computation

In this paper, we specify an algebraic-topological technique for parallel computing a RAG of a given segmentation. This modus operandi have already used in [7,16] for developing a topologically consistent framework for parallel computation in 2D digital image context. Succinctly, starting from a 2-dimensional abstract cell (cubical) complex $C^2$ analogous of a digital image $I$ in which the pixels are the 0-cells, we compute in parallel another cell complex $D^2$ topologically equivalent to the first one, having the same 0-cells but in which the number of face and coface relationships in the canonically associated partial-order set of cells is reduced to a "minimum". Taking into account that $C^2$ is contractible, $D^2$ will have only one cell (critical 0-cell) with no coface neighbors. In [7], it is employed the name of *Morse spanning forest* $(MrSF)$ for $D^2$. Let us note that we use the nickname of $MrSF$ instead of that of $MSF$, due to the fact that $MSF$ is an usual abbreviation for Minimum Spanning Forest in graph theory. If the concrete strategy for "cutting" coface connexions used in any processing unit associated $P$ to each 0-cell mainly depends on the localization in $P$ of the pixels of the "foreground" and the "background" of a given segmentation $S = \{R_i\}_{i=0}^k$ of $I$, the $MrSF$ $D_2$ is, in principle, a good candidate structure for topologically analyzing $S$ and, in particular, to compute its associated RAG. A much better and natural strategy for the RAG-problem is to compute a sort of optimal $MrSF$ (called $HSF$ in [7]) for each region $R_i$ of $S$ and to find an efficient way for "minimally" connecting those HSF structures (interpreted as connected components) between them using adjacency relationships. By "minimal" connectivity, we mean to use only one edge for connecting two adjacent connected components (nodes of the RAG). Since we use an object-based digital image analysis, the design of an HSF framework for 8-connected digital objects can straightforwardly be done simply by slightly changing the external aspect of the processing units employed. An important topological property in the 2D digital setting is that, given a black region-of-interest $R$ of an image, a white maximal connected region surrounded by $R$ ("no there" or hole of $R$ in homology theory) is always 4-connected independently whether $R$ is 4 or 8-connected. We suppose here that all the regions $R_i$ of $S$ are 4-connected. Although this is, in principle, a strong topology restriction that almost never is accomplished in real image segmentation, a suitable mathematical morphological preprocessing of the image can solve this obstacle.

Algorithms of the next section part from the information structures that contain the HSF and the contours of the regions of interest. They can be computed (see [7]) on a time complexity order (for a parallel execution) of $O(log\ c)$, being $c$ the number of corners detected on a 2D digital image. To begin with, a brief summary of the extraction of the HSF and the contours follows.

From now on, in order to favor the computational methods and techniques allowing the practical implementation of a parallel architecture, we reduce the amount of mathematical results to a minimum.

In [7] the processing was focused on detecting in an exhaustive manner the outer and inner contours of the different curves that are present at a presegmented image. Thus, global information could be extracted. The implementation in [7] was essentially a sort of CCL algorithm (Connected-Component Labeling, see [11,15]) only applied to those pixels that form corners. This process was divided in three sections. The first part built the MrSF forest and determine some matrices containing the image corners and their characteristics. The second part was devoted to discover the outer and inner contour curves by following consecutive corners in vertical and horizontal directions. The result was two matrices $H_{cycle}, V_{cycle}$, containing the corner tags of the cycles that stood for the detected curves, and other structures with the information about the sink and sources cells (for the present work they have been comprised into the vector $crit\_idx$). This part seeks for the global information relating the different corners that form the objects inside an image. Finally, a third section finished with the construction of a HSF for the foreground ROI of a binary image, by finding the appropriate pairs of sources and sinks, and by doing the arrow reversing process in parallel for each curve and each line. With previous processing, the contour information of the different image regions is comprised into two matrices. Matrix $C_{row,col,type}$ contains one row per corner and three columns. Column 1 indicates the row index of the corner (or alternatively the Y coordinate). Column 2 holds the column index (or alternatively the X coordinate), and the last column contains the type (number of quadrant, with negative sign if it is external to the current curve, that is, a number among 1, 2, 3, 4, -1, -2, -3, -4). The matrix with the information of closed curves is $H_{cycle}$. This matrix can be reduced to have one row per curve and as many columns as corners have each curve. The numbers contained in the elements of this matrix are indexes to the rows of $C_{row,col,type}$. Finally vector $crit\_idx$ indicates the row index of each critical cell (according to the order given by Matrix $C_{row,col,type}$). Two counters are obtained by previous algorithms: *nof_curves*, which is the number of curves detected, and the vector *nof_corn_curve*, whose elements contain the number of corners of each curve.

In order to clarify this notation, a basic image with two closed curves (each one with a hole) and five curves (one of them is the image border) is depicted in Fig. 1. In this case, *nof_curves* is 5 and the five elements of *nof_corn_curve* contains 4. The elements of these matrices are given in Fig. 2. One of the rows of $H_{cycle}$ includes its corner sequence (16,11,10,5); in particular the first row. Its critical 0-cell has been represented by corner 5. Similarly for the other curves.

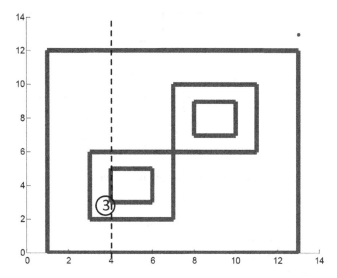

**Fig. 1.** A simple image with three curves (one of them is the image border). The crosses of the different segments with a dotted vertical line that parts from critical cell (tagged as 3) serve to detect inclusions.

An important fact of $H_{cycle}$ is that the corner tags are stored in a sequential order following a "contour" along the curve. This will permit us to find the number of times that a set of segments move in one direction or in the opposite. Moreover, the first hop of this contour is always a horizontal segment, which is important to extract a set of only horizontal pairs of corners (segments).

## 3   Parallel Computation of the Inclusion Relations for the MrSF Structures

Using these matrices, the parallelization of an inclusion searching algorithm can be done in an efficient way, as depicted by the pseudo code of Algorithm 1 (see Fig. 3). Our implementation is inspired by the classical ray-crossing algorithm for the point in polygon problem [14]. However in our case, this problem can

| $H_{cycle}$ | | | |
|----|----|----|----|
| 16 | 11 | 10 | 5 |
| 2 | 7 | 12 | 17 |
| 1 | 6 | 13 | 18 |
| 4 | 9 | 14 | 19 |
| 3 | 8 | 15 | 20 |

| 5 | 12 | 1 | 14 | 3 |
|---|----|---|----|---|

*crit_idx*

| Index | Row coord. | Col. coord | Type |
|-------|-----------|-----------|------|
| 1. . | 6 | 8 | 1 |
| 2. | 7 | 7 | -1 |
| 3. | 10 | 4 | 1 |
| 4. | 11 | 3 | -1 |
| 5. | 13 | 1 | 1 |
| 6. | 6 | 10 | 2 |
| 7. | 7 | 11 | -2 |
| 8. | 10 | 6 | 2 |
| 9. | 11 | 7 | -2 |
| 10. | 13 | 13 | 2 |
| 11. | 1 | 13 | 3 |
| 12. | 3 | 11 | -3 |
| 13. | 4 | 10 | 3 |
| 14. | 7 | 7 | -3 |
| 15. | 8 | 6 | 3 |
| 16. | 1 | 1 | 4 |
| 17. | 3 | 7 | -4 |
| 18. | 4 | 8 | 4 |
| 19. | 7 | 3 | -4 |
| 20. | 8 | 4 | 4 |

$C_{row,col,type}$

**Fig. 2.** Input matrices for a simple image with three curves.

be computed more efficiently because instead of arbitrary polygons, only horizontal and vertical concatenated segments exist. Thus only simple computer operations like comparisons are sufficient to detect crossings. Furthermore, the parallel processing becomes more evident.

Taking into account previous considerations, the codification style and the notation of Algorithm 1, is different from the usual iterative/procedural conventions to describe a pseudo-code. Most studies use an OpenMP-like notation or the *for each* paradigm to express more clearly the thread parallelism that can be exploited (see references along this work). As our aim is to describe the inherent parallelism that can be exploited for extracting the RAG Tree, our notation follows that of OCTAVE/MATLAB, so time complexity orders can be easily computed.

The last stage to compute the RAG Tree consists of the conversion of matrix $T_{inc}$ into another simplified matrix TTM that holds the topological tree (also in a matrix form). This is done by Algorithm 2 (Fig. 4) in a few steps.

The first line computes the number of columns of the TTM, which is given by those curves that have no other inside, by counting the number of columns of $T_{inc}$ that are empty. If the level of "depth" of a curve is the number of curves that it encloses, then the maximum level of "depth" of all the curves plus one gives the number of rows (tree levels) of the TTM (see step 1). Step 2 contains the key point that will serve to order the rows of $T_{inc}$, in order to compute the RAG tree: each row of matrix $C_{idx}$ contains the right sequences. This is due that

---

**Algorithm 1**: Pseudo-code for detecting curve inclusion.

| | |
|---|---|
| Input: | $H_{cycle}$ (1:*nof_curves, 1:nof_corn_curve*): matrix that contain the consecutive corner tags of the cycles that stand for the detected curves |

Input:  $H_{cycle}$ (1:*nof_curves, 1:nof_corn_curve*): matrix that contain the consecutive corner tags of the cycles that stand for the detected curves

$C_{row,col,type}$ (1:*nof_corn*, 3): matrix with the information of corners of quadrants 1, 2, 3, 4. Each matrix contains the row and column indexes and the type (number of quadrant, with negative sign if it is external to the current pixel)

*crit_idx* (1:*nof_curves*): vector containing the corner index of each critical cell.

Outputs:  $T_{inc}$ (1:*nof_curves, 1:nof_curves*): square inclusion matrix. The element $(i, j)$ is set to $j$ if the curve $i$ is included into the curve $j$.

$T_{inc\_min\_row}$(1:*nof_curves, 1:nof_curves*): minimum row coordinates of all the segments of a curve that surrounds another one.

*rows_to_be_deleted*(1:*nof_curves*): vector with the number of times that a curve include any other.

Notation: Comments are preceded with symbol '%'. Matrices are represented by uppercase letters, vectors or variables by cursive lowercase letters.

1

    a.  $F_{extreme} = H_{cycle}$ ( :, 1: 2: *nof_corn_curve*) ;

    b.  $S_{extreme} = H_{cycle}$ ( :, 2: 2: *nof_corn_curve*);

2

    a.  $C_{left} = C_{row,col,type}$ ($F_{extreme}$, 2) ;

    b.  $C_{rigth} = C_{row,col,type}$ ($S_{extreme}$, 2);

3  **for** *crit_cell* = 2: *nof_curves* % curve 1 is the image border, so it is not included in no other. This loop is inserted here to prevent the use of tensors and other complications in the notation. Note that it can be avoided in a parallel implementation because any critical cell can be processed in parallel.

4

    a.  *r_crit_cell* = $C_{row,col,type}$ (*crit_idx* (*crit_cell*), 1) ;

    b.  *c_crit_cell* = $C_{row,col,type}$ (*crit_idx* (*crit_cell*), 2) ;

5

    a.  $CW_{idx}$ = find(*c_crit_cell* > $C_{left}$ && *c_crit_cell* < $C_{rigth}$);

    b.  $AW_{idx}$ = find(*c_crit_cell* < $C_{left}$ && *c_crit_cell* > $C_{rigth}$);

    c.  $E_{idx,left}$ = find(*c_crit_cell* == $C_{left}$);

6

    a.  $ECW_{idx}$ = find(*c_crit_cell* > $C_{left}$ ($E_{idx,left}$-1) && *c_crit_cell* < $C_{rigth}$($E_{idx,left}$));

    b.  $EAW_{idx}$ = find(*c_crit_cell* < $C_{left}$ ($E_{idx,left}$-1) && *c_crit_cell* > $C_{rigth}$($E_{idx,left}$));

7

    a.  $CW_{idx\_tag}$ = $F_{extreme}$ ( [$CW_{idx}$;   $ECW_{idx}$] );

    b.  $AW_{idx\_tag}$ = $F_{extreme}$ ( [$AW_{idx}$;   $EAW_{idx}$] ); % idem if $S_{extreme}$ were chosen as horizontal segments are used.

8

    a.  $CW_{row}$ = $C_{row,col,type}$ ($CW_{idx\_tag}$, 1)

    b.  $AW_{row}$ = $C_{row,col,type}$ ($AW_{idx\_tag}$, 1)

9

    a.  *sup_crosses* = nnz ($CW_{row}$ >= *r_crit_cell*) - nnz ($AW_{row}$ >= *r_crit_cell*);

    b.  *inf_crosses* = nnz ($CW_{row}$ <= *r_crit_cell*) - nnz ($AW_{row}$ <= *r_crit_cell*) ;

    c.  *min_row* = min($CW_{row}$ , $AW_{row}$);

10

    a.  *inclusion* = abs (*sup_crosses* .* *inf_crosses*);

11

    a.  $T_{inc}$ (*crit_cell* , : ) = *inclusion* .* (1:*nof_curves*);

    b.  $T_{inc\_min\_row}$ (*crit_cell* , : ) = *inclusion*.* *min_row* ;

    c.  *rows_to_be_deleted* = *rows_to_be_deleted* + *inclusion*;

12  **end**

**Fig. 3.** Algorithm 1: Pseudo code for the algorithm that computes the inclusion relation of a set of curves.

the minimum row coordinates of a group of nested curves identify the order of inclusions (when sorting them).

Next line reorders $T_{inc}$ using these sequences $C_{idx}$, meanwhile step 4 adds the own curve numbers in a new column. Finally the last step 5 extracts those lines that are the leaves of the RAG tree and transpose the result to obtain TTM. Thus, those curves that do contain any other curve are forgotten in the final TTM matrix.

---

**Algorithm 2**: Pseudo-code for the conversion of the inclusion matrix into a RAT.

| | |
|---|---|
| Input: | $T_{inc}$ (1:*nof_curves*, 1:*nof_curves*): square inclusion matrix. The element $(i, j)$ is set to $j$ if the curve $i$ is included in the curve $j$. |
| | $T_{inc\_min\_row}$(1:*nof_curves*, 1:*nof_curves*): minimum row coordinates of all the segments of a curve that surrounds another one. |
| | *rows_to_be_deleted*(1:*nof_curves*): vector with the number of times that a curve include any other. |
| Outputs: | TTM (1:*nof_curves*, 1:*nof_corn_curve*): matrix that contains the topological tree or RAT |
| | Notation: Comments are preceded with symbol '%'. Matrices are represented by uppercase letters, vectors or variables by cursive lowercase letters. |

% curve 1 is the image border, so it is not included in no other

1

    a.   *nof_col_TTM* (1:*nof_curves*)= *nof_curves* - nnz(sum($T_{inc}$ (:, 1:*nof_curves*) ));

    b.   *nof_row_TTM* (1:*nof_curves*)= 1 + max (sum($T_{inc}$ (1:*nof_curves*, :) ));

2

    a.   [dummy, $C_{idx}$]= sortrows ($T_{inc\_min\_row}$);

3

    b.   $TTM_{extra}$= $T_{inc}$ ($C_{idx}$);

4

    c.   $TTM_{extra}$ (:, *1+nof_curves*) = 1:*nof_curves*;

5

    d.   TTM = $TTM_{extra}$ (not(*rows_to_be_deleted*), :)' ;

**Fig. 4.** Algorithm 2: Pseudo code for the algorithm that computes the inclusion relation of a set of curves.

## 4    An Example of RAG Tree Parallel Computation

In order to explain those Algorithms, let us examine the case of curve 5, whose critical cell is tagged with a 3 (Fig. 1). The searching of the curves that surround any other is based on detecting the crosses of a vertical line with the critical cell of each curve. In Fig. 1, the vertical line is depicted on the column 4, where critical cell of curve 5 was placed by the HSF construction [7].

First step extracts the tags of both extremes of any possible segment, which give us:

$F_{extreme} = (16\ 10\ ;\ 2\ 12\ ;\ 1\ 13\ ;\ 4\ 14\ ;\ 3\ 15)$

$S_{extreme} = (11\ 5\ ;\ 7\ 17\ ;\ 6\ 18\ ;\ 9\ 19\ ;\ 8\ 20)$

After that, those tags are converted into matrices $C_{left}$, $C_{rigth}$, which are filled with the column indexes of all the pair of corners that represent horizontal segments. In our case:

$C_{left} = (1\ 13\ ;\ 7\ 11\ ;\ 8\ 10;\ 3\ 7;\ 4\ 6)$

$C_{rigth} = (13\ 1;\ 11\ 7;\ 10\ 8;\ 7\ 3;\ 6\ 4)$

Step 4 extract the tag of the critical cell of this curve, that is  $crit\_cell$ (5)=3. Coordinates $r\_crit\_cell$=10 and  $c\_crit\_cell$=4 are obtained by accessing to $C_{row,col,type}$. Step 5 gives us the indexes over $C_{left}$ and $C_{rigth}$ (for each curve) of those segments that cross the vertical line on clockwise (CW) or anticlockwise (AW) directions. In our case, the  $find$ function returns:

$CW_{idx} = (1;$ Empty matrix; Empty matrix; 1; Empty matrix)

$AW_{idx} = (2;$ Empty matrix; Empty matrix; 2; Empty matrix)

Matrices $ECW_{idx}$, $EAW_{idx}$ are provided for those cases where the column coordinate is the same for the critical cell and a segment extreme. For those cases, the proper corners that determine this crossing are selected (step 6). At next step 7, the tags of the crosses are found, by indexing on $F_{extreme}$ and $S_{extreme}$. For our example, $CW_{idx\_tag}$ =(10; Empty matrix; Empty matrix; 14; Empty matrix); $AW_{idx\_tag}$ =(6; Empty matrix; Empty matrix; 4; Empty matrix)

The row coordinates of previous tags $CW_{idx\_tag}$ and $AW_{idx\_tag}$ are found by accessing the first column of $C_{row,col,type}$ in the operations of step 8. This gives us:

$CW_{row}$ =(13; Empty matrix; Empty matrix; 7; Empty matrix)

$AW_{row}$ =(1; Empty matrix; Empty matrix; 11; Empty matrix)

The first two operations of step 9 count the number of crosses (non zero elements). Function $nnz$ returns the values:

$sup\_crosses = (1\ ;\ 0\ ;\ 0\ ;\ 1\ ;\ 0)$

$inf\_crosses = (1\ ;\ 0\ ;\ 0\ ;\ 1\ ;\ 0)$

The other operation saves the minimum row coordinates of all the segments, which will be used to find the order in which a curve is surrounded by others (see next algorithm). Finally step 10 computes the vector  $inclusion$, that is, the absolute of the element-by-element product ($sup\_crosses\ .^* \ inf\_crosses$), because $sup\_crosses$ and  $inf\_crosses$ can be 1 or -1 when a segment crosses the vertical line. Note that a curve include the current cell, if and only if there is one cross with this vertical line above this cell and only one below it. Four our case, the fifth row of  $inclusion$ tells us that curves 1 and 4 surround the current curve 5:

$inclusion\ (5,\ :) = (1\ ;\ 0\ ;\ 0\ ;\ 1\ ;\ 0)$

This vector is multiplied element-by-element by the numbers (1: $nof\_curves$), so at step 11 the matrix $T_{inc}$ is marked with these numbers. In our example, the fifth row is set to (1 0 0 4 0). In addition, the matrix $T_{inc\_min\_row}$ is filled with the minimum row coordinates of all the segments of surrounding curves. At the same time, these values serve to fill a vector  $rows\_to\_be\_deleted$ with the

number of times that a curve include any other. This vector will help to delete those rows that must not appear at the final RAG tree. In our example:
$T_{inc} =$

$$\begin{pmatrix} 0\,0\,0\,0\,0 \\ 1\,0\,0\,0\,0 \\ 1\,2\,0\,0\,0 \\ 1\,0\,0\,0\,0 \\ 1\,0\,0\,4\,0 \end{pmatrix}$$

This means that curve 2 is surrounded by 1 (the image borders, in row 1), curve 3 by 1 and 2 (in row 3), curve 4 by 1, and curve 5 by 1 and 4 (row 7).

Using Algorithm 2, it is obvious that the resultant matrix for this example $TTM$ results:

$$\begin{pmatrix} 1\,1 \\ 2\,4 \\ 3\,5 \end{pmatrix}$$

## 5    Implementation and Testing Results

A complete implementation in OCTAVE/MATLAB has been built following previous pseudo codes. In order to check its scalability, a non-fully functional implementation of Algorithm 1 (because its time computing is very much bigger than that of Algorithm 2) has been done in C++ using OpenMP directives. Using previous notation, the next advantages are done evident:

(a) It can be easily demonstrated that Algorithm 1 scales well whit the number of Processing Elements of the target parallel architecture (like multi or manycore, GPUs, SIMD kernels, ...). This also eases the codification for a parallel computer. For similar reasons, those sentences that can be executed in parallel are grouped in the same step (using lines preceded with letters).
(b) OpenMP codes can be written directly through this notation, in most of the cases by converting the matrix processing into nested loops, and preceding the outer loop (usually devoted to the rows) with the directive *#pragma omp parallel for.*
(c) The memory access pattern (which is in most occasions [5] a critical point for the performance that can be achieved in GPUs) can be clearly observed.
(d) Matrix operations that cannot be done in an element-by-element manner (like matrix inversions, matrix multiply, etc.) are avoided.
(e) Only plain matrices have been used, preventing complex data structures (trees, chained lists, stacks, etc.), very inefficient when running on massive data parallel computer architectures.
(f) Finally, Algorithms have no conditional sentences. The avoidance of conditional sentences in the hot spot zones prevents the so-called thread divergence for GPUs, which is one the main reasons why the performance on this platforms diminishes [5].

Two final considerations must be done: (1) the only *for* loop encountered in this algorithm can be avoided in a parallel implementation. In fact its iterations are fully independent, because any critical cell can be processed in parallel using the same input matrices. The reason to insert the loop for is the avoidance of complications in the notation (as the use of tensors and indexations that are not supported by OCTAVE/MATLAB). (2) The only procedures that are not strictly (element-by-element) parallel are those of precompiled functions like *find, nnz, max*, etc. The non-strictly parallel sections of these functions are reduction operations, which can be coded in a binary tree fashion and present a time complexity order of $O(log\ p)$, being $p$ the number of elements involved in the procedure.

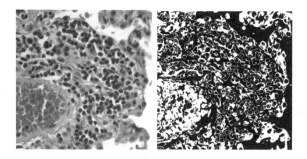

**Fig. 5.** A $300 \times 300$ fragment of a real H & E stained lung tissue sample taken from an end-stage emphysema patient.

For a modest 4-core desktop PC, scalability is almost perfect. Additional tests have been carried out in a server with an Intel Xeon E5 2650 v2, whose main characteristics are: 2.6 GHz, 8 cores (up to 16 threads), $8 \times 32$ KB data caches, Level 2 cache size $8 \times 256$ KB, Level 3 cache size 20 MB, maximum bandwidth to RAM: 59.7 GB/s. For this machine, all tests behave similarly: execution times scale very well for 8 threads (the number of real cores), meanwhile some additional speedup can be achieved above 9 threads, as usual for simultaneous multi-threading technologies. Due that the effects of multitasking in this server are relevant, the OpenMP guided scheduling was preferred.

Timing and speed results (baseline time is that of one thread) are represented in Fig. 6 for the following image from Wikimedia [17]: a $300 \times 300$ fragment of a real H and E (haematoxylin and eosin) stained lung tissue sample taken from an end-stage emphysema patient (Fig. 5, left). This image is segmented (Fig. 5, right) by converting into gray and then posterizing it for the intervals [0,59], [60,119], [120,179], [180,255]. This implementation received input from the output of algorithms in [7], which return a total of 750 curves, 20370 corners (a considerable number, w.r.t to the 90000 pixels of the original image).

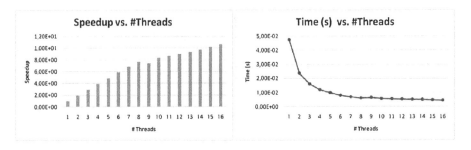

**Fig. 6.** Scalability testing for an Intel Xeon E5 2650 v2. Left: time vs. number of threads. Right: Speedup vs. number of threads

## 6  Conclusions

One important aspect of the RAG tree computation in the algorithm presented here is that we have adopted the MrSF structures so as to determine in a parallel fashion which regions are included or surrounded by others, transforming exhaustively a classical geometric algorithm. From a topological perspective, the intuition seems to lead to the conclusion that the notion of RAG is independent of the 2-dimensional embedding of the image $I$ and it can be efficiently computed in parallel using exclusively global homology information of each region and the local topology of the 1-cells of the cracks between regions (without need to turn to geometric algorithms). To give a correct answer in that direction would allow us to appropriately extend in a topological consistent way the notion of RAG to segmentations of $n$-dimensional ($n \geq 3$) digital images in terms of 0 and $n - 1$ homology generators of the different regions.

**Acknowledgments.** The first author gratefully acknowledges the support of the Spanish Ministry of Science and Innovation (project Biosense, TEC2012-37868-C04-02), the second author the support of the V Plan Propio de la Universidad de Sevilla, project number 2014/753, and the last author the support of the Austrian Science Fund(FWF): project number P27516.

## References

1. Barbu, A., Zhu, S.-C.: Graph partitioning by Swendsen-Wang cuts. In: Ninth IEEE International Conference on Computer Vision, Nice, France, vol. 1, pp. 320–329 (2003)
2. Cucchiara, R., Grana, C., Prati, A., Seidenari, S., Pellacani, G.: Building the topological tree by recursive FCM color clustering. In: Proceeding International Conference on Pattern Recognition, vol. 116(1), pp. 759–762 (2002)
3. Cohn, A., Bennett, B., Gooday, J., Gotts, N.: Qualitative spacial representation and reasoning with the region connection calculus. GeoInformatica 1(3), 275–316 (1997)
4. Costanza, E., Robinson, J.: A region adjacency tree approach to the detection and design of fiducials. In: Video, Vision and Graphics, pp. 63–99 (2003)

5. CUDA C Best Practices Guide Version. NVIDIA. http://developer.nvidia.com/. Accessed 14 July 2015
6. Damiand, G., Bertrand, Y., Fiorio, C.: Topological model for two-dimensional image representation: definition and optimal extraction algorithm. Comput. Vis. Image Underst. **93**(2), 111–154 (2004)
7. Díaz-del-Río, F., Real, P., Onchis, D.: A parallel homological spanning forest framework for 2D topological image analysis. Submitted to Pattern Recognition Letters, July 2015
8. Duarte, A., Sánchez, A., Fernandez, F., Montemayor, A.S.: Improving image segmentation quality through effective region merging using a hierarchical social metaheuristic. Pattern Recogn. Lett. **27**, 1239–1251 (2006)
9. Felzenszwalb, P.F., Huttenlocher, D.P.: Efficient graph-based image segmentation. Int. J. Comput. Vis. **59**(2), 167–181 (2004)
10. Gothandaraman, A.: Hierarchical image segmentation using the watershed algorithm with a streaming implementation. Ph.D. thesis, University of Tennessee, USA (2004)
11. Gupta, S., Palsetia, D., Patwary, M.M.A., Agrawal, A., Choudhary, A.N.: A new parallel algorithm for two-pass connected component labeling. In: 2014 IEEE International Parallel and Distributed Processing Symposium Workshop, pp. 1355–1362 (2014)
12. Haris, K., et al.: Hybrid image segmentation using watersheds and fast region merging. IEEE Trans. Image Process. **7**(12), 1684–1699 (1998)
13. Hernández, S.E., Barner, K.E.: Joint region merging criteria for watershed-based image segmentation. In: International Conference on Image Processing, vol. 2, pp. 108–111 (2000)
14. Hormann, K., Agathos, A.: The point in polygon problem for arbitrary polygons. Comput. Geom. **20**(3), 131–144 (2001)
15. Kalentev, O., Rai, A., Kemnitz, S., Schneider, R.: Connected component labeling on a 2D grid using CUDA. J. Parallel Distrib. Comput. **71**(4), 615–620 (2011)
16. Molina-Abril, H., Real, P.: Homological spanning forest framework for 2D image analysis. Ann. Math. Artif. Intell. **4**(64), 385–409 (2012)
17. Emphysema, H., E. Commons.wikimedia.org File: Emphysema H and E.jpg. Accessed 14 September 2015
18. Pavlidis, T.: Structural Pattern Recognition. Springer, New York (1977)
19. Sonka, M., et al.: Image Processing, Analysis and Machine Vision, 2nd edn. PWS, Pacific Grove (1999)
20. Rosenfeld, A.: Adjacency in digital pictures. Inf. Control **26**, 24–33 (1974)
21. Serra, J.: Image Analysis and Mathematical Morphology. Academic Press, Orlando (1982)
22. Sarkar, A., Biswas, M.K., Sharma, K.M.S.: A simple unsupervised MRF model based image segmentation approach. IEEE Trans. Image Process. **9**(5), 801–811 (2000)
23. Shi, J., Malik, J.: Normalized cuts and image segmentation. IEEE Trans. Pattern Anal. Machine Intel. **22**(8), 888–905 (2000)

# Vision Meets Graphics (VG 2015)

# Two Plane Volumetric Display for Simultaneous Independent Images at Multiple Depths

Marco Visentini-Scarzanella[1]([✉]), Takuto Hirukawa[1], Hiroshi Kawasaki[1], Ryo Furukawa[2], and Shinsaku Hiura[2]

[1] Computer Vision and Graphics Laboratory, Kagoshima University, Kagoshima, Japan
marco.visentiniscarzanella@gmail.com
[2] Graduate School of Information Sciences, Hiroshima City University, Hiroshima, Japan

**Abstract.** We propose a new projection system to visualise different independent images simultaneously on planes placed at different depths within a volume using multiple projectors. This is currently not possible with traditional systems, and we achieve it by projecting interference patterns rather than simple images. The main research issue is therefore to determine how to compute a distributed interference pattern that would recombine into multiple target images when projected by the different projectors. In this paper, we show that while the problem is not solvable exactly, good approximations can be obtained through optimization techniques. We also propose a practical calibration framework and validate our method by showing the technique in action with a prototype system. The system opens up significant new possibilities to extend projection mapping techniques to dynamic environments for artistic purposes, as well as visual assessment of distances.

## 1 Introduction

In Augmented Reality (AR) and/or Mixed Reality (MR) systems, projectors are commonly used to efficiently present information to users by projecting various images onto a scene or object surfaces. Apart from AR/MR applications, projector systems have found extensive artistic applications in the form of projection mapping, where the precalculated scene geometry is used to project an appropriately warped image to be mapped on the scene as an artificial texture. However, in the case of projection mapping the projected pattern is the same along each ray, and what is viewed is therefore spatially invariant up to a projective transformation. Conversely, the potential for practical applications could be significantly broadened if different patterns can be projected at different depths simultaneously. For instance, by considering projection mapping using multiple semi-transparent screens, different movies can be projected on each screen. If different depth layers from a scene are projected on each screen for example, this could effectively increase the users' three-dimensional perception; such volume displays are now intensely investigated [2,6,8,11]. Similarly, in a scene exhibiting

© Springer International Publishing Switzerland 2016
F. Huang and A. Sugimoto (Eds.): PSIVT 2015 Workshops, LNCS 9555, pp. 113–126, 2016.
DOI: 10.1007/978-3-319-30285-0_10

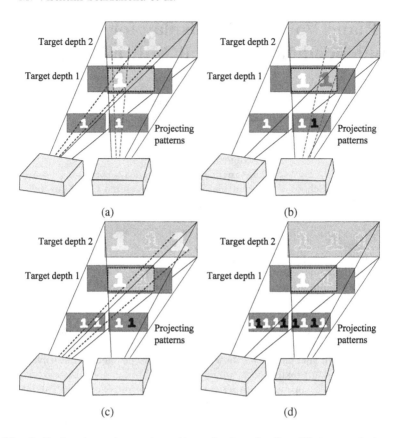

**Fig. 1.** Basic scheme to create patterns for two depths with two projectors.

dynamic, local geometry changes, different patterns could be visualised according to the changing scene depth without the need for explicit 3D reconstruction and/or change of projected images. A system able to project different patterns at different predefined depths can also be used as a non-contact three-dimensional measurement device, which can be used for manufacturing purposes or to aid visual assessment of distances to avoid, for example, vehicle collisions.

In this paper, we propose a technique to realize such a system in practice. Our proposed system consists of multiple projectors coupled with a novel pattern creation algorithm that generates interference patterns to be projected, which recombine at user-defined depths to generate the desired images. The underlying principle of the algorithm can be intuitively understood by considering the following setup. For simplicity, let us assume a system consisting of two projectors and two planes placed at different depths as shown in Fig. 1, where each projector projects its own individual pattern. The aim is to project a single '1' on the first plane and nothing on the second. The patterns are initially designed to project the same image at the same position on the first depth plane as shown in Fig. 1a. Since the patterns' projected position will not coincide on the second depth plane, a compensation pattern should be projected by either projector to remove the duplicate pattern as shown in Fig. 1b. However, since the compensation pattern for the second depth plane will also intersect the first depth plane, this creates another pattern on the first depth plane, which should be removed with another compensation pattern as shown in Fig. 1c. Finally, the final pattern pair can be retrieved by iterating the process until convergence as shown in Fig. 1d. One may consider whether the process always converges to create valid patterns. In this paper, it is revealed that the problem cannot be solved exactly because of the finite field of view of the pattern of projector, however, at the same time, it is shown that close approximations can be created by distributing the approximation error over the whole projected pattern image.

We show a functioning system able to simultaneously project two images at two distinct depths using two conventional LCD or laser projectors. We further contribute by describing a practical geometric and photometric calibration procedure for the system, as well as an automatic procedure for the generation of the distributed interference pattern. The performance of the system is shown both on simulations as well as on our prototype with natural RGB images. The method can also be applied to videos on a per-frame basis. Since this is a brand-new realm of applications, we discuss the limitation of our current version as well as the implementation steps required for replication.

The paper is structured as follows. First, we illustrate related works treating multiple projector systems in Sect. 2. Then, we give an overview of our proposed method in Sect. 3 followed by detailed techniques for projector calibration and distributed pattern creation in Sect. 4. In Sect. 5, simulation results as well as results on our prototype are discussed. Finally, we provide our concluding remarks on the technique in Sect. 6.

## 2   Related Work

Most projection-based augmented reality techniques assume that each single point on the object is illuminated by a single projector. In this case, the color and intensity of the point is determined by the value of the originating pixel of the projector. In contrast, when multiple projectors are considered to illuminate a common scene, we have additional degrees of freedom given by the combination of pixel values to represent a desired intensity on the object. Since the human visual system only concentrates on the center of field of view (FOV), Godin proposed a multi-projector system which projects a high resolution image in the central FOV portion, while a low resolution image is projected to the peripheral areas [5]. Bimber and Emmerling used multiple projectors to improve resolution [4] while Amano to compensate colours [1]. Recently, Nagase et al. [7] used multiple projectors to improve the visual quality of displayed content against defocus, occlusion and stretching artifacts by selecting the best projector for each object point. In this case, binary values are assigned as weights to the projectors and each projector is not used at full capacity. Similarly, in [10] an array of mirrors with a procam system is used to view around occlusions and selectively re-illuminate portions of the scene.

Concerning projection-based stereoscopic and volumetric displays, physically dynamic screen devices such as droplet [2] and moving screens [14] have been proposed, which require special projectors with very high frame rates and are inherently expensive. If the position of the screen is physically moved, the content shown on the screen should be changed electronically by using the depth maps measured by a range finder or alternative 3D tracking methods. In light-field displays [8,11], while multiple projectors are used each light ray is observed separately from specific viewpoints and never mixed. Overall, although the act of combining pixel values cooperatively from multiple projectors that share a common object point could be optimized for numerous tasks, algorithms and applications have not been well explored yet in the community.

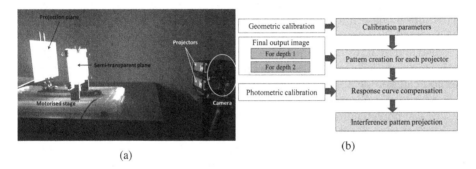

(a)                                (b)

**Fig. 2.** (a) Configuration of our practical system with two projectors and two planes. (b) Overview of the algorithm.

There are two systems that propose techniques for highlighting 3D structure according to its depth using multiple projectors. In [9], structure and depth is highlighted by projecting interfering Moire patterns or complementary colours. In [12], Nakamura *et al.* use a similar matrix formulation to ours to colorise predetermined volume sections and highlight areas in space. However, the technique only crudely exploits the possibilities of light superposition and is therefore unable to produce complex, distinct images at discrete points in space, and only highlights a 3D region with a single colour. Conversely, we propose a novel application for the display of detailed images at distinct locations in space by actively exploiting interference patterns from multiple projectors. Furthermore, in Sect. 4 we highlight the differences in the formulation, which allows us to exploit the sparse structure of the problem and to solve it very efficiently despite very large matrix sizes.

## 3   System Overview

The system consists of two LCD projectors stacked vertically as shown in Fig. 2a and a matte cardboard plane for projection. This was mounted on a motorised rail as to control its position precisely. In order to show the ability to project two different images simultaneously at two different depths, a semi-transparent screen was also included and placed before the matte plane. To calibrate the geometric relationship between projectors, a camera as well as a standard checkerboard calibration plane is required. The main phases of the algorithm are shown in Fig. 2b: first, together with the geometric calibration, prior to projection it is necessary to carry out a photometric calibration procedure in order to compensate for any nonlinearities in the intensity response of the projectors as well as to fix their white balance. Both these phases are described in Sect. 4.1.

Once the system is calibrated offline, the homographies from the geometric calibration together with the desired images to be shown on each plane and positional information about where in space the patterns should recombine are given as the input to our algorithm, which outputs the distributed interference patterns for each projector. This pattern generation procedure is described in Sect. 4.3. Then, the projectors' intensity response curves estimated during the photometric

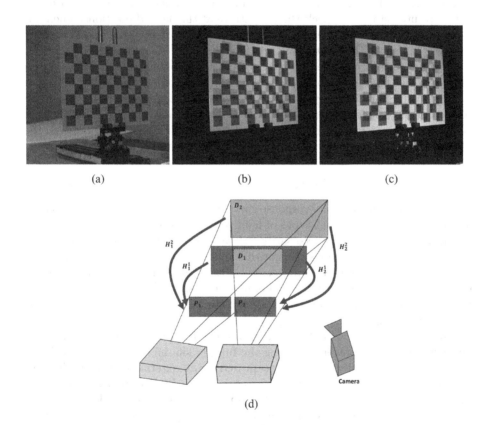

(a)                          (b)                          (c)

(d)

**Fig. 3.** (a) Calibration board for plane/camera homography. (b),(c) Composite images with calibration board and projected checkerboard pattern for camera/projector homography calculation from projector 1 and 2 respectively. (d) Required homographies.

calibration are used to linearise the intensity of the calculated patterns. Finally, all the resulting patterns from each projector are projected simultaneously onto the scene, recombining into the desired images at the requested positions.

## 4   Multiple Simultaneous Image Projections at Multiple Depths

### 4.1   Geometric Calibration

In our method, the homography parameters between each planar board at depths $D_1, D_2$ and each projected pattern $P_1, P_2$, as well as distortion parameters for each projector are required as shown in Fig. 3d. Similarly to projection mapping, the homographies are calculated so that the patterns can be warped in order to be projected to the same area on each plane by both projectors, and to compensate that the planes are not perfectly frontoparallel to the projector array. In order to estimate the homographies, we use an external camera and we place a board with a printed standard checkerboard pattern at the desired positions. Then, for each projector the same checkerboard pattern is projected on the board, and the composite image of the printed and projected patterns is captured by the camera. The two patterns are printed and projected using two different colours as shown in Fig. 3a and b and simple colour thresholding is used to divide the composite image into its constituent patterns. The homographies are found between the plane and the camera as well as between the camera and the projector through chessboard calibration, which allows us to calculate the homography between the plane and the projector. The process is repeated for all projectors and depths.

### 4.2   Photometric Calibration

It is known that the intensity response curve of the projector is nonlinear because of unique features of various types of light sources. More importantly, the intensity response curve is not necessarily the same for all projectors considered in the system. Since our proposed algorithm relies on the precise compensation of the intensity value from both projected patterns, it is crucial for the projected patterns to reflect accurately their nominal intensity. Indeed, experimentally it was found that whenever this stage was omitted, large errors were visible in the recombined images.

For the photometric calibration, we project from each projector a linearly increasing grayscale pattern covering the full [0, 255] intensity range, as shown in Fig. 4c. The projected pattern is captured by an external camera with a linear response and the median value for each of the RGB channels is taken for each intensity bar. The recorded values for both projectors are plotted against their nominal intensity, resulting in characteristic gamma curves as shown in Fig. 4a and b. These are approximated for each channel as $f(x) = ax^b$, where $x$ is the intensity value and $a, b$ are the parameters found through fitting of the observed data. The function is then inverted and kept for compensating the generated pattern prior projection.

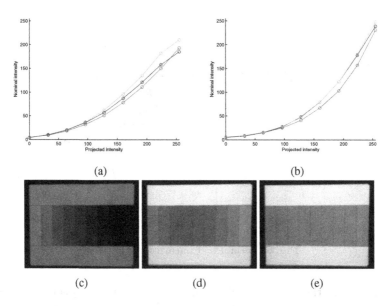

**Fig. 4.** (a),(b) Intensity response curves for projectors 1 and 2 respectively. (c) Projected calibration pattern. (d) Calibration pattern superimposed with its own mirrored version, before and (e) after colour compensation.

To confirm our photometric calibration, we flip horizontally the calibration pattern for one of the projectors and we display it at the same time from both projectors. Since the pattern is linearly increasing, the result of the superposition between the two patterns should be a constant grey value across all bands as shown in Fig. 4e. Conversely, if photometric compensation is not performed, the superposition result shows obvious errors as in Fig. 4d.

### 4.3 Interference Pattern Generation

We formulate the problem of creating the distributed interference patterns for projecting simultaneously different images at different depths, as a sparse linear system. Figure 5 shows the variables definitions. While for clarity we illustrate the process in the case of two projectors and two different images placed at two depth levels, the system can be extended to a higher number of projectors and depth planes.

The two projected patterns from the projectors are denoted as $P_j$ where $j \in \{1, \cdots, J\}$, and the two images to be shown at the two different depths are depicted as $I_k$ where $k \in \{1, \cdots, K\}$, Let pixels on $P_j$ be expressed as $p_{j,1}, p_{j,2}, \cdots, p_{j,m}, \cdots, p_{j,M}$ and let pixels on $I_k$ be $i_{k,1}, i_{k,2}, \cdots, i_{k,n}, \cdots, i_{k,N}$.

The image projection from $P_j$ to $I_k$ can be modeled as a homography with the parameters estimated during calibration. Using these parameters, we can define an inverse projection mapping $q$, where, if $i_{k,n}$ is illuminated by $p_{j,m}$, $q(k, n, j)$ is defined as $m$, and if $i_{k,n}$ is not illuminated by any pixels of $P_j$, $q(k, n, j)$

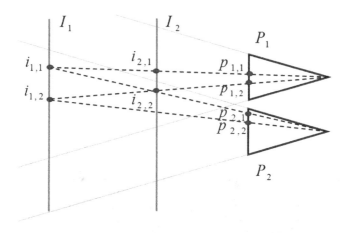

**Fig. 5.** Variables of linear constraints.

is defined as 0. In the example of Fig. 5, $q(2, 2, 1) = 2$ since $i_{2,2}$ is illuminated by $p_{1,2}$, and $q(2, 2, 2) = 1$ since $i_{2,2}$ is illuminated by $p_{2,1}$. $q(2, 1, 2) = 0$ since $i_{2,1}$ is not illuminated by $P_2$.

Let us define $p_{1,0} = p_{2,0} = 0$. Then, using these definitions, the constraints of the projections are expressed as follows:

$$i_{k,n} = p_{1,q(k,n,1)} + p_{2,q(k,n,2)}. \tag{1}$$

By collecting these equations, linear equations

$$\mathbf{I}_1 = \mathbf{A}_{1,1}\mathbf{P}_1 + \mathbf{A}_{1,2}\mathbf{P}_2 \tag{2}$$

$$\mathbf{I}_2 = \mathbf{A}_{2,1}\mathbf{P}_1 + \mathbf{A}_{2,2}\mathbf{P}_2 \tag{3}$$

follow, where $\mathbf{P}_j$ is a vector $[p_{j,1}, p_{j,2}, \cdots, p_{j,M}]$, and $\mathbf{I}_k$ is a vector $[i_{k,1}, i_{k,2}, \cdots, i_{k,N}]$, and the matrix $\mathbf{A}_{k,j}$ is defined by its $(m, n)$-elements as

$$\mathbf{A}_{k,j}(n, m) = \begin{cases} \frac{d_{k,n,j}^2}{\mathbf{L}_{k,n,j} \cdot \mathbf{N}_k} & (q(k, n, j) = m) \\ 0 & (otherwise) \end{cases}, \tag{4}$$

where $d_{k,n,j}$ is the distance between a pixel on the plane and the projector in order to compensate for the light fall-off and $\mathbf{L}_{k,n,j} \cdot \mathbf{N}_k$ is the angle between the normal $\mathbf{N}$ of $I_k$ and the incoming light vector $\mathbf{L}$ at pixel $n$ from $P_j$ to compensate the Lambertian reflectance of the matte plane. By using $\mathbf{I} \equiv \begin{bmatrix} \mathbf{I}_1 \\ \mathbf{I}_2 \end{bmatrix}$, $\mathbf{P} \equiv \begin{bmatrix} \mathbf{P}_1 \\ \mathbf{P}_2 \end{bmatrix}$ and $\mathbf{A} \equiv \begin{bmatrix} \mathbf{A}_{1,1} & \mathbf{A}_{1,2} \\ \mathbf{A}_{2,1} & \mathbf{A}_{2,2} \end{bmatrix}$, we get our complete linear system

$$\mathbf{I} = \mathbf{AP}. \tag{5}$$

The problem to be solved is to obtain $\mathbf{P}$ given $\mathbf{I}$ and $\mathbf{A}$. The length of vector $\mathbf{P}$ is $M \cdot J$, while the length of vector $\mathbf{I}$ is $N \cdot K$. Thus, the matrix $\mathbf{A}$ is a very large sparse matrix. To model the real system, this simple linear model has a problem. Since $\mathbf{I}$ and $\mathbf{P}$ are images, their elements should be non-negative values with a fixed dynamic range. However, the lack of positivity constraints in the solution of the sparse system means that $\mathbf{P}$ may include negative elements. To overcome this issue, we normalize $\mathbf{P}$ by scaling it and adding a constant vector so that the elements are in the range of $[0, 1]$, and obtain the final pixel values of the pattern images by multiplying by the maximum representable pixel value (normally 255). The effect of this is a compression of the resulting dynamic range and a lowering of the contrast. We explore this issue in our results, adding that it can be fixed by using projectors with finer quantisation.

### 4.4  Solving Linear Constraints

Let the number of elements in $\mathbf{P}$ be $Q$, and the number of elements in $\mathbf{I}$ be $R$. $Q$ is also the number of unknown variables in the system, while $R$ is the number of constraints.

To solve the sparse system, our system is set up so that the equation is either well-posed or over-constrained ($R \geq Q$), as under-constrained ($R < Q$) configurations may lead to unstable results. In practice, this entails a system consisting of at least as many projectors as depth planes. For the over-constrained configuration, Eq. (5) can be approximately solved by estimating the pseudo-inverse of $\mathbf{A}$. Since $\mathbf{A}$ is a large sparse matrix, sparse matrix linear calculation package is needed. In this paper, we approximated the solution by using the LSQR solver described in [3,13]. The system can be solved quite efficiently, and in our MATLAB implementation convergence is reached in about 1 second given an input pattern resolution of $1024 \times 768$ on a standard PC running at 2.66 GHz. While the implementation is not real-time yet, the short runtimes make it possible to individually precompute patterns for each frame of a video as well as static images. This is in contrast with the formulation by [12], where the different structure of the matrix $\mathbf{A}$ does not allow the use of sparse solvers, requiring instead a computationally expensive global optimization.

## 5  Experiments

Our setup consists of two stacked EPSON LCD projectors as in Fig. 2a, with an external Point Grey Grasshopper3 camera for calibration. The patterns were projected on a matte plane placed on a motorised stage for fine distance control. Three depths were tested, at 80 cm, 90 cm and 100 cm, referred to as $D_1$, $D_2$ and $D_3$ respectively.

### 5.1  Simulations

To give a quantitative evaluation of the system performance, we use the publicly available test images *Lena*, *Mandrill*, *Peppers* and *Fruits* stretched to the

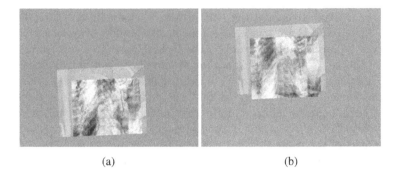

(a)                                    (b)

**Fig. 6.** Projected patterns for (a) top and (b) bottom projectors.

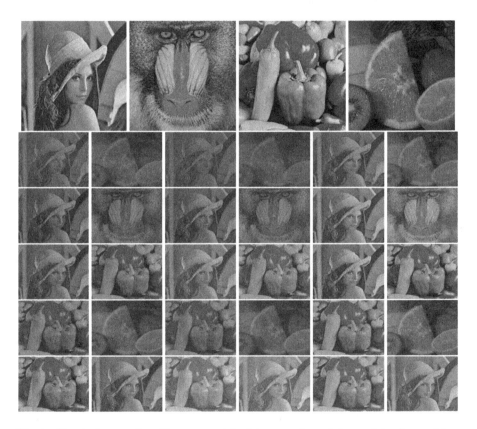

**Fig. 7.** Simulation results. Top row: original images, from left to right: Lena, Mandrill, Peppers, Fruits. From second to last row, showing tests with Lena/Fruits, Lena/Mandrill, Lena/Peppers, Peppers/Fruits, Peppers/Lena. The columns show the simulated recombined images on the two projection planes placed at depths $D_1/D_2$, $D_2/D_3$ and $D_1/D_3$ respectively.

$1024 \times 768$ projector resolution to use all the available pixels, as well as the homographies calculated for our real experimental setup. In our simulations, we include the effect of integer rounding to the standard intensity range $[0, 255]$. In general, we observe that the range of intensity values represented is reduced, thus reducing the overall image contrast. It is important to stress that when

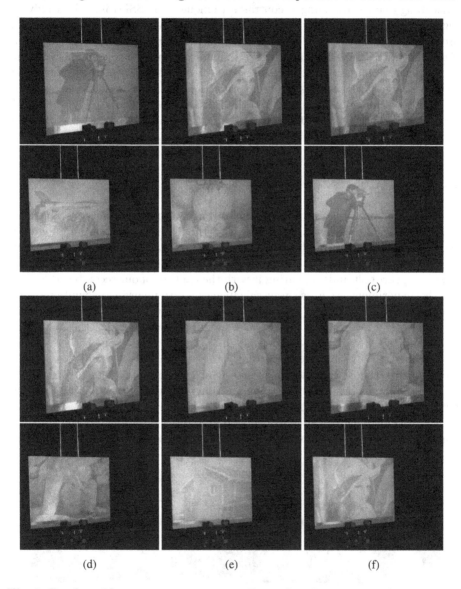

**Fig. 8.** Results with our prototype system. For each pair on consecutive rows, we show the recombined patterns at depths $D_1$ and $D_3$ respectively. The datasets are, (a) *Cameraman/Jetplane*, (b) *Lena/Mandrill*, (c) *Lena/Cameraman*, (d) *Lena/Peppers*, (e) *Peppers/House* and (f) *Peppers/Lena*.

considering the output of the sparse matrix solver without integer rounding and fitting in the $[0, 255]$ range, the PSNR is consistently above 30 dB for all datasets, and the major factor affecting the performance is the dynamic range compression needed to fit into the standard 24-bit per RGB pixel range. Therefore, together with the PSNR values between original and generated images which could be misleading due to the changed contrast, we include the SSIM in order to give a higher-level similarity metric between the original and generated images. Results are reported in Table 1a and b, while examples of generated images are shown in Fig. 7. From the table, we can observe that for all image pair combinations the performance is highest for the combination of depths $D_1/D_3$, which is the one with the largest separations between projection planes. For that combination, for almost all image pairs considered the PSNR exceeds 20 dB, while the SSIM exceeds 0.8, with peaks of 0.93. Examples of the generated patterns are shown in Fig. 6, where it can be seen that no discernible figure can be made out of a single projected pattern.

## 5.2   Real Data

We tested our prototype including a wider range of images from public datasets like *Cameraman*, *Jetplane* and *House* with the $D_1/D_3$ distance pair. Figure 8 the system indeed accurately shows the two images with a good image quality. Numerically, we further tested the system by projecting the original *Peppers* image, capturing it and comparing it with the capture of our recombined image. For this experiment, we chose grayscale images not to incur in any white balance issues. Visually, the results are pleasing and are shown in Fig. 9, however, due to noise in the recapturing process and small calibration errors, the numerical results indicate a PSNR of 14.88 dB and an SSIM of 0.690. Despite the values, the images are clearly visible and importantly, it is striking how suddenly the images recombine at the desired depth as shown in Fig. 9c taken 5 cm before, while outside the predefined depths nothing meaningful is visible, reinforcing the case for visual distance assessment applications of the proposed system. The main issue is one of dynamic range as discussed for the simulations, as the contrast appears reduced in the recombined images. This will be our main focus for future

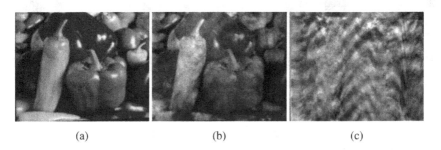

|     (a)     |     (b)     |     (c)     |

**Fig. 9.** Numerical evaluation of the proposed system. (a) Original *Peppers* image. (b) Recombined *Peppers* image. (c) Recombined pattern outside the predefined depths.

**Table 1.** (a) PSNR and (b) SSIM results for combinations of image and depth pairs.

| PSNR | | | | SSIM | | | |
|---|---|---|---|---|---|---|---|
| | D1/D2 | D2/D3 | D1/D3 | | D1/D2 | D2/D3 | D1/D3 |
| Lena-Peppers | 19.76 | 19.04 | 24.34 | Lena-Peppers | 0.825 | 0.796 | 0.930 |
| Peppers-Lena | 20.55 | 14.85 | 19.04 | Peppers-Lena | 0.849 | 0.725 | 0.858 |
| Lena-Fruits | 16.80 | 15.82 | 19.57 | Lena-Fruits | 0.628 | 0.536 | 0.790 |
| Lena-Mandrill | 17.15 | 17.82 | 22.06 | Lena-Mandrill | 0.727 | 0.700 | 0.843 |
| Peppers-Fruits | 18.85 | 17.78 | 22.59 | Peppers-Fruits | 0.749 | 0.692 | 0.896 |

(a)                                    (b)

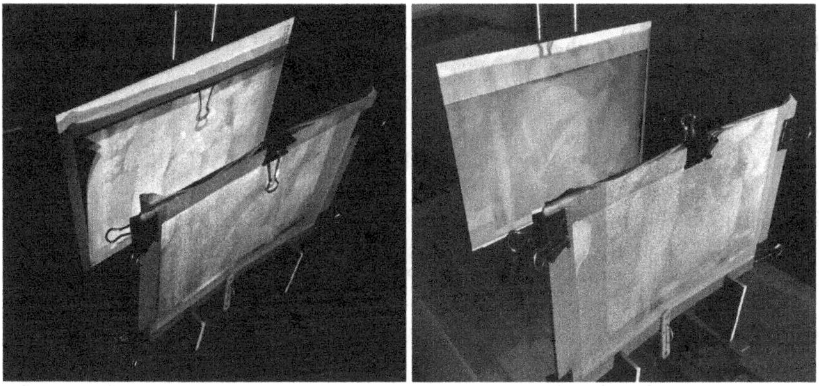

(a)                                    (b)

**Fig. 10.** Prototype showing two images simultaneously projected on a matte and semi-transparent screen for (a) *Lena/Peppers* and (b) *Peppers/Lena*.

investigations. Finally, we show the possibility of showing simultaneously both images using a semi-transparent screen followed by a matte screen in Fig. 10. While the materials used do not allow good definition on the semi-transparent screen, the image of Lena is clearly visible and it successfully demonstrates our concept.

# 6   Conclusion

In this paper, we propose a new pattern projection method which can project different patterns at different depths simultaneously. This novel system is realized by using multiple projectors with an efficient algorithm to create suitable distributed interference patterns. In addition, a practical calibration method for both geometric and photometric parameters is proposed. Experiments were conducted on a working prototype to show the quality of the combined images as well as the calibration and pattern creation method with simulated and real data. Extensions will concentrate on increasing the dynamic range as well as scaling the numbers of patterns and projectors in the prototype.

**Acknowledgments.** This work was supported by The Japanese Foundation for the Promotion of Science, Grant-in-Aid for JSPS Fellows no. 26.04041.

# References

1. Amano, T., Kato, H.: Appearance enhancement using a projector-camera feedback system. In: International Conference on Pattern Recognition (ICPR), pp. 1–4 (2008)
2. Barnum, P.C., Narasimhan, S.G., Kanade, T.: A multi-layered display with water drops. ACM Trans. Graph. (TOG) **29**(4), 76 (2010)
3. Barrett, R., Berry, M., Chan, T.F., Demmel, J., Donato, J., Dongarra, J., Eijkhout, V., Pozo, R., Romine, C., der Vorst, H.V.: Templates for the Solution of Linear Systems: Building Blocks for Iterative Methods, 2nd edn. SIAM, Philadelphia (1994)
4. Bimber, O., Emmerling, A.: Multifocal projection: a multiprojector technique for increasing focal depth. IEEE Trans. Vis. Comput. Graph. **12**(4), 658–667 (2006)
5. Godin, G., Massicotte, P., Borgeat, L.: High-resolution insets in projector-based display: principle and techniques. In: SPIE Proceedings: Stereoscopic Displays and Virtual Reality Systems XIII, vol. 6055 (2006)
6. Hirsch, M., Wetzstein, G., Raskar, R.: A compressive light field projection system. ACM Trans. Graph. (TOG) **33**(4), 58 (2014)
7. Iwai, D.: Extended depth-of-field projector by fast focal sweep projection. IEEE Trans. Vis. Comput. Graph. **21**, 462–470 (2015)
8. Jurik, J., Jones, A., Bolas, M., Debevec, P.: Prototyping a light field display involving direct observation of a video projector array. In: IEEE Conference on Computer Vision and Pattern Recognition Workshops (CVPRW), pp. 15–20 (2011)
9. Kagami, S.: Range-finding projectors: visualizing range information without sensors. In: IEEE International Symposium on Mixed and Augmented Reality (ISMAR), pp. 239–240, October 2010
10. Levoy, M., Chen, B., Vaish, V., Horowitz, M., McDowall, I., Bolas, M.: Synthetic aperture confocal imaging. ACM Trans. Graph. **23**(3), 825–834 (2004)
11. Nagano, K., Jones, A., Liu, J., Busch, J., Yu, X., Bolas, M., Debevec, P.: An autostereoscopic projector array optimized for 3d facial display. In: ACM SIGGRApPH 2013 Emerging Technologies, SIGGRAPH 2013, p. 3:1 (2013)
12. Nakamura, R., Sakaue, F., Sato, J.: Emphasizing 3D structure visually using coded projection from multiple projectors. In: Kimmel, R., Klette, R., Sugimoto, A. (eds.) ACCV 2010, Part II. LNCS, vol. 6493, pp. 109–122. Springer, Heidelberg (2011)
13. Paige, C.C., Saunders, M.A.: Lsqr: an algorithm for sparse linear equations and sparse least squares. ACM Trans. Math. Softw. **8**, 43–71 (1982)
14. Tsao, C.C., Chen, J.S.: Moving screen projection: a new approach for volumetric three-dimensional display. In: SPIE Projection Displays II, vol. 2650, pp. 254–264 (1996)

# Analysis on Coupled Line Cameras Using Projective Geometry

Jinwoo Lee[1], Joo-Haeng Lee[2,3], and Junho Kim[1(✉)]

[1] School of Computer Science, Kookmin University, Seoul, Republic of Korea
junho@kookmin.ac.kr
[2] Human-Robot Interaction Laboratory, ETRI, Daejeon, Republic of Korea
[3] Computer Software, University of Science and Technology,
Daejeon, Republic of Korea

**Abstract.** Recently coupled line cameras (CLCs) have been introduced to calibrate camera parameters solely from a single rectangle with an unknown aspect ratio in the captured image. Even as CLCs are highly related to projective geometry, they have not been analyzed from the framework of projective geometry. In this study, we revisit CLCs using the concepts of projective geometry, such as cross-ratio and projective harmonic conjugate. Finally, we present novel and efficient algorithms to handle off-centered rectangles in CLCs and provide the experimental results of CLC-based reconstructions by using the proposed algorithm for real images.

**Keywords:** Coupled line cameras · Rectangle · Projective geometry · Cross-ratio · Projective harmonic conjugate

## 1 Introduction

Camera calibration is a fundamental tool for estimating the parameters of a given camera from its captured images. The intrinsic parameters depend on the internal characteristics of the camera, such as focal length, principal point, and distortion coefficients, whereas the extrinsic parameters tell us the external 3D pose of the camera against a scene, such as its orientation and position. Because the camera parameters are the basis for analyzing the scene geometry from camera images, they have been extensively studied in computer vision and related areas, including computer graphics and augmented reality.

Recently coupled line cameras (CLCs) have been introduced in [1–3] to estimate the extrinsic parameters of a camera solely from a *single rectangle* with an *unknown aspect ratio* in the captured image. Based on the assumption that the image is captured with a pinhole camera, CLCs provide an analytic solution for the camera pose by reconstructing the projective structure defined between the camera and the plane containing the rectangle. Moreover, it is possible to find the aspect ratio of the unknown rectangle in a scene.

CLCs find the camera pose by using the perspective length distortions captured from two line cameras, each of which belongs to one of two diagonals

© Springer International Publishing Switzerland 2016
F. Huang and A. Sugimoto (Eds.): PSIVT 2015 Workshops, LNCS 9555, pp. 127–138, 2016.
DOI: 10.1007/978-3-319-30285-0_11

in a projected rectangle. By coupling two line cameras a geometrically possible solution space for the camera pose is defined, with an assumption that the center of the projected rectangle is at the center of the image. Because the center of the projected rectangle does not lie on the center of the image in practice, a proxy rectangle is constructed on the center of the image prior to CLCs that is projective similar [1] or congruent [3] to the given off-centered rectangle. Even as CLCs are highly related to projective geometry, especially in defining the line camera and finding a proxy rectangle, CLCs have not been analyzed from the framework of projective geometry.

In this study, we revisit CLCs using the concepts of projective geometry [4] and propose a novel and efficient algorithms to handle off-centered rectangles in CLCs. We firstly show that the lengths of four partial diagonals in any perspectively similar rectangles at arbitrary positions are analytically defined in an up-to-scale manner, by utilizing *projective harmonic conjugate*. Finally, we analytically obtain the lengths of four partial diagonals at the image center directly from an off-centered rectangle and apply them to CLCs for camera calibrations.

## 2    Related Work and Background

### 2.1    Related Work

There are several approaches to exploit the geometry of image quadrilateral for camera calibration. According to [5], we can reconstruct a scene rectangle from a single image without explicit correspondence information between an image quadrilateral and a scene rectangle. However, we need to specify intrinsic parameters such as focal length, which can be computed using a method based on the concept of the image of absolute conic (IAC). Once the rectangle is reconstructed, the external camera parameters can be computed using the method such as [6]. In other approaches [7,8], we need to specify the aspect ratio of a scene rectangle to calibrate the camera. Otherwise, at least two images are required for reconstruction.

In contrast to previous work, CLCs [1–3] provide the geometry of an unknown rectangle from an image qaudrilateral without prior information on the aspect ratio of the rectangle and the focal length of the camera. The initial conception of CLCs in [1] followed the successful formulation of its dual configuration on CLPs (coupled line projectors) that provided a solution to the projector pose estimation problem for a projected quadrilateral in the scene [9]. Through a series of progressive refinements [1–3], CLCs achieved a solution for the problem of estimating camera pose from the single image of an unknown scene rectangle. The solution is unique in that the projective reconstruction and rectangle determination can be performed simultaneously without prior knowledge of correspondences or camera parameters.

The imaging geometry of CLCs is assumed to be a pinhole projection model, which contributes to simplify the underlying geometric configuration and leads to the derivation of simple analytic solutions. The optimized analytic form in [2] is based on the observation of two intersecting solution spheres of line cameras.

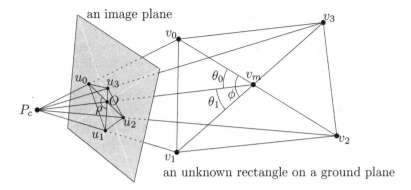

**Fig. 1.** Configuration of a coupled line camera. A unknown rectangle $G$ with vertices $v_0, v_1, v_2, v_3$ is projected on an image plane of a camera $p_c$ as a quadrilateral $Q$ with vertices $u_0, u_1, u_2, u_3$ while the principal axis passes through the centers of $G$ and $Q$.

This was further developed as generalized coupled line cameras (G-CLCs) in [3] to handle any arbitrary scene quadrilateral other than a rectangle. Note that no internal camera parameter is needed for projective reconstruction and the rectangle determination. If required, we can apply a standard calibration method such as in [6,10,11]. This is quite different from the previous method in [12] that requires a prior knowledge of internal camera parameters to reconstruct the scene rectangle.

The CLCs solution is largely composed of three steps: (1) From the given vertices of an image quadrilateral $Q_g$, a centered proxy quadrilateral $Q$ is inferred using the geometric properties of parallel lines in perspective. The computation is solely composed of line-line intersection operations [3] (see Fig. 3). (2) For the centered proxy quadrilateral $Q$ found, the analytic solutions of CLCs in [2] are applied to reconstruct the centered scene rectangle $G$ and to find the position of the principal point $p_c$ in the coordinate system defined by the centered scene rectangle $G$. (3) Once the projective structure defined by $G$ and $p_c$ is reconstructed, the geometry of the target scene rectangle $Q_g$ can be geometrically determined using the method presented in [3]. In [1], a homography between $Q$ and $G$ was used to find $G_g$ from $Q_g$.

This paper focuses on the first step of the CLCs solution that infers a centered proxy quadrilateral from a given off-centered quadrilateral in an image. We propose analytic solutions that define diagonal parameters for CLC-based reconstruction without explicitly inferring a centered proxy quadrilateral.

## 2.2   Background

In this section, we briefly introduce the CLCs and several projective geometry tools to analyze the CLCs based on projective geometry. We refer the readers to [1–3] for more information about CLCs and [4] for details on projective geometry.

**Coupled Line Cameras.** Figure 1 shows a configuration of CLCs. A rectangle $G$ (i.e., $v_0v_1v_2v_3$) is projected on the image plane of a camera $p_c$ as a quadrilateral $Q$ (i.e., $u_0u_1u_2u_3$) while the principal axis passes through the centers of $G$ and $Q$. In this configuration, lengths of partial diagonals of a rectangle are $|v_i - v_m| = 1$ ($i = 0, 1, 2, 3$).

CLCs decompose the projective structure problem into two diagonal problem as *line cameras*. For the line camera, camera pose parameters such as the length of principal axis $\overline{p_c v_m} = d$ and a camera orientation $\angle p_c v_m v_i = \theta_i$, can be represented by lengths of projected partial diagonals $l_i = |u_i - u_m|$ ($i = 0, 1, 2, 3$), as follows:

$$\cos \theta_i = \left( \frac{(l_i - l_{(i+2)})}{(l_i + l_{(i+2)})} \right) d = \alpha_i d \tag{1}$$

where $i = 0, 1$.

In the *pose equation* represented as Eq. (1), the possible positions of the camera are defined on a sphere based on *line division coefficient* $\alpha_i$, for each diagonal ($i = 0, 1$).

To geometrically merge two line cameras with an compliant scale, CLCs introduces a *coupling constraint*:

$$\beta = \frac{l_1}{l_0} \tag{2}$$

Using the geometric configuration specified in Eqs. (1) and (2), the length $d$ of the principal axis can be computed as follows.

$$d = \sqrt{\frac{A_0}{A_1}}$$
$$A_0 = (1 - \alpha_1)^2 \beta^2 - (1 - \alpha_0)^2 \tag{3}$$
$$A_1 = \alpha_0^2(1 - \alpha_1)^2 \beta^2 - (1 - \alpha_0)^2 \alpha_1^2$$

Once the length of principal axis is found, $\theta_i$ can be computed using the pose equation. Next, the $\theta_i$ and an angle of the diagonals $\rho = \angle u_0 O u_1$ are employed to compute a diagonal angle $\phi = \angle v_0 v_m v_1$ as follows.

$$\cos \phi = \cos \rho \sin \theta_0 \sin \theta_1 + \cos \theta_0 \cos \theta_1 \tag{4}$$

Finally, the CLC-based reconstruction computes the camera position $p_c$ as follows.

$$p_c = \frac{d(\sin(\phi)\cos(\theta_0), \cos(\theta_1) - \cos(\phi)\sin(\theta_0), \sin(\rho)\sin(\theta_0)\sin(\theta_1))}{\sin(\phi)} \tag{5}$$

Note that $p_c$ is relatively defined in the coordinates defined by the reconstructed rectangle $G$.

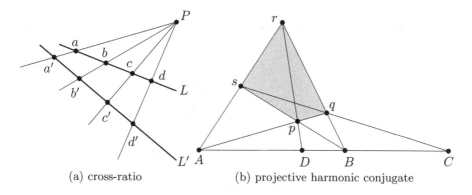

(a) cross-ratio        (b) projective harmonic conjugate

**Fig. 2.** Projective geometric properties used in analyzing CLCs

**Projective Geometry.** The cross-ratio is a ratio between the distances defined by four collinear points on a projective line (see Fig. 2(a)). When four lines starting from a point $P$ intersect a line $L$ at the four points $a$, $b$, $c$, $d$, the cross-ratio of the four points is defined as

$$(a, b; c, d) = \frac{|a, c|}{|a, d|} \bigg/ \frac{|b, c|}{|b, d|}, \tag{6}$$

where $|a, c|$ denotes the directed distance from a to c.

The cross-ratio is the only invariant property that does not affect the projective transformation, meaning that the cross-ratio always holds true for any four collinear points $a'$, $b'$, $c'$, $d'$ on another line $L'$, as follows.

$$(a, b; c, d) = (a', b'; c', d') = \frac{|a, c|}{|a, d|} \bigg/ \frac{|b, c|}{|b, d|} = \frac{|a', c'|}{|a', d'|} \bigg/ \frac{|b', c'|}{|b', d'|} \tag{7}$$

The projective harmonic conjugate comes from a special case of the cross-ratio induced from a quadrilateral (see Fig. 2(b)). Considering a quadrilateral $pqrs$, we can define two intersection points $A$ and $B$, each of which joins a pair of opposite sides in $pqrs$. Once we define a line passing through $A$ and $B$, we can further define $C$ and $D$ from the intersections between the line of $AB$ and each diagonal of $pqrs$. In this case, $D$ is called the harmonic conjugate of $C$, and the cross-ratio of four points $(A, B; C, D)$ is then defined as follows:

$$(A, B; C, D) = \frac{|A, C|}{|A, D|} \bigg/ \frac{|B, C|}{|B, D|} = -1 \tag{8}$$

Let us consider that the arbitrary quadrilateral $pqrs$ is a projected rectangle, i.e., an image of a rectangle in 3D captured from a pinhole camera. Then, the four points $A$, $B$, $C$, $D$ are four vanishing points on a vanishing line defined from the projected rectangle. Moreover, with projective harmonic conjugate one vanishing point can be calculated from the other three vanishing points. In this study, we

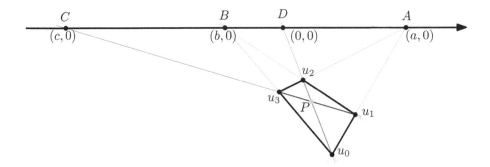

**Fig. 3.** Problem setting: The quadrilateral $u_0u_1u_2u_3$ is an image of an unknown planar rectangle. We can consider the four vanishing points $A$, $B$, $C$, $D$, on a vanishing line, where $A$ and $B$ are the infinity points about two pairs of parallel sides in the rectangle and $C$ and $D$ are the infinity points about two diagonal directions of the rectangle.

utilize this property to analyze the special relationships between the lengths of four partial diagonals in any perspectively similar rectangles at arbitrary positions.

## 3    Analysis

In this section, we analyze the projective structure on the image of a rectangle observed from a pinhole camera. We also show some special relationships among the lengths of the four partial diagonals in any perspectively similar rectangles at arbitrary positions, by using cross-ratios and projective harmonic conjugates.

Let us consider a quadrilateral $u_0u_1u_2u_3$, which is a projective image of a planar rectangle $v_0v_1v_2v_3$ with an unknown ratio in 3D, as shown in Fig. 3. Then, we can define a vanishing point $A$ as the intersection of the extensions of a pair of opposite sides, $\overline{u_0u_1}$ and $\overline{u_2u_3}$. In a similar manner, we can obtain a vanishing point $B$ defined by another pair of opposite sides, $\overline{u_1u_2}$ and $\overline{u_3u_0}$. Next, by defining a vanishing line passing through $A$ and $B$, we further consider two more vanishing points $C$ and $D$, which are the infinity points on the two diagonal directions of the rectangle. Notice that any projective similar rectangles with $u_0u_1u_2u_3$ on the same plane share the same vanishing points, $A$, $B$, $C$, and $D$, on the same vanishing line.

For the sake of simplicity, we define a new coordinate system in the image space, in a way that its origin is located on the vanishing point $D$, its $x$-axis is defined along with the vanishing line, and its $y$-axis is perpendicular to the $x$-axis. We represent the coordinates of other three vanishing points, as $A = (a,0)$, $B = (b,0)$, and $C = (c,0)$, respectively, as shown in Fig. 3. Because the set of the four vanishing points, $A$, $B$, $C$, $D$, is a harmonic range, $c$ can be represented by $a$, and $b$, from the projective harmonic conjugate, as follows.

$$c = \frac{2ab}{a+b} \tag{9}$$

Now, we analyze the length relationships among the four partial diagonals in a quadrilateral $u_0 u_1 u_2 u_3$, whose projective center point is $P = (p^x, p^y)$. The center $P$ of a projective image of a rectangle can be computed as the intersection point between the diagonals, as shown in Fig. 3. The length of a partial diagonal of the quadrilateral is represented as $l_i$, where $i = 0, 1, 2, 3$.

$$l_i = |u_i P| \tag{10}$$

Let us consider the distance from the projective center $P$ and two vanishing points $C$ and $D$, defined by two diagonals. We define the length between $P$ and $D$ as $l_+$ and the length between $P$ and $C$ as $l_-$.

$$l_+ = |DP| = \sqrt{(p^x)^2 + (p^y)^2} \tag{11}$$

$$l_- = |CP| = \sqrt{(p^x - c)^2 + (p^y)^2} \tag{12}$$

Let us represent the unit vectors from $P$ to $D$ as $e_+$ and from $P$ to $C$ as $e_+$.

$$e_+ = \frac{DP}{|DP|} = \frac{DP}{l_+} \tag{13}$$

$$e_- = \frac{CP}{|CP|} = \frac{CP}{l_-} \tag{14}$$

Now, we can represent the coordinates of $u_i$, in terms of the coordinate of $P$, the lengths of partial diagonals, $l_i$, and $l_+$, $l_-$, as follows ($i = 0, 1, 2, 3$).

$$u_0 = \begin{bmatrix} u_0^x \\ u_0^y \end{bmatrix} = P + l_0 e_+ = P + DP \frac{l_0}{l_+} = \frac{l_+ + l_0}{l_+} \begin{bmatrix} p^x \\ p^y \end{bmatrix} \tag{15}$$

$$u_1 = \begin{bmatrix} u_1^x \\ u_1^y \end{bmatrix} = P + l_1 e_- = P + CP \frac{l_1}{l_-} = \frac{l_- + l_1}{l_-} \begin{bmatrix} p^x \\ p^y \end{bmatrix} - \frac{l_1}{l_-} \begin{bmatrix} c \\ 0 \end{bmatrix} \tag{16}$$

$$u_2 = \begin{bmatrix} u_2^x \\ u_2^y \end{bmatrix} = P - l_2 e_+ = P - DP \frac{l_2}{l_+} = \frac{l_+ - l_2}{l_+} \begin{bmatrix} p^x \\ p^y \end{bmatrix} \tag{17}$$

$$u_3 = \begin{bmatrix} u_3^x \\ u_3^y \end{bmatrix} = P - l_3 e_- = P - CP \frac{l_3}{l_-} = \frac{l_- - l_3}{l_-} \begin{bmatrix} p^x \\ p^y \end{bmatrix} + \frac{l_3}{l_-} \begin{bmatrix} c \\ 0 \end{bmatrix} \tag{18}$$

Since $u_0$ and $u_1$ share the vanishing point $A$, the relation $(u_0 \times u_1) \cdot A = 0$ holds true for their homogeneous coordinates and we can obtain the following:

$$(u_0^y u_1^x - u_0^x u_1^y) = a(u_0^y - u_1^y) \tag{19}$$

By using Eqs. (15) and (16), we can represent Eq. (19) with a length relationship, as follows:

$$c(l_+ + l_0)l_1 = a(l_+ l_0 - l_- l_0) \tag{20}$$

By applying the projective harmonic conjugate in Eqs. (9) to (20), we further simplify Eq. (20) as follows.

$$2b(l_+ + l_0)l_1 = (a + b)(l_+ l_1 - l_- l_0) \tag{21}$$

If we apply the similar processes with Eqs. (19) and (20) to the other three sides of the quadrilateral, we can express the length of partial diagonals, $l_1$, $l_2$ and $l_3$, in terms of $a$, $b$, $l_0$, $l_+$, $l_-$, as follows.

$$l_1 = \frac{(a+b)l_- l_0}{(a-b)l_+ - 2bl_0}$$

$$l_2 = \frac{l_+ l_0}{l_+ + 2bl_0} \qquad (22)$$

$$l_3 = \frac{(a+b)l_- l_0}{(a-b)l_+ + 2al_0}$$

Notice that for a given quadrilateral $u_0 u_1 u_2 u_3$, the lengths about $a$, $b$, $l_+$, $l_-$ are fixed. As a result, we can say that the up-to-scale dependencies exists among the lengths of partial diagonals in the quadrilateral, meaning that $l_1$, $l_2$, $l_3$ can be defined from $l_0$, as shown in Eq. (22).

For any projective similar rectangle to a given quadrilateral $u_0 u_1 u_2 u_3$, the lengths about $a$, $b$ are fixed because they share the vanishing points. In that case, once we compute $l_+$ and $l_-$ based on the center of a similar rectangle, we can define $l_1$, $l_2$, $l_3$ from $l_0$, in an up-to-scale manner.

## 4    Algorithm

In this section, we provide specific algorithms to apply our analysis in Sect. 3 to CLCs for camera calibration. For a given off-centered quadrilateral in an image, the goal of the algorithms is to define the lengths of four partial diagonals about a projective similar or congruent rectangle placed on the image center.

*CLCs using a similar rectangle:* For a given off-centered quadrilateral $u_0 u_1 u_2 u_3$, we first compute the four vanishing points $A$, $B$, $C$, and $D$, and measure the directed distances $a$ and $b$, as shown in Fig. 3. Next, for the center point of an image, $O$, we measure $l_+$ and $l_-$, as $|DO|$ and $|CO|$, respectively. We set $l_0$ as a proper value (e.g., 1), and compute $l_1$, $l_2$, and $l_3$ from Eq. (22). We also compute the angle $\angle COD$ to obtain $\rho$ as defined in [1]. Because the lengths of partial diagonals $l_0$, $l_1$, $l_2$, and $l_3$ and the angle between diagonals $\rho$ are computed for a *centered*-case, we can perform the camera calibration with a CLC-based reconstruction.

*CLCs using a congruent rectangle:* We have to explicitly compute $l_0$, to define the projective congruent rectangle placed at the image center from a given quadrilateral $u_0 u_1 u_2 u_3$. First, we consider a new vanishing point $F$, defined from $P$ and $O$ as follows.

$$F = (P \times O) \times (A \times B) \qquad (23)$$

Next, we compute $u_0'$, the projective translation about $u_0$, defined in the *centered* congruent rectangle, as follows.

$$u_0' = (u_0 \times F) \times (C \times O) \qquad (24)$$

Finally, we measure $l_0$ as $|u_0' O|$ and perform the same steps for the case of similar rectangles.

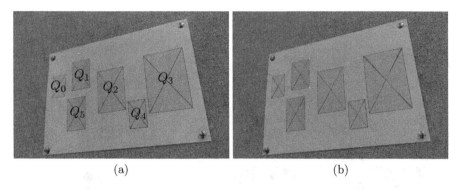

(a)                                            (b)

**Fig. 4.** Experimental verification using Eq. (22): (a) We draw a number of similar rectangles on a plane and take a picture of it in a perspective viewpoint. (b) To experimentally verify the length relationships among the partial diagonals, we calculate the lengths of $l_1$, $l_2$, $l_3$, denoted as blue, from the measured length of $l_0$, denoted as red, in each quadrilateral. In this experiment, we use the four corner points of $Q_1$ (i.e., yellow dots) to define a vanishing line (Color figure online).

## 5  Experiments

Figure 4 shows an experimental verification of our analysis discussed in Sect. 3. First, we draw several similar rectangles on a plane and take a picture of the plane to get the images of the similar rectangles (i.e., the quadrilaterals $Q_0$, $Q_1$, $\cdots$, $Q_5$ as shown in Fig. 4). Next, we *measure* the lengths of partial diagonals, $l_0$, $l_1$, $l_2$, $l_3$, for each quadrilateral in the image space. Next, we select one of the quadrilaterals (e.g., $Q_1$ in Fig. 4) and compute the directed distances $a$ and $b$

**Table 1.** Error analysis

| Quad | Method | $l_0$ | $l_1$ | $l_2$ | $l_3$ | Length error |
|------|--------|-------|-------|-------|-------|--------------|
| $Q_0$ | measured | 64.14 | 53.00 | 63.13 | 51.62 | 0.985 % |
|       | calculated | - | 52.89 | 63.71 | 50.41 | |
| $Q_1$ | measured | 85.96 | 73.24 | 85.09 | 67.42 | 0.536 % |
|       | calculated | - | 72.21 | 85.18 | 67.69 | |
| $Q_2$ | measured | 126.66 | 117.00 | 121.71 | 104.02 | 1.529 % |
|       | calculated | - | 114.96 | 124.96 | 104.53 | |
| $Q_3$ | measured | 175.32 | 181.04 | 166.81 | 154.16 | 3.102 % |
|       | calculated | - | 172.79 | 172.06 | 151.34 | |
| $Q_4$ | measured | 78.71 | 77.62 | 76.48 | 71.84 | 2.096 % |
|       | calculated | - | 75.20 | 78.06 | 70.89 | |
| $Q_5$ | measured | 93.54 | 84.38 | 92.18 | 77.70 | 0.741 % |
|       | calculated | - | 83.01 | 92.62 | 77.42 | |

(a) original images          (b) rectified images

**Fig. 5.** Rectified result for real images. (a) Selected quadrilaterals are denoted as yellow, and their perspectively congruent quadrilaterals are denoted as red. (b) Quadrilaterals and images are rectified by CLC-based reconstruction (Color figure online).

defined on a vanishing line, as described in Sect. 4. Finally, for each quadrilateral $Q_i$, we *calculate* $l_1$, $l_2$, $l_3$, from a measured $l_0$ by using the length relationships in Eq. (22).

Table 1 shows the errors in $l_1$, $l_2$, $l_3$, between measured lengths and calculated ones. We normalize the length differences based on $l_0$, in providing the errors. Notice that all errors are approximately 3 % although we have no prior knowledge of the intrinsic parameters of the camera and the aspect ratio of the similar rectangles. Thus, the CLC-based camera calibrations based on our analysis provides accurate results in most cases.

Figure 5 shows the image rectification based on CLC-based reconstruction by using the proposed method. In Fig. 5(a), We select a quadrilateral, denoted as yellow, assuming that it corresponds to an image of an unknown rectangle. Then, we calculate the lengths of partial diagonals for a perspectively congruent quadrilateral, denoted by red, with the given quadrilateral, by using the algorithm in Sect. 4. Then, we perform the CLC-based reconstruction by using Eqs. (1), (2), (3) and (4), to identify the position of the camera and the diagonal angle of a rectangle. Once the diagonal angle of the rectangle $\phi$ is identified, we can represent the vertices of the rectangle as $v_0 = (1, 0, 0)$, $v_1 = (\cos\phi, \sin\phi, 0)$, $v_2 = -v_0$, $v_3 = -v_1$. Finally we compute a homography $H$ between the quadrilateral and the rectangle, and rectified an image of a quadrilateral included in the whole image using a homography mapping. Figure 5(b) shows the rectified results.

# 6   Conclusion

In this study, we revisited CLCs using the concepts of projective geometry. In this analysis, we showed that four lengths of partial diagonals about an image of an unknown planar rectangle are highly related to the cross-ratio and projective harmonic conjugate defined on its vanishing points. Using this observation, we provided an analytic solution to define the lengths of four partial diagonals in any perspectively similar rectangles at arbitrary positions in an image. Finally, we applied the solution to compute the partial diagonal lengths of a perspectively similar or congruent case at the center from a given off-centered quadrilateral. In the experimental results, we showed the numerical errors and some rectification results using CLC-based reconstructions for camera calibrations.

Although we analyzed CLCs based on projective geometry, we still need to consider a projective similar or congruent rectangle at the image center. For future work, we would like to investigate the analytic solutions for CLCs, where the camera calibration can be solely from an off-centered quadrilateral in a given image.

**Acknowledgements.** This research was supported by Basic Science Research Program through the National Research Foundation of Korea (NRF) funded by the Ministry of Education (NRF-2013R1A1A2010619, 2015R1A5A7037615), MOTIE/KEIT ModMan Project (10048920), and Ministry of Culture, Sports and Tourism (MCST) and Korea Creative Content Agency (KOCCA) in the Culture Technology (CT) Research & Development Program.

# References

1. Lee, J.H.: Camera calibration from a single image based on coupled line cameras and rectangle constraint. In: Proceedings of the 21st International Conference on Pattern Recognition, pp. 758–762 (2012)
2. Lee, J.H.: A new solution for projective reconstruction based on coupled line cameras. ETRI J. **35**, 939–942 (2013)
3. Lee, J.H.: New geometric interpretation and analytic solution for quadrilateral reconstruction. In: Proceedings of the 22nd International Conference on Pattern Recognition, pp. 4015–4020 (2014)
4. Richter-Gebert, J.: Perspectives on Projective Geometry. Springer, Heidelberg (2011)
5. Hartley, R., Zisserman, A.: Multiple View Geometry in Computer Vision, 2nd edn. Cambridge University Press, Cambridge (2004)
6. Zhang, Z.: A flexible new technique for camera calibration. IEEE Trans. Pattern Anal. Mach. Intell. **22**, 1330–1334 (2000)
7. Huang, J., Zhao, C., Ohtake, Y., Li, H., Zhao, Q.: Robot position identification using specially designed landmarks. In: Instrumentation and Measurement Technology Conference, IMTC 2006, Proceedings of the IEEE, pp. 2091–2094. IEEE (2006)
8. Wenhuan, W., Zhanwei, C., Ze-tao, J.: A new camera calibration method based on rectangle constraint. In: 2010 2nd International Workshop on Intelligent Systems and Applications (ISA), pp. 1–4. IEEE (2010)
9. Lee, J.H.: An analytic solution to projector pose estimation problem. ETRI J. **34**, 978–981 (2012)
10. Tsai, R.Y.: A versatile camera calibration technique for high-accuracy 3d machine vision metrology using off-the-shelf tv cameras and lenses. IEEE J. Robot. Autom. **3**, 323–344 (1987)
11. Sturm, P.F., Maybank, S.J.: On plane-based camera calibration: a general algorithm, singularities, applications. In: IEEE Computer Society Conference on Computer Vision and Pattern Recognition, vol. 1. IEEE (1999)
12. Zhang, Z., He, L.W.: Whiteboard scanning and image enhancement. Digit. Signal Process. **17**, 414–432 (2007)

# Real-Time Image Based Lighting for 360-Degree Panoramic Video

Thomas Iorns[1] and Taehyun Rhee[1(✉)]

Victoria University of Wellington, Wellington, New Zealand
taehyun.rhee@ecs.vuw.ac.nz

**Abstract.** This paper presents an effective approach to rendering virtual 3D objects using real-time image based lighting (IBL) with conventional 360° panoramic video. Raw 360° panoramic video captured in a low dynamic range setup is the only light source used for the real-time IBL rendering. Input video data is boosted to high dynamic range using inverse tone mapping. This converted video is then reconstructed into low-resolution diffuse radiance maps to speed up diffuse rendering. A mipmap-based specular sampling scheme provides fast GPU rendering even for glossy specular objects. Since our pipeline does not require any precomputation, it can support a live 360° panoramic video stream as the radiance map, and the process fits easily into a standard rasterization pipeline. The results provide sufficient performance for IBL via stereo head mounted display (HMD), an ideal device for immersive augmented reality films and games using 360° panoramic videos as both the lighting and backdrop for illumination composition.

## 1 Introduction

With the recent rapid growth of interest in stereographic head-mounted displays (HMDs) such as the Oculus Rift [1], content for HMDs is being created at a steadily increasing rate. One important application of content for HMDs is in the creation of virtual reality (VR) and augmented reality (AR) experiences. In particular AR is a live direct or indirect view of a real-world environment whose elements are augmented by computer generated content such as 3D virtual objects. In order to maximize the immersive experience of AR content on HMDs, the seamless composition of the 3D virtual object and the real-world environment is important. Image based lighting (IBL) [2,3] has been used to emulate global illumination (GI) within a real-world scene, where the distant ambient and directional lighting is stored in a single image acting as the radiance map. This method provides high quality, realistic lighting useful for photo-realistic rendering and composition with real-world scenes in live-action films, and augmented reality. The image used for IBL is created by capturing high dynamic range (HDR) 360-degree panoramic images using photographs at various angles and exposure levels. A 360-degree panoramic image can also provide an ideal and intuitive format for HMDs to cover the whole range of viewpoints arising from motion of the viewer's head. Because of this the hardware for capturing

© Springer International Publishing Switzerland 2016
F. Huang and A. Sugimoto (Eds.): PSIVT 2015 Workshops, LNCS 9555, pp. 139–151, 2016.
DOI: 10.1007/978-3-319-30285-0_12

**Fig. 1.** IBL rendering for stereoscopic output using 360° video via our pipeline (left), and the result in head-mounted display (right).

panoramic images and video has become readily available, and as a result many 360° videos (video captured with a full spherical $4\pi$ steradian field of view) can be found on popular video sharing websites such as YouTube [4]. These videos provide a high level of immersion when viewed via HMDs, for a relatively low cost of content production.

The use of 360-degree panoramic images for virtual object lighting in augmented reality has already been proposed [5] and studied in previous research [6]. However when using conventional 360° video as the radiance map for IBL, we need to consider some additional challenges. Firstly IBL requires a high dynamic range (HDR) image of the scene environment to be captured. This requires views of various angles and exposure levels to be provided, and is generated by a user-guided post processing step. Although it is possible to create HDR 360° video using a special device setup such as in [7,8], conventional 360° videos [4] are captured using low dynamic range sensors and cannot provide enough dynamic range data for direct use in IBL. Secondly the IBL technique used must provide real-time rendering of a pair of stereo images shown at high frame rate; HMDs often require stereo rendering of 60 to 90 frames per second (FPS) in order to prevent visual discomfort [9]. Finally, when considering a live 360° video stream for immersive AR applications, precomputation of the radiance map is tricky and limited [10].

In this paper we present a novel pipeline that addresses the above challenges practically. Recent perceptual studies [11,12] have shown that the proper inverse tone-mapping algorithm can reconstruct the dynamic range that is required for IBL, from low dynamic range (LDR) input, and to such a level that the human visual system (HVS) cannot perceive the difference. Chalmers et al. [11] provide a threshold of image resolution that maintains the seamlessness of the final illumination composition. We adapt the perceptual threshold of the HVS to optimize our pipeline. The dynamic range of the LDR 360° video is converted to HDR using an inverse tone mapping operator. By using low-resolution versions of the panoramic video in lighting calculations for which the result is perceptually similar, we are able to emulate various common material properties in real-time. A mipmap-based specular sampling scheme provides fast rendering even for glossy specular objects. Since our pipeline does not require any precomputation, it has the potential to support a live 360-degree panoramic video stream as the radiance map, and the process fits easily into a standard GPU rasterization pipeline. The resulting pipeline reliably provides framerates of over 75 Hz, as required for comfortable viewing on stereo HMDs. The result is the IBL of 3D objects providing a seamless mixture of illumination with the 360-degree panoramic video backdrop. Based on our survey, this is the first practical system that provides interactive IBL from an LDR 360° live video stream suitable for HMDs. The overview of the system pipeline is shown in Fig. 2, and examples of the results for some test video frames can be seen in Fig. 8.

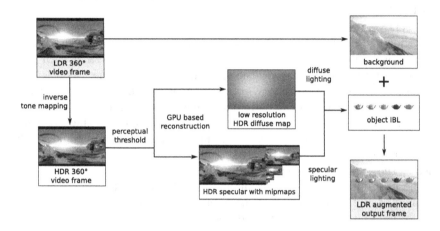

**Fig. 2.** System overview

## 2    Background and Related Work

Image based lighting was described early on by Miller and Hoffman [2] and has been popularized by Debevec [3], who has among other applications used it to convincingly render virtual objects into real-life photographs [13]. Heidrich and Seidel [14] described real-time use of IBL, precomputing diffuse and glossy material lighting integrals to efficiently render these materials by looking up the precomputed values according to surface normal or reflection direction. Kautz and McCool [15] simulated more complex material types by approximating their reflectance properties as a linear combination of glossy reflection from multiple directions. These techniques form the core of many real-time IBL applications (see for example [5,16]).

Ramamoorthi and Hanrahan [17] described an efficient way to represent diffuse radiance maps. They showed that the precomputed lighting integrals for diffuse materials can be described using only a very small number of coefficients in a spherical harmonics basis. These coefficients were shown by King [10] to be able to be calculated in real-time using a dedicated graphics processor, allowing real-time IBL of diffuse materials without precomputation.

An alternate method of calculating material lighting, which has become more performant as graphics hardware has improved, is to approximate the lighting integral directly by sampling from many points on the environment image. Recently this has been used by Kronander et al. [8] to render a virtual object into video in real-time (around 25 frames per second on an Nvidia GeForce 770). For real-time performance it is necessary to use an importance sampling technique (such as [18]) so as to get the most accurate result with the smallest number of samples. To obtain their environment image they used a special device, an additional HDR video camera mounted underneath the primary LDR video camera shooting the scene. This HDR video camera recorded the environment via an attached light probe [3].

Recently Michiels et al. [19] presented a method for IBL using 360° video to provide lighting for virtual objects. They analyze video from a moving 360° video camera in order to determine the position of the camera at each frame. They then use the frames to vary the lighting on a virtual object as it is moved around a reconstructed virtual environment. As well as having a different focus, their technique is also different from ours. They calculate their lighting in terms of spherical radial basis functions [20], which requires precomputing the lighting for each video frame in this basis. According to our survey, we could not find any prior work creating real-time IBL rendering using conventional LDR 360° video as the radiance map without a special device or precomputation.

The main difference in our technique stems from recent perceptual studies. Chalmers et al. [11] observed that the resolution of an environment image being used for lighting could be greatly reduced without causing any noticable difference to the rendered scene. Akyüz et al. [12] found that a simple tonemapping operator is often adequate for believably converting LDR images to HDR. We use these results to perform lighting calculations in real-time, by reducing the resolution of our input and tonemapping LDR to HDR as appropriate.

## 3    Real-Time IBL from 360-Degree Video

We present a real-time IBL system using 360° video. The input video frame can be used to directly represent specular reflection, and along with techniques for representing glossy and diffuse surfaces, a large number of real-world opaque materials are able to be simulated. In order to provide real-time diffuse illumination, we generate a new diffuse radiance map per frame, which can be done in real-time at a perceptually optimized lowered resolution [11]. For specular material types including mirror-like and glossy specular, we sample light from the radiance map according to the reflectance function, at an appropriately reduced resolution using mipmaps [21]. We test our method using three different material setups: diffuse reflection, pure specular reflection, and glossy specular reflection. These properties can be combined to simulate a wide range of believable materials.

## 3.1   Diffuse Illumiation

Diffuse lighting is calculated by generating a diffuse radiance map, as in [2], and sampling from this according to surface normal direction. Assuming fixed aspect ratio, generating the diffuse radiance map is an $O(N^4)$ operation in environment image height. For even fairly low resolution environments this quickly becomes prohibitive. We find viewing on HMDs however, that even when calculated at resolutions as low as 32 by 16 pixels, the diffuse lighting remains visually similar to the full-resolution version when sampled with bilinear filtering as shown in Fig. 3. Most of the output images in this paper were generated using 32 by 16 diffuse maps. A comparison including generation times can be seen in Fig. 3. Even at 128 by 64 pixels the maps can be generated on a low-end graphics card more quickly than standard video framerates require, and as Chalmers et al. show [11] lighting using diffuse maps down to 80 by 40 pixels can be perceptually indistinguishable from lighting using full resolution maps. Once the diffuse radiance map for a frame is generated, the diffuse lighting calculation for any point on an object's surface consists simply of a single texture lookup.

## 3.2   Specular Illumination

Pure specular reflection can be easily achieved by using the input video frame as an environment map. To calculate the specular component of material colour, we simply take the vector from surface to camera, reflect it across the surface

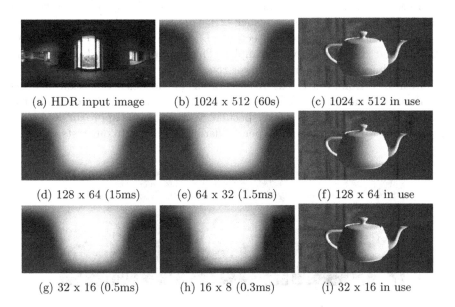

(a) HDR input image          (b) 1024 x 512 (60s)          (c) 1024 x 512 in use

(d) 128 x 64 (15ms)          (e) 64 x 32 (1.5ms)          (f) 128 x 64 in use

(g) 32 x 16 (0.5ms)          (h) 16 x 8 (0.3ms)          (i) 32 x 16 in use

**Fig. 3.** Diffuse radiance maps computed at various resolutions. Generation time on an Nvidia GeForce 730 is given in parentheses. Maps are displayed and sampled using hardware bilinear filtering.

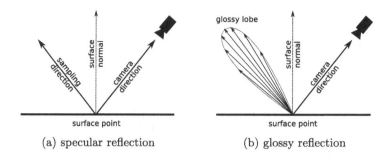

(a) specular reflection          (b) glossy reflection

**Fig. 4.** Specular and glossy specular reflection. The environment is sampled at and around the direction of specular reflection according to the size of the glossy lobe, which is determined by a material roughness parameter.

normal, and sample from the environment map in this direction, as shown in Fig. 4a. Generating accurate glossy specular reflection is computationally expensive. However, it can be approximated by computing glossy environment maps in a similar manner to the diffuse environment map. This is fine for very rough surfaces where the glossy lighting calculation is similar to the diffuse lighting calculation, but it becomes prohibitive as the surface roughness decreases and the gloss level approaches specular. The closer to mirror-reflection the gloss level is, the higher the resolution of the glossy environment map needed to describe it.

An alternative approach is to directly sample from the specular radiance map (in our case the original video frame), which we do efficiently using a technique similar to that of Colbert and Křivánek [21]. We take a small number of samples in a radius around the specular direction, choosing a mipmap level appropriate to the angular distance between samples. The sampling radius depends on the surface roughness parameter. For lower roughness, a higher resolution mipmap level is sampled from, but the decreasing radius of the glossy reflection lobe (see Figs. 4b and 5) means the same number of samples is required independent of roughness level. In this way glossy specular lighting can be approximated using a fixed number of texture lookups per rendering fragment. In our tests we found

**Fig. 5.** To approximate glossy reflection we sample from an appropriate mipmap level of the input environment map, according to the size of the glossy lobe. The number of samples remains constant.

that taking about 18 samples inside the primary glossy lobe, 18 samples outside it, and weighting them by a simple Phong model [22] gave fast and believable glossy surface lighting. While this is sufficient for demonstrating the validity of our pipeline, more complex or efficient techniques such as in [21,23] could easily be substituted (Fig. 6).

**Fig. 6.** Glossy specular reflection for various lobe sizes determined by a roughness parameter of, from left to right: 0.01, 0.05, 0.1, 0.2, 0.5.

## 4   Inverse Tone-Mapping from LDR to HDR

In a typical IBL setup, all lighting calculations will assume HDR lighting input. The difference between scenes rendered using LDR and HDR IBL is immediately apparent (see Fig. 7), with HDR lighting greatly increasing the realism of scenes when compared with LDR lighting. It turns out, however, that simple automatic LDR to HDR conversions can be sufficient for creating believable lighting effects [11,12] when targeting the human visual system. As such we are able to believably light virtual objects using only LDR video.

The tone-mapping operator we use is independent of varying frame properties, applying the same transform to each pixel individually. As such it is easily and efficiently implemented on the GPU. We chose this tonemapping operator as a compromise between those in [11,12], and it appears likely from our experimentation that other simple tonemapping operators would work just as well.

Given an input RGB value we first determine input luminosity as

$$L_i = 0.3 \cdot R_i + 0.59 \cdot G_i + 0.11 \cdot B_i,$$  (1)

(a) LDR          (b) tonemapped LDR          (c) HDR

**Fig. 7.** Comparison of lighting using an LDR environment image (left), an LDR-HDR tonemapped image (middle), and an HDR environment image (right). The simple tonemapping method provides believable results when viewed independently, although it may not perfectly match the HDR lighting result (especially for very high contrast scenes such as the bottom scene here).

where $R_i$, $G_i$ and $B_i$ are the red, green and blue components of the input image, as values between 0.0 and 1.0, and $L_i$ is the calculated input luminosity. We then calculate a desired scaling factor $L_s$ based on this input luminosity as

$$L_s = 10 \cdot L_i^{10} + 1.8. \tag{2}$$

The output red, green and blue components are then determined by

$$[R_o, G_o, B_o] = L_s \cdot [R_i, G_i, B_i]. \tag{3}$$

Parameters here were determined by experiment, and those in Eq. (2) have been used for all examples in this paper. After this operation, the converted image is used as an HDR radiance map in the following rendering steps.

## 5    GPU Implementation

We implemented our method using the GPU, and tested on various consumer-grade video cards including Nvidia GeForce 690, 770 and 980 as well as AMD Radeon 270. The pipeline was laid out as follows.

While GPU instructions are being queued, a separate thread loads and decodes the next video frame. This is passed to the GPU using a pixel buffer object for asynchronous memory transfer. As our target display refresh rate is much higher than typical video framerate (minimum 75 frames per second for HMD, typical 25 frames per second for video) one frame is used for display as the next is being loaded, giving smooth video performance.

```
Input    : LDR 360° video
Input    : 3D mesh data
Output : LDR framebuffer texture for display
while program running do
    if time elapsed > 1 / video FPS then
        /* tonemap next frame to HDR texture                    */
        for pixel ← video frame do
            |  pixel colour *= 10 * (pixel luminance)^10 + 1.8;
        end
        /* render diffuse radiance map                          */
        for outpixel ← diffuse map do
            accumulator = 0;
            weight = 0;
            for inpixel ← low resolution specular map do
                inpixel area = cos(inpixel latitude);
                inpixel weight = inpixel area * angle between(inpixel, outpixel);
                accumulator += inpixel weight * environment colour(inpixel
                direction);
                weight += inpixel weight;
            end
            outpixel colour = accumulator / weight;
        end
        reset elapsed time;
    end
    draw specular environment to output buffer as background;
    rasterize virtual objects into output buffer using IBL shader;
end
```

**Algorithm 1.** Real-Time IBL Process

The main pipeline works as depicted in Fig. 2. The basic procedure is described in Algorithm 1. The diffuse radiance map is upscaled simply by enabling bilinear texture filtering. For head-mounted stereographic display, the display process is executed twice, once for each eye (see Fig. 1 for example output). Object lighting is performed in a GPU fragment shader. Specular and diffuse lighting consist simply of texture lookups into the specular and diffuse radiance maps. Glossy specular lighting uses a somewhat more complicated system of sampling in a fixed pattern from lower-resolution mipmap levels of the specular map. The specific sampling system we used was to take samples in concentric rings around the specular direction, with six samples per ring, three rings inside the glossy lobe (see Fig. 4b), and three rings outside it. Which mipmap level to sample from is determined by taking the distance between samples in a ring, and choosing the level with an equivalent distance between pixels. Samples are weighted by a Phong model [22], and the radius of the glossy lobe is defined to be the distance at which the weighting is 0.5. To reduce discretization artifacts, hardware trilinear filtering is enabled.

## 6   Results

We tested our method on several 360° videos obtained from a popular video sharing website [4]. Video resolutions were between 1920 × 960 and 2048 × 1024, with framerates between 24 and 30 Hz. We tested various 3D objects without texture maps including Teapot (6320 triangles) and Bunny (69451 triangles). Five objects were displayed at once, each using a different combination of the material setups described in Sect. 3. We show that lighting virtual models using this method, with nothing other than LDR 360° panoramic video as input, gives believable results over a wide variety of input lighting conditions (see Fig. 8). We rendered a single camera view at 1280 × 720 resolution. By subjective visual comparison, lighting of the virtual objects seems to match that of the background video in all tested cases.

**Fig. 8.** Output of our pipeline for some of our test video frames. The input 360° video frame is displayed on the top row, and the generated diffuse radiance map on the second.

Rendering with tonemapped LDR to HDR frames seems quite sufficient for believable lighting (see Fig. 7). This is in agreement with [11,12]. Rendering using only the LDR frames for lighting appears dull, and does not match the background scene. Performance of the GPU based IBL is quite efficient, executing at around 90 Hz (11ms per frame) on a GeForce 690 and around 500 Hz (2ms per frame) on a GeForce 980. This leaves plenty of time for additional rendering tasks. Additionally, we tested our method in an Oculus DK2 HMD. Using an Nvidia GeForce 690 we were able to render stereo output at $1182 \times 1464$ resolution for both eyes (see Fig. 1) of the HMD comfortably at 75 Hz.

# 7 Conclusion

This paper presents an effective approach to rendering virtual 3D objects using real time image based lighting (IBL) with conventional 360° panoramic video. Using only low dynamic range 360° panoramic video as input we find that 3D virtual objects can be nicely composited into the panoramic video using IBL rendering. This form of video-based object lighting can be done entirely in real-time and with no precomputation required.

The visual quality of our result is similar to previous IBL techniques requiring precomputation and HDR environment images. This is achieved using the perceptual observation that low resolution environment maps and tonemapped LDR to HDR images can be sufficient for believable lighting.

One aspect of virtual object rendering we do not consider is that of shadowing. A possible extension of this work would be to incorporate an existing real-time shadowing technique such as that of [6]. There is also room for improvement in the compositing technique used to blend the rendered virtual objects with a perspective view of the input video. A potential improvement might be to render the virtual objects directly into the video frame, which we have not yet explored.

Our main contribution is a fully self-contained real-time system for lighting virtual objects so as to match an environment provided via LDR 360° panoramic video content. The novelty of our work is that our system requires no prior analysis of the video stream, can simulate complex materials efficiently, and can work using only readily-available LDR content. The system is efficient enough to render in real-time at the high framerates and resolutions required for immersive head-mounted display. While each component of the pipeline could be improved using more sophisticated methods, a balanced trade-off between perceptible visual quality and sufficient rendering performance is required for practical applications.

**Acknowledgements.** Research reported in this paper was supported by the *Human Digital Contents Interaction for 4D Home Entertainment (HDI4D)* project funded by the *Ministry of Business, Innovation and Employment (MBIE)* in New Zealand.

# References

1. Oculus, V.R.: Oculus rift (2015). http://www.oculusvr.com/rift
2. Miller, G., Hoffman, C.R.: Illumination and reflection maps: simulated objects in simulated and real environments. In: SIGGRApPH 84 Advanced Computer Graphics Animation Seminar notes, vol. 190 (1984)

3. Debevec, P.: Image-based lighting. IEEE Comput. Graph. Appl. **22**(2), 26–34 (2002)
4. YouTube: 360Video (2015). http://youtube.com/360
5. Agusanto, K., Li, L., Chuangui, Z., Sing, N.W.: Photorealistic rendering for augmented reality using environment illumination. In: Proceedings of The Second IEEE and ACM International Symposium on Mixed and Augmented Reality. IEEE, pp. 208–216 (2003)
6. Supan, P., Stuppacher, I., Haller, M.: Image based shadowing in real-time augmented reality. IJVR **5**, 1–7 (2006)
7. Unger, J., Kronander, J., Larsson, P., Gustavson, S., Ynnerman, A.: Temporally and spatially varying image based lighting using hdr-video. In: 2013 Proceedings of the 21st European Signal Processing Conference (EUSIPCO), pp. 1–5. IEEE (2013)
8. Kronander, J., Dahlin, J., Jonsson, D., Kok, M., Schon, T., Unger, J.: Real-time video based lighting using gpu raytracing. In: 2014 Proceedings of the 22nd European Signal Processing Conference (EUSIPCO), pp. 1627–1631. IEEE (2014)
9. Yao, R., Heath, T., Davies, A., Forsyth, T., Mitchell, N., Hoberman, P.: Oculus vr best practices guide. Oculus VR (2014)
10. King, G.: Real-time computation of dynamic irradiance environment maps. GPU Gems **2**, 167–176 (2005)
11. Chalmers, A., Choi, J.J., Rhee, T.: Perceptually optimised illumination for seamless composites. In: Keyser, J., Kim, Y.J., Wonka, P. (eds.) Pacific Graphics Short Papers, The Eurographics Association (2014)
12. Akyüz, A.O., Fleming, R., Riecke, B.E., Reinhard, E., Bülthoff, H.H.: Do HDR displays support LDR content?: a psychophysical evaluation. ACM Trans. Graph. (TOG), **26**(3), Article no. 38 (2007)
13. Debevec, P.: Rendering synthetic objects into real scenes: bridging traditional and image-based graphics with global illumination and high dynamic range photography. In: ACM SIGGRApPH 2008 Classes, p. 32. ACM (2008)
14. Heidrich, W., Seidel, H.P.: Realistic, hardware-accelerated shading and lighting. In: Proceedings of the 26th Annual Conference on Computer Graphics and Interactive Techniques. ACM Press/Addison-Wesley Publishing Co., pp. 171–178 (1999)
15. Kautz, J., McCool, M.D.: Approximation of glossy reflection with prefiltered environment maps. Graph. Interface **2000**, 119–126 (2000)
16. Unger, J., Wrenninge, M., Ollila, M.: Real-time image based lighting in software using HDR panoramas. In: Proceedings of the 1st International Conference on Computer Graphics and Interactive Techniques in Australasia and South East Asia, pp. 263–264. ACM (2003)
17. Ramamoorthi, R., Hanrahan, P.: An efficient representation for irradiance environment maps. In: Proceedings of the 28th Annual Conference on Computer Graphics and Interactive Techniques, pp. 497–500. ACM (2001)
18. Burke, D., Ghosh, A., Heidrich, W.: Bidirectional importance sampling for direct illumination. Rendering Tech. **5**, 147–156 (2005)
19. Michiels, N., Jorissen, L., Put, J., Bekaert, P.: Interactive augmented omnidirectional video with realistic lighting. In: De Paolis, L.T., Mongelli, A. (eds.) AVR 2014. LNCS, vol. 8853, pp. 247–263. Springer, Heidelberg (2014)
20. Wang, J., Ren, P., Gong, M., Snyder, J., Guo, B.: All frequency rendering of dynamic spatially varying reflectance. ACM Trans. Graph. (TOG) **28**, 133:1–133:10 (2009)

21. Colbert, M., Křivánek, J.: Gpu-based importance sampling. GPU Gems **3**, 459–476 (2007)
22. Phong, B.T.: Illumination for computer generated pictures. Commun. ACM **18**, 311–317 (1975)
23. McGuire, M., Evangelakos, D., Wilcox, J., Donow, S., Mara, M.: Plausible Blinn-Phong reflection of standard cube MIP-maps. Technical report CSTR201301, 47 Lab Campus Drive, Williamstown, MA 01267, USA (2013)

# Robot Vision (RV 2015)

# Enhancing Automated Defect Detection in Collagen Based Manufacturing by Employing a Smart Machine Vision Technique

Christopher D. Williams, Manoranjan Paul, and Tanmoy Debnath[(✉)]

Centre for Research in Complex Systems (CRiCS),
Charles Sturt University, Bathurst, Australia
{cwilliams,mpaul,tdebnath}@csu.edu.au

**Abstract.** Machine vision is now being extensively used for defect detection in the manufacturing process of collagen-based products such as sausage skins. At present the industry standard is to use a LabView software environment to manage and detect any defects in the collagen skins. Available data corroborates that this method allows for false positives to appear in the results which is responsible for reducing the overall system performance and resulting wastage of resources. Hence novel criteria were added to enhance the current techniques. The proposed improvements aim to achieve a higher accuracy and flexibility in detecting both true and false positives by utilizing a function that probes for the color deviation and fluctuation in the collagen skins. After implementation of the method in a well-known Australian company, investigational results demonstrate an average 26 % increase in the ability to detect false positives with a corresponding substantial reduction in operating cost.

**Keywords:** Machine vision · Collagen · Defect detection · Robot vision

## 1 Introduction

Machine Vision is a technology used to replace the manual inspection of goods used in a wide area of manufacturing which has already become an increasingly important service. This technology is used in a variety of industries to automate production, increase production yield with greater efficiency, defect detection whilst improving product quality. Although the approach taken by each industry varies depending on the individual products, there are three main approaches for automatic visual inspection (AVI) and defect detection: modelling or referential, inspection or non-referential, and hybrid [7]. The inspection of printed circuit boards (PCBs) [3,4], the defect detection of tiles [5] often use referential and hybrid approaches [1,16]. On the other hand, in agriculture, the common approach for defect detection is by utilizing non-referential approaches [14]. This is mainly because problems arise in analyzing natural objects such as fruits because they have a wide variety of colours and textures [2]. Fruits belonging to the same commercial batch may have different colours depending on the stage of maturity.

© Springer International Publishing Switzerland 2016
F. Huang and A. Sugimoto (Eds.): PSIVT 2015 Workshops, LNCS 9555, pp. 155–166, 2016.
DOI: 10.1007/978-3-319-30285-0_13

**Fig. 1.** (a) Sausages, (b) collagen casing folds, and (c) an image of a flattened collagen casing (taken from bbqhq.net, diytrade.com, and an Australian manufacturing company respectively)

Figure 1 shows sausages and their casings. Casings might have some defects such as creases or folds, black spec, etc. In an automated sausage manufacturing company, a collagen casing needs to be inflated and checked for defect before inserting materials into it. An Australian collagen casing manufacturing company uses a LabView AVI system [15] for accepting or rejecting casings to ensure quality by scanning the casings images. Major causes of the rejected images are due to the existence of creases or folds, black spots, and presence of hairs etc. However, manual inspections afterwards point out the limitations of the Labview program. It is noticed that a number of images are accepted although they should have been rejected and vice versa costing the company thousands of dollars in wasted resources. Our target is to reduce the false rejection rate thereby improving the overall defect detection. In order to achieve this goal an innovative non-referential image processing technique is proposed and implemented through real life experiments to improve the overall defect detection accuracy which is presented in this paper.

We utilize a modified method from PCB inspection [1] to include novel criteria for the defect detection of collagen sausage skins. The method works by locating abnormality in pixel intensity within a sausage image. Here a small abnormality is intensified so that by employing a predefined threshold our proposed method is able to detect it. This solution employs a local merit function to quantify the cost of a pixel that is defective [1]. The function comprises of two components: intensity deviation and intensity fluctuation. It is envisaged to increase accuracy by recognizing creases in the sausage skins created in the inspection process, as a non-defect as well as continuing to recognize black-specs as defects. Experimental results confirm that this approach of intensity deviation and intensity fluctuation improves the defect detection rates of collagen-based sausage skins significantly.

The remainder of this paper is structured as follows. Section 2 provides a brief description of how the defects are defined and inspection process of the collagen based products. Section 3 describes the proposed non-referential model for improving the detection process. In Sect. 4 experimental results and analysis are detailed. Finally Sect. 5 presents conclusions and directions for future work.

## 2     Collagen Skins

### 2.1     Definition and Features of Defects

During the manufacture of collagen-based sausage skins the most common defect is called black spec. These black specs are the remnants of hairs left over from the separation of the animal hide and the collagen film used for creating the sausage skins. All black specs larger than 1 mm are then picked up by the machine vision system and disregarded as defects in the system (Fig. 2).

**Fig. 2.** Black spec defect larger than 1 mm in length.

### 2.2     The Inspection Process in the Existing LabView Defect Detection

Defect detection in the manufacture of collagen sausage skins requires light to be emitted through the bottom of the skin to shine through and illuminate any defects. This illumination technique is known as Transmission (Fig. 3). Here the rolled skins are inflated, flattened, and rolled over the top of a light source. The camera then inspects each region of interest (ROI) and relays the images to the computer system where currently LabView is employed to detect defect. The different steps of the method used by LabView to detect defects are as follows:

- Create a ROI: Using a set-algorithm that finds the edges (Edge Clamps) of the image, LabView determines the edge of the ROI.
- Black Spec Threshold value is determined to differentiate the background noise and the image.
- A LabView Particle Analysis Algorithm is used to determine the size and quantity of black specs.
- Depending on the user determined maximum size of the black spec, the image is then determined to be defective or not.

It can be seen in Fig. 3 that LabView allows the user to place each module in order to achieve the desired defect detection. It also demonstrates the lack of flexibility to manipulate the specific algorithms to customize details. The user can only drag and drop specific modules and add certain parameters for the operation. An issue created from this process occurs when the collagen skin

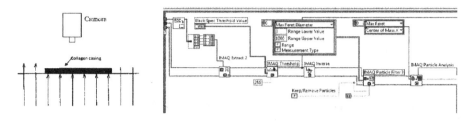

**Fig. 3.** (left)A transmission lighting system and (right) a schematic of LabView defect detection.

**Fig. 4.** A sample of sausage skin folding rejected by the LabView system, however manual inspection identified it as accepted, thus it a false positive case.

creases as it is flattened and rolled through the vision inspection system. These folds are currently being wrongly picked up by the system as a defect and rejected (Fig. 4). This is a costly part of the manufacturing process and can be time consuming and expensive for manufacturers to overcome.

## 3    Proposed Non-referential Model

The proposed model is based on a *localized defects image model* (LDIM) [1], which uses a local merit function to quantify the cost that a pixel is defective. It utilizes two components that look at the intensity deviation and intensity fluctuation within the image. Taking into account of the fact that serious defects occur less often than slight defects, the paper states that further a defect's intensity deviates from the dominant background intensity, the less and less often it is liable to occur. The complete model is expressed as follows:

$$C(x, y) = W_d \times D^2(x, y) + W_f \times F^2(x, y) \tag{1}$$

where the intensity deviation function is $D(x,y) = V(x,y) - H_{x,y}$ and the intensity fluctuation function is $F(x, y) = \sigma(N(x, y)) - 4$. Here -

- $C(x,y)$ is a merit function which represents the cost that a particular pixel is defective. It is the weighted summation of intensity deviation and fluctuation.
- $W_d$ and $W_f$ are weights of $D(x,y)$ and $F(x,y)$ respectively. Both these weights are determined during the experiments which are $\frac{1}{16}$ as suggested in [1].

- Dominant intensity of regional image $H_{x,y}$ can be described by the most frequent intensity of the neighbouring pixels for the position at (x, y). Thus intensity deviation D(x,y) can be expressed as the absolute difference between pixel value of source image V(x,y) and the dominant intensity $H_{x,y}$.
- Thus, intensity deviation D(x,y) at pixel (x,y) can be expressed as the absolute difference between pixel value of source image and dominant intensity.
- Evaluation of intensity fluctuation F(x,y) at (x,y) is based on the neighborhood pixels whereby the value of a pixel and its neighborhood can deviate from the main background intensity. Neighborhood pixels N(x,y) represents (2k+1) pixel at position (x,y). Next standard deviation is applied to the N(x,y) to get the value of total fluctuation $\sigma(N(x,y))$.
- The difference between the intensity deviation, fluctuation and dominant intensity is the localized level: D(x,y) is at the pixel level, F(x,y) is at (2k+1) (2k+1) levels, while $H_{x,y}$ is at regional level [1]. k represents the pixel window size and its value is set as 5 pixels in our experiments as it was observed that this values provides optimum results.

**Pseudo code for the proposed model**

```
Begin image input
Initiate parameters
   For all images
        For all pixel positions at (x,y)
             Calculate  D(x,y) and F(x,y)
             Calculate model  C(x,y)
          End
    End
Calculate cost function above threshold
   Reject or accept image
End.
```

## 4   Experimental Results

The following results are garnered from three groups of test images sourced from a well-known Australian company. The company is a leading supplier of collagen casings for food, creating a range of sausage skins and other meat products. All images procured are from the production of sausage skins and are highly representable of the manufacturing facility. Each image is captured at 2046×800 pixels at 72 dpi grayscale. Three groups of 50 images each were provided to us. After a manual inspection by the company of group 1 s 50 test images, 34 and 16 were declared as defective and non-defective respectively. For group 2 the number of imperfect and perfect images was 30 and 20 respectively. The companys physical inspections have declared 42 and 8 images as faulty and non-faulty respectively in group 3. In order to validate the proposed non-referential model, at first a threshold value of 900 pixels was chosen as this represents the number of pixels greater than the merit function threshold. Also included in our experiments where differing results are achieved through using different threshold pixel values (e.g. 500 and 2500 pixels). It is believed that images of different groups are captured in different times and for different setup of LabView machine and different initial materials, thus the thresholds are varied.

### 4.1 Measurement of Results

To analyse the performance the results were split into the following three categories of classification: Specificity, Sensitivity and Accuracy. Specificity measures the proportion of negatives, which are correctly identified as such. Sensitivity calculates the proportion of actual positives, which are correctly identified as such. Accuracy is defined by the overall accuracy from the specificity and sensitivity.

$$Specificity = (TN/(TN + FP)) \times 100\% \tag{2}$$

$$Sensitivity = (TP/(TP + FN)) \times 100\% \tag{3}$$

$$Accuracy = ((TP + TN)/(TP + TN + FP + FN)) \times 100\% \tag{4}$$

where, TN: True Negatives, TP: True Positives, FN: False Negatives, FP: False Positives.

Figures 5, 6, 8, and 10 in the next pages show graphs of the merit functions and the images that are representative for respective groups samples. Different cases are presented and compared with the LabView results to demonstrate our solutions supremacy. It can be seen from Table 1 that our algorithm has a significantly higher specificity. This demonstrates that it is able to correctly identify false positives. The overall accuracy reaches to 98 % for this batch of images.

Figure 5 shows that our algorithm works well to locate and identify the defect. The graph indicates a clear spike in the cost function, indicating a defect. Both LabView and our algorithm rejected this image correctly.

**Fig. 5.** An analysis of a defect image rejected by LabView, manual inspection, and also our solution. (left) Merit function values, (right) Actual image.

**Table 1.** Results of group 1. This table represents the LabView results, our solution, and the actual confirmed defects vs. false positives in the batch.

|  | LabView | Our results | Actual |
|---|---|---|---|
| Accept | 3 | 14 | - |
| Reject | 47 | 36 | - |
| TP | 34 | 34 | 34 |
| TN | 3 | 16 | 16 |
| FP | 13 | 1 | - |
| FN | 0 | 0 | - |
| Specificity % | 18.75 | 94.12 | - |
| Sensitivity % | 100 | 100 | - |
| Accuracy % | 74 | 98 | - |

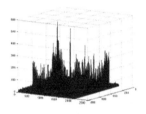 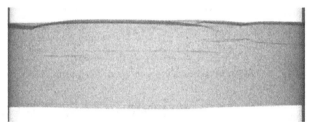

**Fig. 6.** Results of group 1. Showing a false positive defect. This image was found defective by LabView but shown correctly by our solution as non-defective.(left) Merit function values, (right) Actual image

Figure 6 shows a false positive case where the image has a typical creasing effect from the inspection process. The proposed algorithm worked as planned by indicating this image was a non-defect, whereas this image was rejected by the LabView environment.

## 4.2 Threshold Values for Group 1 Images

Two thresholds (Th1 and Th2) were utilized to identify whether a particular image would be accepted or rejected. If the value of the merit function C(x,y) of a pixel position (x, y) is higher than the threshold Th1, that pixel is marked as defected. If the numbers of defect pixels are higher than the threshold Th2, the image is identified as defected. For an image $I$, the Th1 is set as follows based on the difference between the maximum and minimum pixel intensities and the *standard deviation* ($\sigma$) of the image:

$$Th1 = \frac{1}{160}(\alpha^2 + \beta^2) \tag{5}$$

where $\alpha = max(I) - min(I)$ and $\beta = \alpha(I) - 4$. Th1 was kept constant for all groups of images; however Th2 was varied based on the characteristics of the different groups images. The values in Fig. 7 show the different results obtained from changing the threshold (i.e., Th2) values in group 1. It is observed that by increasing the threshold to 2500 pixels the accuracy lowers to 83 % from the default 900 pixels threshold, which scored 98 %, whilst lowering our threshold from the standard 900 pixels to 500 pixels, the accuracy lowers to 87.2 %.

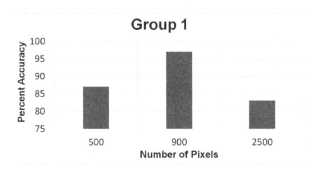

**Fig. 7.** Different accuracy levels at different threshold values for group 1 images.

Figure 8 presents an image which has small dark patches as well as a dark spec making the defect detection harder. The algorithm accepted this image as non-defect incorrectly. It is believed that the darkness of skin has allowed for a higher merit function value which is above the 900 pixels threshold. Thus, it is required to adjust our threshold for this kind of images so that they are accepted in our solution.

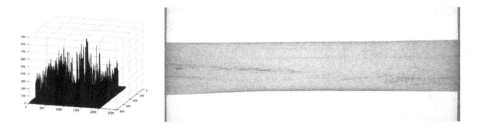

**Fig. 8.** Results of group 2 where it shows a defective image with black spec and creases that was incorrectly identified as a non-defective image. (left) Merit function values, (right) Actual image.

From Table 2 it is observed that the LabView solution rejected all images in this batch resulting in our algorithm having a significantly higher specificity and sensitivity, increasing our overall accuracy to 86 % for this batch of images.

**Table 2.** Results of group 2. This table represents the LabView results, our solution, and the actual confirmed defects vs. false positives in the batch.

|              | LabView | Our Results | Actual |
|--------------|---------|-------------|--------|
| Accept       | 0       | 21          | -      |
| Reject       | 50      | 29          | -      |
| TP           | 30      | 26          | 30     |
| TN           | 0       | 17          | 20     |
| FP           | 20      | 3           | -      |
| FN           | 0       | 4           | -      |
| Specificity %| 0       | 85          | -      |
| Sensitivity %| 60      | 86          | -      |
| Accuracy %   | 60      | 86          | -      |

### 4.3  Different Threshold Values for Group 2 and 3 Images

The values in Fig. 9 show the different results retrieved from changing the threshold values in group 2. It can be seen that by increasing the threshold to 2500 pixels the accuracy increases to 89.5 % from the default 900 pixels threshold which scored 86 %. Whilst lowering the threshold from the standard 900 pixels to 500 pixels, the accuracy decreases to 78 %. It is believed that due to LabViews different parameter settings, a larger threshold is required for this group of images to improve the accuracy.

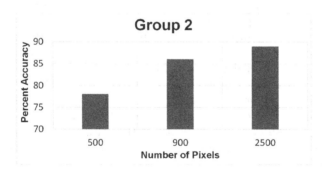

**Fig. 9.** Different accuracy levels at different threshold values for group 2 images.

Table 3 establishes that the LabView solution rejected all images in this batch whilst our algorithm recognized all 8 false positives and 8 true negatives. This resulted in an overall accuracy of 84 %.

Figure 10 shows an image which is correctly accepted by the LabView environment but rejected by our solution, the most probable reason being that background intensity fluctuation was not high enough to breach our threshold level.

**Fig. 10.** The merit function and the corresponding image with creases which is a non-defective image however, it is rejected by our solution. (left) Merit function values, (right) Actual image.

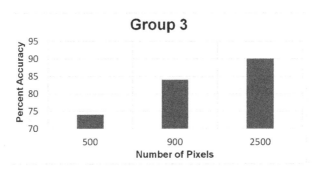

**Fig. 11.** Different accuracy levels at different threshold values for group 3 images.

The values in Fig. 11 show the different results retrieved from changing the threshold values in Group 3. It is observed that by increasing the threshold to 2500 pixels the accuracy increases to 90 % from the default 900 pixels threshold which scored 84 %, whilst lowering the threshold from the standard 900 pixels to 500 pixels the accuracy decreases to 74 %.

In a nutshell, when the pixels threshold was lowered to 500 it yielded lower results consistently, as well as raising the threshold count to 2500 pixels had favourable results for two of the tests (groups 2 and 3). After comparing all the experimental results it can be surmised that although in some cases 2500 pixels threshold improves accuracy, in all cases a threshold of 900 pixels performs reasonably good.

## 5   Conclusions

The experimental results show that the current industry standard LabView environment tends to be less specific in its defect detection rates and would simply reject any product with a fold characteristic. This allows for a greater number of false positive results occurring during the inspection stage of manufacturing. On the contrary the proposed and implemented non-referential model achieves a significant increase in specificity, allowing for a higher proportion of negatives to be correctly identified. The results demonstrate that whilst our solution doesnt fix the problem completely, it improves the overall accuracy of defect detection significantly. It is estimated that a general improvement of approximately 26 % can save for the Australian Food processing company, an average of AUD 260 per day from the current AUD 1000 per day it costs for the wasted time and product involved in false defect detection in a single batch of processing. With factors such as moisture and humidity in the factory environment it is found that settings on the machine are manually adjusted to compensate. Thus, the algorithm threshold would need to be adjusting to suite. It is also noted that differences between results can vary depending on many factors such as:

- Darkness of the skin
- Crease length and amount of creases present in the skin
- Moisture in the collagen skin

Other characteristics for which our solution has detection difficulties include:

- Black spec could be located within the fold or creases of the skin. Depending on the density and amount of folds this defect has the ability to go undetected.
- Black spec could be located within the same frame as a finger defect.
- When a skin is severely creased throughout, our solution may not identify the intensity fluctuation or difference as high enough to trigger the defect threshold thereby rejecting the product.

In future it is envisaged to overcome the limitations of this work by improving the model so that all types of defects could be smartly detected and analysed.

**Acknowledgments.** We acknowledge the Australian Food processing industry to provide images in this analysis and experiments. Due to privacy and business issues we could not name the company in this manuscript.

# References

1. Xie, Y., Ye, Y., Zhang, J., Liu, L., Liu, L.: A physics-based defects model and inspection algorithm for automatic visual inspection. J. Opt. Lasers Eng. **52**, 218–223 (2014)
2. Lpez-Garca, F., Andreu-Garca, G., Blasco, J., Aleixos, N., Valiente, J.M.: Automatic detection of skin defects in citrus fruits using a multivariate image analysis approach. J. Comput. Electron. Agric. **71**, 189–197 (2010)
3. Mar, N.S.S., Yarlagadda, P.K.D.V., Fookes, C.: Design and development of automatic visual inspection system for PCB manufacturing. J. Robot. Comput. Integr. Manufact. **27**, 949–962 (2011)
4. Ibrahim, I., Ibrahim, Z., Khalil, K.: An improved defect classification algorithm for printing defects and its implementation on real printed circuit board images. Int. J. Innovative Comput. Inf. Control. **8**(5), 3239–3250 (2012)
5. Rahaman, A., Hossain, M.: Automatic defect detection and classification technique from image: a special case using ceramic tiles. Int. J. Comput. Sci. Inf. Secur. **1**(1) (2009)

6. Gruna, R., Beyerer, J.: Feature-specific illumination patterns for automated visual inspection. In: 12th IEEE International Instrumentation and Measurement Technology Conference, pp. 360–365, Graz, Austria (2012)
7. Moganti, M., Ercal, F., Dagli, C.H., Tsunekawa, S.: Automatic PCB inspection algorithms: a survey. J. Comput. Vis. Image Underst. **63**(2), 287–313 (1996)
8. Introduction to Machine Vision. http://www.emva.org/cms/index.php?idcat=38
9. Machine Vision. http://www.machinevision.co.uk/what-is-it/4550546879
10. Silva, H.G.D., Amaral, T.G., Dias, O.P.: Automatic optical inspection for detecting defective solders on printed circuit boards. In: 36th Annual Conference on IEEE Industrial Electronics Society, pp. 1087–1091, AZ, USA (2010)
11. Darwish, A.M., Jain, A.K.: A rule based approach for visual pattern inspection. IEEE Trans. Pattern Anal. Mach. Intell. **10**(1), 56–68 (2012)
12. Rokunuzzaman, M., Jayasuriya, H.P.W.: Development of a low cost machine vision system for sorting of tomatoes. J. CIGR **15**(1), 173–180 (2013)
13. Azriel, R.: Introduction to machine vision. Control Syst. Magazines **5**(3), 14–17 (1985)
14. Chen, Y., Chao, K., Kim, M.: Machine vision technology for agriculture applications. J. Comput. Electron. Agric. **36**, 173–191 (2002)
15. LabView Environment. http://www.ni.com/labview/
16. Aye, T., Khaing, A.S.: Automatic defect detection and classification on printed circuit board. Int. J. Societal Appl. Comput. Sci. **3**(3), 527–533 (2014)

# Computer Vision Technology for Vehicular Robot to Follow Guided Track Using Neuro-Fuzzy System

Young-Jae Ryoo[✉]

Mokpo National University, Jeonnam, Korea
yjryoo@mokpo.ac.kr

**Abstract.** This paper describes computer vision technology for a camera-based automatic guided vehicular mobile robot using neuro-fuzzy control system to follow guide lanes with a camera. Without a complicated geometric computing from a camera image to robot-position-localization in conventional researches, the proposed control system transfers the inputs of image sensor into the output of steering values directly. The neuro-fuzzy controller replaces the human driving skill of nonlinear relation between vanishing lines of guide lanes on the camera image and the steering angle of vehicular robot. In straight and curved road, the driving performances by the proposed control scheme are measured in simulation and experimental test.

**Keywords:** Computer vision · Neuro-fuzzy control · Vehicular robot

## 1 Introduction

In recent years, systems that integrate both visual sensors and an autonomous robot together have received a lot of attention, especially in the field of intelligent control [1–3]. Such systems can solve many problems that limit applications in previous robots. An important component of intelligent autonomous robot is to follow the road lane by lateral steering control of the robot. Vision system plays an important role in road following because it has the flexibility and the two-dimensional view. Also, many researchers have discussed possibilities for the application of intelligent control in autonomous robotic systems [4–7].

Several prototype systems of automated vehicles have been developed [3–8]. The lane-following vision control system architecture had developed in Carnegie-Mellon University is a general sample for autonomous vehicle [9, 10]. In the system, the vision system acquires a camera image and uses a typical image processing algorithm to extract road lane segments from the image. These road lane segments are transformed from the image coordinate system to the vehicle coordinate system, and used to the geometric reasoning module. This system has difficulties of heavy computation in given time because the geometric reasoning requires calculation of camera parameters and the lateral control depends on the parameters of road and the vehicular robot. In practical system, a sophisticated processing system might be able to solve these

© Springer International Publishing Switzerland 2016
F. Huang and A. Sugimoto (Eds.): PSIVT 2015 Workshops, LNCS 9555, pp. 167–178, 2016.
DOI: 10.1007/978-3-319-30285-0_14

difficulties. However the challenge of autonomous robot is that there is a limited time for the processing.

Pomerleau proposed ALVNN to overcome the difficulties [11]. The architecture of ALVNN(Autonomous Land Vehicle In a Neural Network) consists of a single hidden layer, feedforward network. The network receives a camera image of the road ahead, and produces the steering command that will keep the vehicle on the road lane. Input layer of the network has 960(32 × 30) units, which many input units require many calculation. To complete the calculation in given time, expensive computer system should be used.

In this paper, a computer vision technology using neuro-fuzzy control system for a camera-based automatic guided robot is presented, which uses a camera image to guide itself along guided lane. The proposed technology of the control system transfers the inputs of camera information into the output of steering angle directly, without a complex geometric reasoning from a visual image to a robot-centered representation in previous studies. The neuro-fuzzy controller replaces the human driving skill of non-linear relation between vanishing lines of road lanes on the camera image and the steering angle of the robot.

## 2    Vision-Based Control

As shown in Fig. 1, the geometrical reasoning between the robot's position and the guided lane can be described on the images using the following parameters:

(1)   The lateral deviation of the vanishing point (VD) describes the lateral position of the current vanishing point (VP) for the reference vanishing point ($VP_{ref}$) as shown in Fig. 1(c) and (d). The parameter, VD depends upon the orientation of the robot on the road as shown in Fig. 1(a).

(2)   The slopes of the vanishing lines ($VL_l$, $VL_r$) are defined by the tangent of the angle between the current vanishing line and the horizontal line as shown in Fig. 1(c). The slope is relative to the lateral position of the robot defined by the lateral distance between the center of the robot and the center of the guide lane.

The camera image contains the vanishing point and the vanishing lines of the guide lane. With these features on the image, the position and orientation of the robot between the guided lanes can be uniquely determined by geometric reasoning. On the basis of the above method, the vision-based-control method is introduced as follows:

Figure 1(c) is the current camera image, and Fig. 1(d) is the desired camera image obtained when the robot reaches the desired relative position and orientation on the guide lanes. The vision-based control system computes the error signals in terms of the lateral position and the slope derived from the vanishing point and vanishing line respectively on the image.

A steering angle generated by the proposed system makes that the vanishing point and the vanishing line on the current image coincide with the desired image. The lateral position of the vanishing point and the slope of the vanishing line computed from the linear vanishing line represent the relative position and orientation of the robot on the road. Then the robot is required to move its center to the lateral center of the guide lane

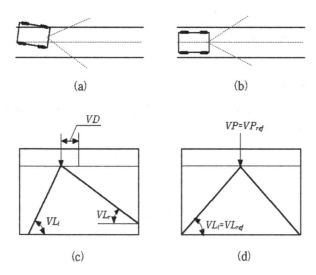

**Fig. 1.** Parameters of the guided lanes on the camera image which depends on the relation between the robot's orientation and position on guided lanes

and to parallel the guide lane by controlling its steering angle. It is significant that the vanishing point moves to the desired point in accordance with human's skill of driving.

# 3  Neuro-Fuzzy System

## 3.1  Neuro-Fuzzy System

The relation between the steering angle and the vanishing point and vanishing line on the camera image is a highly nonlinear function. A fuzzy and neural network is used for the nonlinear relation because it has the learning capability to map a set of input patterns to a set of output patterns. The inputs of the neuro-fuzzy system are the lateral position of the vanishing point and the slope of the vanishing line. The output of the neuro-fuzzy system is the steering angle value. Learning data could be obtained from human skill. After the neuro-fuzzy system learns the relation between input patterns and output patterns sufficiently, it makes a model of the relation between the position and the orientation of the robot, and that of the guide lane. Thus, a good model of the control task is obtained by learning, without inputting any knowledge about the specific robot's position and the guide lanes.

Generally, fuzzy control has a distinguished feature of being able to incorporate expert's control rules using linguistic descriptions of the rules. However, most experts often learn the control rules through trials and errors without clear linguistic expressions and they sometimes learn rules unconsciously. The identification of the control rules from the expert's experience is time consuming. Furthermore, tuning of the membership functions of the fuzzy controller needs "experts of the fuzzy controller".

Thus, neuro-fuzzy can automatically identify the expert's control rules and tune the membership functions from the expert's control data.

## 3.2    Configuration

Figure 2 shows a configuration of the proposed fuzzy controller using a neural network. The fuzzy model is of a linear hybrid model.

$$R^i : \text{if } x_1 \text{ is } A^i_1, \text{ and} \ldots x_j \text{ is } A^i_j, \text{ and } \ldots, x_n \text{ is } A^i_n$$
$$\text{then} \quad y^i = a^i_0 + a^i_1 x_1 + \ldots + a^i_n x_n \tag{1}$$

$$w^i = \prod_{j=1}^{xn} A^i_j(x_j) \tag{2}$$

$$y^o = \frac{\sum_{i=1}^{n} w^i y^i}{\sum_{i=1}^{n} w^i} \tag{3}$$

where $R^i$ is the $i$-th fuzzy rule, $x_j$ is the $j$-th input variable, $A^i_j$ is the $i$-th fuzzy variable for the $j$-th input variable, $n$ is the number of rules, $y^i$ is the $i$-th inferred output value, $a^i_j$ is the coefficient, $w^i$ is the true value in the premise and $y^o$ is the inferred output value.

(A)  $W_{BA}$  (B) $W_{CpB}$ (C$_p$) $W_{DCp}$ (D)  $W_{ED}$  (E)    $W_{FE}$  (F)  $W_{GF}$ (G)

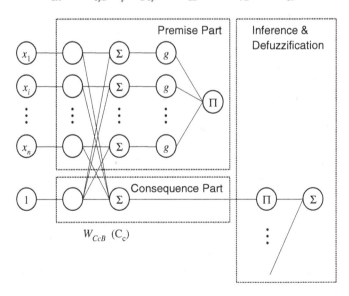

**Fig. 2.** Composition of neuro-fuzzy for a rule unit.

### 3.3 Premise

The network consists of seven layers and uses the back propagation algorithm for learning of the network as shown in Fig. 2. The figure shows the case where the controller has $n$-inputs($x_1$, $x_2$, ..., $x_n$) layer (A layer), one-output layer (G layer), and hidden layer for an unit rule. The outputs of the units with symbols $\sum$ denote sums of their inputs and $\prod$ denote products of their inputs.

The inputs into (A)-layer $x_j$ are normalized by the connection weights $W_{BA}$. Normalized input variables, $\widehat{x}_j$ are given by

$$\widehat{x}_j = \frac{x_j}{Max|x_j|} = W_{BA}x_j \tag{4}$$

The sigmoid function $f(\widehat{x})$ are given by

$$f(\widehat{x}) = \frac{1}{1 + \exp\left(-W_{DCp}\left(\widehat{x} + W_{CpB}\right)\right)} \tag{5}$$

where $W_{CpB}$ and $W_{DCp}$ are to be modified through learning.

The output of the unit in (D)-layer $f(\widehat{x})$ is derived by removing the magnitude of the differentiated value of the sigmoid function $f(\widehat{x})$. The output of (D)-layer $f(\widehat{x})$ is the bell-shaped membership function that has a center of $W_{CpB}$ and slope of $W_{DCp}$.

$$g(\widehat{x}) = \frac{1}{1 + \exp(-W_{DCs}(\widehat{x} + W_{CsB}))} \left(1 - \frac{1}{1 + \exp(-W_{DCs}(\widehat{x} + W_{CsB}))}\right) \tag{6}$$

### 3.4 Consequence

The consequences are expressed by linear equations. As shown in Fig. 2, the neurons of (B)-layer are connected with the neuron of ($C_c$)-layer through weight $W_{CcB}$, which expresses coefficient $a_j^i$ of the linear equations. Therefore, the output of ($C_c$)-layer is expressed as follow:

$$y^i = a_0^i + a_j^i\widehat{x}_1 + \ldots + a_n^i\widehat{x}_n \tag{7}$$

The inferred value of the neuro-fuzzy is obtained from the product of the true values in the premises and the linear equations in the consequences.

$$y^{i\ddagger} = \frac{w^i y^i}{\sum\limits_{n=1}^{n} w^i} \tag{8}$$

The output of (G)-layer can be expressed as follow:

$$y^{i\ddagger} = \sum_{i=1}^{n} y^{i\ddagger} \tag{9}$$

# 4  Computer Simulation

To simulate in computer as shown in Fig. 3, robot dynamic model, transformation of coordinate system, and control algorithms should be determined. The robot dynamic model uses the general model, and has specific parameters. Through transformation of coordinate system, the road could be displayed on the camera image plane visually.

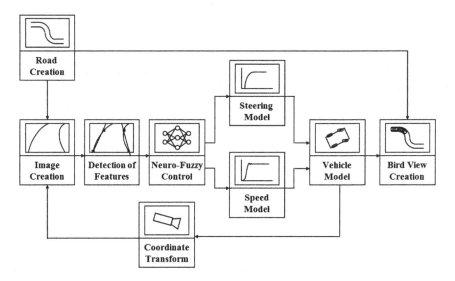

**Fig. 3.** Block diagram of computer simulation.

## 4.1  Robot Model

The general kinematic model of the vehicular robot with 4 wheels in world coordinates is shown in Fig. 4. The reference point $(x_c^W, y_c^W)$ is located at the center point between the rear wheels. The heading angle $\theta$ for $X^W$-axis of the world coordinate system and the steering angle $\delta$ are defined in robot coordinate system.

Since robot coordinate system is used in control of autonomous robots, the current position $(x_c^W, y_c^W)$ of the robot in world coordinate system is redefined as the point of origin for robot coordinate system. When the robot which has the distance $L_v$ between front wheel and rear wheel runs with velocity $v$, the new position of the robot is

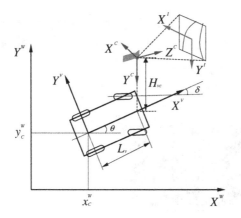

**Fig. 4.** Robot model and camera coordinate transformation model.

nonlinearly relative to steering angle $\delta$ of front wheel and heading angle $\theta$ determined by robot direction and road direction.

## 4.2    Transformation from Ground to Camera Image

In order to simulate in computer visually, the road has to be displayed on the camera image plane. Thus the coordinate transformations along the following steps are needed to determine the road of visual data from the road on the world coordinate system:

(1) Transformation from the world coordinate system to the robot coordinate system. The position $(x_c^W, y_c^W)$ on the world coordinates is redefined as the origin for the robot coordinates.
(2) Transformation from the robot coordinate system to the camera coordinate system.
(3) Transformation from the camera coordinate system to the image coordinate system.

## 4.3    Simulation Results

Simulation results for the autonomous robot are shown in this section. The simulation program is developed from programming of robot's kinematics, transformation of coordinate system, and control algorithms by C++ in computer.

The performance of the proposed visual control system by neuro-fuzzy was evaluated using a robot driving on the track with a straight and curved shape as shown in Fig. 5. Figure 5 shows the bird's eye view of road map and the trajectories of robot's travel.

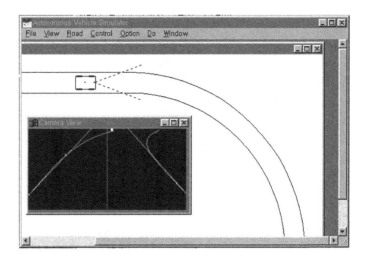

**Fig. 5.** Computer simulation of the proposed vision-based control.

Figure 6 shows the trajectory of the road with guide lanes and the trace of the robot's travel. The road shown as the solid line has the curvature radius of 6 meters and the trace of robot is presented with the solid line and the black square in Fig. 6.

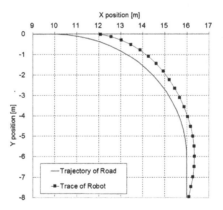

**Fig. 6.** Trajectories of robot's center on curved guide lanes with curvature radius of 6 meters.

Figure 7 shows the robot's steering angle during automatic driving in the simulation of Fig. 6. In Fig. 7, the command steering angle is determined from the neuro-fuzzy controller, the speed controller model, the steering controller model, and the robot model. The controller steers the robot to right (about −10[degree]) at right-turn curve, and to left (about +5[degree]) at left-turn curve. A lateral position error of the robot is defined as the difference between the center of the guide lanes and the center of the robot. As shown in Fig. 8, the driving is completed in lateral error less than 0.5[m].

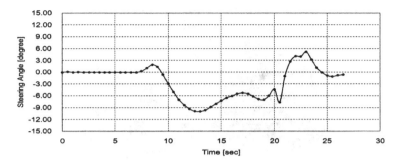

**Fig. 7.** Steering angle.

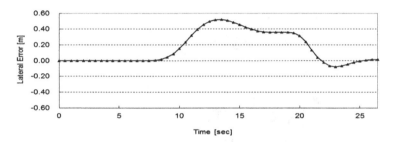

**Fig. 8.** Lateral position error of robot.

# 5    Experimental Driving Test

## 5.1    Setup of Vehicular Robot

The designed robot has 4 wheels, and its size is 1/4 of small passenger car. Driving torque comes from a DC motor set up the trans-axle of the rear wheel. Front wheel is steered by a BLDC motor. Energy source is two batteries connected directly, and each battery has 12 volts. And a camera is used as a vision sensor to get the road information. The control computer of the robot has function to manage all system, recognize the road direction from input camera image by road recognition algorithm, and make control signal of steering angle by the neuro-fuzzy control. And the control computer manages and controls input information from various signal, also it inspects or watches the system state.

The computer is chosen personal computer for hardware extensibility and software flexibility. Electric System to control is compose of vision system, steering control system, and speed control system. Vision system has camera to acquire road image and image processing to detect the guide lanes. Steering control system can convert from control value to analog voltage, read the current steering angle. Figure 9 shows the developed test robot.

**Fig. 9.** Configuration of robot to test vision-based control.

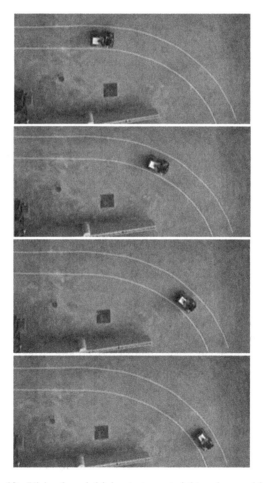

**Fig. 10.** Vision-based driving test on straight and curved lane.

## 5.2  Vision-Based Automatic Driving Test

The proposed vision-base control is tested as shown in Fig. 10. The guide lane's width is about one meter, and the length of the guide lane is set by 15 m with straight lane and curved lane. The curvature radius of curved lane is 6 meters. The robot is confirmed the excellent driving on the straight lane and the curved lane.

## 6  Conclusion

In this paper, a computer vision technology for a camera-based automatic guided robot was described using neuro-fuzzy control system. The nonlinear relation between the camera image and the control signals for the steering angle can be learned by neuro-fuzzy system. The validity of the proposed technology was confirmed by computer simulation. This approach is effective because it essentially replaces human's skill of complex geometric reasoning and control algorithm with a simple mapping of neuro-fuzzy system. This proposed method takes a much less calculation-intensive approach. The proposed control algorithm is available to be embedded in less expensive computer system because of reduction of network unit.

**Acknowledgments.**  This research was financially supported by the Ministry of Science, ICT and Future Planning (MSIP) and Korea Industrial Technology Association (KOITA) through the Programs to support collaborative research among industry, academia and research institutes. (KOITA-2015-5); the Human Resource Training Program for Regional Innovation and Creativity through the Ministry of Education and National Research Foundation of Korea (NRF-2015 H1C1A1035841).

## References

1. Jurgen, R.K.: Smart Cars and Highways Go Global. IEEE Spectr. **28**, 26–36 (1991)
2. Waxman, A.M., LeMoigne, J.J., Davis, L.S., Srinivasan, B., Kushner, T.R., Liang, E., Siddalingaiah, T.: A visual navigation system for autonomous land vehicles. IEEE J. Robot. Autom. **RA-3**(2), 124–140 (1987)
3. Passino, K.M.: Intelligent Control for Autonomous Systems. IEEE Spectr. **32**, 55–62 (1995)
4. Manigel, J., Leonhard, W.: Vehicle Control by Computer Vision. IEEE Trans. Industr. Electron. **39**(3), 181–188 (1992)
5. Tsugawa, S.: Vision-based vehicles in japan: machine vision systems and driving control systems. IEEE Trans. Industr. Electron. **41**(4), 398–405 (1994)
6. Ryoo, Y.-J.: Image technology for camera-based automatic guided vehicle. In: Chang, L.-W., Lie, W.-N. (eds.) PSIVT 2006. LNCS, vol. 4319, pp. 1225–1233. Springer, Heidelberg (2006)
7. Ryoo, Y.-J.: Neural network control for visual guidance system of mobile robot. In: Beliczynski, B., Dzielinski, A., Iwanowski, M., Ribeiro, B. (eds.) ICANNGA 2007. LNCS, vol. 4432, pp. 685–693. Springer, Heidelberg (2007)
8. Ryoo, Y.J.: Smart cars and smart highways from VAV to APOLLO. In: 14th International Symposium on Advanced Intelligent Systems, pp. 18–19 (2013)

9. Kuan, D.: Autonomous robotic vehicle road following. IEEE Trans. Pattern Anal. Mach. Intell. **10**(5) (1988)
10. Thorpe, C.E.: Vision and Navigation, the Carnegie Mellon Nablab. Kluwer Academic Publishers, Boston (1990)
11. Pomerleau, D.A.: Neural Network Perception for Mobile Robot Guidance. Kluwer Academic Publishers, Boston (1997)

# Automatic Matting Using Depth and Adaptive Trimap

Ying Zhao$^{(\boxtimes)}$, Chao Chen, Liyan Liu, and Wei Wang

Ricoh Software Research Center (Beijing) Co., Ltd., Beijing, China
{ying.zhao,chaocc.chen,liyan.liu,wei.wang}@srcb.ricoh.com

**Abstract.** Image matting refers to the problem of accurately extracting the foreground object from an image. The trimap containing labels of known foreground, known background and unknown has been broadly used to reduce solution space of the problem. The matte of an unknown pixel can be solved using samples from its neighbor known foreground and known background. However, the existing methods of color-based sampling may fail when foreground and background share similar colors, meanwhile, automatically generated trimap may not properly cover foreground boundary. In this paper, we propose a novel matting method using depth-assisted sampling and adaptive trimap generation. We use depth to assist color for improving sample selection and generate trimap based on color distribution of local unknown regions to make it cover foreground boundary adaptively. Our experiments show the effectiveness of proposed method.

**Keywords:** Image matting · Trimap · Alpha matte · Depth

## 1 Introduction

Image matting targets to extract foreground object from an image accurately. The process of matting is mathematically modeled by considering the observed color $I_p$ of a pixel $p$ as a combination of foreground $F_p$ and background $B_p$ colors along with its alpha value $\alpha_p$.

$$I_p = \alpha_p F_p + (1 - \alpha_p)B_p, \alpha_p \in [0, 1] \qquad (1)$$

This math model can be solved by adding constraint using trimap which partitions the image into three regions - known foreground, known background and unknown regions that consist of a mixture of foreground and background colors. Due to introducing trimap, $F_p$ and $B_p$ of an unknown pixel p can be estimated by samples of known foreground and known background. Then the $\alpha_p$ of unknown pixel $p$ can be calculated based on Eq. 1.

Therefore, image matting involves generating trimap and calculating alpha values. Manually specifying trimap is a time consuming task for a common user and impractical for real-time application. Simply generating trimap by threshold the depth map may wrongly label the unknown as known, as shown in Fig. 1(b).

© Springer International Publishing Switzerland 2016
F. Huang and A. Sugimoto (Eds.): PSIVT 2015 Workshops, LNCS 9555, pp. 179–191, 2016.
DOI: 10.1007/978-3-319-30285-0_15

Besides that, color-based alpha calculation may not be reliable when foreground and background have similar colors, as shown in Fig. 1(d). Based on this observation, we propose an automatic image matting method using adaptive trimap and depth-assisted sampling. Figure 1(f)-(h) show the overview of proposed method. Firstly, we generate a trimap in which the unknown regions adaptively covering true foreground boundaries. The trimap is initialized by a rough segmentation using depth information, and then refined by analyzing color distribution in local unknown regions. Secondly, a set of foreground and background samples is selected based on depth and color features. Based on the samples, we estimate foreground and background colors for the unknown pixels. Finally, the alpha values are calculated using the estimated colors and their confidences. Our method has two contributions. First, it automatically generates accurate trimap which suits for real-time segmentation without user manually specifying unknown regions. Second, it improves matting quality by using depth to distinguish similar colors of foreground and background.

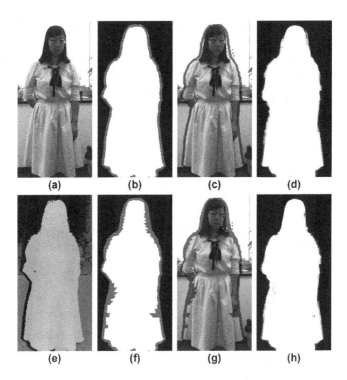

**Fig. 1.** An overview of proposed method comparing with prior art. (a) Color; (b) Automatic trimap; (c) Color-based sampling; (d) Matte using (b), (c); (e) Depth; (f) Adaptive trimap; (g) Depth-assisted sampling; (h) Matte using (f), (g).

## 2   Related Work

Sampling and trimap based image matting method has been proposed for many years. Learning based matting [1], Shared matting [2], Weighted matting [3], Comprehensive sampling matting [4] are recently presented outstanding approaches. They all require user specified trimap as an input. Learning based matting [1] proposes a global learning based approach which learns the model from some nearby labeled pixels for trimap based matting. In Shared matting [2], samples are firstly gathered from rays dividing the image plane into sectors with equal angles and later selected according to their spatial, photometric and probabilistic properties. Pixels in a local region share the selected samples. The Weighted matting [3] uses texture features to complement color to sample. It selects best foreground and background pair among a set of candidate pairs by optimizing an objective function containing color and texture components. In Comprehensive sampling matting [4], sampling is accomplished by expanding the sampling range for pixels farther from the foreground or background boundary and ensuring that samples from each color distribution are included. It selects best samples based on an object function containing measures of chromatic distortion, spatial and color statistics in the image.

There have been other solutions that use depth information for matting purposes. PG2007 [5] uses depth to generate a trimap in steps of upsampling, thresholding, and dilating. It uses depth to improve Bayesian matting [6] and Poisson Matting [7]. ICIP2010 [8] also uses depth map as an extra channel to expand the work of Closed-form matting [9]. Microsoft Kinect [10] provides a background removal method segmenting region of foreground player. CD-matting [13] introduces a user guided object selection method by extending the Closed-form matting [9] to deal with color and range data for robot manipulation system. DAGM2011 [14] provides method of foreground extraction based on one-dimensional histograms in 3D space and further a refinement step based on hierarchical grab-cut segmentation in a video volume with incorporated time constraints.

From these prior arts we can tell that selecting good samples from foreground and background sharing similar colors and generating suitable trimap automatically are still tough tasks. In the following sections, we introduce a depth assisted matting method based on adaptive trimap. By convention, we introduce the details of matting firstly and then discuss how to generate the trimap in Sect. 4. Experiments shown in Sect. 5 verify the effectiveness of our method.

## 3   Depth Assisted Image Matting

In order to automatically process image matting, the algorithm firstly generates a trimap using depth information. The trimap segments the input image into three non-overlapping regions: known foreground $F$, known background $B$ and unknown $U$. Next, the algorithm selects $F$ and $B$ samples for $U$ by optimizing an energy function based on depth and color features, followed by estimating foreground and background colors for $U$. Finally, the alpha values of $U$ are calculated using the estimated colors according to their confidences.

## 3.1  Trimap Initializing

Generally, the goal of trimap generation is to mark out the foreground boundary in which the alpha values are to be calculated. Therefore, we firstly use depth information to find out the target foreground. We use mean shift cluster method to segment the depth map into several blobs. We take the blob with nearest depth and largest size as the target foreground of image matting. After that, we use the foreground depth as a threshold and generate a mask in which the foreground is labeled as 1 while the others are labeled as 0. Since the depth map contains noise and missing data, the found foreground is fairly rough. Therefore, we erode the mask to remove noise and dilate it several times to make true foreground regions are covered as much as possible in non-zero regions. The region got from dilation is the unknown region and labeled as 0.5. Thus, we get the initial trimap and can use it to calculate alpha matte for the image.

## 3.2  Depth Assisted Sampling

Based on Eq. 1, given an unknown pixel, we can calculate its alpha value using its observed intensity and estimated foreground and background colors. And based on the smoothness assumption in [7], an unknown pixels foreground and background colors can be estimated using samples of its neighbors. However, color-based sampling may fail if foreground and background share similar colors. Therefore, we use depth to separate similar colors and select $F$ and $B$ samples for $U$ by optimizing an energy function based on depth and color features.

We refine color image based on depth in following steps. We normalize the clustered depth map and color channels in the range of 0 to 1. Note that the depth value of foreground is larger than background. Then we use it as a gain control parameter of color transform. To avoid making different colors become similar, we use luminance value as an offset control parameter. The parameters of transform are set to be consistent between color channels. After normalization, we compute a new color $C_p$ of pixel $p$ based on depth as indicated in Eqs. 2 and 3.

$$C_p = I_p * D_p + L_p \tag{2}$$

$$C_p = \frac{C_p - \min(C)}{\max(C) - \min(C)} \tag{3}$$

where, $I_p$ is the color of pixel $p$ which contains $R$, $G$ and $B$ channel; $D$ is the depth image; $L_p$ is its luminance value.

Figure 2 shows an example of foreground and background sharing similar colors. The depth map is shown in (a). The original color image is shown in (b) together with its histogram showing overlapping of foreground (Red) and background (Green) color distribution in (d). The color-refined image

**Fig. 2.** Example of color refinement (Color figure online).

and corresponding histogram are shown in (c) and (e) respectively. The process of color refinement has enabled the histograms for the foreground and background regions to be separated. This depth assisted separation of foreground and background helps sample selection.

We select $F$ and $B$ samples for $U$ by optimizing an energy function based on depth and color features. Firstly, we gather a set of candidate $F$ and $B$ samples from neighboring foreground and background regions of unknown pixel $p$. Since pixels in a small region usually share similar colors, we collect samples in a certain step until the number achieves expectation rather than gather all neighbors. Next, we select the best foreground-background sample pairs from the candidates by minimizing the chromatic distortion of observed color and estimated color of pixel p based on energy function $E_p(\tilde{\alpha}_{ij}, f_i, b_j)$.

$$E_p(\tilde{\alpha}_{ij}, f_i, b_j) = \sum_{q \in \Omega_p} ||C_q - (\tilde{\alpha}_{ij} f_i + (1 - \tilde{\alpha}_{ij}) f_j)||^2 \tag{4}$$

where, $f_i$ is the i-th foreground sample of foreground candidates set, $b_j$ is the j-th background sample of background candidates set, $\tilde{\alpha}_{ij}$ is the probability of pixel $p$ belonging to foreground based on taking $f_i$ and $b_j$ as its foreground and background colors, $\Omega_p$ is the unknown region in a small window centered at pixel $p$. Based on Eq. 1, we can use the triplet $(\tilde{\alpha}_{ij}, f_i, b_j)$ to model color of $p$. However, a good sample pair should minimize the chromatic distortion not only for $p$, but also for the unknown pixels in its neighbor. Therefore, we select the best sample pair by minimizing the least squares residual defined by the neighborhood affinity term. We estimated the probability of $p$ belonging to foreground in both chromatic and spatial aspects as in Eq. (5).

$$\tilde{\alpha}_{ij} = \frac{PF_s(p; f_i, b_j) * PF_c(p; f_i, b_j)}{PF_s(p; f_i, b_j) * PF_c(p; f_i, b_j) + (1 - PF_s(p; f_i, b_j)) * (1 - PF_c(p; f_i, b_j))} \tag{5}$$

In chromatic aspect $PF_c$, if pixel p and sample $f_i$ are more similar than pixel $p$ and sample $b_j$ in color, the probability of pixel p belonging to foreground is higher.

$$PF_c(p; f_i, b_j) = \frac{||b_j(R, G, B) - p(R, G, B)||^2}{||f_i(R, G, B) - p(R, G, B)||^2 + ||b_j(R, G, B) - p(R, G, B)||^2} \tag{6}$$

The depth information helps us to consider spatial aspect in 3D. In spatial aspect $PF_s$, if pixel $p$ is closer to sample $f_i$ than pixel p and $b_j$ are in 3D space, the probability of pixel $p$ belonging to foreground is higher.

$$PF_s(p; f_i, b_j) = \frac{||b_j(x, y, z) - p(x, y, z)||^2}{||f_i(x, y, z) - p(x, y, z)||^2 + ||b_j(x, y, z) - p(x, y, z)||^2} \quad (7)$$

Thus, we select the best sample pair $(\tilde{f}_p, \tilde{b}_p)$ of pixel $p$ by minimizing energy function (3). To reduce noise of resulting alpha matte, we average all selected best sample pairs in the small window $\Omega_p$ centered at pixel $p$. Then, we get the estimated foreground and background colors $(\tilde{f}_p, \tilde{b}_p)$ for the unknown pixel $p$.

### 3.3   Alpha Calculation

After we got the estimated foreground and background colors, we can use them to calculate alpha value of the unknown pixel $p$ based on Eq. 1. But the estimated colors may not be reliable if candidate sample sets are noise. Thus, we calculate the confidence of pixel $p$ in its estimated foreground and background colors. Similar with Shared matting [2], we use an exponential function to measure the confidence to ensure that it decreases as the chromatic distortion increased by estimated foreground and background colors.

We calculate mean probability $\tilde{\alpha}_p$ n the set of best samples $(\tilde{f}_{q \in \Omega_p}, \tilde{b}_{q \in \Omega_p})$ and confidence value $CP_p$ of estimated color $(\tilde{F}_p, \tilde{B}_p)$ using Eq. (8).

$$CF_p = \exp(-\lambda M_p(\hat{F}_p, \hat{B}_p)) \quad (8)$$

where, $\lambda$ is the decrease factor. The confidence value expresses the confidence of pixel $p$ in its candidate foreground and background colors. This confidence measure should decrease fast as the foreground and background colors fail to properly model the color of pixel $p$.

Having estimated foreground and background colors with their confidence $CF_p$, we can now compute the final alpha value $\alpha_p$ of pixel $p$.

$$\alpha_p = CF_p \frac{(C_p - \hat{B}_p) * (\hat{F}_p - \hat{B}_p)}{||\hat{F}_p - \hat{B}_p||} + (1 - CF_p)\tilde{\alpha}_{pp} \quad (9)$$

Thus, the alpha value $\hat{\alpha}_{pp}$ stimated from the best sample pair will be accepted if the confidence of estimated color is too low.

### 3.4   Discussion on Trimap

Figure 3 shows two results of matting using different trimaps. Figure 3(a) is color image overlaid by trimap generated in Sect. 3.1 together with corresponding matting result in Fig. 3(b). In Fig. 3(a), we can see that some regions around foreground contour are not labeled as unknown in the trimap. Correspondingly, the matting results in these regions are poor, as shown in Fig. 3(b).

This is mainly because of some background regions are wrongly taken as foreground and the matte of true foreground boundaries have not been estimated. Figures 3(c) and (d) show another problem caused by improper trimap. Figure 3(c) is the same color image overlaid by trimap generated by user strokes together with corresponding matting result in Fig. 3(d). As shown in Fig. 3(c), one cluster of foreground colors is entirely labeled as unknown. This results in missing correct foreground samples in the neighbor of unknown pixels. Therefore, its matting result shown in Fig. 3(d) has low quality. Based on these observations, we propose a trimap generation method to make the unknown regions adaptively covering foreground boundaries.

## 4  Adaptive Trimap Generation

To solve the problems caused by improper trimap, in this section, we present an approach that automatically generates an adaptive trimap in 3 steps: initializing, dividing, and refining. Figure 4 shows examples of matting results based on proposed adaptive trimaps. Comparing with Fig. 3(a) and (c), the unknown regions in Fig. 4(a) and (c) cover true boundaries more properly. The initialization step is described in Sect. 3.1 and not repeated here. Since the foreground proportion in different part of unknown region may not consistent, we divide the trimap into patches before refining it. As discussed in Sect. 3.4, the color distribution in a local region indicates whether the unknown covers foreground boundary properly. Based on our experiments, matting result is good if a local unknown region contains only one cluster of foreground colors. Therefore, we refine the unknown region in each patch based on its color distribution.

(a)            (b)            (c)            (d)

**Fig. 3.** Problems caused by improper trimap.

### 4.1  Trimap Dividing

As shown in Fig. 5, the foreground normally has irregular shape. Directly using equal patch size to divide trimap may produce more than one connected unknown region in one patch. Moreover, using a small size window moving along trimap contour to get patches may still miss real foreground. Inspired by [11], we divide trimap into patches recursively based on KD-tree. This allows each patch to contain only one connected unknown region while cover enough foreground region.

(c)          (d)          (c)          (d)

**Fig. 4.** Adaptive trimaps and their corresponding matting results.

Since nodes of KD-tree should contain foreground as much as possible, we consider unknown together with foreground when calculate splitting center. We calculate average coordinates of non-zero pixels in a node as its splitting center. A node will be divided into two sub-nodes by a line cross the splitting center if these four conditions are satisfied: (I) the node sizes are larger than thresholds; (II) the node has foreground, background, and unknown together; (III) both sub-nodes have unknown; (IV) at least one of sub-nodes has foreground, background, and unknown together. The node is indivisible if one of four conditions is not satisfied. The splitting direction is preferentially decided by larger axis variance. If X (or Y) axis variance is larger, the node will be experimentally divided in vertical (or horizontal) direction. If the node is indivisible in horizontal (or vertical) direction, we will try to divide it in vertical (or horizontal) direction. The leaf nodes of KD-tree are patches of trimap. By doing this, we can get the patch as small as possible. Figures 5(a) and (c) show examples of dividing trimap. We can see that the sizes of KD-elements are different and set automatically based on the object?s size and shape. We only set the termination condition of the division and use same parameter values in all experiments. Once trimap is divided, we can refine the unknown region patch by patch.

## 4.2   Trimap Refining

Firstly, we cluster color to remove the distraction of texture. We apply mean shift cluster method on foreground image since the background color may be cluttered. By doing this, the correct unknown should contain 2 color clusters, one is from background and the other is from foreground. After that, for each patch, we get its cluster number of the unknown region by calculating color histogram of clustered image, recursively merge adjacent bins, and remove bins with sizes smaller than threshold. If the color cluster number is less than 2, the unknown only contains background and doesn't cover foreground boundary. In that case, we expand the unknown region from foreground edge to foreground region. If the color cluster number is more than 2, the unknown may entirely cover one cluster of foreground colors. In that case, we shrink the unknown region from foreground edge to background region. The process is repeated until the color cluster number of the local unknown region is 2. The morphology process of expend or shrink is carried out once for every iteration through loop until the color distribution in one KD-element reaches termination condition.

As mentioned in trimap initialization step, we dilate the foreground mask several times. This allows us to make a limit boundary for refinement. We assume that non-zero region of initial trimap contains all true foreground regions. Therefore, the refinement only happens inside of non-zero region. In this step, we only process the patch having foreground, background and unknown together since we dont have enough information to make a good refinement in other patches. Figure 5(b) and (f) show results of trimap refinement. As the close-up images overlaid by unknown labels shown in Fig. 5(c), (d), (g) and (h), after refinement, the unknown region covers the omitted foreground boundary.

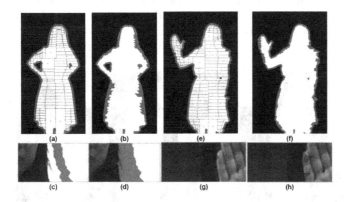

**Fig. 5.** Adaptive trimap generation. (a) and (e) are KD-tree based division results overlaid on initial trimaps; (b) and (f) are refined results of the initial trimaps; ((c), (g)) and ((d), (h)) are close-up color images overlaid by initial and refined trimaps respectively.

## 5 Experiments

In order to evaluate performance of proposed depth-assisted sampling and adaptive trimap generation, we carry out two experiments over two groups of data comparing with four prior arts. First, we test proposed image matting method using depth and adaptive trimap on RGB-D data which consists of depth and color images captured by Kinect v2 sensor. We show visual comparison of prior art results and ours in Fig. 6. In second experiment, we test proposed adaptive trimap generation on benchmark data which contains 13 color images provided by [12]. Figure 7 shows comparison of trimaps generated by user strokes and our method. The visual and quantized comparisons of matting results using Fig. 7 trimaps are shown in Figs. 8 and 9 respectively.

## 5.1    Experiment on RGB-D data

In this experiment, we test proposed image matting method using depth and adaptive trimap on RGB-D data. We generate adaptive trimaps using depth and color images captured by Kinect v2 sensor. The unknown regions of trimaps are overlaid in color images as shown in Fig. 6(a). We use these trimaps as inputs for the other methods, including Learning based matting [1], Shared matting [2], Weighted matting [3] and Comprehensive sampling matting [4]. In the first test image, foreground and background share similar colors. The close-up region in the first row show that our method can produce more accurate result in foreground region which has similar color and texture with background. The second test image has foreground object with holes inside. As shown in close-up of the second row, with the help of depth, our method can select best samples better based on 3D spatial metrics. The last test image has coarse edges in foreground region. The zoomed regions in the third row show that our method relatively keeps more details.

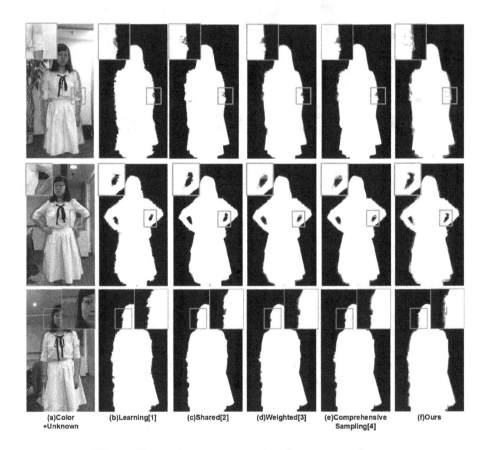

(a)Color +Unknown    (b)Learning[1]    (c)Shared[2]    (d)Weighted[3]    (e)Comprehensive Sampling[4]    (f)Ours

**Fig. 6.** Comparing matting results of prior art with ours.

## 5.2   Experiment on Benchmark Data

To further illustrate the contribution of proposed adaptive trimap, we test the method on a set of 13 benchmark images which has been used more broadly. In Figs. 7 and 8, we show 3 examples of the dataset. The quantized statistic of whole dataset is shown in Fig. 9. Since the dataset only contains color image, in this experiment, we use user strokes-based trimap as initial trimap, as shown in Fig. 7(b). Figure 7(c) shows the color image Fig. 7(a) overlaid by trimap Fig. 7(b) and the red regions corresponding to unknown. It indicates that user strokes omit some foreground boundaries. By using these trimaps, existing matting methods can't produce high quality results which are shown in column (a)s of Fig. 8. Given the trimap, our method refines the unknown regions to cover the omitted foreground boundaries and generates adaptive trimaps which are shown in Fig. 7(d). With the help of our adaptive trimap, the matte quality of existing methods is improved a lot. The comparisons are shown in column (b)s of Fig. 8.

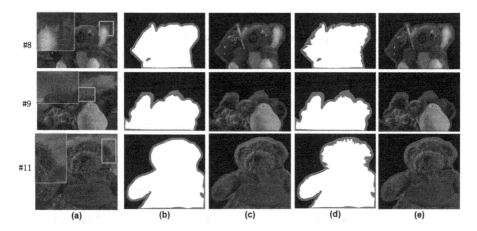

**Fig. 7.** Examples of benchmark data. (a) Color image; (b) User trimap; (c) (b) overlaid in (a); (d) Adaptive trimap; (e) (d) overlaid in (a).

The experiment was carried on a set of benchmark data which doesn't contain depth information. Therefore, we didn't illustrate our matting results in this part. The quantized evaluation results of this experiment are shown in Fig. 9. We calculate the mean square errors (MSEs) according to [12] for matting results generated by user trimap (Red) and adaptive trimap (Blue) of four existing methods. With the help of our adaptive trimap, the MSEs of all methods are reduced. From this experiment we can see that our adaptive trimap generation is effective and can be extended to other methods.

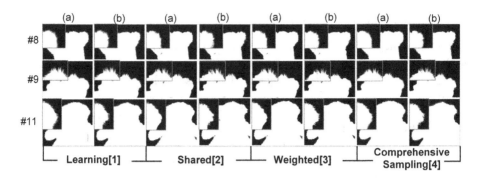

**Fig. 8.** Compare matting results of (a) without and (b) with adaptive trimap.

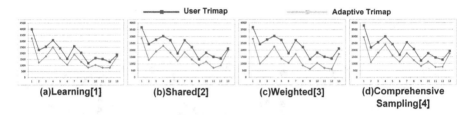

**Fig. 9.** Compare MSE of (Red)without and (Blue)with adaptive trimap (Color figure online).

## 6    Conclusion

In this paper, we propose an automatic image matting method using depth and adaptive trimap. We use depth to complement color to handle the situation of foreground and background sharing similar colors. For adaptive trimap generation, we first use depth to initialize a trimap followed by dividing the trimap into patches based KD-tree. Then, by analyzing color distribution in each patch, we refine its unknown region so as to make it adaptively cover foreground boundary. As shown in experiments, our method produces good matting results and the adaptive trimap generation is also helpful for other matting approaches. However, we only refine the trimap patches containing foreground, background and unknown together which may not work well for object having dense holes. And we simply take the nearest and largest blob as the foreground, assuming that it doesn't contain too many background regions. This may also cause inaccurate results. In the future, we will try utilizing motion information and object detection result to improve the technology.

## References

1. Zheng, Y., Kambhamettu, C.: Learning based digital matting. In: IEEE International Conference on Image Processing (ICIP), pp. 889–896 (2009)

2. Gastal, E.S.L., Oliveira, M.M.: Shared sampling for real time alpha matting. Proc. Eurographics **29**, 575–584 (2010)
3. Shahrian, E., Rajan, D.: Weighted color and texture sample selection for image matting. In: IEEE Conference on Computer Vision and Pattern Recognition (CVPR), pp. 718–725 (2012)
4. Shahrian, E., Rajan, D., Price, B., Cohen, S.: Improving image matting using comprehensive sampling sets. In: IEEE Conference on Computer Vision and Pattern Recognition (CVPR), pp. 636–643 (2013)
5. Wang, O., Finger, J., Yang, Q., Davis, J., Yang, R.: Automatic natural video matting with depth. In: IEEE Pacific Conference on Computer Graphics and Applications (PG), pp. 469–472 (2007)
6. Chuang, Y.Y., Curless, B., Salesin, D.H., Szeliski, R.: A bayesian approach to digital matting. In: IEEE Conference on Computer Vision and Pattern Recognition (CVPR), vol. 2, p. 7 (2001)
7. Sun, J., Jia, J., Tang, C.K., Shum, H.Y.: Poisson matting. ACM Trans. on Graph. (ToG) **23**(3), 315–321 (2004)
8. Piti, F., Kokaram, A.: Matting with a depth map. In: IEEE International Conference on Image Processing (ICIP), pp. 21–24 (2010)
9. Levin, A., Lischinski, D., Weiss, Y.: A closed-form solution to natural image matting. IEEE Trans. Pattern Anal. Mach. Intell. **30**(1), 228–242 (2008)
10. Mutto, D., Zanuttigh, P., Cortelazzo, G.M.: Time-of-Flight Cameras and Microsoft Kinect. SpringerBriefs in Electrical and Computer Engineering. Springer, Heidelberg (2012)
11. He, K., Sun, J., Tang, X.: Fast matting using large kernel matting laplacian matrices. In: IEEE Conference on Computer Vision and Pattern Recognition (CVPR), pp. 2165–2172 (2010)
12. Rhemann, C., Rother, C., Wang, J., Gelautz, M., Kohli, P., Rott, P.: A perceptually motivated online benchmark for image matting. In: IEEE Conference on Computer Vision and Pattern Recognition (CVPR), pp. 1826–1833 (2009)
13. Shibuya, N., Shimohata, Y., Harada, T., Kuniyoshi, Y.: Smart extraction of desired object from color-distance image with users tiny scribble. In: IEEE Conference on Intelligent Robots and Systems, pp. 2846–2853 (2008)
14. Frick, A., Franke, M., Koch, R.: Time-consistent foreground segmentation of dynamic content from color and depth video. In: Mester, R., Felsberg, M. (eds.) DAGM 2011. LNCS, vol. 6835, pp. 296–305. springer, Heidelberg (2011)

# Multi-Run: An Approach for Filling in Missing Information of 3D Roadside Reconstruction

Haokun Geng[1(✉)], Hsiang-Jen Chien[2], and Reinhard Klette[2]

[1] Department of Computer Science, The University of Auckland,
Auckland, New Zealand
hgen001@auklanduni.ac.nz
[2] School of Engineering, Auckland University of Technology,
Auckland, New Zealand

**Abstract.** This paper presents an approach for incrementally adding missing information into a point cloud generated for 3D roadside reconstruction. We use a series of video sequences recorded while driving repeatedly through the road to be reconstructed. The video sequences can also be recorded while driving in opposite directions. We call this a *multi-run* scenario. The only extra input data other than stereo images is the reading from a GPS sensor, which is used as guidance for merging point clouds from different sequences into one. The quality of the 3D roadside reconstruction is in direct relationship to the accuracy of the applied egomotion estimation method. A main part of our motion analysis method is defined by visual odometry following a traditional workflow in this area: first, establish correspondences of tracked features between two subsequent frames; second, use a stereo-matching algorithm to calculate the depth information of the tracked features; then compute the motion data between every two frames using a perspective-n-point solver. Additionally, we propose a technique that uses a Kalman-filter fusion to track the selected feature points, and to filter outliers. Furthermore, we use the GPS data to bound the overall propagation of the positioning errors. Experiments are given with trajectory estimation and 3D scene reconstruction. We evaluate our approach by estimating the recovery of (so far) missing information when analysing data recorded in a subsequent run.

**Keywords:** Multi-run scenario · Motion analysis · Visual odometry · Kalman filter · GPS data · 3D reconstruction · Multi-sensory integration

## 1 Introduction

Scene reconstruction plays an important role in many applications, including urban planning, route navigation, entertainment or gaming industry. Accurately reconstructing the 3D scene is still an extremely complex task in computer vision. Scientists and researchers introduced different methods and types of sensors for improving the egomotion (i.e. rotation and translation) estimation. For instance, a mobile terrestrial *light detection and ranging* (LiDAR) system can deliver

© Springer International Publishing Switzerland 2016
F. Huang and A. Sugimoto (Eds.): PSIVT 2015 Workshops, LNCS 9555, pp. 192–205, 2016.
DOI: 10.1007/978-3-319-30285-0_16

**Fig. 1.** Example of a disparity map (*middle*) generated from a given stereo image pair. Blank spaces in the point cloud (*right*) suggest occlusions or otherwise missing data for high-confidence stereo matching

highly detailed 3D data, the combination with a *global positioning system* (GPS) or an *inertial measurement unit* (IMU) are other examples of techniques that can provide reasonably good egomotion estimation. The use of optical cameras is the most cost-effective option. A camera-based approach can potentially provide reliability in most situations (e.g. for different weather conditions). The Mars Exploration rovers [13] are successful demonstrations of vision-based odometry.

A major problem for stereo vision is the occurrence of the object occlusions. Figure 1 shows a colour-coded disparity map with occlusions and possibly missing data. By using multi-run image sequences, our proposed approach aims at filling in the missing data, typically represented by 3D point clouds prior to surface triangulations or surface rendering.

*Visual odometry* (VO) is the key step of a long production pipeline of our multi-run approach. Scaramuzza et al. [20] indicated that VO methods can provide the trajectory estimation with a small error range between 0.1 % to 2 % of the actual motion. Olson et al. [18] suggested that the error of the VO methods is achievable to be less than 1 % of the total distance travelled. However, tiny errors that are caused by noise from the image data can build-up along a sequence quickly. Therefore, we apply Kalman filters to respond to the noise in the input data, in order to improve the overall egomotion estimation. In our research we also use multi-sensory integration to achieve an optimal and reliable solution for visual odometry in complex and dynamic environments.

In this paper, we propose an approach that reconstructs the scene over multi-run sequences. It takes stereo sequences as the major input, and GPS data as a type of supplementary input. The proposed VO method is the first phase of our approach; it focuses on estimating motion data between subsequent frames within a relatively small time interval. We implemented linear Kalman filter fusion to deal with the errors in the tracked features (i.e. one filter for one tracked feature), in order to ensure that only suitable feature candidates are used for motion estimations. In addition, a single extended Kalman filter is also applied for tracking the cameras' motion altogether.

The rest of the paper is structured as follows: Sect. 2 reviews previous work in the problem domain. Section 3 discusses our proposed approach and its mathematical theories. Section 4 shows how the additional GPS data can be used to bound the build-up error within in a certain range over a long distance. Section 6 explains the design and measures used for the experiments and their evaluations. Section 7 concludes.

## 2  Related Literature

There are serval ways for estimating motion data in computer vision. We choose to focus on a stereo-vision-based method as the basis of our approach. Matthies et al. [14,15] demonstrated the benefits and tradeoffs of using a stereo-vision system over the use of a monocular vision system for calculating motion data. By computing and modelling the errors from the input, they found that the monocular vision system would contribute more errors in depth information. Stereo-matching algorithms are designed to generate disparity images that provide detailed depth information for the given stereo images. Demirdjian et al. [6] presented a method for motion analysis using disparity images generated from a stereo matching algorithm as the only input.

Stereo-matching algorithms commonly require rectified images, which are the output of a calibration procedure. However, calibration is one of the few approaches in computer vision where errors cannot be easily removed in subsequent processes. Hirschmüller et al. [9] state that even sub-pixel calibration errors can cause serious problems for the accuracy of structure reconstruction; they propose a method that can avoid calibration-error amplifications.

The Kalman filter, also known as linear quadratic estimation (LQE), is the most common way of dealing with unexpected errors or noise, which are introduced at different phases of a processing pipeline. With the grown of the complexity of motion analysis, the error-filtering task becomes a non-linear problem. The extended Kalman filter and the unscented Kalman filter have been developed for working with non-linear systems. Julier et al. [10] developed the unscented Kalman filter in 2004. Franke et al. [7] developed a more complex method; they used a Kalman filter fusion to track a number of image features, so that they can distinguish the features into foreground and background by motion data prediction. Based on the theory of Kalman filter fusion, Badino et al. [1] presented a novel method using a least-squares formulation to minimize the reprojection error of the overall egomotion estimation. Badino et al. [2] continued to improve their work into a real-time application. For further and more recent work, see [3].

The *Random Sample Consensus* (RANSAC) method is another commonly used approach for error filtering in feature matching. Kitt et al. [11] show that a RANSAC-based outlier rejection scheme can effectively improve the result of the motion estimation in a dynamic environment. Since feature tracking is considered to be the first step in most of the current visual odometry algorithms, the quality of feature detection directly affects the final estimation result. Song et al. [23] and [12] provide a comprehensive evaluation of mainstream feature detectors; these references discuss the best and worst scenarios for different types of feature detectors.

Roadside reconstruction clearly plays an important role in many advanced technologies and applications, such as navigation, visual reality, or driver-assistance system. Musialski et al. [17] provided an overview of current urban reconstruction methods. They stated that complex reconstruction problems remain to be unsolved to date, and that there is still a long way to go.

## 3   Visual Odometry Estimation

For our visual odometry method, we use a trinocular vision system to collect the image data. The recorded images are with 12-bit depth and $2046 \times 1080$ resolution for each camera. Figure 2(top) shows an example of recorded data. The sequences are usually recorded at $25 \sim 27$ Hz. In order to gain more overlapped regions in the point clouds for the multi-run scenarios, we decided to use the right image rather than the left image as the reference for the disparity map. The trinocular vision system also enables us to have a *third-eye evaluation approach*, see [5], to measure the consistency of any disparity values among the three cameras. Figure 2(bottom) shows the corresponding disparity map and the *transitivity-error-in-disparity-space* (TED) based-disparity-consistency map. The red pixels show the region with high confidence, whereas the blue pixels show the region with low consistency in disparity values.

The proposed visual odometry method mainly follows the traditional work-flow: (1) Feature matching and tracking. (2) Stereo matching. (3) Remove outliers with a RANSAC-based scheme. (4) Disguising foreground and background features. (5) Use static features to obtain the motion data by solving the *perspective-n-point* (PnP) problem. (6) Correct the trajectory with an unscented Kalman filter. (7) Optical and GPS data (i.e. multi-sensory) integration.

**Fig. 2.** *Top*: An input example for trinocular vision. *Bottom*: Corresponding color-enhanced disparity image, and its TED consistency map

The roadside reconstruction and the GPS trajectory will be projected into a left-hand local Cartesian coordinate system, where the origin is the shifted GPS position of the first frame. The $z$-axis is pointing forward into the initial default driving direction. The $x$-axis represents distance shifts from the origin to the left or right. The $y$-axis indicates changes in elevation. A positive value means a more elevated position. In the scene reconstruction coordinate system, we assume that the camera set is at a pre-defined position $[x, y, z]^\top = [\text{left}, \text{height}, 0]^\top$ at the beginning.

# 4   Error Handling and Kalman Filters

Optical cameras can provide fairly robust performance for all situations, but being relatively cheap also comes with some drawbacks (e.g. noise or geometric errors in image data). The ideal environment for egomotion estimation is that all the static features are perfectly detected and matched, and the disparity maps should provide perfect depth information for all the features. In reality, our world is never perfect, every aspects of the approach will bring a certain amount of errors. Noise filtering is an essential step for our algorithm; it should eliminate or at least bound the error propagation within an acceptable range.

In our proposed approach, we use Kalman filter fusion for filtering the errors in the feature matching phase to establish correct correspondences between two feature sets (in the *base* and in the *match image*). In addition, by tracking the features individually with extra depth information, the errors in the disparity and Euclidean space can be minimised. Therefore, the perspective transformation can be estimated more accurately.

We also propose an extended Kalman filter for tracking the rotation (Euler angles) and translation of the vehicle's motion. Julier et al. [10] suggested that the EKF is reliable for solving nonlinear problems that are almost linear. In our proposed method, we use the EKF for tracking changes of the egomotion transformation frame by frame, where the gaps (i.e. the time intervals) between every two frames are relatively small. Therefore, tracking and correcting the camera's trajectory and pose can be considered to be an almost linear problem, solvable with an EKF.

## 4.1   Linear Kalman Filter Fusion for Tracked Features

We propose local linear Kalman filter fusion for feature tracking: one filter for each of the continuously tracked features. Franke et al. [7] firstly used Kalman filter fusion for tracking image features in the 3D space, in order to remove the outliers by measuring the gap between actual and predicted positions of tracked features, and to classify features into foreground or background. This research shows that error minimisation in feature matching and tracking is the key factor that directly influences the quality of the final egomotion estimation. Therefore, we use a set of linear Kalman filters to keep track of all the selected features, and to detect any unexpected change in the tracked features pool. An unexpected change can be, for example, a rapid change in depth or direction; the relevant features are then outliers and need to be discarded. We assume that the noise in the input data is white Gaussian noise, such as the noise introduced by the stereo matching algorithms.

**State Vector.** The state vector is a $12 \times 1$ vector; it contains the 3D positional data $[x, y, z]^\top$ and its velocity $[x', y', z']^\top$. Additionally, it contains the direction data $[\varphi_k, \theta_k, \psi_k]^\top$, and the corresponding angular speed $[\varphi_k', \theta_k', \psi_k']^\top$. Thus, the state vector $\mathbf{x}_k$ is formed as follows:

$$\mathbf{x}_k = [x, y, z, x, y, z', \varphi_k, \theta_k, \psi_k, \varphi_k', \theta_k', \psi_k']^\top \tag{1}$$

**Process Model.** The process model relates to the state vector; it describes the state vector change from the previous moment $k-1$ to the present moment $k$:

$$\mathbf{x}_k = \begin{bmatrix} \mathbf{A}_k & 0 \\ 0 & \mathbf{A}_k \end{bmatrix} \cdot \mathbf{x}_{k-1} + \mathbf{b}_k^\top + \mathbf{n}_k \tag{2}$$

$$\text{where} \quad \mathbf{A}_k = \begin{bmatrix} \mathbf{I}_3 & \Delta t \cdot \mathbf{I}_3 \\ 0_3 & \mathbf{I}_3 \end{bmatrix}$$

$\mathbf{A}_k$ is the state-transition matrix and $\mathbf{b}_k$ is the input-control vector.

**Measure Model.** The measurement is updated by the motion estimated from the last frame. The measurement model observes the current state of the positional and directional data. Thus, the measurement $\mathbf{z}_k$ is given as follows:

$$\mathbf{z}_k = \begin{bmatrix} x_k, y_k, z_k, \varphi_k, \theta_k, \psi_k \end{bmatrix}^\top = \begin{bmatrix} \mathbf{H} & 0 \\ 0 & \mathbf{H} \end{bmatrix} \cdot \mathbf{x}_k + \mathbf{n}_k \tag{3}$$

$$\text{where} \quad \mathbf{H} = \begin{bmatrix} \mathbf{I}_3 & 0 \\ 0 & \mathbf{I}_3 \end{bmatrix}$$

$\mathbf{H}$ is the observation model matrix that translates the state vector to the measurement vector. Noise vector $\mathbf{n}_k$ represents white Gaussian noise.

## 4.2    Extended Kalman Filter for Multi-sensory Integration

The *extended Kalman filter* (EKF) is particularly designed to solve non-linear problems that are "almost" linear. However, the EKF could provide poor results when the prediction and update functions are highly non-linear. In our case, we propose to use the extra GPS data as the major guidance of the positional data of the reconstruction. We still use the continuous image sequences as the major source for motion estimation. The time interval between every two frames is small enough to consider it an 'almost' linear problem. The term 'global' refers to the overall motion transformation into the next state, and it is also refers and compares to the 'local' Kalman filter fusion discussed in Sect. 4.1.

**State Vector.** The state vector is a $12 \times 1$ vector; it contains the 6 elements for positional data and its velocity, and 6 elements for directional information. Thus, the state vector $\mathbf{x}_k$ is formed as above in the local filter, but here with a global meaning:

$$\mathbf{x}_k = [x, y, z, x', y', z', \varphi_k, \theta_k, \psi_k, \varphi'_k, \theta'_k, \psi'_k]^\top \tag{4}$$

**Process Model.** The process model of the EKF is formed by its common $f$ and $h$ functions. So, the state vector can be described by the EKF function

$$\mathbf{x}_k = f(\mathbf{x}_k, \mathbf{u}_k) + \mathbf{w}_k \tag{5}$$

and the measurement vector can be described by

$$\mathbf{z}_k = h(\mathbf{x}_k) + \mathbf{v}_k \tag{6}$$

**Extended Process and Measure Model.** The state vector is given as

$$\mathbf{x} = [\mathbf{p}\top, \mathbf{p}'\top, \mathbf{w}\top, \mathbf{w}'\top]^\top \tag{7}$$

where vector $\mathbf{p}$ represents the positional and velocity information, vector $\mathbf{w}$ represents the angular data. Thus, the positional information can be extracted by the following equation:

$$\begin{bmatrix} \mathbf{p}_k \\ \mathbf{p}'_k \end{bmatrix} = \begin{bmatrix} I & \Delta t \cdot \mathbf{I}_3 \\ 0 & I \end{bmatrix} \cdot \begin{bmatrix} \mathbf{p}_{k-1} \\ \mathbf{p}'_{k-1} \end{bmatrix} \tag{8}$$

The measurement model needs additional normalization as follows:

$$\mathbf{z}_k = h(\mathbf{x}) = \begin{bmatrix} \mathbf{p} \\ normalize(\mathbf{w}) \end{bmatrix} = \begin{bmatrix} \mathbf{p} \\ \frac{\mathbf{w}}{|\mathbf{w}|} \end{bmatrix} \tag{9}$$

Then, the EKF cycle can start to iterate with the two given functions $f$ and $h$.

## 5    Multi-run Merging and Integration

The proposed multi-run approach takes one or more independent sequences for the same street block or area, and uses them to find missing information in the total (so far) reconstructed point cloud. Figure 3 shows trajectories of the GPS signals for the four recorded sequences, each independent sequence is marked by a different colour. Theoretically speaking, taking more image sequences around the same block (more dense information) should allow us that the proposed approach achieves higher quality of the overall roadside reconstruction, but this will also come with performance and accuracy issues.

Multi-sensory integration is a solution to accuracy problems. It enriches the dimensions of the input data, so the different types of input data can be used either to evaluate each other's accuracy, or to increase the information density in the input. For our approach, we use optical cameras (stereo-vision) and a GPS sensor. The image data are the main input of the proposed VO method. For the motion estimation phase, we choose to trust the image data over GPS data. GPS signals usually contain a 0.5 % error, due to a number of approximations, irregularities of the Earth surface, or deviations in GPS readings.

Since the error is irrelevant to travelled distance, so the GPS data can be used to bound the growth of the VO drift error. Once an unusual change is detected, or the growth of the drift error exceeds a tolerance threshold, then the GPS data will be used to correct the overall trajectory by the EKF.

Based on image and GPS data, we propose an approach for the multi-run reconstruction. Figure 4 shows the working pipeline of the proposed multi-run approach. First of all, we use the trinocular vision system to gather the required image data for the VO method, in order to estimate the motion data for every frame, and then create point cloud for 'one run' based on the known motion. Second, we pick the image data recorded in the same street block to construct the point cloud for the 'second run'. Then we use the GPS data of each sequence to roughly guide the merging action of the two point clouds into one 'overall' point cloud. After the rough merging, there are gaps between the two point clouds, so we use an ICP-based method to minimise the transformation between the two given point clouds. However, ICP has its own bottle-neck of performance issues, so we need to reduce the workload to an acceptable level. Thus, we introduce two key interest regions in the 3D reconstruction input: (1) Overlapping regions. (2) Corner regions.

## 5.1 Determination of Overlapping Regions

In order to reduce the processing time and the calculation workload, we need to determine some overlapping regions in the reconstructed point clouds. Then we take only the overlapped region (i.e. the "joint region") as the input to the ICP method to determine the best transformation between the two independent point clouds. The GPS coordinates are used as guidance for finding candidates of overlapped regions.

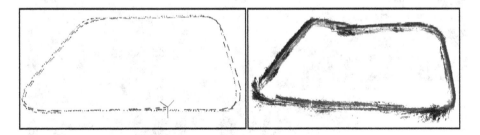

**Fig. 3.** *Left*: Trajectories of four subsequent runs around the same city block, distinguished by colours. *Right*: Corresponding 3D reconstruction of the city block (shown at very low resolution here, just indicating the reconstruction)

1. Trinocular vision-based images

2. Disparity image and TED-based image

3. Proposed Kalman filter fusion

4. PnP method for visual odometry

5. Proposed EKF for GPS integration

6. Detect corner and overlapped regions

7. Use GPS data as the initial guidance

8. Merge two runs with ICP method

**Fig. 4.** The pipeline of the multi-run approach

## 5.2   Corner Region Recognition with GPS

The ICP method is used to find the precise transformation between the two point clouds for the multi-run scenario. However, the ICP method comes with performance limitations. A typical street block usually contains hundreds to thousands frames, which means the size of the point clouds can be too large to process. Due to the limited computation resource, we need to down-sample or reduce the total size of the input data for ICP. Therefore, we choose to use the corners around the block to estimate the transformation. Usually, the corner regions generate point clouds that contain very dense features and textures, because the vehicle needs to slow down at the turning point or corner region of any street block.

A detected corner in a street block

**Fig. 5.** An example of a detected street corner

This action will also gather rich information in all perspective view directions at the corner regions. Figure 5 shows an example of the 3D reconstructed point cloud at one detected corner region. Directly using GPS coordinates is also an efficient and effective way to detect any corners in the trajectory.

# 6   Results and Evaluation

The following assumptions are applied for our experiments: (1) the rectification process of the trinocular system is assumed to be done perfectly; (2) the recording platform is assumed to basically and only travel forward. The experiments have trajectory estimations and 3D scene reconstruction as generated outputs. We evaluate our approach by measuring the overall merging quality of the independent point clouds, and the percentage of the missing information that was recovered from a subsequent run.

The proposed approach and experiments are implemented in Visual C++ with OpenCV and *Point Cloud Library* (PCL). The feature detector used in our method is 'FAST', and the feature descriptor used is 'BRISK'. The 3D roadside reconstruction of the multi-run approach is considered to be the major experimental result. Its quality can be evaluated both visually and also by understanding whether more gaps (in the point cloud) are filled.

Figure 6 illustrates a 3D roadside reconstruction of a city block. The red dots show the projected positions of the trinocular camera set (i.e. its trajectory) for every recorded frame in the sketched 3D scene. This trajectory is estimated by

**Fig. 6.** Result of 3D roadside reconstruction without using GPS data. Red dots indicate the cameras' trajectory in the 3D scene (Color figure online)

**Fig. 7.** Initial result for a multi-run approach (i.e. after the first run)

the proposed feature-matching-based VO method. The trajectory is first estimated by the PnP method, and then corrected and predicted by the proposed
EKF. From the bird's-eye view of the city block, we can see that the roadside reconstruction, obtained from the sequence recorded in the first run, still
contains many gaps and holes in the point cloud. They are inherited from the
disparity images, such as from missing matching pixels, or occlusions.

Figure 7 (left) shows a region which was missing in the first-run point cloud.
Figure 7 (right) illustrates the result of finding the missing data in the reconstructed point cloud after applying the second run sequences. The independent
point cloud from the second run enhanced the overall reconstruction result. It
brings in data, that is missing in the first-run point cloud, but also more noise.

Figure 8 shows the 3D reconstruction result after one run of a multi-run
sequence set. The GPS data is also used here for bounding the total drift-error
growth. However, in our experiments, the drift error is usually not big enough to
activate a correction action of the EKF. The red dots are the projected positions
of the converted GPS signals. The currently used GPS sensor provides discon-
tinuous data, with time gaps of one second. Therefore, we designed the EKF to
be only active when the GPS data is clearly on-line. Once the GPS signals are
dropped, the weight of the GPS signals' reliability will be minimised. The red
dots show the improved camera's trajectory that is done by the EKF.

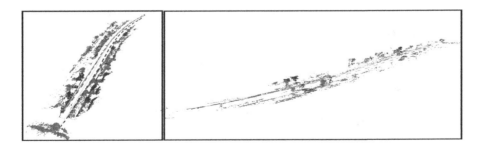

**Fig. 8.** 3D reconstruction by multi-run approach on the same street. Red and blue
point clouds are the features; green and yellow lines are the camera trajectories; red or
blue dotted lines are the GPS trajectories of the first or second sequence, respectively
(Color figure online)

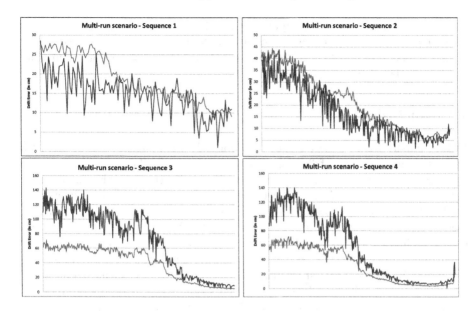

**Fig. 9.** Comparisons of drift errors for the four input sequences of the multi-run approach. The red and blue curve represents the differences in drift errors before and after the application of the EKF (Color figure online)

Figure 9 shows the detailed comparisons of drift errors before and after applying the EKF for the four input testing sequences. Sequences 1 and 2 are in the same direction, and so are Sequences 3 and 4. The figure demonstrates an effect: the testing sequences recorded in the same direction would more likely lead to similar behaviours of drift error generation and EKF correction. It also shows that the EKF correction will gain more control when the drift error gets larger. Each testing sequence contains around 1,400 stereo image pairs.

Our experimental results show that the multi-sensory method is a promising and valuable addition to any stand-alone VO applications. The extra positioning data can be either used as supplementary input or as evaluation measurements. Generally speaking, a stand-alone VO drift error builds up quickly over distance. For instance, even if there is only a small error occurring in the rotation, it will lead to a large drift error in both rotation and translation estimations. The applied filtering methods (e.g. RANSAC, Kalman filters, or bundle adjustment)can improve results for egomotion estimation, but some errors always remain.

Moreover, multi-sensor integration enriches the input data. The resulting visual odometry supports improved reconstruction; it helps to combine street segments according to the GPS data. Therefore, the 3D scene reconstruction can be done at a larger scale (i.e. in different sections in a large area). This demonstrates an alternative method for solving such a kind of problems, compared to other traditional VO methods. However, it also heavily relies on the accuracy of the GPS input. If the GPS is accurate enough, our proposed method could use the extra input to bound the growth of the drift error within a relatively small range. It could also lead to a worse motion estimation if the GPS data has low accuracy.

## 7    Conclusions

In this paper, we propose an effective approach using *multi-run* sequences to fill in the missing data of 3D roadside reconstruction. The point clouds from different directions on the same street are merged together, to solve the missing data problems caused by the occlusion on the disparity images. GPS signals are used as the guidance of the camera set's rough position. It also is an important measurement that could bound the growth of the VO drift errors. The motion data is estimated mainly based on trinocular (stereo vision) image sequences.

In the phase of merging reconstructed point clouds, the ICP-based method appears to be the best option for precisely adjusting the transformation between two independent point clouds. It clearly shows that it can achieve more reliable results when the two point clouds have different perspective angles, compared to the 3D-feature-based method. However, the ICP-based method has performance limitations when the size of the input point clouds is "too large" (obviously a relative measure). Moreover, the ICP-based method can introduce more errors when the overlapped regions are not well-defined; the ICP algorithm will be trapped by the local optimisation problem. It means that the best adjustment description, calculated by the ICP-based method, might not be the *true* best adjustment description.

## References

1. Badino, H., Franke, U., Rabe, C., Gehrig, S.: Stereo vision-based detection of moving objects under strong camera motion. Proc. Comput. Vis. Theor. Appl. **2**, 253–260 (2006)
2. Badino, H., Kanade, T.: A head-wearable short-baseline stereo system for the simultaneous estimation of structure and motion. In: Proceedings IAPR Config Machine Vision Applications, pp. 185–189 (2011)
3. Badino, H., Yamamoto, A., Kanade, T.: Visual odometry by multi-frame feature integration. In: Proceedings of the ICCV Workshop Computer Vision Autonomous Driving, pp. 222–229 (2013)
4. Besl, P., McKay, N.D.: A method for registration of 3-d shapes. IEEE Trans. Pattern Anal. Mach. Intell. **14**, 239–256 (1992)
5. Chien, H.J., Geng, H., Klette, R.: Visual odometry based on transitivity error analysis in disparity space - A third-eye approach. In: Proceedings IVCNZ, pp. 72–77 (2014)
6. Demirdjian, D., Darrell, T.: Motion estimation from disparity images. Proc. ICCV **1**, 213–218 (2001)

7. Franke, U., Rabe, C., Badino, H., Gehrig, S.K.: 6D-Vision: Fusion of stereo and motion for robust environment perception. In: Kropatsch, W.G., Sablatnig, R., Hanbury, A. (eds.) DAGM 2005. LNCS, vol. 3663, pp. 216–223. Springer, Heidelberg (2005)
8. Geiger, A., Lenz, P., Stiller, C., Urtasun, R.: Vision meets robotics: The KITTI dataset. Int. J. Robot. Res. **32**, 1231–1237 (2013)
9. Hirschmüller, H., Gehrig, S.: Stereo matching in the presence of sub-pixel calibration errors. In: Proceedings CVPR, pp. 437–444 (2009)
10. Julier, S., Uhlmann, J.: Unscented filtering and nonlinear estimation. Proc. IEEE **92**, 401–422 (2004)
11. Kitt, B., Geiger, A., Lategahn, H.: Visual odometry based on stereo image sequences with RANSAC-based outlier rejection scheme. In: Proceedings IEEE Intelligent Vehicles Symposium, pp. 486–492 (2010)
12. Klette, R.: Concise Computer Vision. Springer, London (2014)
13. Maimone, M., Cheng, Y., Matthies, L.: Two years of visual odometry on the Mars exploration rovers. J. Field Robot. **24**, 169–186 (2007)
14. Matthies, L.: Dynamic stereo vision. Ph.D. dissertation, Carnegie Mellon University (1989)
15. Matthies, L., Shafer, S.A.: Error modeling in stereo navigation. IEEE J. Rob. Autom. **3**, 239–250 (1987)
16. Milella, A., Siegwart, R.: Stereo-based ego-motion estimation using pixel tracking and iterative closest point. In: Proceedings IEEE International Conference Computer Vision Systems, p. 21 (2006)
17. Musialski, P., Wonka, P., Aliaga, D., Wimmer, M., Gool, L., Purgathofer, W.: A survey of urban reconstruction. J. Comput. Graph. Forum **32**, 146–177 (2013)
18. Olson, C., Matthies, L., Schoppers, M., Maimone, M.: Stereo ego-motion improvements for robust rover navigation. Proc. IEEE Int. Conf. Robot. Autom. **2**, 1099–1104 (2001)
19. Rublee, E., Rabaud, V., Konolige, K., Bradski, G.: Orb: An efficient alternative to SIFT or SURF. In: Proceedings of the ICCV, pp. 2564–2571 (2011)
20. Scaramuzza, D., Fraundorfer, F.: Visual odometry tutorial. Robot. Autom. Mag. **18**, 80–92 (2011)
21. Shakernia, O., Vidal, R., Sastry, S.: Omnidirectional egomotion estimation from back-projection flow. Proc. CVPR Workshop **7**, 82 (2003)
22. Sibley, G., Sukhatme, G.S., Matthies, L.: The iterated sigma point Kalman filter with applications to long range stereo. In: Proceedings Robotics Science Systems (2006)
23. Song, Z., Klette, R.: Robustness of point feature detection. In: Wilson, R., Hancock, E., Bors, A., Smith, W. (eds.) CAIP 2013, Part II. LNCS, vol. 8048, pp. 91–99. Springer, Heidelberg (2013)

# Design and Calibration of Multi-camera Systems for 3D Computer Vision: Lessons Learnt from Two Case Studies

Tom Botterill[1,2]($\boxtimes$), Matthew Signal[2], Steven Mills[3], and Richard Green[1]

[1] Department of Computer Science, University of Canterbury,
Christchurch, New Zealand
tom@hilandtom.com
[2] Tiro Lifesciences, Christchurch, New Zealand
[3] Department of Computer Science, University of Otago, Dunedin, New Zealand

**Abstract.** This paper examines how the design of imaging hardware for multi-view 3D reconstruction affects the performance and complexity of the computer vision system as a whole. We examine two such systems: a grape vine pruning robot (a 4.5 year/20 man-year project), and a breast cancer screening device (a 10 year/25 man-year project). In both cases, mistakes in the initial imaging hardware design greatly increased the overall development time and cost by making the computer vision unnecessarily challenging, and by requiring the hardware to be redesigned and rebuilt. In this paper we analyse the mistakes made, and the successes experienced on subsequent hardware iterations. We summarise the lessons learned about platform design, camera setup, lighting, and calibration, so that this knowledge can help subsequent projects to succeed.

**Keywords:** Multi-view reconstruction · 3D reconstruction · Camera hardware · Camera calibration · Lighting

## 1 Introduction

Computer vision forms an integral part of ever more complex systems, including robot systems, medical imaging systems, smart vehicle systems, and 3D motion capture systems. Each system requires imaging hardware including cameras, lights, and often enclosures to control imaging conditions. This imaging hardware is frequently assembled specifically for the application [1,11,19,23]. In this paper we argue that careful design of the imaging hardware greatly reduces the overall development effort required, hence increasing the likelihood of success and improving overall performance. Computer vision systems chain together many different processes, from low level segmentation and feature extraction, through to high level model fitting, with these models ultimately used to make decisions, e.g. on robot controls, diagnoses. Errors in the imaging process, or limitations of the imaging process, propagate through the different computer vision algorithms

© Springer International Publishing Switzerland 2016
F. Huang and A. Sugimoto (Eds.): PSIVT 2015 Workshops, LNCS 9555, pp. 206–219, 2016.
DOI: 10.1007/978-3-319-30285-0_17

and affect the performance and accuracy of the system as a whole. In our experience, much development effort is spent on compensating for mistakes made when designing the systems and collecting data, and more careful design would simplify and speed up the development process, while improving performance overall.

This paper focusses on the effects of hardware choices on multi-camera systems for 3D reconstruction. Multi-camera systems are popular for applications requiring high-accuracy, high resolution 3D reconstructions. Many design considerations are just as relevant for systems using depth cameras, where similar challenges with lighting[1], image resolution and image quality [8] exist.

The paper is organised as follows: Sect. 2 summarises how the image acquisition process affects the performance of the computer vision system, and Sect. 3 describes two case studies that we use to illustrate these effects. Section 4 reviews the choice of cameras and lenses, camera positioning, illumination, enclosure design and calibration procedures. The impact of each decision, trade-offs required, and lessons learnt from the two case studies are discussed. Recommendations are also summarised in the checklist that is provided as supplementary material, and from http://hilandtom.com/PSIVT2015-Checklist.pdf.

# 2   Effects of Imaging Quality on Computer Vision

The imaging hardware affects a 3D computer vision system's performance in four ways: accuracy, robustness, development cost, and efficiency.

To most straightforward effect of image quality on computer vision systems is on the accuracy of measurements taken from images, e.g. localisation accuracy or the accuracy of a 3D measurement. This is the case for many computer vision methods, including those formulated as a data-plus-spatial energy minimisation (e.g. active shape/contour models, dense stereo, dense optical flow [22]). Improving resolution, focus, pixel signal-to-noise ratios, etc. are straightforward ways to minimise different kinds of image noise [10,19], which enables more weight to be given to the data terms, hence increasing accuracy. By averaging across many pixels, computer vision systems often achieve subpixel or sub-greylevel accuracy [2,19].

A much more challenging class of errors in computer vision are the large discrete errors known as gross errors. These errors are generally too large to average away, and can cause partial or total system failure. Gross errors that create challenges for multi-view 3D computer vision systems include incorrectly detecting and/or matching features, segmentation errors, and errors at depth discontinuities. These errors are prevalent when objects are occluded, partly outside the camera's field of view, or when their appearance is affected by variable lighting, reflections, and shadows. A system's susceptibility to these errors is referred to as its robustness.

An important effect of imaging conditions on computer vision is on development time. When imaging conditions are poor, considerable development time must be spent on modelling shadows and lighting effects [12], and handling the matching ambiguities and increased outlier rates that result (see, for example,

---

[1]  https://support.xbox.com/en-GB/xbox-360/kinect/lighting.

the vast literature on making RANSAC-based robust matching frameworks perform well [9]). In addition, if imaging hardware is redesigned, time consuming code changes may be required throughout the entire system [19], as the errors present and the visual effects to model change.

The imaging process also affects computational efficiency: pixel-level algorithms (e.g. segmentation, dense optical flow or dense stereo) may be slower for higher resolution images, however as soon as a higher-level representation is obtained (e.g. features are extracted) then the resolution no longer affects computation times, and higher quality images may improve performance, e.g. by increasing feature localisation accuracy or by reducing matching ambiguities. Even pixel-level algorithms may be no slower for higher resolution images if fewer iterations are required. Later-stage 3D algorithms can be considerably more efficient when there are fewer outliers: when outlier rates are low, fewer iterations of RANSAC are needed [9] and efficient non-robust quadratic cost functions can be used in bundle adjustment [3]. In our experience, and as is often the case in software [13, Section 25.2], the biggest increases in efficiency come from having more development time available for optimising and parametrising algorithms once the rest of the system is working, and once critical loops are identified. Improving imaging hardware improves computational efficiency by making the development process more efficient.

## 3    Case Studies

In this paper we use two case studies to illustrate the effects of hardware design on system performance and development. The first is a grape vine pruning robot, and the second is a prototype breast cancer screening system. Both use synchronised cameras to image their subject, and use customised imaging enclosures and artificial lighting to control imaging conditions. Both imaging hardware systems have been completely redesigned and rebuilt, at considerable expense, as the importance of the hardware design has become apparent.

### 3.1    Grape Vine Pruning Robot

The first case study is a grape vine pruning robot [5]. Grape vines are pruned by selectively cutting canes on each plant. The robot system, shown in Fig. 1, consists of a mobile platform which straddles a row of vines, and images them with a trinocular stereo camera rig as the platform moves. A computer vision system builds a 3D model of the vines, an AI system decides which canes to prune, and a six degree-of-freedom robot arm makes the required cuts. The main challenge for the computer vision is building a sufficiently complete and structurally correct 3D model of the vines that the AI can make good decisions about where to cut, and so that a path planner can plan a collision-free path for the robot arm to make the required cuts. The project started in 2010, and has employed up-to five full time researchers and developers (including graduate students). 27 people have worked on the project in total.

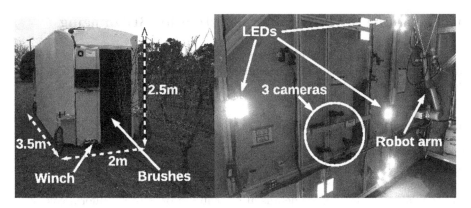

**Fig. 1.** The pruner robot's mobile platform completely covers the vines, blocking out sunlight (left). Inside are high-powered LEDs, three cameras, a robot arm, a generator and the desktop PC that runs all of the software (right).

## 3.2   DIET Machine

The second case study is the Digital Image-based Elasto-Tomography (DIET) system, a prototype breast cancer screening system [2]. A breast is imaged by five cameras while being vibrated, the computer vision system estimates the 3D surface motion, and the observed surface motion is used to infer the internal stiffness of the breast, hence identifying tumours. The computer vision system first identifies the profile of the breast in each image, and reconstructs a 3D surface model from these profiles. The surface motion is measured using dense optical flow, then the 3D surface motion is given by fusing the optical flow with the reconstructed surfaces. The current DIET machine is shown in Fig. 2. The project started in 2005 and has employed up-to five full time researchers and developers.

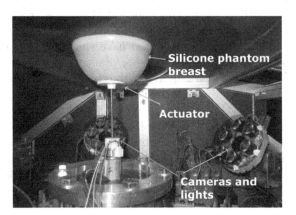

**Fig. 2.** The DIET machine, showing two of the five cameras, the actuator, and a silicone phantom breast. The machine measures 80 cm by 71cm by 38cm.

# 4  Designing a Multi-camera System for 3D Imaging

This section examines each design decision made when building a multi-camera system for 3D reconstruction. The case studies are used to illustrate how each decision affects the performance of the system as a whole.

## 4.1  Imaging Enclosure Design

Imaging enclosures allow lighting levels to be controlled, and provide a uniform background. If lighting levels vary too much, the cameras cannot simultaneously image the brightest parts of the scene (where the sensor is saturated) and the darkest parts (where details are lost in sensor noise). Uniform-coloured backgrounds aid the foreground/background segmentation—the greater the difference between the distributions of colours on the foreground and background, the simpler, and hence more robust, the segmentation will be.

Designing imaging enclosures for 3D imaging is hard because 3D objects cast shadows, different parts are at different distances and angles to different lights (which affects their appearance from different viewpoints), and because multiple overlapping images from different viewpoints are required to give a complete 3D reconstruction.

Canopies are often used by agricultural robots to shade direct sunlight, or to completely control illumination [18,20]. For outdoor applications where it is hard to control lighting, many robots operate only at night, to avoid interference from sunlight, and where active illumination ensures that only subjects close to the light source are illuminated [8,15,21].

The pruner robot's canopy consists of a rigid MayTec[2] aluminium frame with sheet aluminium cladding. Sunlight is excluded with brushes. The inside is lined with corflute corrugated plastic, then covered with photo studio non-reflective chroma-key blue backdrop paper[3]. The background provides a seamless matte blue background behind the vines. The problem with this design is that the background is not sufficiently rigid: sagging causes dark shadows which are detected as vines (especially if background subtraction-based methods are used for segmentation), and wrinkles in the cardboard have similar scale and appearance to wires. These artefacts increase the number of incorrectly detected vines, and increase the levels of robustness required throughout the computer vision software. In addition, the background is fragile and prone to damage, rendering the entire system is unusable. A more robust design would use a rigid backing.

The first pruner robot did not use brushes, and was unusable during daylight, as sunlight shone on both the vines and background. The current design can be used in all weather, however small shafts of sunlight get through gaps in the brushes (Fig. 7). These saturated regions are detected and masked out before foreground/background segmentation.

---

[2] http://www.maytec.org/.

[3] http://savageuniversal.com/products/seamless-paper/studio-blue-seamless-paper.

The first DIET machine used a shiny black perspex background. The segmentation was unreliable, as the measured colour of specular reflections off the background was often the same as the breast, because the boundary between the machine and breast was in shadow, and because seams close to the breast edge were detected instead of the breast edge. The current machine uses a matte black perspex background and adds a marker to the actuator (a black and white circle). Together with lighting improvements, (Sect. 4.3) this makes the segmentation far simpler and more reliable (Fig. 6).

## 4.2  Camera Positioning and Lens Selection

Lenses should be selected and cameras should be positioned so that enough of the subject is visible, and so that stereo baselines are sufficient to achieve the required accuracy. This can be a challenging trade-off, as longer baselines give greater accuracy only if feature matching and localisation errors do not also increase (e.g. because of appearance changes).

To design the pruner robot, we built a software model of the canopy, and tested lenses and camera positions within this model so that the entire height of the vine was visible, from the highest canes down to the middle of the trunk, with the blue background behind the vines. Vine dimensions were provided by vineyard managers. Unfortunately vines are often lower than the system was designed for, and some rows cannot be modelled because the vine's head regions are outside the camera's field of view. Moving cameras is not simple, because positions are restricted by the frame, lenses and background position. Even when the vines can be modelled, reconstruction is more likely to fail for important low canes that are only partially visible. This introduces structural errors into the reconstruction, and affects pruning decisions. The next iteration of the pruner robot will be designed based on field measurements.

The first DIET machine also missed data because of poor camera positioning—data from one-in-three patients from an early clinical trial were unusable because the breast was partly outside the camera's field of view.

## 4.3  Lighting Design

Lighting must be setup so that scenes are evenly illuminated, so that objects' appearances do not change depending on their position [12]. This is challenging when imaging 3D scenes where the camera's field of view or depth of field are large, where shadows and occlusions are common, or where object's are shiny and show specular reflections—these make the same object appear differently in different cameras, and may saturate the sensor. Even when objects are pure Lambertian reflectors (their colour appears the same from any viewpoint), obtaining even illumination is challenging, because light intensity drops quadratically with distance from the light source, and because many light sources' (including "wide angle" machine vision lights) intensities drop as the angle from the light's centre increases. [4] used a computer model of the pruner robot and the DIET machine to design more effective lighting configurations, which give more even lighting throughout the scene. For the pruner robot, the optimal configuration of 14 light sources provides illumination levels that vary by 48 % across the vines, whereas a simpler configuration (a regular grid) give 70 % variation, and a single point source gives 96 % variation. The most effective configurations position lights in a 2 m wide ring around the cameras. Having more light sources provides more robustness to shadows, and positioning most light sources further away from cameras mitigates the effect of light intensity decreasing with depth.

For the DIET machine, the optimal configuration of five light sources is a large circle just above the cameras. The existing machine was modified to obtain this configuration: lighting variation between the top and bottom of the breast fell from 40 % to 30 % when 5 of 30 LEDs were masked out.

## 4.4   Light Sources

Machine vision lights and strobes are widely available, however current commercial solutions don't have the wide-angle and high intensity that the pruner robot and DIET machine require [4]. It is straightforward to build suitable lights from high-power wide angle (or "unlensed") LEDs, heat sinks, and commercially-available "constant current" LED power supplies, however obtaining constant light levels is challenging, due to artefacts remaining from the mains AC power input [12], and because power supplies modulate the voltage to keep the current constant while the LED's resistance changes with temperature. On the pruner robot, an additional capacitor on each power supply smooths out high frequency flickering[4]. On the DIET machine, the amount of light is not proportional to the strobe duration, and varies with the LED's temperature. Updates to the strobe duration are damped to prevent large lighting fluctuations.

## 4.5   Camera Data Acquisition

Camera manufacturers provide APIs and example programs for grabbing images from cameras onto a PC, and these example programs are easy to adapt for particular applications. The challenges in data acquisition are synchronising cameras and getting large amounts of image data onto the computer and saved to disk. Camera APIs also provide control of colour balance, shutter time, etc. (see supplementary material[5] for a summary of trade-offs required). Auto-exposure and auto white balance cause image changes that make registering views more challenging. The pruner robot has controlled lighting, so these settings can be fixed. The DIET machine also fixes these settings, but controls brightness and saturation by changing the strobe duration.

When imaging moving objects, cameras are usually triggered simultaneously so that images are captured at the same moment. Images may also need to be synchronised with strobes, or other events. The most common synchronisation method is to use the camera's external trigger input. Alternatively, several

---

[4] http://www.red.com/learn/red-101/flicker-free-video-tutorial.
[5] Also available from http://hilandtom.com/PSIVT2015-Checklist.pdf.

Firewire (1394a/b) cameras using the same card, or multiple cards[6], can be synchronised in software. External triggering is used by commercially-available multi-camera systems[7]. The synchronisation methods used in the pruner robot and DIET machine are summarised in Fig. 3. Note that modern computer hardware allows uncompressed or losslessly-compressed high resolution (1.3 megapixel) images from three cameras to be saved to disk at over 30 frames per second, without the need for specialised hardware or video capture cards. Although the pruner robot's computer vision system only requires 2.5 frames per second, the high framerates provide data that is useful for evaluating the effects of different robot speeds [5].

**Fig. 3.** Examples of image acquisition hardware setups. Modern USB3 and 1394b cameras allow high data-rate uncompressed imaging without specialised hardware (i.e. capture cards).

## 4.6   Lens Focus

Important properties of machine vision lenses are their focal length, or zoom (which is usually fixed), and their aperture and focus (which are either fixed, have manual control, or can be controlled automatically). The aperture controls how much light the sensor receives, and the focus setting controls the range of depths for which the image is in focus, for a given aperture. The wider the aperture, the more light is received, but the narrower the range of depths for which the subject is in focus. Setting up lenses so that objects are in focus

---

[6] https://www.ptgrey.com/KB/10574.

[7] e.g. http://www.4dviews.com/.

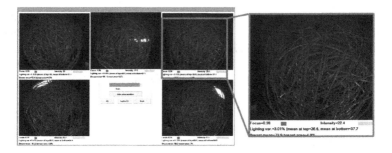

**Fig. 4.** The DIET machine's GUI for setting camera focus. The wire ball has sharp edges at a range of depths. The focus and aperture are set to maximise the sum of squared differences between neighbouring pixels.

wherever they appear is challenging: if one part of the scene is in focus, others might not be, and manually inspecting an entire high-resolution image for focus is hard (inspecting edges to verify they aren't blurred requires zooming-in). A slight loss of focus might be acceptable for some applications (although spatially-varying focus is generally undesirable) as many computer vision methods, e.g. optical flow, invariant features, use Gaussian blurring to reduce the effects of noise and quantisation.

Contrast detection autofocus [14] is commonly used in consumer cameras. The camera scans across a range of focus settings, and selects the setting that maximises a measure of focus. The effect of a lens being out of focus is to blur the image, and hence an image that is out of focus has smaller differences between neighbouring pixels. For a fixed aperture, a simple and effective [14] measurement of focus is the sum of squared differences between neighbouring pixels. If this focus measure is displayed as a camera captures images, the lens's focus can be adjusted until this measure is maximised (Fig. 4).

The challenge in using fixed-focus cameras for 3D machine vision is that the range for which they are in focus must include the full range of depths where the object might be visible, across the entire image. A sum-of-squared-differences focus measure is only valid for a fixed scene, so this scene should contain textured objects at a suitable range of depths, across the entire image.

The pruner robot's cameras were setup by imaging vines (which have many sharp edges at the required range of depths), using both a GUI that automatically measures focus, and manual inspection of the images. There are still regions of the images which are not well focussed throughout the required depth range, and the wire detector performs poorly in these regions, impacting the completeness of the 3D reconstruction of the scene.

The first DIET machine was focussed manually. Images from an early clinical trial are out of focus in places, which probably impacts the accuracy of skin motion tracking. The current DIET machine uses a GUI to automatically measures focus. The focus is set while imaging a wire ball (Fig. 4), because the wire ball has sharp edges at the entire range of depths where the breast surface could be. The optimal parametrisation for optical flow estimation has a larger kernel size (blur size) for computing derivatives for the current machine than the old machine, because images are now sharper.

Autofocus cannot generally be used for 3D computer vision because changing the focus may change the camera calibration. Objects move around the image when the focus on the lenses on the pruner robot is adjusted (10MP, $\frac{2}{3}''$, 5mm Goyo C-mount lenses).

## 4.7   Camera Calibration

Camera calibration is the process of finding a transform (a camera matrix, and possibly distortion parameters) that maps the position of objects in the world to their coordinates in the image. Zhang's [24] widely-used method for camera calibration involves imaging a calibration target of known dimensions (often a checkerboard pattern), locating the calibration target in each image, then optimising calibration parameters and estimated target positions to minimise the image distance between projected and measured target positions (e.g. using Levenberg-Marquardt optimisation). The calibration models the effects of the lens and sensor size (intrinsic parameters), and the position and orientation of each camera (extrinsic parameters).

OpenCV [16] has routines for detecting calibration targets, and for calibrating pairs of stereo cameras. Both the pruner robot and the DIET machine use OpenCV's target detection routines, then use Zhang's method to estimate the intrinsic and extrinsic parameters for all of the cameras jointly, avoiding any loss of accuracy from combining multiple pairwise calibrations.

OpenCV's calibration pattern detector is most reliable when calibration targets have a large white border[8]. A problem with checkerboard and dot-pattern targets is that their orientation is ambiguous—the target can be detected in different orientations (180 degrees out) in images from two cameras. If undetected, this will cause the calibration to fail. Either marking the calibration target (e.g. adding a coloured mark to one corner, which can be detected and used to resolve the ambiguity), or using a non-symmetric pattern (e.g. [17]) prevents this problem. Some printers scale the width and height of a target differently; this is another potential point-of-failure to check.

Capturing calibration target images in a range of poses throughout the region where objects are imaged is important for obtaining accurate calibrations [17]. Robot Operating System (ROS) has guidelines for capturing target images for stereo calibration[9]. Figure 5 shows the effect of the number of target images on the accuracy of the calibration of one pair of cameras on the pruner robot. For ground truth, we assume that a calibration with 802 targets detected in both images is accurate (so the error estimates are actually lower bounds). We

---

[8] http://docs.opencv.org/modules/calib3d/doc/camera_calibration_and_3d_reconstruction.html.

[9] http://wiki.ros.org/camera_calibration/Tutorials/StereoCalibration.

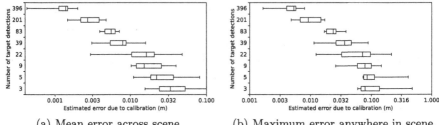

(a) Mean error across scene.    (b) Maximum error anywhere in scene.

**Fig. 5.** Effect of the number of targets detected in both images of a stereo pair on the accuracy of reconstructed 3D points. Box plots show the range, quartiles, and median errors, from 15 calibrations for each number of targets. The scene is 2 m wide, with a depth of field of 0.5 m to 1.75 m.

then estimated calibrations from randomly-selected subsets of the detected targets. The accuracy of the subset calibrations is measured by sampling 3D points throughout the region of interest, projecting to 2D using the accurate calibration, reconstructing with the subset calibration, and comparing to the original 3D points. Higher accuracy is obtained when more images are used: capturing less than fifty images gives average errors of more than 1 cm in the 3D reconstruction due to calibration alone. The ROS guidelines, and [17], note that common practice is to capture dozens of target images, to give a suitable distribution of pattern positions for every pair of cameras. For multi-camera systems, we recommend capturing up-to a thousand images of a pattern, so that hundreds of targets are detected for every pair of cameras. In our experiment, 1352 stereo images of the target were captured, and the target was detected in both images 802 times. For the DIET machine, over 600 images are needed to ensure there are at least 40 detections for every pair of cameras. Capturing this many images is an inexpensive way of reducing the errors in the 3D reconstruction.

Obtaining an accurate camera calibration is challenging. [17] write that "Reliable and accurate camera calibration usually requires an expert intuition to reliably constrain all of the parameters in the camera model", and conduct human trials to show that accurate calibrations are rarely obtained by novices. They propose using a software tool to guide users through the calibration process for a single camera. Much early research on the DIET project was on camera calibration with various calibration objects ([7], Chaps. 4 and 5), however the methods were ill-conditioned (often using only two faces of a single object), and an accurate calibration was rarely obtained [6]. We recommend capturing images of standard calibration targets whenever data is collected, both to validate that the calibration is unchanged, and so that cameras can be calibrated retrospectively if necessary.

For multi-camera systems for 3D reconstruction, an extra consideration is the choice of the origin. Often one camera is chosen to be at the origin (e.g. in OpenCV's routines), but it may be more appropriate to choose an origin which aligns the 3D model with the machine. The pruner robot selects the origin so

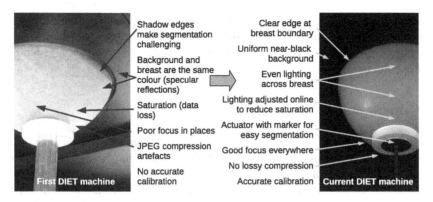

**Fig. 6.** Hardware changes have improved several different aspects of the DIET machine, so that the images can now be used to track skin texture rather than requiring markers.

that the volume in which the vines move is an axis-aligned box. This simplifies the application of constraints on the 3D reconstruction, which come from the physical dimensions of the machine, and means that if one camera moves and loses calibration, other calibrations (the robot arm position, and a laser line structured light scanner) do not change. The DIET machine's origin is in the machine's centre, and is aligned with the patient, so that tumour positions can be matched between the patient and the 3D model.

## 4.8 Camera Mounting

Calibrating cameras is time consuming, and undetected calibration changes are a potential source of error. It is important to attach cameras securely so that the calibration does not change. Most machine vision cameras are mounted with either a single $\frac{1}{4}''$ tripod screw, or four small bolts. The tripod mount screws

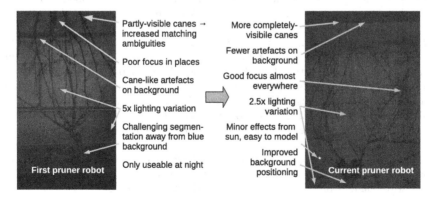

**Fig. 7.** Hardware changes have improved several different aspects of the vine images from the first pruner robot to the current system.

are prone to loosening if cameras are knocked, and are easy to over-tighten, so we recommend using the four small bolts. The pruner robot has a metal guard protruding beyond the lens (Fig. 1) to prevent people or vines from accidentally knocking the lenses.

## 5   Conclusion

Designing camera systems for 3D computer vision is challenging because of the many factors affecting image quality. Carefully designed hardware systems result in simpler and more robust computer vision systems, and shorter development times. In two case studies, two different teams of engineers made similar mistakes when setting up multi-camera systems for 3D reconstruction, and these mistakes have unnecessarily delayed both projects. In this paper we have listed and analysed many of the design considerations that must be taken into account when designing multi-camera systems, so that future projects don't make the same mistakes. These recommendations are summarised in a checklist and a list of trade-offs, which is provided as supplementary material[10].

## References

1. Bac, C.W., van Henten, E.J., Hemming, J., Edan, Y.: Harvesting robots for high-value crops: State-of-the-art review and challenges ahead. J. Field Robot. **31**(6), 888–911 (2014)
2. Botterill, T., Lotz, T., Kashif, A., Chase, G.: Reconstructing 3D skin surface motion for the DIET breast cancer screening system. IEEE Trans. Med. Imaging **33**(5), 1109–1118 (2014)
3. Botterill, T., Mills, S., Green, R.: Refining essential matrix estimates from RANSAC. In: Proceedings Image and Vision Computing New Zealand, pp. 1–6. Auckland (2011)
4. Botterill, T., Mills, S., Green, R., Lotz, T.: Optimising light source positions to minimise illumination variation for 3D vision. In: 3D Imaging, Modeling, Processing, Visualization and Transmission (3DIMPVT), Second International Conference on, pp. 222–229, Zurich. IEEE (2012)
5. Botterill, T., Paulin, S., Green, R., Williams, S., Lin, J., Saxton, V., Mills, S., Chen, X., Corbett-Davies, S.: A robot system for pruning grape vines. Pre-print under review (2015). http://hilandtom.com/tombotterill/pruner-preprint.pdf
6. Brown, R., Chase, J., Hann, C.: A pointwise smooth surface stereo reconstruction algorithm without correspondences. Image Vis. Comput. **30**(9), 619–629 (2012)
7. Brown, R.G.: Three-dimensional motion capture for the diet breast cancer imaging system. Ph.D. thesis, Department of Mechanical Engineering, University of Canterbury (2008)
8. Chéné, Y., Rousseau, D., Lucidarme, P., Bertheloot, J., Caffier, V., Morel, P., Belin, É., Chapeau-Blondeau, F.: On the use of depth camera for 3D phenotyping of entire plants. Comput. Electron. Agric. **82**, 122–127 (2012)

---

[10] Also available at http://hilandtom.com/PSIVT2015-Checklist.pdf.

9. Chum, O.: Two-view geometry estimation by random sample and consensus. Ph.D. thesis, Czech Technical University in Prague (2005)
10. Czeranowsky, C., Schwr, M.: How do you assess image quality? Technical Report, Basler (2015)
11. Erol, A., Bebis, G., Nicolescu, M., Boyle, R.D., Twombly, X.: Vision-based hand pose estimation: A review. Comput. Vis. Image Underst. **108**(1), 52–73 (2007)
12. Jahr, I.: Handbook of Machine Vision, chap. Lighting in Machine Vision, pp. 73–203. Hornberg, A (ed.) Wiley (2006)
13. McConnell, S.: Code Complete, 2nd edn. Microsoft Press, Redmond (2004)
14. Mir, H., Xu, P., van Beek, P.: An extensive empirical evaluation of focus measures for digital photography. In: Sampat, N., Tezaur, R., Battiato, S., Fowler, B.A. (eds.) IS&T/SPIE Electronic Imaging Digital Photography X, vol. 9023, pp. 90230I. International Society for Optics and Photonics (2014)
15. Nuske, S., Wilshusen, K., Achar, S., Yoder, L., Narasimhan, S., Singh, S.: Automated visual yield estimation in vineyards. J. Field Robot. **31**(5), 837–860 (2014)
16. OpenCV Computer Vision Library. http://opencv.org/
17. Richardson, A., Strom, J.P., Olson, E.: Aprilcal: Assisted and repeatable camera calibration. In: Intelligent Robots and Systems (IROS), pp. 1814–1821. IEEE, Tokyo (2013)
18. Silwal, A., Gongal, A., Karkee, M.: Apple identification in field environment with over the row machine vision system. Agric. Eng. Int.: CIGR J. **16**(4), 66–75 (2014)
19. Telljohann, A.: Introduction to building a machine vision inspection. In: Hornberg, A (ed.) Handbook of Machine Vision, pp. 35–71. Wiley (2006)
20. Vision Robotics Corporation (2015). http://visionrobotics.com/
21. Wang, Q., Nuske, S., Bergerman, M., Singh, S.: Automated crop yield estimation for apple orchards. In: Desai, J.P., Dudek, G., Khatib, O., Kumar, V. (eds.) Experimental Robotics. STAR, vol. 88, pp. 745–758. Springer, Heidelberg (2013)
22. Wedel, Andreas, Pock, Thomas, Zach, Christopher, Bischof, Horst, Cremers, Daniel: An improved algorithm for TV-$L^1$ optical flow. In: Cremers, Daniel, Rosenhahn, Bodo, Yuille, Alan L., Schmidt, Frank R. (eds.) Statistical and Geometrical Approaches to Visual Motion Analysis. LNCS, vol. 5604, pp. 23–45. Springer, Heidelberg (2009)
23. Zhang, B., Huang, W., Li, J., Zhao, C., Fan, S., Wu, J., Liu, C.: Principles, developments and applications of computer vision for external quality inspection of fruits and vegetables: A review. Food Res. Int. **62**, 326–343 (2014)
24. Zhang, Z.: A flexible new technique for camera calibration. T. Pattern Anal. Mach. Intell. **22**(11), 1330–1334 (2000)

# Attribute Based Affordance Detection from Human-Object Interaction Images

Mahmudul Hassan$^{(\boxtimes)}$ and Anuja Dharmaratne

School of IT, Monash University Malaysia,
Jalan Lagoon Selatan, 47500 Bandar Sunway, Malaysia
{mahmudul.hassan,anuja}@monash.edu

**Abstract.** The detection of functional classification of an object, which is also referred as affordance is a prevalent researched topic in the domain of robotics and computer vision. Typically, the approaches regarding fine level affordance (affordance related to core traits of an object i.e. graspability, rollability etc.) detection are often disjoint from the techniques in higher level affordance detection (i.e. drinkability or pourability of a glass). In this paper, we have proposed an attribute based technique for higher level affordance detection which integrates methods from both fine level and high level affordance detection, and takes three prominent contexts (Human, Object and the ambience) into account. It further represents each of these contexts as a cluster of attributes rather than singular entities thus making the affordance detection process more semantic, efficient, dynamic and general.

**Keywords:** Affordance · Attribute transfer · Modelling mutual contexts

## 1 Introduction

The astonishing stature that separates humans from other forms of biological entities is its inherited capability of learning. Our ancestors were been able to excavate the potentiality of fire woods, coals and other objects that afford, not only to lit fire but also cooking. In plain context the tacit knowledge of learning the usability of different objects is an integral part of the success story of the human race. In the domain of Computer vision and Artificial intelligence, it is a very important topic of research. Though it sounds very linearly simple, but the research paradigm in this field is quite multidimensional and encompasses both fine level and high level layers. For example in practical robotics the premier focus is to master the identification of fine level usability of the objects (i.e. rolling ability, graspability etc.) in contrast in computer vision the focus is on some higher tones. Here researchers are more inclined to detect higher level usage of objects (i.e. how a human performs interaction with a computer). The way these two streams of researches are approached is often disjoint. In this paper we have tried to portray the benefits of combining the techniques from these two sects of researches. In broader terms we have used objects basic visual features

© Springer International Publishing Switzerland 2016
F. Huang and A. Sugimoto (Eds.): PSIVT 2015 Workshops, LNCS 9555, pp. 220–232, 2016.
DOI: 10.1007/978-3-319-30285-0_18

(SIFT, textons, edges, color histograms etc.) to infer some higher level attributes such as its material, shape, size, visual parts etc. to find the objects usability. We have also tried to boost the detection process of objects usability by using different contexts such as the human demonstration (i.e. body poses) and ambient objects (i.e. the induced effects of one object to others). We believe this integration of attributes and contexts make the detection process more robust, semantic and general.

### 1.1 Psychological Perspective of Affordance

The theory of affordances [1] was introduced as a theory of direct perception, which can account for findings in development psychology. According to [2,3] An affordance is an intrinsic property of an object. In broader sense, affordance is the functional classification of objects. Affordance is neither subjective nor objective. It depends on the object being interacted, the human who interacts and the ambient objects. For example, a chair is meant for sitting for an adult but for a toddler it does not have the sitting affordance rather, it has the climbing affordance. On the other hand when we see a mug alone, we infer its affordance as drinkable but as soon as we see a pitcher on top of it, its affordance space accumulate the pourable affordance as well. Hence, it is evident to state that, the affordance of an object is basically the mapping of these three contexts.

### 1.2 Ontological Classification of Affordance Detection Techniques

Generally affordance prediction has been approached from two different prospective. Firstly, the methods that learn the affordances passively by observing the humans interacting with the objects [4–6] and on the other hand methods that use objects visual features (appearance) to learn the objects affordance [7,8]. Usually the first category of works does focus on the high level affordance detection where the later works concentrate on the finer level affordances. But these conventional views towards affordance detection are now changing and there is a new trend where the researchers are combing both human actions and objects perception for affordance detection [9–13]. These mixed approaches are primarily used for higher level affordance detection [4], [9–12], [14–16]. Apart from robust affordance detection, these blended techniques, emerging substantially as an adequate tool for solving different problems in the computer vision domain, such as: classifying object categories [9,10,17], scene understanding [18–20], segmenting sub-activities from continues high level activity [21], robot navigation [22], robot-object placement [23], anticipation of human action [24–26] etc.

There is also a variant ontological prospective in the fine level affordance modeling approaches. It is visual features [7,8] versus the physical attributes of the objects [27–29]. In the visual features based approaches, finer features like Corner points (SIFT, HOG), edges, texture (textons), colour (Histograms) etc. are extracted from the objects and directly mapped with affordances. In contrast with that, in the attribute approaches, the finer level visual features are used to predict mid-level physical attributes [27] such as size, shape, material, weight etc. A key advantage of attribute based detection is the ability to leverage object properties which are shared by multiple affordances, leading to more effective generalization to novel examples and the ability to learn new affordances with limited training data.

### 1.3  Challenges in Affordance Detection

There are fundamental difficulties in both the above mentioned approaches. Regarding direct perception approaches, there are three major issues. Firstly, affordances are not actually determined-in the physical sense, by visual features, rather by the physical properties of the objects [30]. Whether an object can roll or not depends on the shape of the object; whether it can be pushed is influenced by its material properties. Secondly, the visual features are very much vulnerable from different imaging and viewing phenomenon. Thirdly, a liability of the direct perception based methods is that there is no form of knowledge transfer between the object classes. In contrast, problems with the approaches related to human demonstration (both considering the objects and without it) are that, human could perform same actions with different objects (like mopping a table has similar body pose of ironing). Moreover a single object can have multiple affordances, therefore it is required to train the system with each action-object pair and consequently the training process becomes very complex and lacks the generalization (Systems usually suffers if an unseen object or body poses are considered). Another challenge in demonstration based affordance detection is that affordance depends on the 'attributes' of a person; it will not remain same for all the humans with same object. For example if the height of the human changes, than the possible actions that can be performed with a certain object will vary. Even the attributes of the objects and the ambient environment (other objects nearby) influence the affordance of an object.

## 2  Overview and Contribution of Our Approach

The core competency of our model is that it takes into account mutual contexts of the attributes of the object, the human and the ambient environment. We believe the affordance detection process of an object can improve substantially by considering the mutual relations of these contexts and their attributes. For example a knife has the primary affordance of cutting. But if the knife is made of plastic, it does not afford to cut harder objects. Here, we can see the change in the attributes can change the affordance space of that object. Similarly if we see a human is performing a stirring action with a knife, than the affordance space of the knife again changes and accumulate stirring. It shows that the body poses of the human helps us to infer the affordance of an object. Again if we see a knife is near to a food can or a biscuit tin, it may afford opening them. Here the ambient object induced the change in the affordance space of the object. Especially from static images, where unlike the video no temporal references are available this process of mutual context analysis helps the system to develop a knowledge base and detect affordance more robustly. Furthermore, since our approach of affordance detection represents these contexts as sets of different attributes rather than considering them stand alone entities. It ensures the system to be more semantic, efficient, dynamic and general. For instance, in accordance with the previous example, we do not detect/classify the object as knife rather we describe it as a rectangle, metal object with sharp edges. We describe the objects with different attributes according to [30]. Simultaneously we also describe the mutual relations of the objects with human and the other ambient objects by a number of attributes [29]. Have used this attribute based representation for unseen object class detection, and they claim that this method does possess knowledge transfer mechanism and helps to recognize unseen and untrained objects. We have find that attributes are shared between the spectrums of different affordance classes also. For instance most of the objects that afford drinking (i.e. mug, cup, bottle, flask etc.) are cylindrical in shape and may have a handle (i.e. a mug handle).

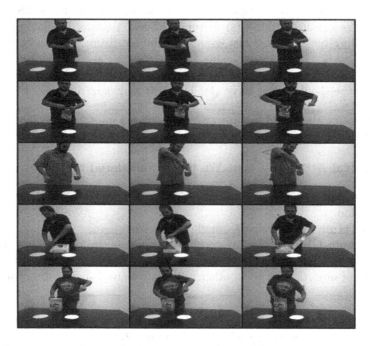

**Fig. 1.** Opening a jar (top row), Opening a poly(2nd row), Opening a drinks can (3rd row), Opening packet (4th row) and opening a tin with knife (bottom row).

In this paper, we have portrayed the importance the attributes in detecting human object interactions robustly. For instance, in Fig. 1 we consider opening object actions. We have multiple opening scenarios, like: opening a can, opening a packet of potato chips, opening a flask, opening a box etc. We analyzed and inferred that, we have different opening body poses for different object classes due to the difference in the attributes of the objects. At the same time the attributes related to the human and the ambient objects are also important. Our work is inspired by the works of [27] and [31]. The main focus of this research is to combine the different notions of affordance modeling in order to achieve a robust affordance model. We are using the visual features to predict mid-level physical attributes of the objects and as well as the human and the environment (the other nearby objects). After that we use the physical attributes as the features to learn (both as parameters and the structure) our high level affordance detection model.

Our novel attribute based affordance model, encompasses two types of features related to the human, object and the environment in order to model objects affordances, namely: visual features and physical attributes [27]. The visual features are the basic image features extracted from images.

**The Visual Features that We have Considered are:**

- **For the Objects:** SURF(speeded up robust features) features, HOG (Histograms of oriented gradients) features, Edges, Textons, Region properties of bounding boxes, Image histograms, Euclidian distances between multiple objects.
- **For the Subjects:** Human body joint coordinates from kinect, the angles between the shoulder-arm-wrist (for both left and right hand).

After extracting the visual features, we have created multiple classifiers to classify physical attributes related to both objects, human and ambient objects.

**The Physical Attributes that We have Considered are:**

- **For the objects:** Material, Aspect ratio, Height, Objects shape, Color, Orientation.
- **For the Human:** Body poses, angle of the arms.
- **For Human-Object:** The distance of the object(s) from each body joints.
- **For Object-Object:** Euclidean distance between multiple objects, the spatial location of objects relative to other objects, relative aspect ratio of multiple objects.

The flow of our system is as follow: First, given images with human interacting with different objects, we select the bounding boxes of the object(s). After that we extract the base features from the selected bounding boxes (objects). We also extract the body joint coordinates of the human and the angles of the arms. Then we use these base features to train mid-level attribute classifiers. Subsequently we use these mid-level attributes as the features of our overall affordance model. In the test scenario, given the bounding boxes (the user provide the bounding boxes), the system can detect affordance of the selected objects more semantically and robustly.

# 3  Attribute Based Affordance Model

Our affordance model can be formalized by the following statements:

- The affordance space as $(\lambda)$ where $(\lambda)$ is a m dimensional vector.
- Objects visual features are $(\theta)$ where $(\theta)$ is a t dimensional vector.
- Objects physical attributes are $(\alpha)$ where $(\alpha)$ is a p dimensional vector.
- Body pose features are $(\beta)$ where $(\beta)$ is a q dimensional vector.
- Humans physical attributes are $(\gamma)$ where $(\gamma)$ is a r dimensional vector.
- Ambient environment attributes are $(\varepsilon)$ where $(\varepsilon)$ is a s dimensional vector.

Then, we can formalize the model as:

$$(\lambda) = f(\alpha, \beta, \gamma, \varepsilon, \theta) \tag{1}$$

So, if we want to represent the relations of these components in a joint distribution form:

$$p(\lambda, \alpha, \beta, \gamma, \varepsilon, \theta) = p(\lambda \mid \alpha, \beta, \gamma, \varepsilon, \theta)p(\alpha \mid \beta, \gamma, \varepsilon, \theta)p(\beta \mid \gamma, \varepsilon, \theta)p(\gamma \mid \varepsilon, \theta)p(\varepsilon \mid \theta)p(\theta) \tag{2}$$

$$p(\lambda, \alpha, \beta, \gamma, \varepsilon, \theta) = p(\lambda \mid \alpha, \gamma, \varepsilon)p(\alpha \mid \theta)p(\gamma \mid \beta)p(\varepsilon \mid \beta, \theta) \tag{3}$$

So, for finding the affordance, we can marginalize $\lambda$, and we get by the variable elimination method:

$$p(\lambda \mid \alpha, \beta, \gamma, \varepsilon, \theta) = \sum_{\alpha}\sum_{\beta}\sum_{\gamma}\sum_{\varepsilon}\sum_{\theta} p(\lambda, \alpha, \beta, \gamma, \varepsilon, \theta) \tag{4}$$

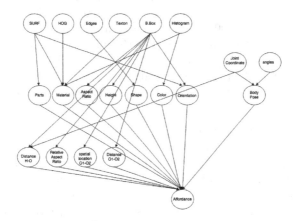

**Fig. 2.** The Bayesian network representation of the proposed model.

Currently we have implemented our attribute based affordance model with Bayesian network (Fig. 2). We have compared two different scoring methods for learning the structural model of the Bayesian network, (1) Bayesian Information Criterion and (2) Greedy hill climbing (optimization). For inference we have used junction tree algorithm. Apart from the Bayesian network, we have also implemented our model with a multi-dimensional SVM and K-Nearest neighbor algorithm. In the case of the KNN, we have tested the model with Euclidean, Cityblock and Minkowski distances. We have used the N-fold validation for cross validation of the model.

## 3.1   Attribute Classifiers

As we have stated earlier the mid-level attributes are classified from the base features. We have implemented separate classifiers for each of the mid-level physical attributes.

**Parts Classification.** We have introduced a novel physical attribute called Parts. It is basically distinct image patches of objects which are common in all the objects in a single affordance class. Different object classes can have a single affordance, we argue that though these object classes are dissimilar in visual aspects but they do share some common parts. For example the objects which have affordance of drinking or pouring usually have visual patches of a handle. These parts have proved to be a robust cue in our affordance detection model. For the part class detection, first we manually selected distinct parts of different objects (5 parts per affordance class) class that has a common affordance, and then these parts (patches) are cropped out from the object images (we have used 750 patches for each part class). In Fig. 3, different selected parts of the sitting affordance class is shown. These cropped patches are finally used as features for our part class detection classifier. We have trained our parts detection classifier with Bag of features algorithm, where we have trained the classifier with vocabulary sizes from 1000 to 4000 with 500 interval and final set the vocabulary size to 1500 (1500 clusters) since it has given us the highest accuracy. Patch size was set to [64 128 192 256] for the optimal efficiency. Finally a multiclass SVM is used as classification algorithm. The grid points (SURF points) were selected densely for the bag of features algorithm. For the part classification, we have achieved 71 % accuracy.

**Material Classification.** For the material detection of different objects (what the object is made of), we have extracted SURF points, HOG features, Textons [32] and image histograms from object images. These features are then subsequently given as inputs into a K-nearest neighbor classifier to detect materials. We have considered material type of: paper, metal, plastic, poly, food, glass and cloth. We have tested and compared our classifier with [32] and [33] where Textons and Fractals are used, and found that, our classifier is more suitable in detecting materials of real life objects. Real life objects have a lot of labeling and undesired interest points. Though [32] performs better with basic surface texture images of different materials but loses accuracy for real life objects. For the material classification images of each object class (1200 images per object class).

**Fig. 3.** The common parts in diverse objects that afford sitting.

**Aspect Ratio and Height.** Aspect ratio is a popular measurement that gives us a cue about the size of an object with some sort of scale invariance perspective. We have calculated the aspect ratio as the width over height of the selected bounding boxes. On the other hand height is simply the vertical height of the selected bounding box. We have simply used the measurements of the object bounding boxes as features for our aspect ratio and the height classifier, where a multi class SVM is used for training and classification.

**Shape Classification.** Shape is a very prominent feature of the object. Most of the time, the objects which share same affordances have their shape in common. We have classified shapes as Square, Cylindrical, round and 3D-boxy. We have first extracted the edges of the objects via Prewitt edge detector filter. Then we performed some morphological operations on the edges and the Hough matrix is calculated. Finally a curve fitting algorithm is used to find the similarities in shapes. We have compared our algorithm with [34], and observed that our efficiency is lower than it, but due to the complexity, we remained with our algorithm as the difference of the efficiency is not substantial. Currently, our shape detection classifiers accuracy is 78 %.

**Color and Orientation Classification.** For color classification, we have used simple histograms of the object images as features. The histograms of all Red channel, Green channel and Blue channel are used. The KNN algorithm is used to implement the classifier.

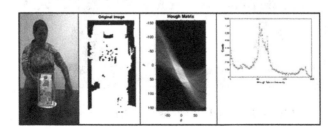

**Fig. 4.** The process of shape detection.

For the orientation, we have initially used rotating patches of object images with 900 variations and trained a SVM based object classifier to classify the Horizontal and Vertical version of the objects. But the classifier has not performed optimally due to different traits of object poses. Moreover, the object detection itself is a substantial challenge to handle and increases the complexities of the overall system to a significant. For time being, as the main focus of the current work is to depict the effects of attributes in the overall affordance detection we have manually input the orientation values of the object in our final affordance classifier.

**Body Pose Classifier.** For the objective to implement a robust body pose classifier, we had to first identify and segment human body from a cluttered scene. Then we had to acquire the body joint locations. We have first tried to use simple Part based method [35], where week classifiers are trained with HOG features to detect and track the body parts, but the results were not optimal. Later we have used the Microsoft Kinect sensor to capture RGBD images and got the articulated human skeleton by Kinect SDK. The Kinect Skeleton viewer function, that is a part of the support package of Kinect SDK, provides coordinates 20 body joints of detected human body robustly. We have considered only the 10 joints of the upper body (Shoulder center, Head, Left shoulder, Right shoulder, Left elbow, Right elbow, Left wrist, Right wrist, Left hand, Right hand). We have used these coordinates as the base features for human action pose detection. Our novel action pose detection classifier is inspired by the concept of [34]. We have represented the body poses not by the mere coordinates of the body joints but by the distance of each body joints from the head. This method helped us to offset view point variance and translation variance to some extent. For the classification we have used the K-NN algorithm.

For the human action pose classifier, we have also used the inner angles of the elbows as base features. The vector dot products were used to determine the angle (Fig. 5).

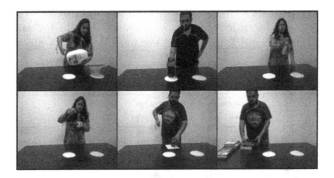

**Fig. 5.** Detected skeletons in different actions.

**Human-Object Distance Classifier.** For Human-Object distance attribute classifier, we have used the Euclidian distance between the object centroid and the human body joints (Skeleton joints, acquired by Kinect) as base features. A multidimensional SVM is used for the classification.

**Relative aspect Ratio and Relative Spatial Location Classifier.** Relative aspect ratio and relative spatial locations are the attributes which are only used in the case of multiple objects. Relative aspect ratio implies the comparison of the aspect ratio of one object to other. We have find that the relative aspect ratio gives us a useful insight of objects affordance in a multiple object setting. For instance for a pouring action, most of the time the larger object is Pour from object and the smaller object is pour to object. For the relative spatial location, we have decomposed each image frames into nine cells as: Center, Above, Bottom, Left, Right, Upper left, Upper right, Bottom left, Bottom right. We index the locations of each object by these cells and use them as base features.

## 4   Training and Inference

For training the affordance classifier, we have used 9632 images of different actions being performed. There are 22 action classes performed with 43 objects. 4 subjects (person) were used to perform the actions. The action classes are: (1) Spraying in the body (2) Chopping (3) Cutting (4) Drinking with both hands (5) Drinking with single hands (6) Eating snacks (7) Eating fruit (8) Ironing (9) Mopping (10) Opening poly (11) Opening box (12)Opening can (13) Opening jar (14) Opening packet (15) Opening tin (16) Pouring with both hands (17) Pouring with single hands (18) Spraying in the air (19) Stacking with both hands (20) Stacking with a single hand (21) Waving (22) Answering mobile phone.

For the training of the attributes (material, shape, color and parts) classifiers, we have used features extracted from objects images from different datasets such as 'Caltech 256' and SHORT-100 and also downloaded images from the web. For testing our model we have used Human-Object-Interaction images from known object classes (The affordance classes which are trained) and also novel object classes. In the test dataset, there are also instances where the objects are partially occluded and the human body poses are unknown.

## 5   Model Evaluation

We have tested our model with a test dataset of 3 subjects performing 22 actions with 18 objects. Total instances of the test dataset are 528. We have initially implemented our model with SVM, KNN and Bayesian networks to find the most suitable algorithm for our model (pilot testing). Due to the best empirical results, a Bayesian Network based method is used for constructing the final affordance model. For comparing these three algorithms a prototype test dataset was used which is different from the actual testing dataset.

We have compared our model with two baseline models. For baseline (a) we tested the models which used only human body pose as features for Human-Object-Interaction detection and for base line (b), the models which used the mutual contexts of human body poses and detected object classes for affordance detection.

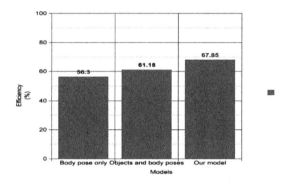

**Fig. 6.** The comparison of our model with the base lines.

Figure 6 shows the comparative results of our attribute based affordance model with the base lines. The overall accuracy of our model is 67.85 %. This accuracy is acquired by testing the model with both known and unseen object classes. It shows the accuracy and generalization improves a substantial amount with our model. The overall accuracy of the base line algorithms are 61.18 % (Objects and body poses) and 56.3 % for body pose only.

# 6    Conclusion

In contrast with the current affordance detection models in the computer vision and robotics domain, we have implemented our model by considering mutual contexts of Human-Object and ambient environment. Moreover we have represented each context with a cluster of attributes. Due to the inclusion of multiple contexts and knowledge sharing capability within the attributes our model proved to perform more efficiently, semantically and has generalization quality.

# References

1. Gieseking, J.: The People, Place, and Space Reader. Hilldale, New Jersey (2014)
2. Helbig, H.: Action observation can prime visual object recognition. Exp Brain Res. **200**(3–4), 251–258 (2009)
3. Kjellstrm, H.: Visual object-action recognition: Inferring object affordances from human demonstration. Comput. Vis. Image Underst. **115**(1), 81–90 (2011)
4. Manuela, V., Rybski, P., von, F.: FOCUS: A generalized method for object discovery for robots that observe and interact with humans. In: Proceedings of the 2006 Conference on Human-Robot Interaction, IEEE Press, Salt Lake City (2006)

5. Zhu, Y., Fathi, A., Fei-Fei, L.: Reasoning about object affordances in a knowledge base representation. In: Fleet, D., Pajdla, T., Schiele, B., Tuytelaars, T. (eds.) ECCV 2014, Part II. LNCS, vol. 8690, pp. 408–424. Springer, Heidelberg (2014)
6. Grabner, H., Gall, J., Gool, V.: What makes a chair a chair? In: 2011 IEEE Conference on Computer Vision and Pattern Recognition (CVPR), Colaradao (2011)
7. Castellini, C., Tommasi, T., Noceti, N., Odone, F., Caputo, B.: Using object affordances to improve object recognition. IEEE Trans. Auton. Mental Dev. **3**, 207–215 (2011)
8. Moldovan, B., Moreno, P., van Otterlo, M., Santos-Victor, J., De Raedt, L.: Learning relational affordance models for robots in multi-object manipulation tasks. In: 2012 IEEE International Conference on Robotics and Automation (ICRA), pp. 4373–4378, Minnesota (2012)
9. Roudposhti, K.K., Dias, J.: Probabilistic human interaction understanding. Pattern Recognit. Lett. **34**, 820–830 (2013)
10. Desai, C., Ramanan, D., Fowlkes, C., Kesselman, C.: Discriminative models for static human-object interactions. In: 2010 IEEE Computer Society Conference on Computer Vision and Pattern Recognition Workshops (CVPRW) (2010)
11. Bangpeng, Y., Fei-Fei, L.: Modeling mutual context of object and human pose in human-object interaction activities. In: 2010 IEEE Conference on Computer Vision and Pattern Recognition (CVPR), San Francisco (2010)
12. Bangpeng, Y.H., Liu, M., Philipose, M., Pettersson, H., Sun, M.: Subsequences. J. Vis. Commun. Image Representation **25**, 719–726 (2014)
13. Bangpeng, Y., Xiaoye, J., Khosla, A., Lin, A.L., Guibas, L., Fei-Fei, L.: Human action recognition by learning bases of action attributes and parts. In: 2011 IEEE International Conference on Computer Vision (ICCV), pp. 1331–1338, Barcelona (2011)
14. Packer, B., Saenko, K., Koller, D.: A combined pose, object, and feature model for action understanding. In: 2012 IEEE Conference on Computer Vision and Pattern Recognition (CVPR), pp. 1378–1385. Rhode Island (2012)
15. Ikizler-Cinbis, N., Sclaroff, S.: Object, scene and actions: combining multiple features for human action recognition. In: Daniilidis, K., Maragos, P., Paragios, N. (eds.) ECCV 2010, Part I. LNCS, vol. 6311, pp. 494–507. Springer, Heidelberg (2010)
16. Peursum, P., Venkatesh, S., West, G.A.W., Bui, H.H.: Object labelling from human action recognition. In: Proceedings of the First IEEE International Conference on Pervasive Computing and Communications, pp. 399–406, Dallas (2003)
17. Jakkula, V., Diane, J.C.: Mining sensor data in smart environment for temporal activity prediction. In: Poster session at the ACM SIGKDD, San Jose, CA (2007)
18. Jiang, Y., Saxena, A.: Infinite latent conditional random fields. In: 2013 IEEE International Conference on Computer Vision Workshops (ICCVW), pp. 262–266. IEEE (2013)
19. Jiang, Y., Saxena, A.: Modeling high-dimensional humans for activity anticipation using Gaussian process latent CRFS. In: Robotics: Science and Systems, San Francisco (2014)
20. Koppula, H., Gupta, R.: Saxena: ILearning human activities and object affordances from rgb-d videos. Int. J. Rob. Res. **32**, 951–970 (2013)
21. Sun, J., Moore, J., Bobick, A., Rehg, J.: Learning visual object categories for robot affordance prediction. Int. J. Robot. Res. **29**, 174–197 (2009)
22. Jiang, Y., Koppula, H., Saxena, A., Kesselman, C.: Hallucinated humans as the hidden context for labeling 3D scenes. In: 2013 IEEE Conference on Computer Vision and Pattern Recognition(CVPR), pp. 2993–3000, Portland (2013)

23. Koppula, H., Ashutosh, S.: Learning spatio-temporal structure from rgb-d videos for human activity detection and anticipation. In: Proceedings of the 30th International Conference on Machine Learning (ICML-13). Atlanta (2013)

24. Koppula, H.S., Saxena, A.: Anticipating human activities for reactive robotic response. In: 2013 IEEE/RSJ International Conference on Intelligent Robots and Systems (IROS), p. 2071, Tokyo (2013)

25. Jiang, Y., Saxena, A.: Modeling high-dimensional humans for activity anticipation using gaussian process latent CRFs. In: Proceedings of Robotics: Science and Systems, San Francisco (2014)

26. Hermans, T., Rehg, J.M., Bobick, A.: Affordance prediction via learned object attributes. In: IEEE International Conference on Robotics and Automation (ICRA): Workshop on Semantic Perception, Mapping, and Exploration, pp. 181–184. IEEE Press, New York (2011)

27. Lampert, C.H., Nickisch, H., Harmeling, S.: Learning to detect unseen object classes by between-class attribute transfer. In: IEEE Conference on Computer Vision and Pattern Recognition, pp. 951–958. Florida (2009)

28. Farhadi, A., Endres, I., Hoiem, D., Forsyth, D.: Describing objects by their attributes. In: IEEE Conference on Computer Vision and Pattern Recognition, pp. 1778–1785, Florida (2009)

29. Sun, J.: Learning visual object categories for robot affordance prediction. Int. J. Robot. Res. **29**, 174–197 (2010)

30. Gupta, A., Davis, L.S.: Objects in action: An approach for combining action understanding and object perception. In: IEEE Conference on Computer Vision and Pattern Recognition, 17–22, Minnesota (2007)

31. Leung, T., Malik, J.: IRepresenting and recognizing the visual appearance of materials using three-dimensional textons. Int. J. Comput. Vis. **43**, 29–44 (2001)

32. Varma, M., Zisserman, A.: A statistical approach to texture classification from single images. Int. J. Comput. Vis. **62**, 61–81 (2005)

33. Salve, S.G., Jondhale, K.C.: Shape matching and object recognition using shape contexts. In: 2010 3rd IEEE International Conference on Computer Science and Information Technology (ICCSIT), pp. 471–474 (2010)

34. Lu, X., Chia-Chih, C., Aggarwal, J.K.: Human detection using depth information by kinect. In: 2011 IEEE Computer Society Conference on Computer Vision and Pattern Recognition Workshops (CVPRW), Colarado (2011)

# Mathematical and Computational Methods in Biomedical Imaging and Image Analysis (MCBMIIA 2015)

# Hardware Acceleration of SVM-Based Classifier for Melanoma Images

Shereen Afifi[1(✉)], Hamid GholamHosseini[1], and Roopak Sinha[2]

[1] Department of Electrical and Electronics Engineering,
School of Engineering, Auckland University of Technology,
Private Bag 92006, Auckland 1142, New Zealand
{safifi, hgholamh}@aut.ac.nz
[2] School of Computer and Mathematical Sciences,
Auckland University of Technology, Auckland 1142, New Zealand
rsinha@aut.ac.nz

**Abstract.** Melanoma is the most aggressive form of skin cancer which is responsible for the majority of skin cancer related deaths. Recently, image-based Computer Aided Diagnosis (CAD) systems are being increasingly used to help skin cancer specialists in detecting melanoma lesions early, and consequently reduce mortality rates. In this paper, we implement the most compute-intensive classification stage in the CAD onto FPGA, aiming to achieve acceleration of the system for deploying as an embedded device. A hardware/software co-design approach was proposed for implementing the Support Vector Machine (SVM) classifier for classifying melanoma images online in real-time. The hybrid Zynq platform was used for implementing the proposed architecture of the SVM classifier designed using the High Level Synthesis design methodology. The implemented SVM classification system on Zynq demonstrated high performance with low resources utilization and power consumption, meeting several embedded systems constraints.

**Keywords:** SVM · CAD · Melanoma · FPGA · Hardware implementation

## 1 Introduction

Computer Aided Diagnosis (CAD) systems have been widely used in practical clinical settings to support detecting of a variety of cancers. Melanoma is considered the most dangerous form of skin cancer, in which early diagnosis could help in dramatically decreasing morbidity and mortality [1]. Therefore, CAD of medical images should be efficiently exploited for improving early detection of melanoma lesion. Developing such systems for this kind of applications is extremely computationally demanding with high inherent parallelism. Systems with parallel processors could be useful for accelerating such computations, but they are energy intensive and have prohibitively high costs. Special purpose hardware such as reconfigurable hardware is promising for speeding up computations, and provides High Performance Computing (HPC) at lower cost and lower power consumption [2].

© Springer International Publishing Switzerland 2016
F. Huang and A. Sugimoto (Eds.): PSIVT 2015 Workshops, LNCS 9555, pp. 235–245, 2016.
DOI: 10.1007/978-3-319-30285-0_19

Field-Programmable Gate Arrays (FPGAs) are powerful massively parallel processing reconfigurable devices which are used for achieving necessary performance of embedded systems with efficient utilization of hardware resources. FPGAs have recently shown very high performance for many applications in image processing [3]. Accordingly, FPGA is considered to be a suitable hardware platform with HPC for implementing image processing algorithms with inherent parallelism essential for developing CAD of medical images.

This work is based on our previous work and experimental results achieved for diagnosis of melanoma [4]. A dataset of benign and malignant melanoma images was used for our CAD system which was collected from available web resources. The typical structure of a CAD system includes image pre-processing, segmentation techniques, features extraction, and classification schemes. Some methods were employed for the pre-processing, segmentation, and feature extraction stages in our previous work. Regarding the classification stage, five different classifiers (k-Nearest Neighbors, Multi-Layer Perceptron, Naive Bayes, Random Forest and Support Vector Machine (SVM)) were tested and evaluated for their classification performance for the selected melanoma dataset. From the performance comparison of the five classifiers that was based on different feature selection sets, the SVM classifier demonstrated a better accuracy than others for classification and diagnosis of melanoma [4]. Therefore, the SVM classifier is considered in this work as being one of the best classifiers with high accuracy level of classifying medical images targeting melanoma detection. Also, the SVM model is a powerful machine learning tool that was used for efficient classification in various applications [5].

Regarding acceleration of the CAD system, the classification scheme is the most compute-intensive task among the diagnosis process. For that reason, this work proposes hardware acceleration for the SVM classifier by implementing its time-consuming computation part on FPGA as a coprocessor targeting deployment in an embedded environment.

A hardware/software co-design is proposed for running the compute intensive task included in the SVM algorithm on the FPGA. The system is implemented on the recent Xilinx Zynq device using the High-Level Synthesis (HLS) design methodology. Experimental results demonstrated minimal hardware resources utilization and low power dissipation which increases the potential of developing an embedded CAD system.

The main contribution of this paper is proposing a hardware/software co-design of the SVM classifier implemented on the hybrid Zynq platform using HLS, targeting melanoma detection.

This paper is organized in five sections. Related work of hardware implementations for the SVM classifier on FPGA is briefly introduced in Sect. 2. The proposed hardware accelerated SVM classification system is presented in Sect. 3, followed by experimental results and discussion presented in Sect. 4. Finally, Sect. 5 provides the conclusion and future work.

## 2 Related Work on FPGA-Based Implementation of SVM Classifier

There are several research works that aim to speed up SVM classification in hardware. Various techniques of hardware architectures and designs have been implemented on FPGAs achieving high level of parallelization as well as high performance computing. Many work exploit the FPGA-based parallel systolic array architecture in their implementations [6–10], resulting in good results of classification speedups that mostly outperformed implementations on GPPs/CPUs. In addition, other work employed the Dynamic Partially Reconfiguration (DPR) technique [7, 11], achieving higher flexibility and design space expansion besides gaining speedups. Some research work also recorded relatively good results of power consumption reduction [6] as a result of using the DPR technology.

Interestingly, many studies adopted the multiplier-less approach [9, 12–14], where expensive multipliers required for computations are replaced with conventional adders and/or shifters in order to decrease hardware complexity. Similarly, others [15, 16] utilized the hardware-friendly kernel function for simplifying the hardware design by using also the simple shift and add operations instead of resource consuming multiplications. As a result of multiplier-less implementation, significant reduction in hardware resources utilization was achieved. In addition, remarkable power consumption decrease was demonstrated [9, 12, 13, 17].

Moreover, the common pipelining technique was used in many previous hardware designs [11–13, 17–26], taking advantage of the parallel processing capabilities of the FPGA that led to throughput increase of the implemented classification process. Some researchers designed a pipeline stage for common and shared multipliers required for computations to decrease usage of duplicate multiplications [19, 20]. Some pipelined designs [21, 23] were based on exploiting the embedded Intellectual Property (IP) cores in the FPGA device for efficient resources utilization. Furthermore, a pipelined adder structure was used by various designs [11–13, 17, 18, 24].

To summarize, existing implementations in literature for SVM classification target improvement in accelerating the classification process. However, there is a trade-off between classification accuracy and high performance, and meeting embedded systems constraints of low level of area and power consumption. Due to some simplifications performed for the hardware implementation, some loss in accuracy rating occurs [12, 13, 17, 26, 27]. Moreover, most designs in existing literature were implemented on old versions of FPGAs and only a very limited number used recent ones [9, 28].

To the best of our knowledge no implementation for SVM classification phase exists in literature that applies a hardware/software co-design technique taking advantage of the hybrid architecture of the Zynq platform. In addition, all previous implementations were designed by using the traditional Hardware Description Language (HDL), which is time consuming and requires expert hardware designers. However, HLS design methodology has been lately recommended for simplifying hardware designs for coprocessors on FPGAs [29]. Moreover, no hardware implementation on FPGA exists in literature for the SVM model to classify melanoma clinical images. Consequently, this work proposes a hardware/software co-design method for implementing SVM classifier on Zynq device using HLS method targeting detection of melanoma with high performance and low cost.

# 3  The Hardware Accelerated SVM Classification System

## 3.1  Selected Platform and Design Tools

One of the most recent platforms; Zynq-7000 was selected for implementing the SVM classifier on hardware, complying with latest technology to reach an efficient embedded system. The Zynq-7000 All Programmable System on Chip (SoC) is one of the recent platforms provided by Xilinx [30]. It has a hybrid structure of combining an ARM Cortex-A9 dual-core as a Processing System (PS) with the hardware programmability of an FPGA as a Programmable Logic (PL) in a single SoC, which simplifies embedded systems realization. Accordingly, the Zynq-7000 SoC is considered to be a promising platform for creating hand-held medical imaging systems with high performance and low cost.

Additionally, Xilinx offers very efficient and powerful software tools; Vivado Design Suite that simplifies the embedded system design process on a single device, integrating a SoC with an FPGA [31]. Interestingly, Xilinx provides an efficient tool employing the HLS design methodology, which simplifies programing FPGA with high-level language than using the traditional HDL [29]. Thus, using the HLS method is recommended for significantly decreasing FPGA development time and effort [32]. Therefore, the Xilinx Vivado HLS tool was exploited to develop a hardware accelerator for speeding up the SVM classification process to be integrated within a single SoC and realized on the recent Zynq device.

## 3.2  The Employed SVM Classifier

One of the common SVM classifiers algorithms; SVM-light was used to implement a case study to classify given melanoma images. SVM-light is an available simple classifier implemented in C language which is used for classification in different domains [33]. The C source code of the SVM-light classification phase was adopted for the hardware implementation using the HLS method in order to reach hardware acceleration.

The classification code of a binary SVM-light model with linear kernel was studied for customization in order to reach a synthesizable code capable of realization on hardware. Thus for synthesizing, the dynamic memory allocation scheme that applies in the C code for flexibility was changed for static fixed sizes targeting our case study. As a result, the algorithm became dependent on the maximum number of selected features (vector size) which should be defined before implementation.

The most time and resource consuming part in the classification algorithm is the accumulation/summation of multiplication of vectors that exists in the main decision function (1) using linear kernel (dot product) [34].

$$\text{Class (s)} = \text{sign} \left( \sum \alpha_i y_i (x_i \cdot s) + b \right) \tag{1}$$

To classify a new pattern known as $s$ in (1), the dot product between $s$ and every support vector known as $x_i$ should be computed (the other parameters $\alpha$, $y$, and $b$ are specified from the training phase). Therefore, the hardware/software co-design technique was applied to partition the algorithm efficiently between software and hardware, reaching acceleration of the accumulation of vectors multiplication part via running on hardware.

### 3.3    The Hardware Implemented Classification System

The structure of the proposed SoC is depicted in Fig. 1, where the HLS IP module is developed first with Vivado HLS tool and then extracted to be implemented as a hardware coprocessor onto the PL part of the Zynq platform. By using the HLS tool with C/C++ language, a top function module was designed as an HLS IP for executing the complicated for loop of the multiplication process. However, the rest of the code was designed as a test bench calling the top function by passing the vectors as formal parameters after reading data of trained SVM model from a file and doing some processing for preparing data.

For optimizing the formal parameters of the top function as being ports of the hardware IP, the AXI4-Stream interface was assigned for the IO interfaces by using the Vivado HLS Directives in order to stream the data of the two vectors for the multi-plication into the HLS IP. Also, the AXI-lite bus was assigned for the designed function for controlling the IP core and data flow for the system via communicating with the ARM processor in PS part of the Zynq platform as shown in Fig. 1. The double data type of the vectors was replaced by float to be able to generate an AXI4-Stream interface for streaming data between the ARM CPU in PS and the hardware coprocessor in PL. Also, the source file was changed to a CPP file instead of C as to support HLS stream protocol. As a result, some minor changes in the code were placed using the Vivado HLS tool to satisfy the above reaching high parallelism.

In order to achieve a good level of optimization, some of the different available directives in the HLS tool for optimization were applied for the top module. Pipelining and unrolling the loop for the accumulation of multiplication process were assigned and tested targeting an increase in data throughput rate. Based on synthesis results, **333** clock cycles were required for processing without applying any optimization directives for the loops in the proposed function. However, **169** and **204** clock cycles were required when using unroll and pipeline directives respectively.

Regarding hardware resources utilization estimated from synthesizing, **1514** FF slices, **1794** LUTs and **5** DSP48Es were utilized from using unroll directive, whilst **650** FF slices, **878** LUTs and **5** DSP48Es from using pipeline one. Actually, there is a trade-off between the data throughput and area, as by using the unroll directive more utilization of FF and LUT resources took place than using the pipeline one. However by using the recent Zynq device of large optimized size, the main aim is to increase

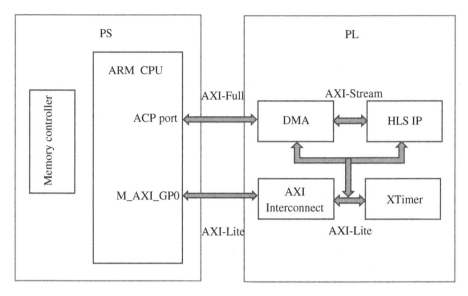

**Fig. 1.** The block diagram of the proposed system on Zynq

data throughput with reasonable resources utilization. Accordingly, the unrolling technique was exploited for the implementation, reaching throughput improvement.

After successfully synthesizing the code and applying optimization and interfaces directives, the HLS IP core for the classifier was successfully co-simulated and exported as an RTL implementation using the Vivado HLS tool. Then, the exported HLS IP was integrated into a proposed system that was designed by the help of Vivado Design tool as shown in Fig. 2.

The HLS IP core was connected as a Zynq coprocessor to be implemented in the PL with the ARM processor in PS via ACP (Accelerator Coherency Port) using DMA (Direct Memory Access). The DMA controller IP was used to control the data transfer between the ARM processor and the HLS IP through the AXI4-Stream protocol. The ACP is a 64-bit AXI slave interface on the snoop control unit, which provides an asynchronous cache-coherent access point directly from the Zynq PL to the PS with low latency path [35]. Also, an AXI-Timer is instantiated for measuring the number of clock cycles required by the cores for performance comparisons.

Finally after synthesizing, implementing and generating the bitstream of the proposed design using the Vivado tool, it was exported for the Software Development Kit (SDK) to be ready for running the application on Zynq device.

## 4    Experimental Results

Considering the SVM-light source code as a case study, it was tested first in the Microsoft Visual Studio before using for hardware implementation. The trained model was generated and tested targeting detection of melanoma using a dataset of 356 clinical images (168 melanoma images). The trained data consists of feature extracted

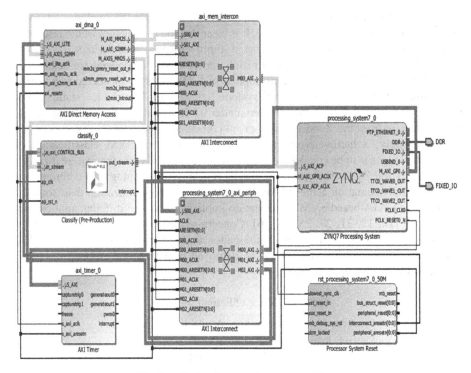

**Fig. 2.** The implemented system on Zynq

data based on HSV color channels after applying some of the pre-processing and segmentation schemes for the images, with maximum number of features equal to 27 [4]. The default linear kernel function and default parameters for the SVM-light program were used for the training and classification phases. The trained model generated was exploited by the classification phase for the hardware implementation.

The recent Xilinx Vivado 2015.1 Design Suite was used for implementing the proposed system on the Xilinx XC7Z020CLG484-1 target device of the Zynq-7 ZC702 Evaluation Board. An application of classifying a test image was written in C as a test bench to run the exported implementation on the Zynq device by the aid of the Xilinx SDK tool. The experimental results for the hardware accelerator were the same as the software classification results, which showed that the classification accuracy level is preserved without any reduction from the hardware acceleration in contrast to some previous work in literature [13, 17].

In addition, the AXI Timer IP core was used to compare the total computing time between running the designed code for the accumulation of multiplication process on ARM processor in PS and on hardware downloaded in PL part. The ARM processor was running at 666.67 MHz, whilst the computing logic was running at 50 MHz. The total number of clock cycles for the software on ARM processor was **64998**, while for the AXI DMA and hardware accelerator it was **549** cycles. Accordingly, the acceleration factor was greater than **110**, which showed significant acceleration from the implemented hardware accelerator for the proposed SVM classification system.

Table 1 summarizes the hardware resources utilization for the implementation of the proposed system on the Zynq device. It is clear that the percentages of the resources utilization are very low, showing significant improvement in area savings.

Moreover, the power consumption results reported by Vivado tool are detailed in Table 2. The on-chip total power consumption of **1.738** watts is considered to be small reasonable value, meeting embedded systems constraints. The device static power consumes 9 % of the total, whilst the remainder 91 % was dissipated by the dynamic activity mostly from the Zynq PS component compared to other on-chip components.

Interestingly, a hardware/software co-design method of SVM classification of melanoma images is to be considered as an added work in literature that was realized on the recent hybrid Zynq platform using the HLS design methodology. In addition, our proposed implementation achieved lower hardware resources utilization than some of the previous FPGA-based SVM classification implementations of different applications in literature [10, 12, 21, 23, 25, 34, 36]. Concerning power consumption, our implementation demonstrated lower power dissipation than other related work [6, 12, 25]. Therefore, our proposed system could be deployed as a real-time embedded system dedicated for melanoma detection.

**Table 1.** Device utilization summary.

| Resource | Utilization | Available | Utilization % |
|---|---|---|---|
| Slice FF Registers | 5584 | 106400 | 5.25 |
| Slice LUTs | 4373 | 53200 | 8.22 |
| Memory LUT | 173 | 17400 | 0.99 |
| BRAM | 3 | 140 | 2.14 |
| DSP48 | 5 | 220 | 2.27 |
| BUFG | 1 | 32 | 3.13 |

**Table 2.** On-Chip components power consumption summary.

| On-Chip Component | Power (mW) |
|---|---|
| Clocks | 9 |
| Logic | 3 |
| Signals | 4 |
| BRAM | 2 |
| DSPs | <1 |
| PS7 | 1565 |
| Total Dynamic Power | 1584 |
| Device Static Power | 154 |
| Total On-Chip Power | 1738 |

## 5  Conclusion

A hardware/software co-design was realized for the SVM classification of melanoma images on the hybrid Zynq platform. The system, implemented on a recent Zynq device, achieved higher throughput and significant savings in area and power consumption. The implemented SVM classifier was significantly accelerated by hardware, preserving the classification accuracy without any loss. Additionally by using the HLS design methodology, the development time and effort was reduced and embedded system design was simplified.

Hardware implementation results of higher performance, lower resources utilization and less power consumed meet the embedded systems constraints. Consequently, a real time embedded system for efficient melanoma images classification could be realized by the proposed system, achieving high performance and low cost.

For future work, the proposed embedded system of the SVM classifier could be applied for different classification problems. Also, additional work on hardware architectures would be explored targeting an increase in the SVM classification accuracy. Additionally, the proposed hardware/software co-design realized on Zynq with the HLS design method could be adopted by hardware designers for implementing their embedded systems. Moreover, other optimization techniques like DPR technique could be employed for further design optimizations.

Finally, the hardware implementation on FPGA could be extended in the future for other computationally demanding parts in the process, aiming to reach an efficient real-time CAD system for enhancing early detection of melanoma with high performance and low cost.

# References

1. Sathiya, S.B., Kumar, S.S., Prabin, A.: A survey on recent computer-aided diagnosis of melanoma. In: International Conference on Control, Instrumentation, Communication and Computational Technologies (ICCICCT), pp. 1387–1392. IEEE Press (2014)
2. Véstias, M.P.: High-performance reconfigurable computing granularity. In: Encyclopedia of Information Science and Technology, pp. 3558–3567 (2015)
3. Saegusa, T., Maruyama, T., Yamaguchi, Y.: How fast is an FPGA in image processing? In: International Conference on Field Programmable Logic and Applications, FPL 2008 pp. 77–82. IEEE Press (2008)
4. Sabouri, P., GholamHosseini, H., Larsson, T., Collins, J.: A cascade classifier for diagnosis of melanoma in clinical images. In: 36th Annual International Conference of the IEEE Engineering in Medicine and Biology Society (EMBC), pp. 6748–6751. IEEE Press (2014)
5. Nayak, J., Naik, B., Behera, H.: A comprehensive survey on support vector machine in data mining tasks: applications & challenges. Int. J. Database Theory Appl. **8**, 169–186 (2015)
6. Patil, R., Gupta, G., Sahula, V., Mandal, A.: Power aware hardware prototyping of multiclass SVM classifier through reconfiguration. In: 2012 25th International Conference on VLSI Design (VLSID), pp. 62–67. IEEE Press (2012)
7. Hussain, H.M., Benkrid, K., Seker, H.: Reconfiguration-based implementation of SVMclassifier on FPGA for classifying microarray data. In: Proceedings of the Annual InternationalConference of the IEEE Engineering in Medicine and Biology Society (EMBS), pp. 3058–3061 (2013)
8. Hussain, H., Benkrid, K., Seker, H.: Novel dynamic partial reconfiguration implementations of the support vector machine classifier on FPGA. Turkish Journal of Electrical Engineering and Computer Sciences (2014)

9. Mandal, B., Sarma, M.P., Sarma, K.K.: Implementation of systolic array based SVM classifier using multiplierless kernel. In: Proceedings of the 16th International Conference on Automatic Control, Modelling & Simulation (ACMOS 2014), pp. 288–294. WSEAS Press (2014)

10. Kyrkou, C., Theocharides, T.: A parallel hardware architecture for real-time object detection with support vector machines. IEEE Trans. Comput. **61**, 831–842 (2012)

11. Papadonikolakis, M., Bouganis, C.: Novel cascade FPGA accelerator for support vector machines classification. IEEE Trans. Neural Netw. Learn. Syst. **23**, 1040–1052 (2012)

12. Kyrkou, C., Theocharides, T., Bouganis, C.-S.: An embedded hardware-efficient architecture for real-time cascade support vector machine classification. In: 2013 International Conference on Embedded Computer Systems: Architectures, Modeling, and Simulation (SAMOS XIII), pp. 129–136. IEEE Press (2013)

13. Kyrkou, C., Bouganis, C.-S., Theocharides, T., Polycarpou, M.M.: Embedded hardware-efficient real-time classification with cascade support vector machines. IEEE Trans. Neural Netw. Learn. Syst. **27**, 99–112 (2015)

14. Shuai, X., Yibin, L., Zhiping, J., Lei, J.: Binarization based implementation for real-time human detection. In: 2013 23rd International Conference on Field Programmable Logic and Applications (FPL), pp. 1–4 (2013)

15. Ruiz-Llata, M., Guarnizo, G., Yébenes-Calvino, M.: FPGA implementation of a support vector machine for classification and regression. In: The 2010 International Joint Conference on Neural Networks (IJCNN), pp. 1–5. IEEE Press (2010)

16. Jallad, A.H.M., Mohammed, L.B.: Hardware Support Vector Machine (SVM) for satellite on-board applications. In: 2014 NASA/ESA Conference on Adaptive Hardware and Systems (AHS), pp. 256–261 (2014)

17. Kyrkou, C., Theocharides, T., Bouganis, C.S.: A hardware-efficient architecture for embedded real-time cascaded support vector machines classification. In: Proceedings of the 23rd ACM international conference on Great lakes symposium on VLSI, pp. 341–342. ACM (2013)

18. Papadonikolakis, M., Bouganis, C.-S.: A novel FPGA-based SVM classifier. In: International Conference on Field-Programmable Technology (FPT), pp. 283–286. IEEE Press (2010)

19. Kim, S., Lee, S., Cho, K.: Design of high-performance unified circuit for linear and non-linear SVM classifications. J. Semicond. Technol. Sci. **12**, 162–167 (2012)

20. Koide, T., Anh-Tuan, H., Okamoto, T., Shigemi, S., Mishima, T., Tamaki, T., Raytchev, B., Kaneda, K., Kominami, Y., Miyaki, R., Matsuo, T., Yoshida, S., Tanaka, S.: FPGA implementation of type identifier for colorectal endoscopie images with NBI magnification. In: 2014 IEEE Asia Pacific Conference on Circuits and Systems (APCCAS), pp. 651–654 (2014)

21. Ago, Y., Nakano, K., Ito, Y.: A classification processor for a support vector machine with embedded DSP slices and block RAMs in the FPGA. In: 2013 IEEE 7th International Symposium on Embedded Multicore Socs (MCSoC), pp. 91–96 (2013)

22. Mizuno, K., Terachi, Y., Takagi, K., Izumi, S., Kawaguchi, H., Yoshimoto, M.: Architectural study of HOG feature extraction processor for real-time object detection. In: 2012 IEEE Workshop on Signal Processing Systems (SiPS), pp. 197–202 (2012)

23. Komorkiewicz, M., Kluczewski, M., Gorgon, M.: Floating point hog implementation for real-time multiple object detection. In: 2012 22nd International Conference on Field Programmable Logic and Applications (FPL), pp. 711–714. IEEE Press (2012)

24. Liu, C., Qiao, F., Yang, X., Yang, H.: Hardware acceleration with pipelined adder for support vector machine classifier. In: 2014 Fourth International Conference on Digital Information and Communication Technology and it's Applications (DICTAP), pp. 13–16. IEEE Press (2014)

25. Pietron, M., Wielgosz, M., Zurek, D., Jamro, E., Wiatr, K.: Comparison of GPU and FPGA implementation of SVM algorithm for fast image segmentation. In: Kubátová, H., Hochberger, C., Daněk, M., Sick, B. (eds.) ARCS 2013. LNCS, vol. 7767, pp. 292–302. Springer, Heidelberg (2013)

26. Kryjak, T., Komorkiewicz, M., Gorgon, M.: FPGA implementation of real-time head-shoulder detection using local binary patterns, SVM and foreground object detection. In: 2012 Conference on Design and Architectures for Signal and Image Processing (DASIP), pp. 1–8 (2012)

27. Qasaimeh, M., Sagahyroon, A., Shanableh, T.: FPGA-based parallel hardware architecture for real-time image classification. IEEE Trans. Comput. Imag. **1**, 56–70 (2015)

28. Kelly, C., Siddiqui, F.M., Bardak, B., Woods, R.: Histogram of oriented gradients front end processing: an FPGA based processor approach. In: 2014 IEEE Workshop on Signal Processing Systems (SiPS), pp. 1–6. IEEE Press (2014)

29. Vivado High-Level Synthesis, http://www.xilinx.com/products/design-tools/vivado/integration/esl-design.html

30. Zynq-7000 All Programmable SoC, http://www.xilinx.com/products/silicon-devices/soc/zynq-7000.html

31. Vivado Design Suite, http://www.xilinx.com/products/design-tools/vivado.html

32. Ning, M., Shaojun, W., Yeyong, P., Yu, P.: Implementation of LS-SVM with HLS on Zynq. In: 2014 International Conference on Field-Programmable Technology (FPT), pp. 346–349. IEEE Press (2014)

33. Joachims, T.: Making large-scale SVM learning practical. In: Schölkopf, B., Burges, C., Smola, A. (eds.) Advances in Kernel Methods: Support Vector Learning. MIT Press, Cambridge (1999)

34. Mahmoodi, D., Soleimani, A., Khosravi, H., Taghizadeh, M.: FPGA simulation of linear and nonlinear support vector machine. J. Softw. Eng. Appl. **4**, 320–328 (2011)

35. Zynq-7000 All Programmable SoC Acccelerator for Floating-Point Matrix Multiplication using Vivado HLS, http://www.xilinx.com/support/documentation/application_notes/xapp1170-zynq-hls.pdf

36. Qasaimeh, M., Sagahyroon, A., Shanableh, T.: FPGA-based parallel hardware architecture for real-time image classification. IEEE Trans. Comput. Imag. **1**, 56–70 (2015)

# Automatic Pose Estimation Using Contour Information from X-Ray Images

Erik Soltow[(✉)] and Bodo Rosenhahn

Institut Für Informationsverarbeitung, Leibniz Universität Hannover,
Hannover, Germany
`soltow@tnt.uni-hannover.de`

**Abstract.** An automatic approach to model-based pose estimation is presented that only uses given, segmented contours in X-ray images. The pose estimation based on Fourier Descriptors is extended to an arbitrary, calibrated stereo setup and eliminates the need for a manually given initialization. To further refine the pose, local and global optimization schemes that minimize the distance between the segmentation and the projected object over the six pose parameters are compared. Experiments show that a sampling-based optimization outperforms gradient-based methods and the sampling can be further improved to fit the given imaging setup and the object of interest. Simulated data shows that the pose can be estimated nearly perfect in stereo setups and yields highly accurate results on single-view setups. Clinical data supports these findings.

**Keywords:** Pose estimation · Fourier descriptors · Simulated Annealing

## 1 Introduction

Inferring three-dimensional information from two-dimensional images is an important part of bio-medical image analysis. Three-dimensional data is rarely acquired in clinical routine due to higher costs, the additional time to gather and process the data or simply because the imaging device is not available. Nevertheless, this particular information is often needed in image guided surgery and preoperative planning [3] or the evaluation of three-dimensional movements like implant migration [4] and knee kinematics [5].

Pose estimation is one part of the challenging task of relating two-dimensional and three-dimensional data. Given a model of the object of interest and at least one projection, the goal is to determine the pose of the model that best explains the projections. Using rigid objects the pose consists of six parameters: the location (three translations) and orientation (three rotations) of a known object. In a bio-medical context bones or endoprostheses are usually of interest.

Many algorithms have been developed to assess the problem of pose estimation in a clinical context [6]. Typically, these methods require a manual initialization to start a minimization process that aligns the segmented and the projected contours [4,7]. Depending on the amount of data that has to be processed, this

© Springer International Publishing Switzerland 2016
F. Huang and A. Sugimoto (Eds.): PSIVT 2015 Workshops, LNCS 9555, pp. 246–257, 2016.
DOI: 10.1007/978-3-319-30285-0_20

can be a time-consuming task, limiting the usability in clinical routine. Additionally, stereo setups with orthogonal cameras are often used to ideally represent the three-dimensional space. In a clinical environment this may be impracticable. Monocular setups or smaller angles between the cameras have to be considered.

Automatic or semi-automatic pose estimation are commonly proposed for fluoroscopic images [8]. Temporal relations are used to initialize the following frame. However, a manually provided pose is still required to start the process at the first frame or to guide it during certain key frames.

Another often neglected problem are projective characteristics of objects of interest in a clinical context. Human long bones and many endoprostheses may show little rotational variation about one axis and radiopaque objects like metal implants can only be processed by their contour, further limiting usable features.

In our work we provide a fully automatic method for the pose estimation of rigid objects from X-ray images in a monocular or stereo imaging setup. Given the segmented contour of the object in the images an initial pose is computed using Fourier Descriptors and a matching to a database of simulated projections. The pose is further refined by minimizing the distance between the given segmentation and the projection of the model over the pose parameters. We combine local and global optimization schemes, such that properties of the imaging setup and the object of interest are considered.

## 2   Methods

### 2.1   Fourier Descriptor

The Fourier Descriptor (FD) offers a representation of a two-dimensional shape that is invariant to translation, scale and rotation if properly normalized. It allows to easily compare similar objects and is mostly used for shape discrimination and retrieval [9]. The FD uses the discrete Fourier transform to convert a two-dimensional closed contour into the one-dimensional frequency domain (Fig. 1).

The boundary of the object is sampled by $N = 2^m$ equidistant points $(x_n, y_n)$ given in the complex plane:

$$c_n = x_n + j y_n, \ n = 0, \ldots, N-1 \,. \tag{1}$$

The Fourier transform of this closed contour is given by

$$C_k = \sum_{n=0}^{N-1} c_n \exp\left(-j \frac{2\pi k n}{N}\right), \ k = 0, \ldots, N-1 \,. \tag{2}$$

Properties of the transform are exploited to normalize the coefficients $C_k$. Translations of the contour in the image plane only have an effect on the coefficient $C_0$. Setting

$$\hat{C}_0 = 0 \tag{3}$$

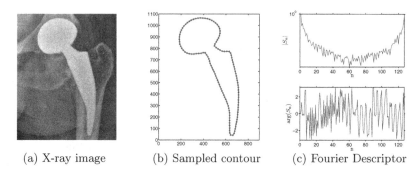

(a) X-ray image          (b) Sampled contour          (c) Fourier Descriptor

**Fig. 1.** X-ray image of a total hip implant (a), sampled contour (b) and its normalize Fourier Descriptor (c). Displayed are magnitude $|S_n|$ and phase angle $\arg(S_n)$ of the FD computed with 128 equidistant points.

centers the contour and normalizes for translational differences. The size of the object affects the magnitude of the coefficients $C_k$. Ensuring that $|C_1| = 1$ holds, normalizes for the scale of the shape. Rotational differences and the respective starting point of the contour affect the phase of the coefficients $C_k$. Thus, the normalized FD are given by

$$\hat{C}_k = \frac{C_k}{|C_1|} \exp\left(j\frac{\arg(C_1) + \arg(C_{N-1})}{2}\right) \exp\left(jk\frac{\arg(C_1) - \arg(C_{N-1})}{2}\right), \quad (4)$$

where $\arg(z)$ denotes the phase of the complex number $z$. Rotations are normalized by the main ellipse of the shape, the starting point is shifted to ensure that $\arg(\hat{C}_1) = \arg(\hat{C}_{N-1}) = 0$ always holds. However, a rotation of the ellipse about $\pm\pi$ remains indeterminable and thus, a second normalization

$$\hat{C}_k^\pi = \hat{C}_k \exp\left(j\pi(k - 1)\right) \quad (5)$$

has to be considered.

## 2.2    Pose Estimation with Fourier Descriptors

The properties of the Fourier Descriptor enable a relatively fast and intuitive approach to estimate the pose without the need for a manual initialization. We follow the work of Banks et al. [1] and extend it to an arbitrary, calibrated imaging setup.

By using the normalized FD to describe a projection of an object, the six-dimensional pose space can be reduced to two rotational parameters. Translations in the three-dimensional space are covered by the invariance of the descriptor to scale and translation in the image plane. The rotational invariance limits the distinguishable three-dimensional rotations. By sampling over the remaining two rotations the whole pose space can be covered. In the following we briefly explain our pose estimation procedure.

A database of views of the object over two rotations is built. Visually speaking, we obtain all possible FD of the projected object by viewing the object from positions lying on a sphere with the object located at the center. Missing parameters of the pose are inferred by the normalization factors, the known pose in the database and the geometric properties of the imaging setup after finding the best matching view in the database.

The database is built by simulating the imaging process with a known three-dimensional model of the object of interest. With a simulated camera at the $z$-axis the object centered on the same axis is first rotated around the $x$-axis by an angle $\omega_x \in [-\pi/2, \pi/2]$, followed by a rotation around the $y$-axis by an angle $\omega_y \in [-\pi, \pi]$ (see Fig. 2). To each pair of angles $(\omega_x, \omega_y)$ the normalized FD $\hat{C}(\omega_x, \omega_y)$ and the normalization factors are stored.

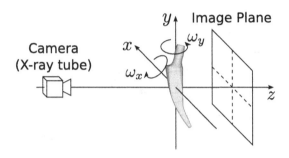

**Fig. 2.** Simulation setup to build the database of model views.

The pose estimation is carried out using a single view of the object in a calibrated setup, e.g. we know the projection matrix $P$ that projects three-dimensional points into the image plane. In particular, the focal length $f$ (distance from the x-ray tube to the X-ray cassette), the camera center (location of the focus of the x-ray tube), the pixel size $(s_x, s_y)$ of the detector and the principal point $(p_x, p_y)$ are needed. Intrinsic camera parameters of the simulated and the real imaging setup do not need to coincide, but should be roughly comparable.

After segmenting the object of interest in the image the normalized Fourier Descriptors $\hat{C}^{input}$ and $\hat{C}^{\pi,input}$ are computed. For the sake of simplicity, we only refer to $\hat{C}^{input}$. However, it should be noted that both possible normalizations have to be considered. In order to find the most similar FD of our database to $\hat{C}^{input}$, we search for the closes FD in terms of the Euclidian distance:

$$\hat{C}^{db} = \arg\min_{(\omega_x, \omega_y)} \sum_{i=2}^{N-1} \left\| \hat{C}_i(\omega_x, \omega_y) - \hat{C}_i^{input} \right\|_2 . \tag{6}$$

The in-plane rotation, i.e. the rotation about the $z$-axis, is estimated by

$$\omega_z = \frac{\arg(C_1^{input}) + \arg(C_{N-1}^{input})}{2} - \frac{\arg(C_1^{db}) + \arg(C_{N-1}^{db})}{2}, \tag{7}$$

the difference in the rotations used for normalization. The angle has to be adjusted by $\pi$ if the second normalization $\hat{C}^{\pi}$ was used for the input contour. With the intercept theorem the distance of the object from the camera center, i.e. the translation in direction of the $z$-axis, is given by

$$t_z = \left( \frac{|C_1^{db}|}{|C_1^{input}|} \frac{f^{input}}{f^{db}} - 1 \right) d_z^{db} . \tag{8}$$

The formula uses the scale factor as magnification factor in the projection and the distance $d_z^{db}$ of the object to the camera center in the database setup. Figure 3 shows the geometric explanation of (8).

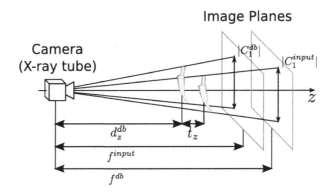

**Fig. 3.** Geometric explanation of depth estimation using FD. Simulated and real camera are aligned and the depth is related to the apparent size of the object in the image planes.

The remaining parameters are estimated in a similar fashion using the in-plane rotation and the different magnification factors. Translational parameters can be estimated by

$$\begin{pmatrix} t_x \\ t_y \end{pmatrix} = \frac{1}{N} \frac{d_z^{db}}{f^{db}} \left( \frac{|C_1^{db}|}{|C_1^{input}|} \begin{pmatrix} x^{input} \\ y^{input} \end{pmatrix} - R(\omega_z) \begin{pmatrix} x^{db} \\ y^{db} \end{pmatrix} \right) , \tag{9}$$

where

$$\begin{pmatrix} x^{input} \\ y^{input} \end{pmatrix} = \begin{pmatrix} s_x^{input} \left( Re(C_0^{input}) - p_x^{input} \right) \\ s_y^{input} \left( Im(C_0^{input}) - p_y^{input} \right) \end{pmatrix} \tag{10}$$

relates the perceived translation in the image plane to the scale of the camera coordinate system. The database entry is adjusted analogously. Lastly,

$$\begin{pmatrix} \omega_x \\ \omega_y \end{pmatrix} = \begin{pmatrix} \omega_x^{db} \\ \omega_y^{db} \end{pmatrix} - R(-\omega_z) \begin{pmatrix} \arctan \left( x^{input} / f^{input} \right) \\ \arctan \left( y^{input} / f^{input} \right) \end{pmatrix} \tag{11}$$

uses the inclination to define the left rotational parameters. In a final step, the object has to be transformed to the world coordinate system by using the extrinsic parameters of the real camera setup.

## 2.3  Pose Estimation Using Contour Distance

The Fourier Descriptors allow for an approximate estimation of the object pose dependent on pose space coverage. A more exact pose can be derived by directly minimizing the distance between the segmented contour $c^{seg}$ in the image and the projection of the object $c^{proj}$. For each point on the segmented contour the closest point on the projected contour is identified and the sum the distances is minimized over the pose of the object:

$$E(\omega, t) = d\left(c^{seg}, c^{proj}(\omega, t)\right) = \frac{1}{n} \sum_{i=1}^{n} \min_{j} \left\| c_i^{seg} - c_j^{proj}(\omega, t) \right\|^2 \rightarrow \min! \,. \quad (12)$$

In a stereo setup the energy for both views is simply added.

A standard procedure in pose estimation is the Iterative Closest Points (ICP) algorithm that estimates the optimal transformation between two point clouds. A variant directly relates the two-dimensional points of the contour to the three-dimensional model to infer the pose [11]. ICP solves the problem in (12) indirectly by minimizing the distance between the correspondences in each step.

In general, the ICP method is fast and fairly robust. However, the solution is a local minimum and depends on the starting point. Especially objects with low rotational variance suffer from an energy function with many broad, local minima. Unfortunately, those objects are common in the bio-medical context. Long bones or many implants fall in this category and often lack the desired accuracy in the estimated pose.

Other methods solve (12) by directly optimizing over the six pose parameters in an iterative manner. Given a starting pose $\left(\omega^{(0)}, t^{(0)}\right)^{\mathsf{T}} \in \mathbb{R}^6$ we search for a series of updates

$$\begin{pmatrix} \omega^{(i+1)} \\ t^{(i+1)} \end{pmatrix} = \begin{pmatrix} \omega^{(i)} \\ t^{(i)} \end{pmatrix} + \begin{pmatrix} \Delta\omega \\ \Delta t \end{pmatrix}, \, i \geq 0 \quad (13)$$

that gradually minimizes the energy (12). Non-linear optimization schemes are either derivative-free like the Nelder-Mead method or use the (approximated) gradient to define a descending direction like Sequential Quadratic Programming [10]. Again, these methods guarantee only a local minimum.

Global optimization schemes like Simulated Annealing [2] often incorporate a stochastic component and the search direction is found randomly to further explore the function.

## 2.4  A Combined Approach

Finally, we aim to combine the approaches introduced above. Fourier Descriptors and a database matching are used to estimate an initial pose which is further refined by minimizing the contour distance. Firstly, we extend the descriptor-based pose estimation to a stereo setup. Afterwards, we briefly explain the additional refinement steps.

In the single-view setup the segmented contour is compared to each database entry and the best matching entry is used to estimate the pose as described in

Sect. 2.2. For a stereo setup the known geometry of the imaging setup can be incorporated to solve for ambiguities in the database matching. The two contours are matched to pairs that are feasible, i.e. the views in the database differ in the same angle as the cameras. One pose is estimated for each view and the poses are combined to preserve reliable pose parameters.

Without loss of generality, we assume both cameras lie in the $xz$-plane with one camera centered on the $x$-axis and the second camera rotated by an angle $\alpha$ around the $y$-axis. For the first camera the $x$- and $y$-coordinates are related to in-plane pose parameters. Translations along these axes and a rotation around the $z$-axis induce high changes in the image and these parameters are typically estimated more accurate. The $z$-coordinate on the other hand corresponds to depth information and often lacks precision.

Given two different sets of points $X^1 = \{(x_i^1, y_i^1, z_i^1)^\mathsf{T}, i = 1, \ldots, n\}$ and $X^2 = \{(x_i^2, y_i^2, z_i^2)^\mathsf{T}, i = 1, \ldots, n\}$ that describe the model in the estimated pose for each camera, we compute a mixed model

$$X_m = \left\{ \begin{pmatrix} \frac{1}{1+|\cos\alpha|}(x_i^1 + |\cos\alpha|x_i^2) \\ \frac{1}{2}(y_i^1 + y_i^2) \\ \frac{1}{1+|\cos\alpha|}(|\cos\alpha|z_i^1 + z_i^2) \end{pmatrix}, i = 1, \ldots, n \right\} . \tag{14}$$

For an angle of $\alpha = 90°$ between the cameras the depth information of each camera is mainly ignored. Smaller camera angles require the usage of more depth information.

The computed model is topologically not identical to the original model. Either the first or the second model has to be rigidly transformed to match the model $X_m$. This yields the initial pose in the stereo setup as shown in Fig. 4. The initial pose is estimated using mostly two-dimensional information. To account for possible errors we use this pose to start an ICP-based pose estimation, relating three-dimensional model points to the two-dimensional contours from all available cameras.

Finally, the contour distance is minimized directly over the six pose parameters. We use a sampling-based optimization scheme and incorporate a priori information about the object and the imaging setup to guide the minimization process. The initial pose estimation yields errors that are, in general, not equally distributed among the pose parameters. Out-of-plane parameters are prone to errors and reflection planes or axes of symmetry induce further difficulties. To improve the sampling we estimate the errors that are typically induced in the initial pose estimation step. Random poses are generated in the simulation setup and pose estimation is performed using Fourier Descriptors. The measured errors in rotation and translation indicate suitable search directions, i.e. mean and standard deviation for the sampling step in the Simulated Annealing. Since those errors mostly depend on the angle between the cameras and the shape characteristics of the model the trained sampling parameters transfer well to comparable real setups.

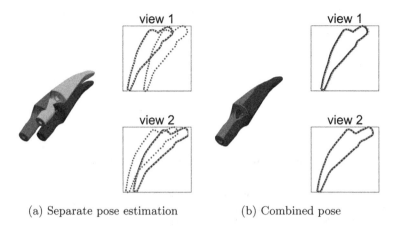

| (a) Separate pose estimation | (b) Combined pose |

**Fig. 4.** Pose estimation using fourier descriptors in a stereo setup. Examples are shown for an individual (a) and combined estimation (b), with estimated models and their projections in green or red and the ground truth in blue (Color figure online).

## 3 Experiments and Results

We test our method on both simulated and real clinical data with a comparable X-ray setup.

### 3.1 Simulated Data

The simulations are carried out to demonstrate the ability of our method to automatically estimate the pose of the femoral part of a hip implant and the distal part of the femur. The used surface model of the implant is a three-dimensional scan of a short-stem total hip replacement manufactured by Aesculap, Germany. The model of the femur was reconstructed from a computed tomography. Figure 5 shows that both objects offer a relatively low amount of rotational variance around one axis and the estimation of an accurate pose is typically challenging even if a user generated input is given to guide the process.

Pose estimation of these models is an integral part of the Model-based Roentgen Stereophotogrammetric Analysis [4]. The simulated imaging setup resembles a real clinical setup in this context. We assume the projective model of a pinhole camera to approximate a radiography and generate contours. A focal length of $1200\,mm$, an average distance of the object to the camera center of $1000\,mm$ and an image resolution of $0.2\,mm$ per pixel are used as standard imaging setup. We generate 200 random poses of the implant and the femur for evaluation. Rotations are drawn from an uniform distribution without further limitations to fully explore the capabilities of the method, translations are limited to a maximum of $100\ mm$. Additionally, we added a $5\,\%$ noise to the parameters of the base imaging setup for each generated pose.

Initial pose estimation was carried out with Fourier Descriptors computed with a database generated in the standard imaging setup. In a refinement step

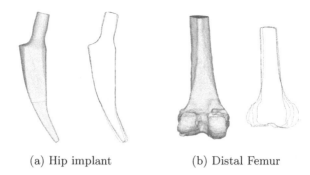

(a) Hip implant          (b) Distal Femur

**Fig. 5.** Models used for experiments on simulated data and selected projections. The depicted contours are generated by rotating each model by an angle $\alpha \in \{-30°, -10°, 10°, 30°\}$ to visualize the low rotational variance.

the energy (12) is minimized with Sequential Quadratic Programming (SQP) as described in [4], a state of the art approach in model-based implant migration analysis. Furthermore, we show the results of the Nelder-Mead method (NM) and two sampling-based optimization schemes: Simulated Annealing with equally distributed search directions (SA) and empirically estimated distributions (SA$^{est}$) as explained above. Results are listed in Table 1 showing the rotational errors (angle of rotation about one axis) and translational errors (Euclidean distance between object center).

**Table 1.** Mean and standard deviation of rotational and translational errors using simulated data (200 random poses) of the hip implant and the distal femur using different pose estimation methods.

|  | FD | SQP | NM | SA | SA$^{est}$ |
|---|---|---|---|---|---|
| **Stereo setup, angle between cameras: 90°** | | | | | |
| $\bar{R}_{err}$ (deg) | $3.87 \pm 2.62$ | $1.28 \pm 1.38$ | $0.78 \pm 1.13$ | $0.22 \pm 0.68$ | $0.01 \pm 0,01$ |
| $\bar{t}_{err}$ (mm) | $1.28 \pm 0.85$ | $0.38 \pm 0.39$ | $0.09 \pm 0.15$ | $0.02 \pm 0.06$ | $0.01 \pm 0.05$ |
| **Stereo setup, angle between cameras: 30°** | | | | | |
| $\bar{R}_{err}$ (deg) | $4.83 \pm 6.91$ | $2.15 \pm 3.76$ | $1.58 \pm 2.79$ | $0.41 \pm 2.41$ | $0.04 \pm 0.22$ |
| $\bar{t}_{err}$ (mm) | $5.58 \pm 6.88$ | $2.33 \pm 2.44$ | $0.53 \pm 1.66$ | $0.30 \pm 0.87$ | $0.02 \pm 0.05$ |
| **Monocular Setup** | | | | | |
| $\bar{R}_{err}$ (deg) | $6.35 \pm 4.86$ | $3.94 \pm 3.49$ | $2.61 \pm 2.54$ | $2.05 \pm 2.43$ | $0.49 \pm 1.04$ |
| $\bar{t}_{err}$ (mm) | $10.1 \pm 11.3$ | $6.06 \pm 8.26$ | $3.73 \pm 4.19$ | $2.78 \pm 3.87$ | $0.84 \pm 0.43$ |

We sampled the views in the database at approximately 5° which corresponds to the computed error using Fourier Descriptors. Translational errors in the initial pose estimation are highly dependent on the imaging setup and show that the FD lack precision in the depth estimation. Subsequent refinement steps are capable of eliminating most of the error in the pose in a stereo setup, so the FD typically generate a reasonable starting pose.

The SQP approach yields results that are in the scope of the accuracy reported in the literature for stereo setups even without a manually initialization of the pose. Derivative-free optimization schemes outperform the gradient-based SQP in our test. Sampling-based optimization is the method of choice if a highly accurate pose is needed. Simulated Annealing shows the best results with nearly perfectly estimated poses in a stereo setup and acceptable poses in a monocular setup. Limiting the search direction by estimating possible errors does not only further improves the accuracy, but the minimum is typically found faster as well. However, computation time remains a disadvantage of these methods.

### 3.2 Clinical Data

In a second step we evaluate our method on 40 clinically acquired images. The used X-ray stereo images are from a short-stem total hip replacement study. The X-ray tubes are placed with an angle of approximately 40°. Every image is calibrated with the help of a calibration box. In the evaluation we focus on the pose estimation of the femur implant.

A few difficulties have to be addressed: the implant varies in size and the neck of the implant is often occluded by the hip socket. We ignore the neck part of the implant model and build a separate database for each size to apply the pose estimation via Fourier Descriptors. The implant contour is segmented by simple thresholding and automatically adjusted accordingly by analyzing the curvature along the contour. A sample of a segmented contour is displayed in Fig. 6a.

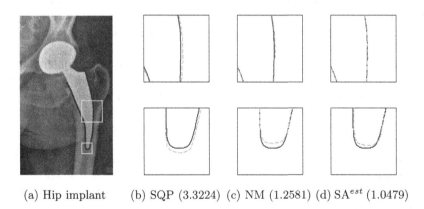

(a) Hip implant    (b) SQP (3.3224) (c) NM (1.2581) (d) $SA^{est}$ (1.0479)

**Fig. 6.** Effect of different energy minima on the computed pose. A sample image with the used segmented contour is shown in (a). Red rectangles show areas of interest, depicted in (b)–(d) with comparisons between segmented (blue) and projected (green) contours. The provided values show the energy (12) (Color figure online)

Unfortunately, no ground truth is known for the pose estimation of the implant in this study. We provide the found minimal energy (12) to compare different approaches and assume that errors in the pose and final energy are dependent as Fig. 6 suggests. However, the relation is highly non-linear. Even small improvements on the energy function may induce qualitatively better poses if out-of-plane parameters are optimized. The poses estimated by NM and $SA^{est}$ differ in about $2°$ and $9°$ compared to the SQP pose, but the energy of both poses is similar.

On average, we achieved a minimal energy of $3.16 \pm 0.94$ using SQP, $1.29 \pm 0.37$ using NM, $1.22 \pm 0.35$ using SA and $1.14 \pm 0.34$ using our proposed, adapted Simulated Annealing $SA^{est}$. Similar to the finding on the simulated data, the Nelder-Mead method and Simulated Annealing are superior to the SQP method typically used to solve this problem. On average, SA yields a minimal energy $10\%$ lower than NM. Although the improvement seems small, the mean of the pose differences are about $3°$ in rotation and $0.8\,mm$ in translation. Main differences are rotations about the longitudinal axis and translations in out-of-plane direction. As Fig. 6 indicates the resulting poses of the SA typically show a qualitatively better agreement with the segmented contour.

## 4    Conclusion

We presented an automatic approach to model-based pose estimation in a clinical setup that utilizes X-ray images. No user-provided initial pose is needed. Given the contour of the object in one image the starting pose can be estimated by using Fourier Descriptors and a database of predefined, simulated views of the object.

The pose estimation process was extended to an arbitrary, calibrated imaging setup, so simulations to generate the database and the real setup do not have to share the same projective parameters. Monocular pose estimation is possible, however, if a second view of the object is provided the estimated poses can be combined using their known relation to greatly increase the quality of the estimation. In our simulated experiments sampling-based methods clearly outperformed the state of the art method used to assess implant migration. The space of probable search directions can be effectively limited by generating test samples and the optimization generally provides better results especially in a monocular test setup.

Experiments on clinical data further support the findings on simulated data. On general, the Simulated Annealing generates poses with lowest energy that agrees best with the segmented contour. The computational overhead justifies the higher accuracy.

The initial pose estimation presented in this paper requires that the object is fully visible in the image. Occlusions can only be handled by reducing the object to a common part displayed in all data as shown in the clinical experiments. Therefore, our proposed method is particularly suited for the pose estimation of radiopaque implants with clearly visible boundaries. Additional experiments are needed to further evaluate the applicability to pose estimation of bones, a more challenging task since the image contour is more prone to segmentation errors due to a lower contrast to its surrounding. Effects of these errors on the pose estimation process need to be investigated and incorporated accordingly.

**Acknowledgments.** We would like to thank the Laboratory for Biomechanics and Biomaterials, Dept. of Orthopaedics, Hannover Medical School for providing the models and the clinical data used in the evaluation.

# References

1. Banks, S.A., Hodge, W.A.: Accurate measurement of three-dimensional knee replacement kinematics using single-plane fluoroscopy. IEEE Trans. Biomed. Eng. **43**, 638–649 (1996)
2. Davis, L.: Genetic Algorithms and Simulated Annealing. Morgan Kaufman Publishers Inc., Los Altos (1987)
3. Gamage, P., Xie, S.Q., Delmas, P.: Pose estimation of femur fracture segments for image guided orthopedic surgery. In: 24th International Conference Image and Vision Computing New Zealand, pp. 288–292 (2009)
4. Kaptein, B., Valstar, E., Stoel, B., Rozing, P., Reiber, J.: A new model-based RSA method validated using CAD models and models from reversed engineering. J. Biomech. **36**, 873–882 (2003)
5. Li, G., de Velde, S.K.V., Bingham, J.T.: Validation of a non-invasive fluoroscopic imaging technique for the measurement of dynamic knee joint motion. J. Biomech. **41**, 1616–1622 (2008)
6. Markelj, P., Tomazevic, D., Likar, B., Pernus, F.: A review of 3D/2D registration methods for image guided interventions. Med. Image Anal. **16**, 642–661 (2012)
7. Zhang, B., Sun, J.W., Chi, Z.Y., Sun, S.B., Meng, S., Zhang, Y., Rolfe, P.: Estimation of 3D pose of femurs in bi-planar digital radiographs. In: Long, M. (ed.) World Congress on Medical Physics and Biomedical Engineering May 26-31, 2012 Beijing, IFMBE Proceedings, vol. 39, pp. 1313–1316. Springer, Heidelberg (2013)
8. Yamazaki, T., Kamei, R., Tomita, T., Sato, Y., Yoshikawa, H., Sugamoto, K.: Improved semi-automated 3D kinematic measurement of total knee arthroplasty using x-ray fluoroscopic images. In: Jaffray, D.A. (ed.) World Congress on Medical Physics and Biomedical Engineering, June 7-12, 2015, Toronto, Canada, IFMBE Proceedings, vol. 51, pp. 322–325. Springer, Heidelberg (2016)
9. Zhang, D., Lu, G.: A comparative study of fourier descriptors for shape representation and retrieval. In: Proceedings of 5th Asian Conference on Computer Vision (2002)
10. Nocedal, J., Wright, S.J.: Numerical Optimization. Springer, New York (2006)
11. Wunsch, P., Hirzinger, G.: Registration of CAD-models to images by iterative inverse perspective matching. In: Proceedings of the 1996 International Conference on Pattern Recognition (1996)

# A Study on Model Selection
# from the $q$-Exponential Distribution
# for Constructing an Organ Point
# Distribution Model

Mitsunori Yamada$^{(\boxtimes)}$, Hidekata Hontani, and Hiroshi Matsuzoe

Nagoya Institute of Technology, Gokiso-cho, Showa-ku,
Nagoya-shi, Aichi 466-8555, Japan
yamada@iu.nitech.ac.jp

**Abstract.** A method is proposed that improves generalization performance of a point distribution model (PDM) of a target organ. Representing the PDM with a directed graphical model (DGM), the proposed method selects an appropriate model for each of the unary terms and of the pairwise terms of the DGM from a $q$-exponential distribution. The $q$-exponential distribution has a parameter, $q$, which controls the tail length, and its representation includes both a Gaussian distribution and a student's $t$-distribution: The distribution is identical with a Gaussian distribution when $q = 1$ and the distribution with a larger value of $q$ has heavier tails. The proposed method selects a value of $q$ for each of the distributions appeared in the DGM based on an Akaike's information criterion (AIC), which is employed for selecting a model that will minimize the generalization error. The proposed method is applied for the construction of a PDM of the liver and the results show that larger values of $q$ are selected in the posterior region, which contacts with other soft organs.

**Keywords:** Point distribution model · Model selection · AIC · $q$-exponential distribution

## 1 Introduction

Point distribution models (PDMs) of target organs play important roles in the segmentation of 3D medical images (e.g. [1,2]). A PDM that represents statistical variety of the shape of a target organ is constructed from a set of training data and the model is registered to given new images for segmenting the target organ region in each of the images. In this study, employing a PDM for representing the statistical variety of the shapes, the authors focus on the improvement of the generalization performance of the model.

A PDM represents a target organ surface in an image with a set of $N$ points on the surface. Let the three-dimensional coordinates of the $i$-th point in an image be denoted by $\boldsymbol{x}_j = [x_j, y_j, z_j]^T$ $(j = 1, 2, \ldots, N)$. Then an $3N$-vector,

© Springer International Publishing Switzerland 2016
F. Huang and A. Sugimoto (Eds.): PSIVT 2015 Workshops, LNCS 9555, pp. 258–269, 2016.
DOI: 10.1007/978-3-319-30285-0_21

$X = [x_1^T, x_2^T, \ldots x_N]^T$ denotes the location and the whole shape of the target organ. A statistical shape model of the target organ represents the prior probability distribution of these $3N$ variables $p(X) = p(x_1, x_2, \ldots, x_N)$ and a Gaussian distribution is widely employed implicitly and explicitly for this representation. A Gaussian distribution has two kinds of parameters, the mean $\mu$ and the covariance $\Sigma$, and you can represent the prior probability distribution with a Gaussian one by estimating the values of these parameters from a given training data set. You can estimate these parameter values straightforwardly from a set of training data but the estimated values are often degraded by outliers in the data, which are not well described by a Gaussian distribution, and often overfit to the training data when the number of the data is not large enough. These cause poor generalization performance for the resultant model. The objective of this study is *not* to estimate the true prior probability distribution $X$ but to improve the generalization performance.

For example, an active shape model (ASM) [3,4], which is one of the most popular model used for the target organ segmentation in given medical images, implicitly employs a Gaussian distribution for representing the statistical variety of the shape of a target organ. Let a covariance matrix empirically estimated from a given training data set be denoted by $\hat{\Sigma}$ and let its eigenvectors and the corresponding eigenvalues be denoted by $u_1, u_2, \ldots$ and $\lambda_1, \lambda_2, \ldots$, respectively, where the eigenvalues are in decreasing order. Then, you can represent the statistical variety as follows:

$$X(\theta) = \hat{\mu} + U\theta, \tag{1}$$

where $\hat{\mu}$ denotes the estimated mean vector, $U = [u_1|u_2|\ldots|u_r]$ is a $3N \times r$ matrix where $r < 3N$, and $\theta$ is a $r$-vector that controls the shape described by the model. $X$ in (1) obeys a Gaussian distribution, of which the mean is $\hat{\mu}$ and the covariance matrix is $\Sigma = U\Lambda U^T$ where $\Lambda = \mathrm{diag}(\lambda_1, \lambda_2, \ldots, \lambda_r)$, when $\theta$ obeys a $r$-dimensional Gaussian distribution with zero mean and unit covariance. When you register the ASM to a given image, you firstly detect $N$ points, $\tilde{x}_j$ ($j = 1, 2, \ldots, N$), from the image that correspond to $x_j$ of the model and then estimate $\hat{\theta}$ in (1) so that $X(\hat{\theta})$ fits to the measured points, $\tilde{X} = [\tilde{x}_1^T, \tilde{x}_2^T, \ldots, \tilde{x}_N^T]^T$. You can estimate $\hat{\theta}$ by minimizing a cost function, $C(\theta)$, such that

$$C(\theta) = \lambda \|X(\theta) - \tilde{X}\|^2 + \|\theta\|^2. \tag{2}$$

The cost function of $\theta$ in (2) comes from $-\log\{p(\tilde{X}|\theta)p(\theta)\}$, where the prior probability distribution, $p(\theta)$, is represented by the Gaussian with zero mean and unit variance and where the likelihood, $p(\tilde{X}|\theta)$, is also the Gaussian of which the mean is zero and the variance is $\lambda^{-1}I$. It is a MAP estimation to minimize $C(\theta)$ in (2). You need to estimate the covariance matrix, $\hat{\Sigma}$, for constructing the model in (1) and the estimated covariance matrix often overfits to training data especially when the number of the data is not large [5]. This overfitting worsens the generalization performance [6].

You have at least two approaches to improve the generalization performance: In one approach, some regularizers or priors are introduced to the estimation of $p(X)[6]$. In other approach, a model function of which the generalization performance would be the best is selected from a set of functions prepared in advance. In this study, the latter approach is employed: The proposed method selects an appropriate probability distribution model from $q$-exponential distribution, which can represent both a Gaussian distribution and a student's $t$-distribution, so that the generalization performance is improved. For the model selection, the authors employ an Akaike's information criterion. The $q$-exponential distribution and the AIC are described in the next section.

## 2   Proposed Method

Let the surface of a target organ in the $i$-th training image be denoted by $\mathcal{S}^i$ $(i = 1, 2, \ldots, M)$ and let the three-dimensional coordinates of the $j$-th corresponding point generated on $\mathcal{S}^i$ be denoted by $x_j^i$ $(j = 1, 2, \ldots, N)$. Given a set of the training data, $\{x_j^i | i = 1, 2, \ldots, M; j = 1, 2, \ldots, N\}$, we estimate the prior probability distribution, $p(x_1, x_2, \ldots, x_N)$, as a model.

### 2.1   Graphical Model Representation

In this study, the prior probability distribution is represented as shown in (3). You can represent the probability distribution model (3) with a directed graphical model (DGM).

$$p(x_1, x_2, \ldots, x_N) = \prod_j p(x_j) \prod_{(j,k)\in\mathcal{E}} p(x_j | x_k), \tag{3}$$

where each node in the corresponding graph represents $x_j$ $(j = 1, 2, \ldots, N)$ and $\mathcal{E}$ denotes a set of directed edges in the graph. Using the model shown in (3), you can register the model to a given image by computing the posterior probability or by maximizing it. You can of course employ an undirected graphical model for the representation such that

$$p(x_1, x_2, \ldots, x_N) = \prod_j p(x_j) \prod_{(j,k)\in\mathcal{E}'} p(x_j, x_k), \tag{4}$$

where $\mathcal{E}'$ denotes a set of undirected edges in the corresponding graph. A directed graphical model is often employed when there exist causal relationships between the variables and it looks natural to employ an undirected one for representing a PDM [6,7] because the points on an organ surface do not have any causality. The authors, though, employ a DGM because it is not straightforward to compute a conditional probability distribution, $p(x_j | x_k)$, from a simultaneous one, $p(x_j, x_k)$ in case the simultaneous distribution is represented by a $q$-exponential distribution. You need to compute $p(x_j | x_k)$ when you infer the posterior probability distribution on the graphical model by using, e.g. a belief propagation or MCMC. If you employ a $q$-exponential distribution, the pairwise term, $p(x_j, x_k)$, in (4) is represented by a six-dimensional $q$-exponential distribution but the conditional probability distribution, $p(\boldsymbol{x}_j|\boldsymbol{x}_k)$, computed from the pairwise term is *not* represented by a $q$-exponential distribution. When you employ $q$-exponential distribution, it is not easy to represent the prior with an undirected graphical model as shown in (4).

Each unary term, $p(\boldsymbol{x}_j)$ in (3), is estimated from a set of the training data, $\{\boldsymbol{x}_j^i | i = 1, 2, \ldots, M\}$. The pairwise term, $p(\boldsymbol{x}_j|\boldsymbol{x}_k)$, is assumed to satisfy $p(\boldsymbol{x}_j|\boldsymbol{x}_k) = p(\boldsymbol{x}_j - \boldsymbol{x}_k)$ in this study and is estimated from a set of the data, $\{\boldsymbol{d}_{jk}^i | i = 1, 2, \ldots, M; (j, k) \in \mathcal{E}\}$, where $\boldsymbol{d}_{jk}^i = \boldsymbol{x}_j^i - \boldsymbol{x}_k^i$. The $q$-exponential distribution, which has three different kinds of parameters, is employed for representing these terms, and the parameters except $q$ are estimated by using an EM algorithm. The last parameter, $q$, controls the shape of the distribution and is determined based on an AIC.

## 2.2   $q$-Exponential Distribution

A $d$-dimensional $q$-exponential distribution is represented as follows:

$$p_q(\boldsymbol{x}; \boldsymbol{\mu}, \boldsymbol{\Sigma}) = Z \left[ 1 + \frac{1}{\nu}(\boldsymbol{x} - \boldsymbol{\mu})^T \boldsymbol{\Sigma}^{-1}(\boldsymbol{x} - \boldsymbol{\mu}) \right]^{1/1-q}, \tag{5}$$

where

$$Z = \frac{\Gamma((\nu + d)/2)}{(\pi\nu)^{d/2}\Gamma(\nu/2)|\boldsymbol{\Sigma}|^{1/2}},$$

$\nu = -d - 2/(1 - q)$, $\boldsymbol{\mu}$ is a $d$-vector and denotes the mean, and $\boldsymbol{\Sigma}$ is a $d \times d$ symmetry matrix and corresponds to the covariance matrix of a Gaussian distribution. The distribution is integrable if $q < 1 + 2/d$ and converges to a Gaussian distribution when $q \to 1$. Figure 1 shows graphs of one-dimensional $q$-exponential distributions that have identical values of $\boldsymbol{\mu}$ and $\boldsymbol{\Sigma}$ and have different values of $q$. As you can see, the distributions with larger values of $q$ have heavier tails.

## 2.3   EM Algorithm for Parameter Estimation

Fixing the value of $q$, you can estimate the values of $\boldsymbol{\mu}$ and $\boldsymbol{\Sigma}$ that maximize the likelihood from a given training data by using an EM algorithm. The likelihood of $\boldsymbol{\mu}$ and $\boldsymbol{\Sigma}$ to a given set of training data, $\{\boldsymbol{x}^i | i = 1, 2, \ldots, M\}$, is represented as shown in (6)[8].

$$L_q(\boldsymbol{\mu}, \boldsymbol{\Sigma}) = M \log(Z) + \frac{1}{1 - q} \sum_{i=1}^{M} \log \left( \frac{\nu + s^i}{\nu} \right), \tag{6}$$

where $s^i = (\boldsymbol{x}^i - \boldsymbol{\mu})^T \boldsymbol{\Sigma}^{-1}(\boldsymbol{x}^i - \boldsymbol{\mu})$. Maximizing $L_q$ in (6), you obtain the following equations:

$$\hat{\boldsymbol{\mu}}_{\text{ML}} = \frac{\sum_i w_i \boldsymbol{x}^i}{\sum_i w_i}, \tag{7}$$

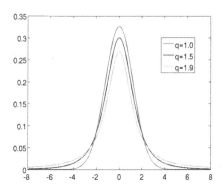

**Fig. 1.** The shapes of the $q$-exponential distributions with different values of $q$. The distributions with larger values of $q$ have heavier tails. The distribution is identical with a Gaussian one when $q = 1$.

$$\hat{\boldsymbol{\Sigma}}_{\mathrm{ML}} = \frac{1}{M} \sum_i w_i (\boldsymbol{x}^i - \hat{\boldsymbol{\mu}}_{\mathrm{ML}})(\boldsymbol{x}^i - \hat{\boldsymbol{\mu}}_{\mathrm{ML}})^T, \tag{8}$$

where $w_i = (\nu + d)/(\nu + s^i)$. As shown in the above equations, you need to compute the values of *weights*, $w_i$, in order for the estimation. Interpreting $w_i$ as latent variables, you can estimate $\hat{\boldsymbol{\mu}}_{\mathrm{ML}}$ and $\hat{\boldsymbol{\Sigma}}_{\mathrm{ML}}$ with an EM algorithm [8]. The outline of the algorithm is described below.

1. Set initial values of $\boldsymbol{\mu}$ and $\boldsymbol{\Sigma}$ as $\boldsymbol{\mu}^{(0)}$ and $\boldsymbol{\Sigma}^{(0)}$, respectively and set $m = 0$.
2. E-step:
   Calculate the weight, $w_i^{(m)}$, as follows:

$$w_i^{(m)} = \frac{\nu + d}{\nu + (\boldsymbol{x}^i - \boldsymbol{\mu}^{(m)})^T (\boldsymbol{\Sigma}^{(m)})^{-1}(\boldsymbol{x}^i - \boldsymbol{\mu}^{(m)})}. \tag{9}$$

3. M-step:
   Update the values of the parameters as follows:

$$\boldsymbol{\mu}^{(m+1)} = \frac{\sum_i w_i^{(m)} \boldsymbol{x}^i}{\sum_i w_i^{(m)}}, \tag{10}$$

$$\boldsymbol{\Sigma}^{(m+1)} = \frac{1}{M} \sum_i w_i^{(m)} (\boldsymbol{x}^i - \boldsymbol{\mu}^{(m+1)})(\boldsymbol{x}^i - \boldsymbol{\mu}^{(m+1)})^T. \tag{11}$$

4. Check if the values of the parameters are converged. If not, increase $m$ as $m \leftarrow m + 1$ and back to E-step. Otherwise output the final values as $\hat{\boldsymbol{\mu}}_{\mathrm{ML}} = \boldsymbol{\mu}^{(m)}$ and $\hat{\boldsymbol{\Sigma}}_{\mathrm{ML}} = \boldsymbol{\Sigma}^{(m)}$.

Replacing $\boldsymbol{x}^i$ with $\boldsymbol{d}^i_{jk}$, you can estimate $p(\boldsymbol{x}_j | \boldsymbol{x}_k)$ in the same manner.

## 2.4 Model Selection with AIC

The shape of the $q$-exponential distribution changes with respect to $q$. Given an identical set of training data, you obtain different estimations, $\hat{\boldsymbol{\mu}}_{\mathrm{ML}}$ and $\hat{\boldsymbol{\Sigma}}_{\mathrm{ML}}$ depending on the value of $q$ and the generalization performance of the resultant statistical model changes with respect to $q$. In the proposed method, an appropriate value of $q$, which will minimize the generalization error, is selected for each of the distributions, $p(\boldsymbol{x}_j)$ and $p(\boldsymbol{x}_j|\boldsymbol{x}_k)$, based on an AIC.

An Akaike's Information Criterion (AIC) is derived from a KL-divergence between an employed probability distribution model and the true distribution and is used for selecting a model that will minimize the generalization error from a set of models [9]. The AIC of the $q$-exponential distribution is a function of $q$:

$$\mathrm{AIC}(q) = -2L_q(\hat{\boldsymbol{\mu}}_{\mathrm{ML}}, \hat{\boldsymbol{\Sigma}}_{\mathrm{ML}}) + 2l, \tag{12}$$

where $l$ denotes the number of the parameters. The $q$-exponential distributions with different values of $q$ have identical number of the parameters and the second term of the right hand side in (12) is constant with respect to $q$. You can hence select the best model that minimizes AIC by selecting the value of $q$ at which the likelihood, $L_q(\hat{\boldsymbol{\mu}}_{\mathrm{ML}}, \hat{\boldsymbol{\Sigma}}_{\mathrm{ML}})$, is maximum with respect to $q$. An algorithm for the selection of $q$ for each of the distributions, $p(\boldsymbol{x}_j)$ and $p(\boldsymbol{x}_j|\boldsymbol{x}_k)$, is as follows:

1. Set $q = 1$ and set a small positive step size $\Delta_q$.
2. Estimate $\hat{\boldsymbol{\mu}}_{\mathrm{ML}}$ and $\hat{\boldsymbol{\Sigma}}_{\mathrm{ML}}$ by using an EM-algorithm and estimate the likelihood $L_q(\hat{\boldsymbol{\mu}}_{\mathrm{ML}}, \hat{\boldsymbol{\Sigma}}_{\mathrm{ML}})$ by means of a cross-validation.
3. Update $q$ as $q \leftarrow q + \Delta_q$. If $q < 1 + 2/d$, back to 2.
4. Select the value $q^*$, which maximizes $L_q$.

## 3 Experimental Results

Sets of artificial data were used for evaluating if the proposed method improved the generalization performance and a set of CT images was used for constructing a PDM of the liver and for studying what values of $q$ were selected for the probability distributions in (3).

### 3.1 Experiments with Artificial Data

Two families of data were generated by drawing them from an identical $d$-dimensional Gaussian probability distribution for examining if the model selection improved the generalization performance. The former family consisted of sets of training data and the latter one consisted of a set of data for evaluating the constructed models. Multiple sets of training data were generated in order to investigate the relationships between the number of training data and the selected value of $q$.

Let $\mathcal{X}_{n_{\mathrm{T}}}^m$ denote a set of $n_{\mathrm{T}}$ training data: $\mathcal{X}_{n_{\mathrm{T}}}^m = \{\boldsymbol{x}_1^m, \boldsymbol{x}_2^m, \ldots, \boldsymbol{x}_{n_{\mathrm{T}}}^m\}$ where $\boldsymbol{x}_n^m$ $(n = 1, 2, \ldots, n_{\mathrm{T}})$, are $d$-vectors and denote the training data. For statistically evaluating the constructed models, we generated $M_{\mathrm{T}}$ sets of $n_{\mathrm{T}}$ training data, $\mathcal{X}_{n_T}^1, \mathcal{X}_{n_T}^2, \ldots, \mathcal{X}_{n_T}^{M_T}$, by drawing the data from an identical Gaussian distribution. By changing the value of $n_T$ as $n_T = n_T^1, n_T^2, \ldots, n_T^{N_T}$, we generated $N_T \times M_T$ sets of training data. The proposed method was then applied to each of the training data sets: $\hat{\boldsymbol{\mu}}_{ML}$ and $\hat{\boldsymbol{\Sigma}}_{ML}$ were estimated at each $q$ and then $q^*$ at which the AIC was minimum was selected.

The generalization performances of the constructed models, $p_q(\boldsymbol{x}|\hat{\boldsymbol{\mu}}_{ML}, \hat{\boldsymbol{\Sigma}}_{ML})$, were evaluated by using the set of the data for the evaluation. Let the set for the evaluation be denoted by $Y = \{\boldsymbol{y}_1, \boldsymbol{y}_2, \ldots, \boldsymbol{y}_{N_E}\}$, where $\boldsymbol{y}_i$ $(i = 1, 2, \ldots, N_E)$ are $d$-vectors and are drawn from the Gaussian distribution. The generalization error is evaluated as follows:

$$E(q) = -\sum_{i=1}^{N_E} \log p_q(\boldsymbol{y}_i|\hat{\boldsymbol{\mu}}_{ML}, \hat{\boldsymbol{\Sigma}}_{ML}). \tag{13}$$

The error shown in (13) comes from a KL-divergence between a true probability distribution from which the data are derived and a model probability distribution. Let the true probability distribution be denoted by $\bar{p}_T(\boldsymbol{x})$, which is assumed to be a Gaussian distribution in the experiments, and let the model probability distribution be denoted by $p_q(\boldsymbol{x})$. The KL-divergence between $\bar{p}_T(\boldsymbol{x})$ and $p_q(\boldsymbol{x})$ is given as

$$\mathrm{KL}[\bar{p}_T(\boldsymbol{x})||p_q(\boldsymbol{x})] = \int \bar{p}_T(\boldsymbol{x}) \log \bar{p}_T(\boldsymbol{x}) d\boldsymbol{x} - \int \bar{p}_T(\boldsymbol{x}) \log p_q(\boldsymbol{x}) d\boldsymbol{x}. \tag{14}$$

The first term in the right hand side in (14) is independent of the model and cannot be evaluated in general. The second term can be approximately evaluated by using a set of observed data, $\{\boldsymbol{y}_i|i = 1, 2, \ldots, N_E\}$, which are derived from $\bar{p}_T(\boldsymbol{x})$, as $-\sum_i \log p_q(\boldsymbol{y}_i)$. The generalization error shown in (13) hence decreases when the KL divergence between the true distribution, $\bar{p}_T(\boldsymbol{x})$, and the model $p_q(\boldsymbol{x})$ is smaller.

The experimental results demonstrated in this subsection were obtained when $d = 3$ and when the mean and the covariance matrix of the Gaussian were $\bar{\boldsymbol{\mu}} = [0, 0, 0]^T$ and $\bar{\boldsymbol{\Sigma}} = \mathrm{diag}(10, 10, 5)$, respectively. The number of the data used for the evaluation of (13) was set as $N_E = 1000$ and the step size of $q$ was set as $\Delta_q = 1/100$. The graphs in Fig. 2 show the relationships between the value of $q$ and the generalization error, $E(\hat{\boldsymbol{\mu}}_{ML}, \hat{\boldsymbol{\Sigma}}_{ML})$, obtained when $n_T = 10, 20, 40$, and 50. The bars in the graphs demonstrate one-sigma of the generalization errors evaluated by using $N_E = 1000$ evaluation data. $E(q = 1)$ indicates the generalization errors of a (classical) Gaussian distribution model. The green dots indicate the value of $q = \bar{q}$ at which the generalization error, $E$, is minimum. The blue dots indicate the average value of $q^*$s that were selected from $M_T = 100$ training data sets based on the AIC. The average value was not identical with $\bar{q}$ but the selected model $(q = q^*)$ had better generalization performance than the Gaussian one $(q = 1)$ even though all of the data obeyed the Gaussian probability distribution. As shown in Fig. 2, $\bar{q}$ and $q^*$ decreased to one as the number of the training data, $n_T$, increased. The proposed method successfully selected a model that had the generalization performance better than a Gaussian one.

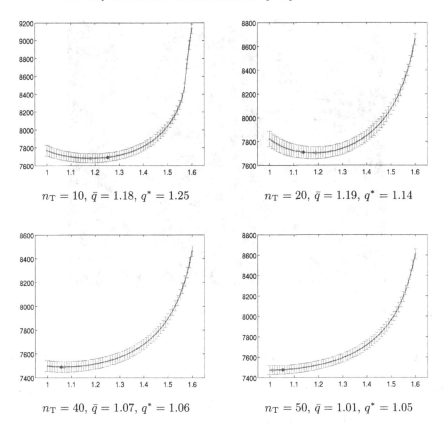

$n_T = 10,\ \bar{q} = 1.18,\ q^* = 1.25$       $n_T = 20,\ \bar{q} = 1.19,\ q^* = 1.14$

$n_T = 40,\ \bar{q} = 1.07,\ q^* = 1.06$       $n_T = 50,\ \bar{q} = 1.01,\ q^* = 1.05$

**Fig. 2.** Results of the simulation experiments. In each graph, the horizontal axis shows the value of $q$ and the vertical one shows the evaluated generalization error, $E$ in (13). The green dot indicates $\bar{q}$ where the error is minimum and the blue dot indicates the average value of $q^*$.

## 3.2 Experiments with CT Images

A PDM of the liver in a CT image was constructed from a set of 40 training CT images each in which the liver region was manually labeled. The statistical variety of the liver was represented by a directed graphical model as shown in (3) and $q^*$ was selected for each of the unary terms and the pairwise ones, $p(\boldsymbol{x}_j)$ and $p(\boldsymbol{x}_j|\boldsymbol{x}_k)$ based on the AIC. The step size of $q$ was set as $\Delta_q = 1/1000$.

The locations and the shapes of the patients' bodies in the training images were normalized in advance by firstly automatically detecting 198 landmarks from each training image by a MCMC-based method [10,11] and by secondly deforming each image so that the detected landmarks were registered to their average locations. Figure 3 shows an example of the locations of the landmarks. Then, a set of 1300 corresponding points was generated on the surface of each labeled liver region in the deformed images by using a generalized multi-dimensional scaling (GMDS)[12] (see Fig. 4). Let $\boldsymbol{x}_j^i$ denote the $j$-th

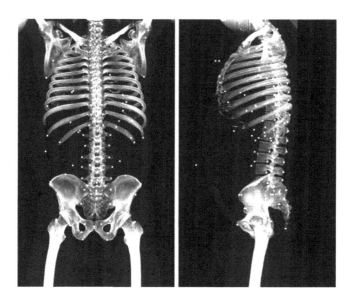

**Fig. 3.** The locations of the landmarks used for the image normalization (red dots)

corresponding point generated on the surface in the $i$-th training image. It should be noted that you will obtain a different statistical model from an identical set of the training images if you normalize the images in a different way or if you employ a different method for the generation of the corresponding points.

In this study, the structure of the directed graphical model was determined after $q^*$ for each unary term, $p(\boldsymbol{x}_j)$, was selected. A pairwise term, $p(\boldsymbol{x}_j|\boldsymbol{x}_k)$, is represented by a directed edge that links from $\boldsymbol{x}_k$ to $\boldsymbol{x}_j$ and the set of the edges, $\mathcal{E}$ in (3), was determined by the Delaunay diagram of the points on the average surface. You can obtain the average surface by computing the average of the training data of each point, $\hat{\boldsymbol{x}}_j = (\sum_{i=1}^{N} \boldsymbol{x}_j^i)/N$ and two nodes in the graphical model were linked by an edge if the corresponding two points in the PDM were linked by an edge in the Delaunay diagram. The direction of each edge was in the increasing order of $q^*$. Then, you obtain an acyclic directed graph. Once you determine $\mathcal{E}$, you can estimate $p(\boldsymbol{x}_j|\boldsymbol{x}_k)$ ($[j,k] \in \mathcal{E}$) from a set of training data, $\{\boldsymbol{d}_{jk}^i | i = 1, 2, \ldots, M\}$, where $\boldsymbol{d}_{jk}^i = \boldsymbol{x}_j^i - \boldsymbol{x}_k^i$.

**Fig. 4.** Examples of the corresponding points generated by GMDS [12]. The colors indicate the correspondence between different surfaces.

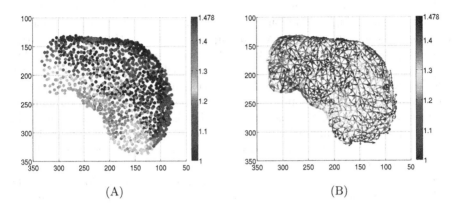

(A)                                    (B)

**Fig. 5.** $q^*$ selected for the unary terms (A) and for the pairwise terms (B). The training data set for each point marked by a circle is shown in Figs. 6 and 7

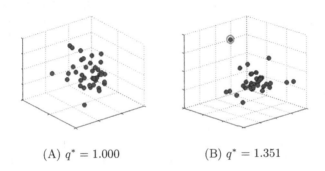

(A) $q^* = 1.000$                    (B) $q^* = 1.351$

**Fig. 6.** Examples of the training data sets for the two points marked in Fig. 5. $q^* = 1.000$ was selected from (A) and $q^* = 1.351$ from (B).

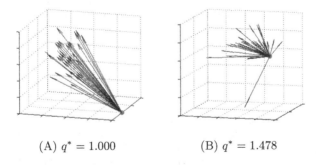

(A) $q^* = 1.000$                    (B) $q^* = 1.478$

**Fig. 7.** Examples of the training data sets for the two edges marked in Fig. 5. $q^* = 1.000$ was selected from (A) and $q^* = 1.478$ from (B).

Figure 5 shows the experimental results: The panel (A) demonstrates $q^*$ selected for each single point on the liver surface and the panel (B) demonstrates $q^*$ for each edge in the directed graph. As shown in the panel (A), larger values of $q$ were selected at the points in the posterior portion of the liver: The shape of the probability distribution selected at each point in the posterior liver portion had heavier tails. Figure 6 shows two examples of the training data sets. The panel (A) shows a training data set of a point in the anterior portion of the liver at which $q^* = 1.000$ and the panel (B) shows a training data set in the posterior portion at which $q^* = 1.351$. As shown, some *outliers* (circled in the figure) were found in the training data set when larger $q^*$ was selected. It should be noted that the location of the anterior portion of the liver is constrained more strongly than that of the posterior portion because of the locations of the landmarks used for the image normalization. The anterior portion of the liver is located near the anterior portion of the abdominal cavity, of which location in a normalized image is more strongly constrained by a set of the landmarks detected at the rib cage and the navel. As shown in Fig. 5(B), probability distributions with heavier tails were selected for representing the pairwise terms in the right portion of the liver. Two examples of the training data for the pairwise terms are shown in Fig. 7. Larger values of $q$ were selected when the training data sets include outliers, of which the Mahalanobis distance from the mean are large.

## 4   Conclusion

The authors propose to represent the statistical variety of a target organ with a directed graphical model and to select an appropriate model from $q$-exponential distribution for representing the unary terms and the pairwise ones in order to improve the generalization performance. For the model selection, the AIC is employed. Simulation experiments demonstrated that the model selection improved the generalization performance and the experiments with clinical images showed that the distributions with heavier tails were selected for the representation of the unary terms in the posterior portion of the liver. The future works include to implement a method for registering the PDM constructed in this study and to compare it with a Gaussian model in regard to the registration performance.

## References

1. Cootes, T.F., Taylor, C.J.: Statistical models of appearance for medical image analysis and computer vision. In: SPIE Medical Imaging, pp. 236–248. International Society for Optics and Photonics (2001)
2. Heimann, T., Meinzer, H.P.: Statistical shape models for 3D medical image segmentation: a review. Med. Image Anal. **13**(4), 543–563 (2009)
3. Cootes, T.F., Taylor, C.J., Cooper, D.H., Graham, J.: Active shape models-their training and application. Comput. Vis. Image Underst. **61**(1), 38–59 (1995)

4. Blake, A., Isard, M.: Active Contours: The Application of Techniques from Graphics, Vision, Control Theory and Statistics to Visual Tracking of Shapes in Motion. Springer Science & Business Media, New York (2012)
5. Friedman, J., Hastie, T., Tibshirani, R.: Sparse inverse covariance estimation with the graphical lasso. Biostatistics **9**(3), 432–441 (2008)
6. Sawada, Y., Hontani, H.: A study on graphical model structure for representing statistical shape model of point distribution model. In: Ayache, N., Delingette, H., Golland, P., Mori, K. (eds.) MICCAI 2012, Part II. LNCS, vol. 7511, pp. 470–477. Springer, Heidelberg (2012)
7. Hontani, H., Tsunekawa, Y., Sawada, Y.: Accurate and robust registration of non-rigid surface using hierarchical statistical shape model. In: IEEE Conference on Computer Vision and Pattern Recognition (CVPR), pp. 2977–2984. IEEE (2013)
8. Kotz, S., Nadarajah, S.: Multivariate t-Distributions and Their Applications. Cambridge University Press, Cambridge (2004)
9. Akaike, H.: A new look at the statistical model identification. IEEE Trans. Autom. Control **19**(6), 716–723 (1974)
10. Nemoto, M., Masutani, Y., Hanaoka, S., Nomura, Y., Yoshikawa, T., Hayashi, N., Yoshioka, N., Ohtomo, K.: A unified framework for concurrent detection of anatomical landmarks for medical image understanding. In: SPIE Medical Imaging, p. 79623E. International Society for Optics and Photonics (2011)
11. Hanaoka, S., Masutani, Y., Nemoto, M., Nomura, Y., Yoshikawa, T., Hayashi, N., Yoshioka, N., Ohtomo, K.: Probabilistic modeling of landmark distances and structure for anomaly-proof landmark detection. In: Proceedings of the Third International Workshop on Mathematical Foundations of Computational Anatomy-Geometrical and Statistical Methods for Modelling Biological Shape Variability, pp. 159–169 (2011)
12. Bronstein, A.M., Bronstein, M.M., Kimmel, R.: Numerical Geometry of Non-rigid Shapes. Springer Science & Business Media, New York (2008)

# Passive and Active Electro-Optical Sensors for Aerial and Space Imaging (EO4AS 2015)

# Recent Progress in In-Flight Radiometric Calibration and Validation of the RapidEye Constellation of 5 Multispectral Remote Sensing Satellites

Andreas Brunn[✉], Sara Bahloul, Dietrich Hoffmann, and Cody Anderson

BlackBridge AG, Kurfürstendamm 22, 10719 Berlin, Germany
{andreas.brunn,sara.bahloul,dietrich.hoffmann,
cody.anderson}@blackbridge.com
http://www.blackbridge.com

**Abstract.** BlackBridge AG is a geospatial data provider which operates a constellation of five identical multispectral remote sensing satellites. These satellites cover five spectral bands in the visible (VIS) and near infrared (NIR) spectral range. Radiometric calibration of multispectral and hyperspectral instruments like those operated by BlackBridge AG is of fundamental importance if the data e.g. should be used for remote sensing applications or if the atmospheric influence to the data should be corrected using methods based on atmospheric transfer codes. For the RapidEye constellation three goals are achieved using calibration. First, spatial calibration corrects response differences for the individual CCD elements in one CCD array. Second, temporal calibration provides a comparable measurement of the five different cameras over time. Finally, absolute calibration links the relative digital number (DN) outputs of the sensors to absolute at-sensor radiance levels.

This paper explains in detail the methodologies used for radiometric calibration of the five satellite constellation.

## 1 Introduction

To extract reliable information from remote sensing imagery they need to be corrected for systematic defects or undesirable sensor characteristics [1].

The level of the calibration necessary is highly dependent on the intended application of the data. If the data is envisaged for a visual inspection or interpretation a correction for the pixel response non uniformity (PRNU) is most important to make the detector response equal when exposed to the same amount of light. In addition to the PRNU correction most applications like time series analysis or automatic change detection [2] rely on a very stable data quality and accuracy over time. For the application of physically based atmospheric correction models like MODTRAN [3,4] an absolute calibration of the data is essential.

The RapidEye system initially was designed to support accurate and automated analysis of vegetated areas. Such targets usually require the detection of

© Springer International Publishing Switzerland 2016
F. Huang and A. Sugimoto (Eds.): PSIVT 2015 Workshops, LNCS 9555, pp. 273–284, 2016.
DOI: 10.1007/978-3-319-30285-0_22

very subtle spectral features and in consequence a very accurate correction and calibration of the multispectral satellite data.

The initial radiometric calibration concept [5] planned statistics based methods for on-orbit PRNU correction and temporal calibration after a pre-launch calibration and characterization phase. In the course of the operation of the system, the calibration methods have been adjusted significantly to reflect the actual needs of the customers. Finally, absolute calibration using the reflectance based vicarious calibration method [6,7] has been added to the calibration process and applied successfully for several years [8].

## 2    The RapidEye Constellation of Satellites

RapidEye is a full end-to-end commercial Earth Observation system comprising a constellation of five satellites carrying identical multispectral cameras and their dedicated spacecraft control and data processing centres. The system is owned and operated by BlackBridge AG.

The constellation of satellites was launched into orbit on August 29, 2008 from Baikonur Cosmodrome on one Dnepr launch rocket and injected into a sun synchronous orbit at a nominal altitude of 630 km and an inclination of 97.9°. The spacecraft follow each other in their orbital plane at about 19 min intervals. These orbital characteristics allow the system to image any place on earth between ±84° daily with a satellite roll angle up to ±20°.

The satellite platform is a Micro Satellite platform developed and built by Surrey Satellite Technology (SSTL) (Fig. 1(a)). The multispectral imager (MSI) observes the Earth in five discrete spectral bands. The instrument is composed of an all-reflective three mirror anastigmat telescope that is mounted on a thermally controlled optical bench, and a focal-plane assembly (FPA) containing five linear CCD arrays, each integrated with a dichroic filter to provide spectral separation into discrete bands [8] (Fig. 1(b)).

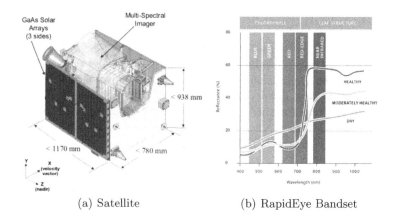

(a) Satellite                (b) RapidEye Bandset

**Fig. 1.** RapidEye satellite bus sketch (left) and RapidEye band sets (right)

The shown bandset is mainly adjusted for applications of vegetation analysis like agriculture and forestry. The RapidEye constellation carries the first multispectral imagers containing Red-Edge bands, which are especially useful for detecting subtle differences in the health status of plants. Figure 1(b) emphasizes the usefullness of the Red-Edge band as it helps to characterize the difference between healthy green vegetation and vegetation showing an already reduced vitality.

The native spatial resolution of 6.5 m at nadir, together with a broad swath width of 75 km and the imaging capacity of up to 1 500 km per orbit, results in a total of up to 6 million sqkm of high quality and high resolution remote sensing imagery per day. As of 2015 the growing image archive owned by BlackBridge holds more than 6 billion sqkm of imagery.

# 3   Calibration of the Cameras

The radiometric calibration of the RapidEye Constellation is broken into three different calibration goals, each performed following distinct methods and procedures. These methods are:

- Spatial Calibration
- Temporal Calibration
- Absolute Calibration

These methods are described in the following section.

## 3.1   Spatial Calibration

The purpose of spatial calibration is to maintain homogeneous spectral responses among all of the 12 000 CCD detectors in each of the five spectral bands of the five RapidEye satellites. Visually this calibration step prevents from visible banding and striping effects in the imagery. To adjust the individual sensor responses to each other, the detectors are assigned with individual gain and offset values, resulting in one radiometric correction table (RCT) per band containing 12 000 offset and 12 000 gain values.

At the beginning of operations for this purpose a purely statistical method has been used. This method used the detector mean and standard deviation values of all operational images to calculate the correction values. As for this method imagery worth of sometimes several weeks have been necessary to create useful correction values a new method has been adopted.

With this side slither method the correction factors are obtained by evaluating two special types of images, dark shots and side slither images, which are acquired by every satellite every three months [9]. The update resulting from the quarterly dark shots and side slither images is performed as a regular maintenance measure even if there is no apparent quality issue. In case of sudden detector changes, which can occur for various non-critical reasons, the offsets can be taken from the latest available dark shot and the gains can be derived statistically from the latest operational imagery, overlaid with the last (up to three months old) side slither gains. Hence, this eliminates the need for special acquisitions during fast troubleshooting.

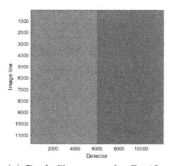

(a) Dark Shot over the Pacific Ocean

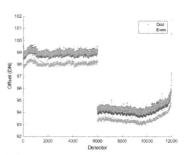

(b) Derived Detector Offsets, Separated for Odd and Even Detector Numbers

**Fig. 2.** Calculation of the detector offsets using a dark shot.

A dark shot, as seen in Fig. 2(a), is acquired over the Pacific Ocean at night and is used to calculate the detector offsets. The offsets are the detectors' response to a zero input. As blinding the detectors is not possible, a zero input image is simulated by a dark shot. Figure 2(b) shows the calculated offsets, which correspond to the detector-wise (column) means of the dark shot data. The difference between the left and the right sides of the detector means is due to the readout mechanism used on-board.

A side slither image, as seen in Fig. 3(a), is acquired over a bright homogeneous target while the satellite is yawing by 90° and allows for the calculation of the detector gains. During northern hemisphere summer time, side slither images are acquired over Greenland, whereas during southern hemisphere summer time the target area is Dome C in Antarctica. The premise behind a 90° yawed image is that each detector captures the same spot on the ground, which allows for a comparison of the detectors' responses to the exact same incoming radiation. It is desirable to have as bright a target as possible since the differences in detector gain become more apparent at the high end of the response curve. Figure 3 shows a small extract from a (shifted) side slither and the resulting detector gains.

To obtain the detector gains the individual detector responses are shifted to align the ground samples. Following this, the previously calculated detector offsets are subtracted from the corresponding column and the remaining detector (column) means are divided by the overall side slither image mean, resulting in the detector gains shown in Fig. 3(b).

These gains and offsets must be adjusted before they meet the form needed for the RapidEye RCTs. This adjustment is briefly explained at the end of this section. However, there is a second way to calculate the detector gains, used

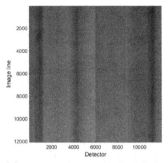

(a) Extract from a Shifted Side Slither over Greenland

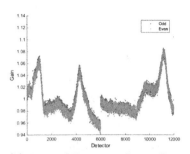

(b) Derived Detector Gains, Separated for Odd and Even Detector Numbers

**Fig. 3.** Calculation of the detector gains using a side slither.

especially in cases of sudden detector changes and gradual changes over time. In those cases it is not feasible to perform a side slither maneuver every few days.

Sudden detector changes usually affect only a few thousand detectors and become visible as a banding in the imagery. As the sudden change leaves the rest of the detectors unaltered, only the gains of the affected detectors need to be updated. The detector offsets can be taken from the last quarterly update and the detector gains for the affected detectors are derived from statistics of the most recent operational imagery. It is assumed that data taken during a side slither maneuver provides the most accurate detector gains, which is why those are kept for the unaffected detectors. This combination method finds the affected detectors, uses statistics collected after the sudden detector change to estimate new gains for these detectors, and combines the new gains for the affected detectors with the previous side slither gains for the unaffected detectors.

During normal operation, the detector means of every acquired image are stored. For the combination method, those stored means are retrieved for a period of at least one week, starting after the sudden detector change.

Figure 4(a) shows the latest side slither gains compared to the gains derived from the statistics of the detector means. The statistical gains are only displayed roughly between detectors 9 000 and 11 000, which is where the sudden detector change took affect. The exact location of the banding is determined by the zero crossing points of the difference of two curves fitted to the side slither and the statistical gains for 12 000 detectors each. Two individual bandings which are separated by less then 1 000 detectors are treated as one. In order to blend the statistical gains into the side slither gains, a buffer of 500 detectors on either side of the banding is used to guarantee a smooth transition between the two datasets.

The final combined gains for the 12 000 detectors, which are valid after the sudden detector change, are displayed in Fig. 4(b). They equal the last side slither gains anywhere which is further than 500 detectors away from the banding, equal

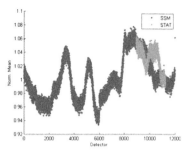

(a) Side Slither Gains with Adjusted and Merged Statistical Gains

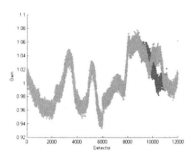

(b) Combined Side Slither and Adjusted Statistical Gains

**Fig. 4.** Collecting and merging the side slither gains and the statistical gains

the statistically derived gains within the banding and form a smooth transition between both datasets in the 500 detector wide buffer on either side of the banding.

As a last step, the gain and offset values have to be adjusted to be applicable to the RapidEye data. The hitherto calculated gains and offsets correct the preprocessed input signal $Q$ as follows,

$$Q'_i = (Q_i - o_i) \cdot g_i , \tag{1}$$

where $Q'$ is the corrected digital signal, $o$ is the offset, $g$ is the gain and the identifier $i \in \{1, \ldots, 12\,000\}$ denotes the individual detectors. Before filling out the RCTs that are applied to the RapidEye data, the gains and offsets are adjusted to correct $Q$ in the following way

$$R = (Q_i \cdot g'_i) - o'_i, \tag{2}$$

where $R$ is the corrected signal in DNs, $o'$ is the adjusted offset, $g'$ is the adjusted gain and $i$ is as above.

## 3.2    Temporal Calibration

The objective of the temporal radiometric calibration is to achieve homogenous sensor responses between all five satellites of the constellation over the entire mission time. This is impaired by a degradation of sensitivity of the sensors. The degradation mainly depends on the quality of the assembled components and their life-time, but can be also affected by certain incidents like overblending. The temporal calibration tries to figure out the magnitude of this degradation. So as a result of this, adjustment-parameters can be applied.

This procedure is performed for all five bands on each satellite. This allows BlackBridge to generate image-products with comparable radiance since the start of operations and to ensure high radiometric quality for all products.

To evaluate the degradation of a sensor BlackBridge uses a network of 27 pseudo-invariant calibration-sites all over the world. An overview of these sites is given in Fig. 5. The sites have a size of about 50 × 200 km each and cover approximately 20 to 30 RapidEye-Product-tiles per site. All calibration-sites are located in areas with a stable and dry surface, essentially deserts.

Each calibration-site is scheduled for acquisition every fourteen days. The acquisition of these was started at the beginning of the mission and meanwhile more than 300 000 RE-tiles have been acquired for calibration purposes.

Based on this amount of imagery, statistical means are calculated for certain points in time. The assumption behind this calculation is that mean values of a set of images covering pseudo-invariant calibration-sites are stable over time and will be only affected by a sensitivity decrease of the sensor. So, from the behavior of these mean values the degradation of the sensor can be derived.

To ensure that the changing mean reflects only the degradation, all unsuitable images, that contain blackfill, clouds, haze, snow etc., must be excluded from the calculations. This is done by an incremental filtering process that sorts all inappropriate images out. In a first step all acquisitions of a single tile-id are filtered against their mean, then the remaining tiles of a single calibration-site are filtered against their mean and finally all sites are filtered together. The benchmark for filtering is always the current mean value of the section and its standard deviation.

**Fig. 5.** BlackBridge calibration sites

Since all images in the database are affected by previously applied radiometric correction parameters, the image-means must be reduced to normalized values. This step is done before the filtering process starts.

In addition to this the images show seasonal differences. These are visible in larger mean values between April and September and smaller means between October and March. The reason for this is that the majority of the calibration-sites are located in the Northern hemisphere. Therefore, the filtering process and data-analysis is applied only on intervals of multiples of 12 months.

After all filtering a line is fitted through all remaining mean-values, where the gain of the line shows the degradation with respect to time. This gain is called "DailyTemporalFactor (T)".

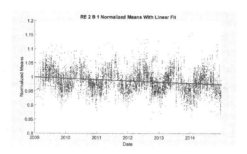

**Fig. 6.** Linear fit of tile means for RE2B1

Figure 6 shows an example of the result of the filtering process and the line-fit for RE2 Band1.

In addition to this continuous, but small, degradation for some of the sensors an abrupt decline in sensitivity was found. This can happen after special events, like down-time for a satellite. Knowing an event has occurred, the sensor-sensitivity before and after the event is analyzed in detail, to determine, whether a discontinuity occured. If so a Temporal Discontinuity Factor $(D)$ is calculated as:

$$D = \frac{(T_{before\ event} - T_{after\ event})}{T_{after\ event}}$$

To keep the sensor responses over time constant the DailyTemporalFactor $(T)$ and the TemporalDiscontinuityFactor $(D)$ are applied on all images. $T$ as a daily factor is multiplied by the number of days between image acquisition and system commissioning. $D$ is applied as constant factor for all images that are taken after the date of the discontinuity.

Finally, the sensor-degradation for all five RapidEye satellites are displayed as a decline in percentage since mission start. The current values from the end of July 2015 can be seen in Fig. 7.

The maximum value for degradation is nearly 5 % for RE1 Band1. With respect to seven years mission operations, this is a very respectable status. The numbers have a bit-depth of 16 bit, unsigned.

## 3.3 Absolute Calibration

Absolute calibration means to convert the digital counts provided by the camera into physical radiance units. This procedure is essential for a wide variety of applications.

Usually the instruments are characterized and calibrated very accurately before integration with the spacecraft and launch into the Earth's orbit. During the assembly and mostly the launch but also during the whole mission lifetime the spectral characteristics of the instruments including the detector sensitivity is not completely stable. This sensor behaviour requires a proper validation and calibration throughout the full mission lifetime.

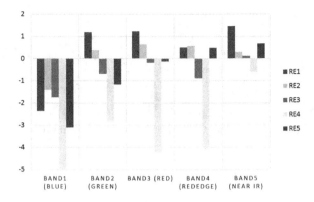

**Fig. 7.** Degradation [%] of RE-sensors July 2015

In the calibration and validation community many different methods are used to achieve the goal of an absolutely calibrated satellite. For the Landsat 8 Operational Land Imager the calibration teams are using on-board calibration equipment like lamps, solar diffusors or shutter doors, celestial objects like the moon [10] or ground based vicarious calibration [11].

For commercial and small satellite programs it is usually not practically feasible to integrate on-board calibration equipment or use celestial objects. Therefore, BlackBridge uses a reflectance based vicarious calibration approach for absolute calibration.

The reflectance based vicarious calibration methodology relies on ground-based surface reflectance measurements of a selected site and atmospheric conditions over that site [12]. The ideal sites for vicarious calibration activities show a homogeneous surface and a stable atmosphere with as little scatterers as possible. Therefore the ideal sites are high elevation flat desert areas. However, such sites are usually very bright and the effort to access them is high. Hence other sites like pastures are used successfully for vicarious calibration, too [7].

For the RapidEye satellites BlackBridge AG has maintained support contracts with the College of Optical Sciences, University of Arizona (UoA) since 2009. UoA is using the very bright Railroad Valley site [13] (Fig. 8(a)) as a ground target. To achieve a proper absolute calibration over as wide a dynamic range as possible a further contract with the Image Processing Lab of the South dakota State University (SDSU) has been added in 2013. SDSU uses a pasture site which is, compared to the RRV site, significantly darker at least in the visible bands (Brookings 3M site) [14] (Fig. 8(b)).

In addition to the manned site at Railroad Valley, an automated Radiometric Calibration Test Site (RadCaTS) has been used since 2015 [15]. Table 1 summarizes the yearly volumes of the simultaneous field and image collects.

Since 2011 the reference information has been collected for all 5 RapidEye sensors, while in 2009 and 2010 only 2 sensors were used. To characterize the full

(a) Railroad Valley Calibration site    (b) Brookings Calibration site

**Fig. 8.** Used calibration sites

**Table 1.** Number of collects since 2009

|              | Railroad Valley | Brookings |
|--------------|-----------------|-----------|
| 2009 - 2010  | 10              | -         |
| 2011         | 5               | -         |
| 2012         | 25              | -         |
| 2013         | 5               | 9         |
| 2014         | 10              | 12        |
| 2015 *       | 105**           | 10        |

\* expected; ** incl. RadCaTS

constellation after these two initial years the statistics based temporal calibration approach was used to extend and supplement the absolute calibration to the other sensors.

The vicarious calibration process measures the hyperspectral upwelling radiance using a field spectrometer (Fig. 9(b)) simultaneously with the satellite overpass. In addition, the atmospheric transmittance is measured in the interval surrounding the overpass (Fig. 9(a)). Extinction values, calculated from the atmospheric transmittance measurements, together with the overpass geometry information is used to support the transformation of the hyperspectral top of canopy reflectance data into at-sensor radiance. After the accurate resampling of the hyperspectral data to the actual sensor spectral response this simulated at-sensor radiance is compared to the satellite measured at-sensor radiance. The differences between the simulated and satellite measurements from all references on both of the sites are used to calculate adjusted gain and offset values for a linear correction of the satellite measurements to reflect absolute radiance measurements in the RapidEye products.

The current settings of these linear correction parameters reflect the results of all reference measurements until the end of 2014. With these measurements the remote sensing data is in sync in an absolute manner. The new measurements from 2015 will be incorporated as soon as they are available as a whole. This is expected to be early 2016.

(a) Sun Pho-    (b) Field Spectrome-
tometer         ter

**Fig. 9.** Measurement devices

## 3.4 Conclusion and Outlook

The methods described above are showing a distinct improvement in accuracy and responsiveness compared to the methods initially designed for the constellation of the satellites. The side slither method described in Sect. 3.1 makes it possible to take corrective action right after response changes of a group of detectors have been detected. Additionally the result of the flat fielding using this method is visually clearly better than those using the original statistical method. With the addition of the dark Brookings calibration site to the absolute calibration an improvement in accuracy especially in the darker regions could be achieved.

For the next update taking place in 2016 it is planned to add another darker water site to achieve a further improvement in the dark region of the dynamic range especially for the red-edge and NIR bands.

**Acknowledgments.** The authors thank the engineering and operations teams at BlackBridge AG, especially Brian D'Souza, Tom Haylock, Roland Schulze and the mission planning team for their support in performing the side slither maneuvres, planning the spacecraft imaging the right areas for the field campaigns and for other contributions.

Additionally the authors thank the teams from South Dakota State University and the University of Arizona for performing the field campaigns on the Brookings and Railroad Valley sites.

## References

1. Schowengerdt, R.A.: Remote Sensing, Models and Methods for Image Processing, 3rd edn. Academic Press, Burlington (2006)
2. Lunetta, R.S., Elvidge, C.D.: Remote Sensing Change Detection: Environmental Monitoring Methods and Applications. Taylor & Francis Ltd., London (1999)
3. Berk, A., Bernstein, L.S., Robertson, D.C.: MODTRAN: A Moderate Resolution Model for LOWTRAN. Airforce Geophysics Laboratory, Hascom Air Force Base (1987)

4. Berk, A., Anderson, G.P., Bernstein, L.S.: MODTRAN4 radiative transfer modeling for atmospheric correction. Proc. SPIE **3756**, 348–353 (1999)

5. Brunn, A., Naughton, D., et al.: The calibration procedure of the multispectral imaging instruments on board the rapideye remote sensing satellites. In: Proceedings of EuroCow (2010)

6. Slater, P.N., Biggar, S.F., Thome, K.J., Gellmann, D.I., Spyak, P.R.: Vicarious radiometric calibrations of EOS sensors. J. Atmos. Oceanic Technol. **13**, 349–359 (1996)

7. Thome, K.J.: In-flight inter sensor radiometric calibration using vicarious approaches. In: Morain, S., Budge, A. (eds.) Post-Launch Calibration of Satellite Sensors, pp. 95–100. Taylor & Francis Group, London (2004)

8. Naughton, D., Brunn, A., et al.: Absolute radiometric calibration of the RapidEye multispectral imager using the reflectance-based vicarious calibration method. J. Appl. Remote Sens. **5**(1), 53544-1–53544-23 (2011)

9. Anderson, C., Brunn, A., Thiele, M.: Combining imaging statistics and side slither imagery to estimate relative detector gains. In: Proceedings of the CalCon, Logan (2012)

10. Markham, B., Barsi, J., et al.: Landsat-8 operational land imager radiometric calibration and stability. Remote Sens. **6**(12), 12275–12308 (2014)

11. Czapla-Myers, J., Anderson, N.J., Biggar, S.F.: Early ground-based vicarious calibration results for Landsat 8 OLI. In: SPIE Optical Engineering + Applications, pp. 88660-1–88660-10 (2013)

12. Thome, K.J.: Sampling and uncertainty issues in trending reflectance-based vicarious calibration results. In: SPIE Optics & Photonics 2005, pp. 588216–1–588216–11 (2005)

13. Thome, K.J., McCorkel, J., Czapla-Myers, J.: Inflight intersensor radiometric calibration using the reflectance-based method for LANDSAT-type sensors. In: Proceedings of the Pecora 17, The Future of Land Imaging - Going Operational (2008)

14. Aaron, D.: Radiometric calibration assessment of commercial high spatial resolution multispectral image products. In: Civil Commercial Imagery Evaluation Workshop (2006)

15. Czapla-Myers, J., Leisso, N.P.: Recent results from the radiometric calibration test site (RadCaTS) at Railroad Valley, Nevada. In: Proceedings of the SPIE 7807, pp. 78070R–78070R-9 (2010)

# Verification of a Spectrometer Breadboard for Characterization of a Future Spaceborne Sensor

Horst Schwarzer[1], Andreas Eckardt[1], and Ralf Reulke[2(⊠)]

[1] DLR German Aerospace Center, Institute of Optical Sensor Systems,
Rutherfordstraße 2, 12489 Berlin, Germany
andreas.eckardt@dlr.de

[2] Computer Vision, Humboldt-Universität zu Berlin,
Unter den Linden 6, 10099 Berlin, Germany
reulke@informatik.hu-berlin.de

**Abstract.** German Aerospace Center **DLR** is involved in several hyperspectral missions for Earth remote sensing (e.g. EnMAP) but also for deep space and planetary missions (e.g. the Mercury mission Bepi Colombo). Hyperspectral instruments are designed for characterization of planetary surfaces, oceans and the atmosphere.

These spectrometers operate in the visible (VIS), near infrared (NIR), short wave infrared (SWIR) up to thermal infrared (TIR) spectral range with a spectral sampling below 10 nm up to 100 nm. In the spatial domain these instruments have more then 1000 pixels with a Ground Sampling Distance (GSD) of about 30 m up to 90 m.

The paper describes the calibration and performance verification of a breadboard model for future spectrometer on space-borne platforms. These procedures include measurements of the dark signal (DS), the linearity and deviation from linearity, noise behavior and signal to noise ratio (SNR) as well as photon transfer curve (PTC), the absolute radiometric calibration and the spectral imaging performance or the spectral resolution.

## 1 Introduction

In this paper the verification process of a breadboard solution (BB) for the DESIS instrument will be explained. An example for a space-borne instrument is DESIS (DLR Earth Sensing Imaging Spectrometer). This instrument will be installed on International Space Station (ISS). The instrument will be installed on the Multi-User System for Earth Sensing (MUSES) platform of Teledyne Brown Engineering.

DESIS was designed and developed to deliver precise data from the Earth surface and the atmosphere in the VIS/NIR spectral range with high spectral, high radiometric and moderate spatial resolution. To meet the sophisticated radiometric and spectral requirements and to guaranty a high reliability for detection of changes in the Earth ecosystem, a qualified in-flight calibration

© Springer International Publishing Switzerland 2016
F. Huang and A. Sugimoto (Eds.): PSIVT 2015 Workshops, LNCS 9555, pp. 285–295, 2016.
DOI: 10.1007/978-3-319-30285-0_23

concept including internal calibration, based on LED illumination and ground target based calibration have been established. A description of this instrument can be find in the paper from Eckardt [1].

With BB is to be shown that the test setup and the sensor is suitable in principle for the future measurement system on the Space Station.

This paper is organized as follows. Section 2 describes the DESIS hyperspectral imaging instrument. Section 3 introduces terminology and performance parameter, which has to be verified. Section 4 describes some measurements and their results. Finally, Sect. 5 presents our conclusions.

## 2    Instrument Description

DESIS is a hyperspectral instrument in a spectral range of 400 nm up to 1000 nm (VIS-NIR) and based on a modified Offner-Design for the Spectrometer. The telescope has a TMA (three-mirror anastigmat) design. Instead of the TMA, in the BB a telecentric glass-optics is used. The optical scheme of BB is shown in Fig. 1. The incoming light will be imaged by the objective into spectrometer slit plane. The slit defines the observed swath on the observed scene. The light enters the mirror and will be reflected onto the grating where the light is spectral dispersed and reflected back to the mirror. Then the mirror focuses the 2D spectrum of the scene into the focal plane of the spectrometer.

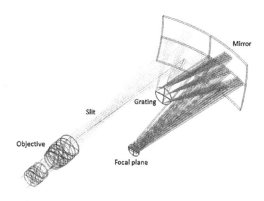

**Fig. 1.** Optical scheme of the BB

In the following Table 1 the design parameter of DESIS and BB are collected.

The DESIS-Detector is a sCMOS array. The pixel size is $24 \cdot 24 \, \mu m^2$. 235 columns were used to perform the spectral channels and 1024 pixels (rows) were used in spatial direction. The radiometric resolution is 13 bit. A description of this detector can be found in the paper from Eckardt, [10].

For DESIS BB2 the GT3300 camera from Allied [8] was used. This camera is based on the Truesense KAI-08050 CCD-chip (see [9]).

**Table 1.** Optical performance data of DESIS and BB

|  | DESIS | DESIS BB |
|---|---|---|
| Telescope | 2.8/320 mm | 4/100 mm |
| FOV | 4.4 | 7.6° |
| IFOV | 0.004° | 0.0074° |
| Spectrometer type | Offner | Offner |
| Spectral range | 400 nm–1000 nm | 450 nm–950 nm |
| Spectral channels | 235 | |
| Spectral sampling | 2.55 nm | < 0.5 nm |
| In-orbit calibration | 2 Internal LED field | 2 internal lamps |
| Pointing (along-track) | ±40° | |

## 3   Radiometric Calibration

### 3.1   General Consideration

Overview about sensor performance consideration can be found in Kopeika [3], Janesick [4,5]. Following radiometric performance parameter are measured and derived for system verification.

– System gain determination (necessary for QE and DC determination)from Photon transfer curve (PTC),
– Linearity, saturation and non-linearity correction parameter,
– Signal to Noise Ratio (SNR),
– Dark Current (DC) and read noise measurements,
– Quantum efficiency (QE) determination.

### 3.2   Signal Calculation

The wavelength dependent incident radiance $L_{rad}(\lambda)$ causes irradiance $E(\lambda)$ on the detector chip ($f_\#$ is the f-number of the telescope, $T_{opt}$, $R_{mir}$ and $\eta_{gr}$ are the optics transmission, the Offner mirror reflection and grating efficiency):

$$E\left(\lambda\right) = \frac{\pi}{\left(4 \cdot f_\#^2\right)} \cdot T_{opt}\left(\lambda\right) \cdot R_{mir}^2 \cdot \eta_{gr}\left(\lambda\right) \cdot L_{rad}\left(\lambda\right) \tag{1}$$

$< n_{ph} >$ is the average number of photons incident on the detector surface $A_{pix}$ during integration time $\tau_{int}$. $\cdot\eta_{disp}$ is the linear dispersion of the grating and defines the extent to which a spectral interval is spread out across a pixel in the focal plane (with the center wavelength $\lambda$) and is expressed in [nm/pixel].

$$\langle n_{ph}\rangle = \tau_{int} \cdot A_{pix} \cdot \eta_{disp} \cdot \frac{\lambda}{hc} \cdot E \tag{2}$$

The photons generate with a probability $\eta_\lambda^{qu}$ electron - hole pairs in the semi-conductor (quantum efficiency). This is the prerequisite for the stored electrons in the read-out register.

The measured digital gray value is $s$. It consists of the average (expectation-) value $\langle s \rangle$ and the noise.

$$s = \langle s \rangle + \eta_{DV} \cdot \left( \eta_V \cdot \left( \xi_{el} + \xi_{el}^D \right) + \xi_k \right) + \xi^{ADU} \tag{3}$$

The equation include the three noise- components: photon noise, dark current, and the read- or read-out noise. The last one are noise sources related to the sensor read out and amplifier circuits and can be described by a normal distribution with variance $\sigma_k^2 = \left\langle (\xi_k)^2 \right\rangle$. Photon noise and dark current are Poisson distributed.

The ADU noise (quantization noise) $\xi^{ADU}$ will be neglected in this presentation. The average signal is

$$\langle s \rangle = \eta_{DV} \cdot \eta_V \cdot \eta_\lambda^{qu} \cdot \tau \cdot A_{pix} \cdot \eta_{gr} \cdot \frac{\lambda}{hc} \cdot E + DS \tag{4}$$

$\eta_{DV} \cdot \eta_V \cdot \left\langle n_{el}^D \right\rangle$ is the dark signal $DS$.

In this (linear) signal model the total variance $\sigma_s^2$ of the digital signal $s$ is given according to the propagation of uncertainty (or propagation of error) by

$$\sigma_s^2 = \eta_{DV}^2 \cdot \eta_v^2 \cdot \left( \langle n_{el} \rangle + \left\langle n_{el}^D \right\rangle \right) + \eta_{DV}^2 \cdot \sigma_k^2. \tag{5}$$

With Eq. (4)

$$\langle s \rangle = \eta_{DV} \cdot \langle U \rangle = \eta_{DV} \cdot \eta_V \cdot \left( \langle n_{el} \rangle + \left\langle n_{el}^D \right\rangle \right)$$

Eq. (5) can be written in the following form:

$$\sigma_s^2 = \eta_{DV} \cdot \eta_V \cdot \langle s \rangle + \eta_{DV}^2 \cdot \sigma_k^2 \tag{6}$$

This linear equation is a relation between variance of measured noise and averaged signal. The slope is the system gain $G_s$ and the offset is the read noise. The equation is related to the photon transfer method (see Janesick [5]) and can be use for characterization of the sensor.

### 3.3    Test Facility and Configuration

Experimental Setup was installed on an optical bench with a light-tight box. The measurements performed using a calibrated integrating sphere (IS) from Gigahertz Optics (see Fig. 2) with an output port diameter of 20 cm.The spatial homogeneity of the radiometric sphere is better than 1 %; the intensity stability is better than 0.06 % within 30 min The absolute radiometric calibration was provide by national metrological institute PTB. The irradiation level of this radiometric sphere can be varied over a large range by the shutters in front of the four Quartz Tungsten Halogen (QTH) lamps and additional metal filters

**Fig. 2.** Test setup for measuring the radiometric performance data with UMBB500var (IS) and interference filter (IF).

without changing the spectral behavior of the irradiation in contrast to current controlled radiometric spheres. This is essential for linearity measurements. The reference detector is a Hamamatsu.

The spectral performance measurements and calibrations will be performed using Penray lamps (e.g. from company **Newport**). To cover the spectral region from 400 nm to 1000 nm Hg, Ar, Ne and Kr spectral lamps were used.

# 4   Calibration and Performance Verification of BB

## 4.1   Photon Transfer Curve and Conversion Gain

The measurement concept is based on an analysis of detector signal and the corresponding noise by variation of input exposure (= irradiance x exposure time). With Eq. (6) the conversion gain can be derive from the slope between noise variance and signal. Figure 3 shows the result. The overall system (conversion) gain is $0.808\,[DN/e^-]$.

## 4.2   Linearity and Linearity Error

The principle of the measurement is to increase the incident exposure $E[i] = T_i \times E_0^i$ by changing either on the integration time ($T_i$) or the irradiance ($E_0^i$). Integration time can be measured with high accuracy and a large range of different $T_i$ can be obtained. To test the entire measurement set-up the change of irradiance should also be taken into account. In this case the spectral behavior of the radiation source should not changes.

The straight line is a least squares fit. Below saturation (i.e. on the straight line part of the linearity plot), it can normally be arranged that the correlation coefficient between the data and the fitted line should normally be greater than e.g. 0.995.

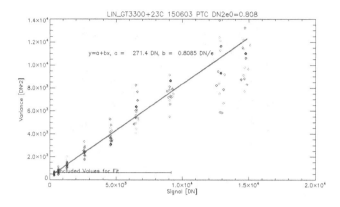

**Fig. 3.** Photon Transfer Curve. Results of the conversion gain determination and the error ranges.

Left Fig. 4 shows an example for the test results. The conversion gain was determined from PTC analyses as describes in the previous Sect. 4.1. The maximum signal of $2^{14}$ corresponds to $FWC = 20Te^-$. From the same data set the SNR can be derived (Fig. 4, right). A $SNR > 100$ can be realized with this detector for $DN \geq 10^4$.

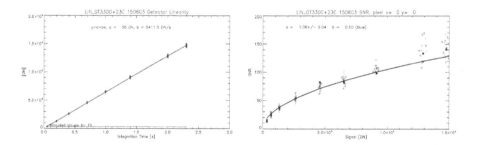

**Fig. 4.** Linearity and linear full well (left), SNR (right).

Non-linearity is significant, but can described by a polynomial fit. In the following figures (Fig. 5), non-linearity estimation are shown.

### 4.3 Dark Current

Dark current DC or dark current rate in $[e^-/pixel/sec]$ is calculated from averaged dark signal and is related to conversion gain and integration time.

With changing integration time, the dark signal noise rises. This relation is linear. In Fig. 6 the dark signal for different pixels is shown. The red line is a linear interpolation. The integration time range is from 0.1 s up to 2 s. To convert

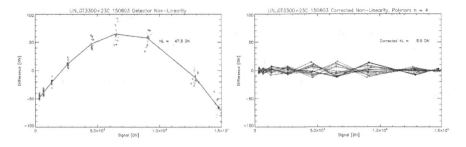

**Fig. 5.** Non-linearity (left) and and polynomial based correction (right). The remaining error is less than 1 %.

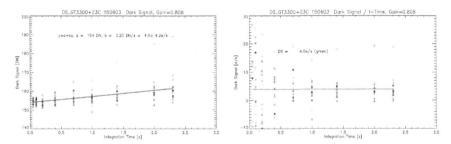

**Fig. 6.** Dark signal (left) and dark current (right) behavior for varying integration time at different locations on the chip. Dark current is $4\,e/p/s$ or $2.1\,pA/cm^2$.

dark signal $D_R$ from $[e/p/s]$ to $[pA/cm^2]$ we use the following equations ($Q = 1.6 \cdot 10^{-19}$ and $A = 5.5 \cdot 5.5\mu m^2$):

$$D_R\,[e/p/s] = \frac{J_d\,[A/cm^2] \cdot A\,[cm^2]}{Q} \quad J_d\,[A/cm^2] = \frac{Q \cdot D_R\,[e/p/s]}{A\,[cm^2]} \quad (7)$$

### 4.4    Spectral Responsivity and Quantum Efficiency (QE)

*Spectral Responsivity* is the ratio of measured signal (with substracted dark signal) to incident illumination measured in various spectral bands (responsivity measurement). A comprehensive curve gives the shape of the responsivity in a broad spectrum containing each measured spectral band.

The *quantum efficiency* (QE) at a given wavelength expressed as a percentage is the ratio of the number of photoelectrons at the detector output (signal with subtracted dark signal) to the number of incident photons in a given integration time.

The QE is measured at various wavelengths using narrow band filters. QE is being calculated using the formula (4) [%] and $G_s$ from Subsect. 4.1. The description of the variables and constants can be found in Subsect. 3.2.

$$\eta_\lambda^{qu} = \frac{(\langle s \rangle - DS) \cdot h \cdot c}{G_S \cdot \tau_{\text{int}} \cdot E \cdot A_{pix} \cdot \lambda} \cdot 100\,\% \quad (8)$$

The overall system gain $G_S$ is determined by using Eq. (6). The irradiance $E$ of the IS is measured using a calibrated photodiode with a reference to the National Standards situated in the same plane as the detector array. The measured QE (see Fig. 7) is calculated as a mean signal value over the number of pixels. The QE is very small. The reason is that in determining the QE, the fill factor was not taken into account.

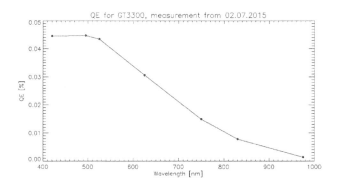

**Fig. 7.** Results for QE

## 4.5 Spectral Calibration

The spectral performance measurements and calibrations will be performed using Penray lamps. Figure 8 shows the spectral lines of the Ar(Hg)-Penray lamp measured in the BB focal plane using a camera with $5.5\,\mu m \cdot 5.5\,\mu m$ pixel size. The connection to the wavelengths can be found in the corresponding catalogs (see e.g. web-site [6,7]).

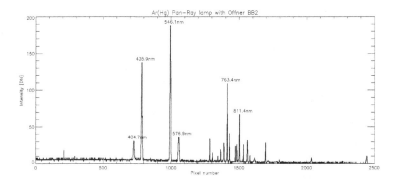

**Fig. 8.** Spectrum of the Ar Penray lamp measured in the DESIS focal plane

In Fig. 9 the linear relationship between the pixel position and the corresponding wavelength is shown. The deviation from the linear behavior (standard deviation) is 4 pixels (this corresponds to 2 nm in the wavelength region of 500 nm). This relationship also allows to determine the linear dispersion of the test setup. 500 nm are mapped to 1000 pixels on the chip ($\sim$ 0.5 nm/pixel).

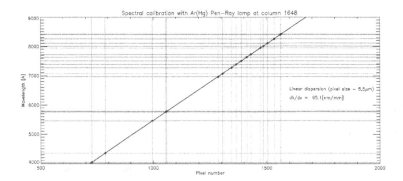

**Fig. 9.** Linear dependence between known wavelength and position on the chip. The linear dispersion is 95.1 nm/mm or 0.52 nm/pixel.

Individual spectral lines allow an investigation of the spectral resolution of the spectrometer. For evaluation we use an approach from Reulke [2] for determination of the spatial resolution of a camera. To determine the resolution the Rayleigh criterion is used. Instead of the Bessel function, the normal distribution (Gaussian) is employed. The Gaussian is characterized by the dispersion $\sigma_\lambda$. Resolution is then the distance between two normalized and superimposed normal distributions that have a minimum of 0.73. The sigma dependent distance is $2.84 \times \sigma_\lambda$. Therefore the resolution corresponds to three times $\sigma_\lambda$.

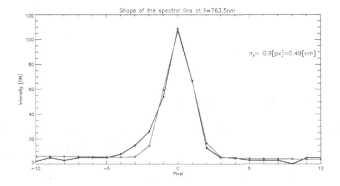

**Fig. 10.** Spectral distribution of the Ar-line at $\lambda = 736.5$ nm.

The following Fig. 10 shows the fit of a spectral line. The spectral resolution is about 1.5 nm. The dominant share is the telescope and the spectrograph. The pixel influence can be neglected. This can be explained from the square sum of the individual standard deviations. Assuming for the pixel on a $\sigma_{pix} = 0.5$, then it follows for the rest of the system $\sigma_{spec} = 0.8$ or 1.1. nm.

**Table 2.** Summary of calculated and measured parameter.

|  | System parameter | Measured values | Remarks |
|---|---|---|---|
| Optics |  |  |  |
| f-Number $f_\#$ | 4 |  |  |
| Transmission | 0.88 |  |  |
| Spectrometer |  |  |  |
| Mirror reflection | 0.92 |  |  |
| Grating efficiency | 0.37 |  |  |
| Dispersion |  | 0.523 nm/pixel | Sect. 4.5 |
| Spectrom. slit | 13 μm |  |  |
| Detector |  |  |  |
| Array | 3296 × 2472 |  |  |
| Pixel size | 5.5 μm × 5.5 μm |  |  |
| Conversion gain |  | 0.808 DN/e$^-$ | Sect. 4.1 |
| QE (522 nm) |  | 0.0432 % | Sect. 4.4 |
| Measurement condition |  |  |  |
| Wavelength | 522 nm |  |  |
| Radiance (IS) | 300 W/m$^2$ · μm · sr |  |  |
| Integration time | 1.4 s |  |  |
| Results |  |  |  |
| Signal | 8290 DN | 9090 DN | calculated |
| FWC at $2^{14}$ DN |  | $20Te^-$ | see Sect. 4.2 |
| SNR for $DN > 10^4$ |  | $\geq 100$ |  |
| Dark current |  | 4 e/s or 2.1 pA/cm$^2$ |  |

# 5    Summary and Conclusion

The breadbord model of the DESIS instrument was tested, calibrations were carried out and performance data were verified. A summary of the measured parameter can be found in Table 2.

With the known system parameters and measured quantities in Table 2, allows the comparison of the measured and calculated signal. The incident radiance is known from the calibrated light source. Irradiance can calculated from

Eq. (1). The resulting number of electrons and conversion to digital numbers is related with Eq. 4. With optics transmission of $T_{opt} = 0.8778$ and mirror reflection $R_{mir} = 0.92$ the calculated signal is 8300 DN. The measured value is 9090 DN (see Fig. 4 at $\tau_{int} = 1.4$ ms).

It is worth noting that it is possible to calculate directly the expected signal from the known and measured parameters. It can also be derived parameters of the spectroscope, for example, the real resolution in spectral direction. Thus the design and future verification and calibration of DESIS can be carried out.

**Acknowledgements.** The authors would like to thank all the colleagues who have supported this work, especially Karl-Heinz Degen for performing the measurements.

# References

1. Eckardt, A., Horack, J., Lehmann, F., Krutz, D., Drescher, J., Whorton, M., Soutullo, M.: DESIS (DLR Earth Sensing Imaging Spectrometer) for the ISS-MUSES platform. In: Proceedings of IEEE International Geoscience and Remote Sensing Symposium, IGARSS, Milano, Italy (2015)
2. Reulke, R., Sebastian, I.: Bestimmung der Bodenaufloesung der WAOSS-Kamera. Bild und Ton **45**, 271–275 (1992)
3. Kopeika, N.S.: A System Engineering Approach to Imaging. Morgan Kaufmann, SPIE Press Book, Bellingham (1998)
4. Janesick, J.R.: Scientific Charge-Coupled Devices. SPIE Press Book, Bellingham (2001)
5. Janesick, J.R.: Photon Transfer. SPIE Press Book, Bellingham (2007)
6. Optomechanics Research, Echelette Spectrograph. http://www.echellespectrographs.com/gallery.htm
7. L.O.T.-Oriel UK, Pen-Ray Line Sources. http://pas.ce.wsu.edu/CE415/PenRay_lamp_spectra.pdf
8. GT3300 camera from Allied. http://www.alliedvision.com/en/products/cameras/detail/3300.html
9. KAI-08050 Image Sensor. http://www.ccd.com/pdf/ccd_8050.pdf
10. Eckardt, A., Reulke, R., Schwarzer, H., Venus, H., Neumann, C.: sCMOS detector for imaging VNIR spectrometry. In: Proceedings of SPIE, vol. 8870 (2013)
11. Jahn, H., Reulke, R.: Systemtheoretische Grundlagen optoelektronischer Sensoren. Wiley-VCH, Berlin (2009)

# Video Surveillance (VSWS 2015)

# Moving Shadow Detection from Background Image and Deep Learning

Jong Taek Lee[✉], Kil-Taek Lim, and Yunsu Chung

Electronics and Telecommunications Research Institute (ETRI),
Daegu, South Korea
jtlee@utexas.edu, {ktl,yoonsu}@etri.re.kr

**Abstract.** We present a novel approach for moving shadow detection, which is applicable to various environments. Although there have been extensive studies of shadow detection since 1980s, the problem is still considered as a challenging and important issue in the most visual surveillance systems. Herein, we propose a shadow region learning method using a deep structure for moving shadow detection. Unlike previous approaches which are usually based on hand-crafted features using chromacity or physical properties of shadow regions, our approach is able to automatically learn features of shadow region from input source and its background image. The proposed approach is relatively simpler to implement than previous approaches as we don't need to consider intensity and color properties of video sequences. However, its performance is comparable to that of state-of-the-art approaches. Our algorithm is applied to five different datasets of moving shadow detection for comprehensive experiments.

**Keywords:** Moving shadow detection · Convolutional deep neural network · Visual surveillance

## 1 Introduction

Shadows are always present both in-door and out-door environments. The effect of shadows varies depending on light sources, but it has a high impact on the most surveillance systems. Shadows often make scene analysis more difficult rather than help scene understanding. Although shadow detection is a difficult problem, detected shadows can help analyzing the direction of light sources and the geometry of scenes. Also, shadow removal aids the localization, segmentation, and tracking of interesting objects in surveillance systems. A substantial number of studies for shadow detection ever exist, but the shadow detection is an important and challenging problem in the computer vision field.

Therefore, we propose a new general approach for shadow detection. By using convolutional deep neural network (ConvNets), we can learn features for shadow regions from both input images and background images. Without adjusting parameters for environments, we are able to learn our network with sufficient amount of input data.

© Springer International Publishing Switzerland 2016
F. Huang and A. Sugimoto (Eds.): PSIVT 2015 Workshops, LNCS 9555, pp. 299–306, 2016.
DOI: 10.1007/978-3-319-30285-0_24

The rest of the paper is organized as follows: Sect. 2 shortly introduces previous works. Section 3 presents a detailed description of our approach. Section 4 exhibits quantitative and qualitative experimental results. Section 5 concludes the paper.

## 2    Related Work

### 2.1    Moving Shadow Detection

Prati et al. [1] and Sanin et al. [2] classified and presented comparative evaluation of moving shadow detection methods developed until 2000 and 2010, respectively. Sanin et al. [2] placed shadow detection methods in a feature-based taxonomy comprised of four categories such as chromacity, physical properties [3], geometry [4] and textures [5]. As our method learns features from regions of the input frame and its background frame, it combines a spectral feature-based method and a texture-based method. Yet, none of methods introduced in [2] used convolutional networks for feature learning in a moving shadow detection framework.

### 2.2    Deep Learning

Many deep representation learning architectures have been proposed in the last decade and the successes of these deep learning methods in speech recognition [6] and image classification challenge [7] have motivated its use in computer vision applications. Khan et al. [8] proposed a ConvNets architecture to learn the most relevant features for shadow detection instead of using hand-crafted features. The learned features are further fed to conditional random field (CRF) model for shadow edge detection. Shen et al. [9] also proposed a structured ConvNets for shadow detection, but its output spaces are high dimensional to learn shadow edge structure. Both approaches are able to learn features of shadow boundaries to segment shadow regions from the other regions.

On the other hand, our approach learns shadow regions instead of shadow edges. Our approach can be less accurate than these two approaches for detecting shadow edges and their surrounding pixels, but our approach can efficiently localize shadow blobs without significant errors. Also, to the best of our knowledge, no studies have tried to use both input image and background image to learn features for shadow region classification.

## 3    Approach

### 3.1    System Overview

This subsection provides an overview of our shadow detection method. Given an input image, we first generate an over-segmented image. For superpixels containing positive pixels from foreground mask, their locations are measured to extract patches of an input image, a foreground mask, and a background image. Input

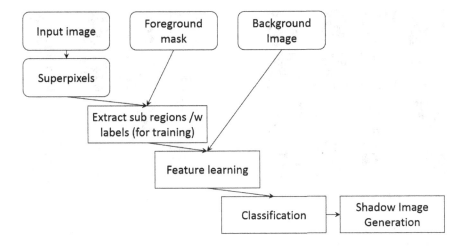

**Fig. 1.** The framework of our shadow detection.

image patches and background image patches are merged so that the number of channels of input source for our ConvNets is six. (three from input image and three from background image) The number of output from the ConvNets is three: foreground class, shadow class, and invalid class. From the superpixels of input image and their shadow classification results, we can generate a foreground/shadow map. This system overview is summarized in Fig. 1.

### 3.2 Sub-region Extraction

The size of shadow blobs and foreground blobs varies depending on the size of interesting objects and light conditions. In the case that we use a grid of uniformly spaced cells as a sub-region, the quantization error will increase if the grid is sparse, and the computational requirements will increase if the grid is dense. Therefore, we use a over-segmented image by using a superpixel algorithm. To form superpixels, we use the *Superpixels Extracted via Energy-Driven Sampling* (SEEDS) algorithm [10] because the algorithm runs in real-time and performs a comparable achievement to the state-of-the-art. The extracted superpixels are further resized to a fixed size window for feature learning, as shown in Fig. 2.

### 3.3 Deep Shadow Region Learning with ConvNets

Our ConvNets consists of seven layers as shown in Fig. 3. The first four layers are two convolutional layers and two subsampling layers, and the other three layers are fully-connected layers. The last fully-connected layer can generate a probability for 3 classes such as foreground, shadow, and the others. The Rectified Linear Unites (ReLUs) nonlinearity is applied to the output of two convolutional layers and two fully-connected layers to reduce the training time. The first and second convolutional layers consist of twenty and sixty 5 × 5

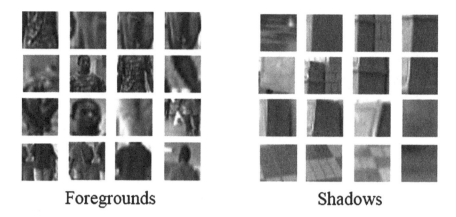

Foregrounds                    Shadows

**Fig. 2.** A collection of resized sub-regions with label - foregrounds (not shadows) on the left side and shadows on the right side.

kernels, respectively, with unit pixel stride. The pooling size is $2 \times 2$ with unit-pixel stride. Also, the fully-connected layers have 500 units each.

The dimension of input source of our ConvNets is 32 (width) $\times$ 32 (height) $\times$ 6 (channels) by integrating an input image and background image. We trained our ConvNets without background image (i.e. $32 \times 32 \times 3$ input source), but the network could not learn features for shadow detection. The network may be able to learn boundaries near shadows, but classifying shadow regions only depending on image patch seems impractical.

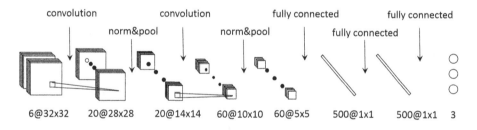

**Fig. 3.** An illustration of our ConvNet architecture.

## 4   Experiments

### 4.1   Datasets

To evaluate the proposed approach, we used a challenging video sequences introduced in [1,11,12]: The Campus, Hallway, Lab, Room, and CAVIAR sequences. The details of the video sequences are present in [2]. These video sequences are challenging because of variations in the scene, illumination, and type/size of objects and shadows. The Campus sequence is an outdoor sequence where some of the shadows are extremely long and the Hallway sequence is an indoor sequence which has a textured background. The Lab sequence has a dynamic scene of two people crossing each other and the Room sequence is taken by a wide-angle camera with distortion. show two laboratory rooms in two different perspectives and lighting conditions. The CAVIAR sequences has a reflective background and human clothing appearance varies significantly. Our shadow detection method does not need to change any parameters for different sequences, which implies our method is applicable to wide range of shadow detection problem. The first row of Fig. 4 shows a sample images for shadow detection. We implemented an shadow detection system using the Caffe [13] implementation of the ConvNets.

## 4.2   Experimental Framework

**Network Configuration.** The input layer corresponds to input image patch and background image patch, and the output layer corresponds to class probability measure whether the image patch is of shadows or not. The size of input image patch has an impact on the efficiency and accuracy of the shadow detection system. We tested three shadow detection image sizes ($32 \times 32$, $20 \times 20$, $48 \times 48$) to find the optimal solution. Using a $20 \times 20$ sized detection window, each iteration takes less time than the others and the network converges faster. However, the accuracy rate of the network is too low for shadow detection. For a $48 \times 48$ window, the performance of the network is slightly better than using a $32 \times 32$ window after 4 times of computational load is used.

**Optimization and Class Balancing.** We trained our network using the standard stochastic gradient descent with momentum. Initial learning rate is 0.0001, momentum is 0.9, and weight decay is 0.0005. We used drop-out layers in the first two fully-connected layers to learn more robust features. The performance of our network was not improved by class balancing, while our labels are slightly unbalanced.

**Table 1.** Comparison of percentage (%) of shadow detection rate ($\eta$) and shadow discrimination rate ($\xi$).

| Sequence | Campus | | Hallway | | Lab | | Room | | CAVIAR | |
|---|---|---|---|---|---|---|---|---|---|---|
| Method | $\eta$ | $\xi$ | $\eta$ | $\xi$ | $\eta$ | $\xi$ | $\eta$ | $\xi$ | $\eta$ | $\xi$ |
| DNM [1] | 82.9 | 86.7 | – | – | 76.3 | 89.9 | 78.6 | 90.3 | – | – |
| SILTP [5] | 62.6 | 43.1 | 82.3 | 91.1 | – | – | – | – | 87.5 | 94.8 |
| RMSDAP [14] | 33.8 | 91.0 | 88.3 | 96.4 | – | – | – | – | 89.7 | 96.4 |
| Proposed | 74.3 | 84.9 | 89.6 | 92.2 | 86.2 | 84.3 | 80.9 | 93.7 | 84.0 | 93.7 |

## 4.3   Quantitative Comparisons

To compare the accuracy of our proposed method with the baseline moving shadow detection method, we tested our network on five different video sequences and present the two terms for analyzing shadow detection performance: shadow detection rate $(\eta)$ and shadow discrimination rate $(\xi)$ [1]. The two metrics are defined as follows:

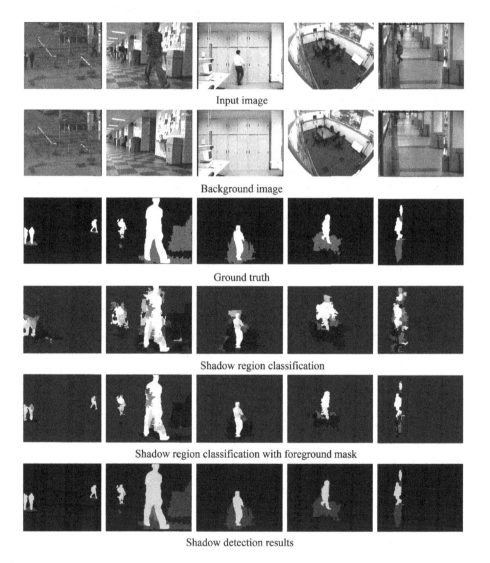

Input image

Background image

Ground truth

Shadow region classification

Shadow region classification with foreground mask

Shadow detection results

**Fig. 4.** Qualitative results of our methods on five video sequences: Campus, Hallway, Lab, Room, and CAVIAR from left to right (Color figure online).

$$\eta = \frac{TP_S}{TP_S + FN_S}; \xi = \frac{TP_F}{TP_F + FN_F}, \tag{1}$$

where $TP$ and $FN$ denote true positive and false negative, respectively, and the subscript $S$ stands for shadow and $F$ stands for foreground. Shadow detection rate can be calculated by the ratio of the number of the correctly classified shadow pixels to that of the number of the shadow pixels. Shadow discrimination rate can be calculated by the ratio of the number of the correctly classified foreground pixels (not shadow) to that of the number of foreground pixels. The performance of our method and baseline methods are compared in Table 1. Our method performs as good as other methods.

### 4.4   Qualitative Results

Figure 4 shows successful examples of the proposed method detecting shadows in various environments. The images of the first three rows are given in the datasets. The fourth row shows the probability map, where brighter pixels are more likely foregrounds (not shadows) and darker pixels are more likely shadows. The pixels of dark green color indicate regions which are neither foregrounds nor shadows. The fifth row shows the probability map with foreground (including shadows) mask. The sixth row presents how many shadow/foreground pixels are correctly classified. The pixels of blue, teal, red, and yellow indicate true positive of shadows, true positive of foregrounds, false negative of shadows, and false negative of foregrounds, respectively.

## 5   Conclusion and Future Work

We proposed a novel shadow region learning method using a deep structure for moving shadow detection in various environments. Due to the simplicity and generality of our method, it can easily incorporate other existing methods. However, our system requires sufficient amount of labeled training data. In future work, we consider to use autoencoder neural networks [15] to increase learning rates for scenarios where small labeled training data and large unlabeled training data. To enhance our shadow detection, we could incorporate a CRF model [16], which is able to enforce label consistency and local smoothness. Also, we consider a fully convolutional network for shadow detection as it is proven effective for semantic segmentation.

## References

1. Prati, A., Mikic, I., Trivedi, M.M., Cucchiara, R.: Detecting moving shadows: algorithms and evaluation. IEEE Trans. Pattern Anal. Mach. Intell. **25**(7), 918–923 (2003)
2. Sanin, A., Sanderson, C., Lovell, B.C.: Shadow detection: a survey and comparative evaluation of recent methods. Pattern Recogn. **45**(4), 1684–1695 (2012)

3. Huang, J.-B., Chen, C.-S.: Moving cast shadow detection using physics-based features. In: IEEE Conference on Computer Vision and Pattern Recognition (CVPR), Miami, pp. 2310–2317 (2009)
4. Lalonde, J.-F., Efros, A.A., Narasimhan, S.G.: Detecting ground shadows in outdoor consumer photographs. In: Daniilidis, K., Maragos, P., Paragios, N. (eds.) ECCV 2010, Part II. LNCS, vol. 6312, pp. 322–335. Springer, Heidelberg (2010)
5. Qin, R., Liao, S., Lei, Z., Li, S.Z.: Moving cast shadow removal based on local descriptors. In: 20th International Conference on Pattern Recognition (ICPR), Istanbul, Turkey, pp. 1377–1380 (2010)
6. Hinton, G.E., Deng, L., Yu, D., Dahl, G.E., Mohamed, A.R., Jaitly, N., Kingsbury, B.: Deep neural networks for acoustic modeling in speech recognition: the shared views of four research groups. IEEE Signal Process. Mag. **29**(6), 82–97 (2012)
7. Krizhevsky, A., Sutskever, I., Hinton, G.E.: Imagenet classification with deep convolutional neural networks. In: Advances in Neural Information Processing Systems (NIPS), Lake Tahoe, pp. 1097–1105 (2012)
8. Khan, S.H., Bennamoun, M., Sohel, F., Togneri, R.: Automatic feature learning for robust shadow detection. In: IEEE Conference on Computer Vision and Pattern Recognition (CVPR), Columbus, pp. 1939–1946 (2014)
9. Shen, L., Wee Chua, T., Leman, K.: Shadow optimization from structured deep edge detection. In: IEEE Conference on Computer Vision and Pattern Recognition (CVPR), Boston, pp. 2067–2074 (2015)
10. Van den Bergh, M., Boix, X., Roig, G., de Capitani, B., Van Gool, L.: SEEDS: superpixels extracted via energy-driven sampling. In: Fitzgibbon, A., Lazebnik, S., Perona, P., Sato, Y., Schmid, C. (eds.) ECCV 2012, Part VII. LNCS, vol. 7578, pp. 13–26. Springer, Heidelberg (2012)
11. Martel-Brisson, N., Zaccarin, A.: Kernel-based learning of cast shadows from a physical model of light sources and surfaces for low-level segmentation. In: IEEE Conference on Computer Vision and Pattern Recognition (CVPR), Anchorage, pp. 1–8 (2008)
12. CAVIAR: Context Aware Vision using Image-based Active Recognition. http://homepages.inf.ed.ac.uk/rbf/CAVIAR/
13. Jia, Y., Shelhamer, E., Donahue, J., Karayev, S., Long, J., Girshick, R., Guadarrama, S., Darrell, T.: Caffe: Convolutional Architecture for Fast Feature Embedding. arXiv preprint (2014). arxiv:1408.5093
14. Dai, J., Han, D.: Region-based moving shadow detection using affinity propagation. Int. J. Signal Process. Image Process. Pattern Recogn. **8**(3), 65–74 (2015)
15. Hinton, G.E., Osindero, S., Teh, Y.W.: A fast learning algorithm for deep belief nets. Neural Comput. **18**(7), 1527–1554 (2006)
16. Zhu, J., Samuel, K.G.G., Masood, S.Z., Tappen, M.F.: Learning to recognize shadows in monochromatic natural images. In: IEEE Conference on Computer Vision and Pattern Recognition (CVPR), San Francisco, pp. 223–230 (2010)

# Extracting Player's Stance Information from 3D Motion Data: A Case Study in Tennis Groundstrokes

Boris Bačić[(⊠)]

School of Computer and Mathematical Sciences,
Auckland University of Technology, Auckland, New Zealand
boris.bacic@aut.ac.nz

**Abstract.** This study presents a novel approach towards computing elements of balance, movement fluidity and reaction time, the foundations of which are commonly introduced in tennis as swing stance. The achieved results utilising presented algorithms, show 100 % recognition of tennis swings (forehands and backhands) and swing stance angle extractions from the 3D test data set. The data set was captured at 50 Hz without ball impact information using a stationary multi-camera setup. The next generation of exergames and augmented coaching technologies, utilising the presented approach for processing players' footwork and stance will enable research advancements in human performance and further developments towards improving proprioception and kinaesthetic awareness. Determining body orientation within a temporal and spatial activity pattern to predict the follow-up action(s) may also enable advancements such as improving safety in surveillance, robot and automotive vision.

**Keywords:** Exergames · Sport and rehabilitation · Biomechanics · Augmented coaching systems (ACS) · Human motion modelling and analysis (HMMA)

## 1 Introduction

With the increase of cross-disciplinary research interest in development in *exergames* and coaching systems technology, it is expected that end-users will soon benefit from advancements aimed to improve/regain *kinaesthetic awareness*, skills and technique of motion patterns that require balance, fluidity and control. Coaching *proprioception* and kinaesthetic awareness by incorporating stance of the body with specific movements has a potential to advance sport performance, rehabilitation and related areas promoting an active life and to reach broad audience including busy, aging or less-physically active population. In tennis, stance coaching foundations (as body position during the swing) is aimed at improving performance and safety associated with balance, agility, movement fluidity and reaction times. The objective of this study is to quantify and extract the stance angle of body position in tennis groundstrokes from captured 3D motion data without ball impact information. It is expected that extraction of body orientation information during recognised activity pattern is transferrable to future

© Springer International Publishing Switzerland 2016
F. Huang and A. Sugimoto (Eds.): PSIVT 2015 Workshops, LNCS 9555, pp. 307–318, 2016.
DOI: 10.1007/978-3-319-30285-0_25

exergames, augmented coaching systems (ACS) and other disciplines including surveillance, robot and automotive vision.

The following sections cover exergames and tennis domain-specific backgrounds related to stance. The mid-section includes 3D motion capture, data set analysis, developed algorithms with intermediate results and customisation tasks visualisation. The last section provides discussion, critique, results and concluding remarks.

## 1.1 Motion Capture, Exergames and Augmented Coaching Systems

Increasing popularity in exergames and 3D-based augmented coaching technology is attributed to various factors such as: advancements in computer vision (CV), open source CV, multi-camera DLT systems, and various ICT infrastructures with available SDKs that can capture and process human motion. From a pioneering Nintendo's hand-held motion capture device to the advanced concept of Microsft's Kinect using the body as a controller, the research community has benefited with available development platforms with SDKs for low-cost motion data capture. In this study, it is contended that variable accuracy of Xbox 360 Kinect depth mapping 0.4−8 m [1] and sampling frequency at 30 Hz, will improve with the next generations of exergames. Although the main advancement of the second generation of the Kinect sensor [2] may be perceived as having improved video resolution, the next generation of motion capture devices are expected to capture larger volumes, higher frequency, accuracy and precision of human motion data to allow further research advancements in coaching capabilities of exergames and early prototypes of ACS [3–6].

At present, to the best of our knowledge there are no available exergames that are able to reward performance of player's solid base of support or assess body stance.

## 1.2 Tennis and Sport Science Backgrounds

Stance is a concept associated with body position during the swing action relative to the intended target line. In coaching practice, stance variations are typically introduced as a player progresses beyond beginner or advanced-beginner level. The basic stance, known as 'side-on' or 'square stance' is empirically considered in coaching practice as the most favourable body position to help novice players to find their optimal swing power and stable body position. Historically, in the era of wooden racquets and predominant single-hand backhands, players were generally thought to execute their groundstrokes from square stances while today's forehands and predominant two-hand backhands are generally executed from all four common stances, mostly from semi-open and open stances [7–11].

To gain a competitive advantage, players of all skill levels aim to optimise and personalise stance selection associated with weight transfer, impact speed, and ball rebound height as a response to the opponent's actions. For example, the 'square' stance (or slightly 'closed' stance approach to the ball) towards the target line generally offers more stability relative to the 'open' stance at ball impact. Furthermore, hitting the ball on the run along the baseline with e.g. 'closed stance' makes it harder to accelerate the racquet before impact, compared to the optimal stance for a player when hitting 'winners' [8, 12]. On the other hand, the potentially less-safe, 'open stance', allows extended court coverage and fast response to opponents actions at the expense of balance and produced impact velocity of the racquet on the ball [7, 13].

In coaching practice there is a known phenomenon of disagreements over decision boundaries (e.g. 'is it square or closed stance?') or prioritising feedback and intervention [14]. Given the subjective and qualitative analytical nature of coaching, this study provides methods and algorithms that could quantify i.e. extract the feet angle from a groundstroke stance and determine the groundstroke category (i.e. forehand or backhand) from captured 3D motion data for exergames and ACS.

## 2 Experimental Data Collection, Annotation and Analysis

The tennis motion data set was recorded at 50 Hz by nine video cameras from fixed locations. The data set contained 3D coordinates of a set of retro-reflective markers ($q = 22$) attached to anatomical body landmarks and a racquet (ASCII text data exported from SMART-e 900 eMotion/BTS). A rigid topology of interconnected marker's trajectories was used to represent an avatar for an animated interactive 3D stick figure player. The tennis experts and end-users were able to visually assess diverse hitting stances (Figs. 1 and 2) with no recorded contact with the ball. The motion data set contained forehand and backend tennis swings with a balanced distribution of relatively good and bad swings that were considered as *common errors* [14].

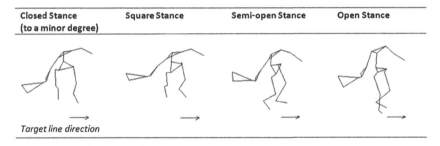

**Fig. 1.** Visualising stance relative to the target line

Stance assessment heuristics and utilised concept:

- Extracting the stance angle from a hitting position is possible by comparing the imaginary line connecting the tips of the tennis shoes and the target line direction.
- The extracted stance angle must have only one value associated with the swing type. Therefore, as a concept, for a right handed player, the *front leg* for forehands is the left leg, while for backhands it is the right leg, regardless of the player's stance.

The captured multi-time-series of motion data are denoted as:

- Human motion is represented via 3D marker position trajectories $m_p(t) = (x_p(t), y_p(t), z_p(t))$ in the captured volume.
- Marker's projections into x, y and z axis are denoted as: $\overrightarrow{Xm}, \overrightarrow{Ym}, \overrightarrow{Zm}$ .
- Each motion data sample is a frame of constituent markers $M = (m_1, m_2, ..., m_q)$.
- A frame $M$, representing a static stick-figure (shown in Fig. 3) is an interconnected finite set of three-dimensional marker positions in Euclidean space.
- Each swing event $S_j$ is a set of $k$ consecutive frames: $S_j = (t, ..., t + k; M_{1, ..., q})$, or $S_j = \{M(t) | t_0 \leq t \leq t_{k-1}\}$, where $m_p \in M$; $p = 1, ..., q$; $i, j, k, p, q \in \mathbb{N}$.

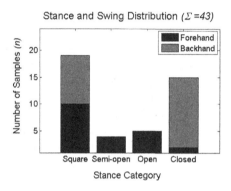

**Stance and Swing Distribution ($\Sigma$ =43)**

Number of Samples (n)

Forehand
Backhand

Square  Semi-open  Open  Closed

Stance Category

**Expert's stance analysis**

| | |
|---|---|
| 0 – Square stance: | 19 |
| 1 – Semi open stance: | 4 |
| 2 – Open stance: | 5 |
| 3 – Closed stance: | 15 |

Note:
Introducing or encouraging open-stance in single-hand backhand was not considered as safe practice for the objective of this study.

**Fig. 2.** Data set analysis: Stance distribution and expert-based classification into four output labels (0 – square stance, 1 – semi-open, 2 – open and 3 – closed stance).

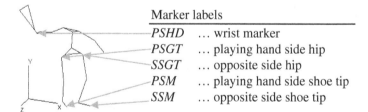

**Marker labels**

| | |
|---|---|
| PSHD | ... wrist marker |
| PSGT | ... playing hand side hip |
| SSGT | ... opposite side hip |
| PSM | ... playing hand side shoe tip |
| SSM | ... opposite side shoe tip |

**Fig. 3.** Constructed 3D stick figure in right-handed Euclidean space

## 3   Methods and Experimental Results

Swing type and stance angle extraction are considered as temporal and spatial composition of computational steps. The presented algorithms are optimised to work with a minimalistic subset of markers (Fig. 3). As such, the hip markers *PSGT* and *SSGT* (*great trochanter*) are used as the equivalent concept of front leg heuristic by computing the front and rear hip position for stance angle extraction. Although the captured data contained only right-handed swing actions, the presented approach is based on the hand holding a racquet (i.e. *PSHD* marker).

## 3.1    Swing Type Recognition and Stance Angle Extraction

Before computing a stance angle, the output of the swing type algorithm (Table 1) is used to determine front and rear hip sides of the pelvis in relation to swing type.

**Table 1.**  Pseudo code for computing swing type recognition.

| Swing type recognition algorithm |
| --- |
| 1: **Initialise** marker numbers (**Fig. 3**): *PSGT, SSGT* and *PSHD*; |
| 2: **Input:** multi-time-series of swing event $S_j$<br>$\quad S_j = \{M(t) \mid t \in \{1,...,lastFrame\}; M = (PSGT, SSGT, PSHD);$<br>$\quad S_j[1,...,lastFrame; PSGT, SSGT, PSHD]$; |
| 3: Determine a frame number *iFrame* of the current swing $S_j[1,...,lastFrame;$ *PSHD*] as maximum scalar distance max(·) towards the estimated target projection *ValuesX* of *PSHD* marker trajectory:<br>$\quad iFrame = \max(ValuesX[1,...,lastFrame; PSHD]);$ |
| 4: Determine the shortest distance in x-z plane between the *PSHD* and hip markers [*PSGT,SSGT*] as:<br>$\quad$ **if** *ValuesX*[*iFrame*; *PSGT*] < *ValuesX*[*iFrame*; *SSGT*] **then**<br>$\qquad swing\_type = FOREHAND$<br>$\quad$ **else**<br>$\qquad swing\_type = BACKHAND$<br>$\quad$ **end if;** |
| 5: **Output:** *swing_type* |

Note: The algorithm is not designed to classify all possible tennis swings such as swing between the legs or other possible variations of e.g. lob recovery.

Before the stance angle extraction within the swing $S_j$ event, the swing type algorithm (Table 1) includes determining a leading hip for forehand and backhand from the existing markers' time-series and relative pelvis centre (*greater sciatic notch*). Derived markers (in Eqs. (1) and (2)) are labelled as *near_rear_hipM* and x–z plane body centre i.e. computed pelvis centre *PelvisC_GT*. The *near_rear_hipM* is assigned after the swing type recognition (Table 1) to initialise stance angle algorithm (Table 2).

$$near\_rear\_hipM = \begin{cases} PSGT : near\_front\_hipM = SSGT, if\,(swing\_\text{type} = FOREHAND) \\ SSGT : near\_front\_hipM = PSGT, if\,(swing\_\text{type} = BACKHAND) \end{cases}$$

$$(1)$$

**Table 2.** Pseudo code for static and dynamic stance as body position relative to the target line.

| |
|---|
| **Stance angle extraction algorithm** |

1: **Initialise** parameters:

Marker numbers (**Fig. 3**): *PSHD, PSGT, SSGT, PSM* and *SSM*;

Target line – by default, it is considered that x-axis is parallel to i.e. $\delta = 0$;

2: **Input:** multi-time-series of swing event *Sj*, swing_*type*, *near_rear_hipM*

$$S_j = \{M(t) \mid t \in \{1,...,lastFrame\}; M = (PSHD, PSGT, SSGT, PSM, SSM);$$

3: **if** initialised $\delta \neq 0$ **then**

rotate markers' data around *y-axis* until x-axis is parallel to the intended target line (**Table 3**):

$$\forall M = rotate(\{\overrightarrow{Xm}, \overrightarrow{Ym}, \overrightarrow{Zm}\}, \delta)$$

**end if**;

4: Compute pelvis centre (2) being a virtual marker inside a human body as:

$$PelvisC\_GT \in \{\overrightarrow{Xbody\_centre}, \overrightarrow{Ybody\_centre}, \overrightarrow{Zbody\_centre}\};$$

5: Extract temporal ROI $St_j \subset S_j$ where playing hand displacement from

$S_j[1,...,lastFrame; PSHD]$ is $\overrightarrow{Xstroke\_displacement}$ as a difference between furthest and closest hand swing position relative to target line and relative to pelvis centre *PelvisC_GT*:

$$St_j \equiv f_1^{ROI}(S_j);$$

$$St_j = \{M(i) \mid startFrameNo \leq i \leq endFrameNo\};$$

$$\overrightarrow{Xstroke\_displacement} = |\overrightarrow{Xpshd} - \overrightarrow{Xbody\_centre}|;$$

$$startFrameNo = \max(\overrightarrow{Xstroke\_displacement});$$

$$endFrameNo = \min(\overrightarrow{Xstroke\_displacement});$$

6: Further temporal ROI extraction $Sttr_j \subseteq St_j \subset S_j$ and distance vector

$\overrightarrow{Xh\_dist}$ computed as functional composition $Strr_j \equiv f_1^{ROI}(S_j) \circ f_2^{ROI}(St_j)$:

$$St_j = \{M(i) \mid newStartFrameNo \leq i \leq newEndFrameNo\};$$

$$\overrightarrow{Xh\_dist} = |\overrightarrow{Xnear\_front\_hipM} - \overrightarrow{Xpshd}|;$$

$$newEndFrameNo = \min(\overrightarrow{Xh\_dist});$$

$$newStartFrameNo = startFrameNo;$$

$$no\_of\_frames = newEndFrame - newStartFrame;$$

producing intermediate results as shown in **Fig. 4**;

7: Calculate the average stance angle $\alpha$ between shoe markers *PSM* and *SSM* positions in transverse plane:

$$\{\forall i \in N \mid newStartFrameNo \leq i \leq newEndFrameNo\};$$

$$\alpha = transf\left( swing\_type, \frac{\sum_{newStartFrameNo}^{newEndFrameNo} \arctan\left(\frac{\overline{Zssm[i]} - \overline{Zpsm[i]}}{\overline{Xssm[i]} - \overline{Xpsm[i]}}\right)}{no\_of\_frames} \right)$$

where *transf*(·) is further customisable angle transformation (3);

8: **Output:** $\alpha$

Note:

Step 6: *newStartFrameNo = startFrameNo* could be modified if the *no_of_frames* may be too small e.g. due to low capture frame rate and personal idiosyncrasies in racquet sporting nature.

$$\overrightarrow{Xbody\_centre} = \frac{\left|\overrightarrow{Xssgt} - \overrightarrow{Xpsgt}\right|}{2} + \overrightarrow{Xnear\_rear\_hipMarker}$$

$$\overrightarrow{Ybody\_centre} = \frac{\left|\overrightarrow{Yssgt} - \overrightarrow{Ypsgt}\right|}{2} + \overrightarrow{Ynear\_rear\_hipMarker} \qquad (2)$$

$$\overrightarrow{Zbody\_centre} = \frac{\left|\overrightarrow{Zssgt} - \overrightarrow{Zpsgt}\right|}{2} + \overrightarrow{Znear\_rear\_hipMarker}$$

Temporal filtering in tennis groundstrokes (shown in Table 2), is implemented as two-stage reduction of temporal Region of Interest (ROI) of a swing interval $S_j[startFrame, ..., endFrame]$. Temporal filtering is defined as composition of temporal and spatial operations of ROI to obtain stance angle: $\alpha = f_1^{ROI}(S_j) \circ f_2^{ROI}(St_j)$ $\circ f_3^{ROI}(Sttr_j)$, where $Sttr_j \subseteq St_j \subset S_j$.

The video capture system was initialised so that x-axis is parallel to the target line.

The intermediate experimental results in Fig. 4 show stance computing as angle extraction from temporal region of interest within recognised motion patterns.

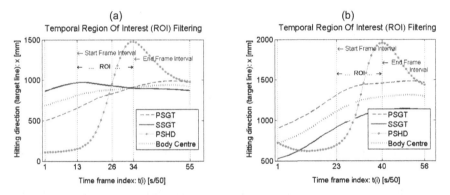

**Fig. 4.** Results of multi-stage temporal filtering of marker's trajectories for hips and hand/wrist that holds a racquet. Characteristic discriminant motion patters for selected swing intervals of: (a) forehand and (b) backhand. Vertical lines indicate selected time period of playing hand marker displacement around the pelvis centre (virtual Body Centre) relative to target line.

### 3.2    Angle Transformations Issues, Customisations and Visualisations

The need for angle transformation function *transf*(·) is to: (1) produce monotone angle transformation; and (2) convert from 3D to 2D and to positive oriented angles in transverse x–z plane (i.e. top 3D view) for viewing and algorithm validation that would be intuitive to a domain expert (as depicted in Fig. 5).

To accommodate intuitive angle expert's validation for cases where 'closed-stance' forehand would change sign (in IV[th] quadrant) the *transf*(·) function would increase computed negative angle by $2\pi$ (e.g. comparable to compass north bearing between 1° and 359°) (Fig. 6).

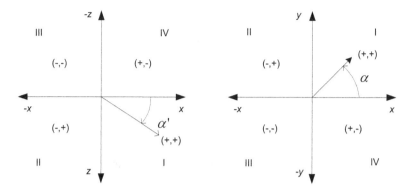

**Fig. 5.** Visualising right-handed 3D transverse x-z plane compared to x–y 2D system

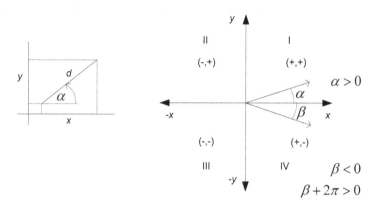

**Fig. 6.** Customisation of positive and negative stance quadrants (x, y) by increasing angle by $2\pi$

Similarly, the developers may choose an arbitrary angle of e.g. ideal square stance parallel to x-axis to be calculated and reported to user either as 0° or 90°.

Considering that the feet position angle within a swing event $S_j$ may not be restricted to the tangent function domain ($-\pi/2$, $\pi/2$) then tan(·) could result in producing zero-division at $\pi/2$ dividable angles, given that $\tan(x) = \frac{\sin(x)}{\cos(x)}$ (Fig. 7).

Customising transformation task to provide angle reporting alternative:

Enabling customisation alternatives to stance angle extraction supports mediating coaches' disagreements e.g. associated with decision boundaries between square stance and closed stance of forehand. The transformation function (3), was customised so that the negative angles of forehand stance to be increased by $\pi$ (instead of $2\pi$ as generally proposed). The outcome of customised transformation function (3), would result in angles $\alpha \geq 0$ for the open, semi-open and square stances, while $\alpha < 0$ would indicate the closed stance. Nonetheless the closed stance single hand backhands would result in angles $\alpha > 0$.

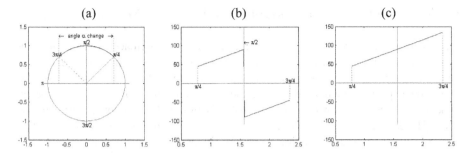

**Fig. 7.** Positive monotone angle transformation example of arctan($\cdot$) function for selected angle $\alpha$ change (a) from non-monotone (b) to monotone function (c).

$$
\alpha = \begin{cases}
\dfrac{\displaystyle\sum_{i=newStartFrame}^{newEndFrame} arctan\left(\dfrac{\overrightarrow{Zssm}_{[i]} - \overrightarrow{Zpsm}_{[i]}}{\overrightarrow{Xpsm}_{[i]} - \overrightarrow{Xssm}_{[i]}}\right)}{no\_of\_frames} & , if\{BACKHAND\} \\[4ex]
\dfrac{\displaystyle\sum_{i=newStartFrame}^{newEndFrame} arctan\left(\dfrac{\overrightarrow{Zpsm}_{[i]} - \overrightarrow{Zssm}_{[i]}}{\overrightarrow{Xssm}_{[i]} - \overrightarrow{Xpsm}_{[i]}}\right)}{no\_of\_frames} & , if\{FOREHAND\}\cap\{\overrightarrow{(Xssm}[i] - \overrightarrow{Xpsm})[i]) \geq 0\} \\[4ex]
\dfrac{\displaystyle\sum_{i=newStartFrame}^{newEndFrame} arctan\left(\dfrac{\overrightarrow{Zpsm}_{[i]} - \overrightarrow{Zssm}_{[i]}}{\overrightarrow{Xssm}_{[i]} - \overrightarrow{Xpsm}_{[i]}}\right)}{no\_of\_frames} + \pi & , if\{FOREHAND\}\cap\{\overrightarrow{(Xssm}[i] - \overrightarrow{Xpsm})[i]) < 0\}
\end{cases}
$$

$$(3)$$

## 4   Discussion, Limitation and Critique

Stance assessment may be assessed by a coach as holistic body position. To extend this study, hip rotation for example could reveal additional information related to stance an even to grip preferences (way holding a racquet to execute a particular swing type). In addition, shoulder turn pattern could improve safety, performance and help assessing e.g. serve return technique. When players are hitting the ball on the run, comparing the shoe tips position relative to the target line may not always be a reliable method in particular for low frame rate systems. Although two-hand backhand data were not captured, the applied concept of playing arm crossing the virtual centre of the body is applicable to both single- and two-handed backhands. To aid in customisation of stance classification and to address the issue raising from the running positions the future algorithm extensions may also take into account average hip angle and feet position before the intended impact with the ball.

## 5 Conclusions, Recommendations and Future Work

The experiments on presented analytical computational approaches show that it is possible from multi-camera video to: (1) quantify body stance orientation by extracting the angles around the swing impact zone and (2) recognise the groundstrokes from 3D motion data specific to tennis. For exergames and augmented coaching system development, the presented concepts, stance customisation and extraction experiments on tennis 3D data are generally applicable to diverse disciplines and activities nature including dancing, hitting, kicking, throwing, blocking, shooting and balancing. In general, body orientation towards arbitrary direction during a specific movement pattern may provide valuable information in predicting intended activity development. Body orientation monitoring and processing is also applicable to other cross disciplinary research, including surveillance and machine vision safety monitoring, e.g. pedestrian traffic collision avoidance. Future work will include advancing and extending application to rehabilitation devices to extract, monitor, assess and provide feedback in near-real time from captured kinematic chain sequence and other human ineligible parameters that may guide functions of augmented coaching systems. Future work on assessment of balance, kinetic/kinematic chain and movement fluidity would benefit from availability of big motion data sets, 3D motion acquisition systems and cross disciplinary surveillance research such as in the areas of sporting activities, human action and semantic interpretations of events [15–17].

**Acknowledgements.** The author wishes to express his appreciation to Dr. Ana Marsanasco for her critique. Tennis data have been obtained in Peharec polyclinic for physical therapy and rehabilitation, Pula (Croatia) during afterhours with support, rigour, watchful critical observations and general biomechanics assistance of Petar Bačić (biomechanics lab specialist and professional tennis coach).

## Appendix

For systems that would require aligning 3D data with the target line, the algorithms for rotation around y-axis (Table 3) and animated 3D stick figure player are based on affine transformations to work with supplied 3D data.

**Table 3.** Pseudo code for 3D marker rotation around y-axis.

| Marker rotation algorithm |
|---|
| 1:   **Input:** $m_i, \delta$ |
| 2:   $p_{transf} \leftarrow \begin{bmatrix} x \cdot \cos(\delta) & 0 & z \cdot \sin(\delta) \\ 0 & y & 0 \\ -x \cdot \sin(\delta) & 0 & z \cdot \cos(\delta) \end{bmatrix} \cdot \begin{bmatrix} 1 \\ 1 \\ 1 \end{bmatrix};$ |
| 3:   **Output:** $p_{transf}$ |

For validation purposes, the implemented algorithms produced a list of the swing files with numeric results. Selected samples were visually inspected from the identical virtual point of view by using the animated 3D stick figure player; for example a semi-open stance, rotated around y-axis is evident from the front view (Fig. 8).

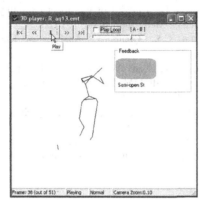

**Fig. 8.** Example of interactive 3D player reporting simple feedback on classified semi-open stance (in green text). Stick figure is rotated around y-axis and a line on the ground denotes the target line for visual assessment of extracted angles. Feedback not related to stance is masked in grey (Color figure online).

# References

1. Mota-Gutierrez, S.A., Hayet, J.-B., Ruiz-Correa, S., Hasimoto-Beltran, R.: Efficient reconstruction of complex 3-D scenes from incomplete RGB-D data. In: Huang, F., Sugimoto, A. (eds.) PSIVT 2013. LNCS, vol. 8334, pp. 71–82. Springer, Heidelberg (2014)
2. Kinect for Windows Features, www.microsoft.com/en-us/kinectforwindows/meetkinect/features.aspx
3. Bacic, B.: Bridging the gap between biomechanics and artificial intelligence. In: XXIV International Symposium on Biomechanics in Sports (ISBS 2006), pp. 371–374. Salzburg (2006)
4. Bacic, B.: Evolving connectionist systems for adaptive sports coaching. In: Ishikawa, M., Doya, K., Miyamoto, H., Yamakawa, T. (eds.) Neural Information Processing, vol. 12, pp. 53–62. Springer, Heidelberg (2008)
5. Bačić, B.: Connectionist Methods for Data Analysis and Modelling of Human Motion in Sporting Activities. Ph.D. Thesis, School of Computer and Mathematical Sciences, AUT University, Auckland (2013)
6. Bačić, B.: Prototyping and user interface design for augmented coaching systems with MATLAB and delphi: implementation of personal tennis coaching system. In: MATLAB Conference 2015. Auckland (2015)
7. Bollettieri, N.: Bollettieri's tennis handbook. Human Kinetics, Champaign (2001)
8. Crespo, M., Higueras, J.: Forehands. pp. 147–171. Human Kinetics, Champaign (2001)
9. Roetert, P., Groppel, J. (eds.): World-Class Tennis Technique. Human Kinetics, Champaign (2001)

10. Knudson, D., Blackwell, J.: Trunk muscle activation in open stance and square stance tennis forehands. Int. J. Sports Med. **21**, 321–324 (2000)
11. Reid, M., Elliott, B., Crespo, M.: Mechanics and learning practices associated with the tennis forehand: a review. J. Sports Sci. Med. **12**, 225–231 (2013)
12. Open Stance vs. Closed Stance Tennis Forehand, https://www.youtube.com/watch?v=FDFYvkk-e84
13. Bahamonde, R.E., Knudson, D.: Kinetics of the upper extremity in the open and square stance tennis forehand. J. Sci. Med. Sport **6**, 88–101 (2003)
14. Knudson, D.V., Morrison, C.S.: Qualitative Analysis of Human Movement. Human Kinetics, Champaign (2002)
15. Wang, J., Kankanhalli, M.S., Yan, W., Jain, R.: Experiential sampling for video surveillance. In: First ACM SIGMM International Workshop on Video Surveillance (IWVS 2003), pp. 77–86, Berkeley, CA (2003)
16. Yan, W., Kieran, D.F., Rafatirad, S., Jain, R.: A comprehensive study of visual event computing. Multimedia Tools Appl. **55**, 443–481 (2011)
17. Zhang, J., Lin, H., Nie, W., Chaisorn, L., Wong, Y., Kankanhalli, M.S.: Human action recognition bases on local action attributes. J. Electr. Eng. Technol. **10**, 1264–1274 (2015)

# Fusion of Foreground Object, Spatial and Frequency Domain Motion Information for Video Summarization

Md. Musfequs Salehin[1(✉)] and Manoranjan Paul[1]

School of Computing and Mathematics, Charles Sturt University,
Bathurst 2795, Australia
{msalehin,mpaul}@csu.edu.au

**Abstract.** Surveillance video camera captures a large amount of continuous video stream every day. To analyze or investigate any significant events from the huge video data, it is laborious and boring job to identify these events. To solve this problem, a video summarization technique combining foreground objects as well as motion information in spatial and frequency domain is proposed in this paper. We extract foreground object using background modeling and motion information in spatial domain and frequency domain. Frame transition is applied for obtaining motion information in spatial domain. For acquiring motion information in frequency domain, phase correlation (PC) technique is applied. Later, foreground objects and motions in spatial and frequency domain are fused and key frames are extracted. Experimental results reveal that the proposed method performs better than the state-of-the-art method.

**Keywords:** Background modeling · Motion information · Phase correlation · Video summarization

## 1 Introduction

Every day an enormous amount of surveillance video is captured 24 hours throughout the whole world for providing security, monitoring, preventing crime, and controlling traffic. In general, a number of surveillance video cameras are set up in a number of difference places of a building, business area, or congested area. These cameras are connected to a monitoring cell for storing and investigating. To store this huge volume of video data requires tremendous memory space. In addition to this, to find out any important events from the stored video for investigating or performing analysis, operators need to access the stored videos. This process is very tedious, lengthy and expensive. To solve these problems, a method for generating the shorter version of original video containing important events is highly desirable for memory management and information retrieval.

*Video summarization* (VS) is the technique to select the most informative frames so that it can contain all the necessary events and reject unnecessary contents to make the summarized video as concise as possible. Therefore, a good video

© Springer International Publishing Switzerland 2016
F. Huang and A. Sugimoto (Eds.): PSIVT 2015 Workshops, LNCS 9555, pp. 319–331, 2016.
DOI: 10.1007/978-3-319-30285-0_26

summarization method is one that has several important properties. First, it must have the capability to include all significant incidents within the original video. Second, it should be able to generate a smaller version of the provided long video. Third, it should not contain repetitive information. The main purpose of VS is to represent a long original video in a condensed version in such a way that a user can get the whole idea of the entire video in a constrained amount of time.

In a video, foreground objects generally contain more detail information [1]. Again, human usually concentrate more on the movements of objects [2]. Consequently, objects as well as their motion are important features for a video. Motivated by these findings, a video summarization scheme is proposed in this paper based on objects and their motion in a video. To include foreground object information, Gaussian mixture-based parametric background modeling (BGM) [3–7] has been applied. To acquire the complete information of object motion in a video, object motion is extracted not only in spatial domain but also in frequency domain. To obtain motion information in spatial domain, consecutive frame difference is applied. For achieving object motion in frequency domain, phase correlation technique [8,9] is applied. To the best of our knowledge, phase correlation is not applied for video summarization methods. Therefore, the main contribution of this paper is to apply phase correlation in video summarization method. The computational time of phase correlation is very low and rich motion information is obtained by phase correlation technique [8].

The structure of the remaining paper is as follows. Section 2 reviews related research. The proposed method is described in Sect. 3. Experimental results as well as detail discussions are provided in Sect. 4. Finally, a concluding remarks and future direction are drawn in Sect. 5.

## 2   Related Research

In the literature, different approaches have been proposed for summarizing various types of videos. For egocentric video summarization, region saliency is predicted in [10] using a regression model and storyboard are generated based on region importance score. In the method proposed in [11], story driven egocentric video is summarized by discovering the most influential objects within a video. Gaze tracking information is applied in [12] for summarization. In case of user generated video summarization, adaptive submodular maximization function is applied in [13]. A collaborative sparse coding model is utilized in [14] for generating summary of the same type of videos. Web images are used in [15] to enhance the process of summarizing the user generated video. To summarize movie, aural, visual and textual are merged in [16]. Role community network is applied in [17]. Film comic is generated using eye tracking data in [18].

However, the importance of surveillance video for industrial application is very higher than other types of videos (e.g., egocentric, user generated, movie). To summarize surveillance video, object centered technique is applied in [19]. Dynamic VideoBook is proposed in [20] for representing the surveillance video in a hierarchical order. Learned distance metric is introduced in [21] for summarizing nursery school surveillance video. In [22], salient motion information is applied. Maximum a posteriori probability (MAP) is used in [23] for synopsis generation. Recently, a method is proposed in [1] for a multi-view surveillance video summarization. Firstly, a single view summarization is generated in this approach for each sensor independently. For this purpose, MPEG-7 color layout descriptor is applied to each video frame and an online-Gaussian mixture model (GMM) is used for clustering. The key frames are selected based on the parameters of cluster. As the decision of selecting or neglecting a frame is performed based on the continuously updates of these clustering parameters, a video segment is extracted instead of key frames. Lastly, multi-view summarization is produced by applying distributed view selection method using the video segments extracted for each sensor in the previous step.

To the best of our knowledge, phase correlation technique has not been applied for video summarization. In this proposed approach, phase correlation technique is applied to incorporate motion information in frequency domain and fused with moving foreground object and spatial motion information.

## 3   The Proposed Method

The proposed scheme is based on area of moving foreground objects and their motion information in spatial and frequency domain. The main steps of the proposed method are (1) moving foreground object extraction (2) motion information calculation in spatial domain, (3) motion estimation in frequency domain, (4) fusion of foreground object area and spatial as well as frequency motion information, and (5) video summary generation. The flow chart of the proposed method is shown in Fig. 1. The detail of each step is explained in the subsequent sub-section.

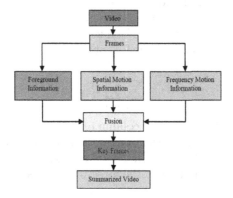

**Fig. 1.** Framework of the proposed method

## 3.1   Foreground Object Extraction

In the proposed method, Gaussian mixture-based parametric BGM [3–7] is applied. In this parametric BGM, each pixel is modeled by the $k$ Gaussian distributions ($k$=3) and each Gaussian model represents either static background or dynamic foreground object during time frame. For instance, suppose a pixel intensity $X_t$ at time $t$ is modeled by $k$th Gaussian with recent value $\gamma_k^t$, mean $\mu_k^t$, standard deviation $\sigma_k^t$ and weight $\omega_k^t$ such that $\sum \omega_k^t = 1$. The learning parameter is used to update parameter values, such as mean, standard deviation, and weight. At the beginning, the system contains empty set of Gaussian models. After observing the first pixel ($t$=1), a new Gaussian model ($k$=1) is generated with$\gamma_k^t = \mu_k^t = X_t$, standard deviation $\sigma_k^t = 30$ and weight $\omega_k^t = 0.001$. Then for each new observation of pixel intensity $X_t$ of the same location at $t$, it tries to find a matched model from the existing models such that $|X_t - \mu_k| \leq 2.5\sigma_k$.

To obtain gray scale background frame, background modeling [3–7] is applied after converting each color-frame into gray scale image. Then, A color video frame at time $t$ is converted into gray image $I(t)$ and subtracted from the corresponding gray background frame $B(t)$ obtained by the background modeling. A pixel is considered foreground pixel and set the value to one, if the pixel intensity difference between $I(t)$ and $B(t)$ is greater than or equal to a certain threshold (*Thr1*). If the pixel intensity does not satisfy this condition, it is regarded as a background pixel and set to zero. In this way, a foreground pixel $G_{i,j}(t)$ is obtained as follows

$$G_{i,j}(t) = \begin{cases} 1, & \text{if } |I_{i,j}^r(t) - B_{i,j}^r(t)| \geq Thr1 \\ 0, & \text{otherwise} \end{cases} \tag{1}$$

where $(i, j)$ is the pixel position. The value of $Thr1$ is set to 20 to avoid subtle changes between background and foreground. This is a common practice to set the threshold value to 20 to identify object from the background as mentioned in [4]. After that, the total number of non-zero pixels in $G_{i,j}(t)$ is used as area of foreground object feature $F(t)$ which is obtained by the following equation

$$G(t) = \sum_{i=1}^{r} \sum_{j=1}^{c} G_{i,j}(t), \tag{2}$$

where $r$ and $c$ represent the row and column of $F$ respectively. According to the psychological theories of human attention, motion information is more significant than the static attention clues [2]. Therefore, motion information is included in the proposed method in addition to the foreground object.

## 3.2   Motion Information Calculation in Spatial Domain

Human usually concentrate more on the movements of objects in a video [2]. In order to obtain object motion information in spatial domain, frame-to-frame difference is applied. Consider two consecutive frames $I(t-1)$ and $I(t)$ at time

$t-1$ and $t$ in video. To find out spatial motion information, the color difference in red, green, and blue channel between these frames is calculated. If the differences at each pixel in three different channels are greater than or equal to a threshold ($T2$), this pixel is considered as motion pixel and set to value one. Otherwise, it is sure that this pixel does not contain any motion information. Therefore, the spatial motion information $S_{i,j}(t)$ in pixel $(i,j)$ at time $t$ can be obtained by the following equation

$$S_{i,j}(t) = \begin{cases} 1, & \text{if} \quad |I_{i,j}^r(t) - I_{i,j}^r(t-1)| \geq T2 \\ & \text{and} \quad |I_{i,j}^g(t) - I_{i,j}^g(t-1)| \geq T2 \\ & \text{and} \quad |I_{i,j}^b(t) - I_{i,j}^b(t-1)| \geq T2 \\ 0, & \text{otherwise} \end{cases} \tag{3}$$

where $I_{(i,j)}^r$, $I_{(i,j)}^g$, and $I_{(i,j)}^b$ represent red, green and blue color at $(i,j)$ channels respectively. This is a common practice to set 20 as a threshold value to obtain information between two consecutive frames [4]. Therefore, the value of $T2$ is set to 20. The spatial motion information $S(t)$ is obtained at time t by summing all values in $S_{i,j}(t)$ as follows

$$S(t) = \sum_{i=1}^{r} \sum_{j=1}^{c} S_{i,j}(t), \tag{4}$$

where $r$ and $c$ represent row and column of $S$ respectively. However, motion extracted in spatial domain is not sensitive to diffuse phenomena [24]. For example, it does not work well when global illumination changes occur. Additionally, spatial motion estimation is prone to local inaccuracies and small motion discontinuities [25].

### 3.3   Motion Estimation in Frequency Domain

To overcome the problem of spatial motion calculation, motion information is calculated in frequency domain. Motion estimated in frequency domain has some advantages over spatial domain [24]. It is efficient for global changes of illumination and robust to motion estimation near object boundaries. To obtain motion information in frequency domain, each frame is divided into a number of blocks of $16 \times 16$ pixels size. Then, phase correlation technique [8] is applied between the current block and reference block. The phase correlation peak $\beta$, the magnitude of the motion accuracy, extracted from phase correlation method is used as motion indicator for that block. The phase difference $\phi$ is calculated between the current block and its co-located reference block after applying *Fast Fourier transformation FFT* on each block. The inverse FFT is performed on the calculated phase difference and finally two dimensional ( 2-D) motion vector ($dx$, $dy$) is obtained [26]. This 2-D motion vector contains peaks $\beta$ where there are shift between the current and reference blocks.

$$\phi = fftshift|ifft(e^{j(\angle F_r - \angle F_c)})|, \tag{5}$$

M.M. Salehin and M. Paul

where $F_r$ and $F_c$ represent FFF of current and reference block respectively.

$$(dx, dy) = \max(\phi) - b/2 - 1 \tag{6}$$

$$\beta = \phi(dx + b/2 + 1, dy + b/2 + 1) \tag{7}$$

where $b$ is block size. For example, $b$ will be 16 if $16 \times 16$ is used. If the value of $\beta$ of a block greater than a threshold ($T3$), it is considered that this block contains sufficient motion information. In this method, the value of $T3$ is set to 0.6. All the values greater than $T3$ are summed to obtain motion information F(t) in frequency domain.

$$F(t) = \sum_{n=1}^{N} \sum_{m=1}^{M} F_{n,m}(t), \tag{8}$$

where $N$ and $M$ represent row/$b$ and column/$b$ of $F$ respectively. The motion information obtained in frequency domain applying phase correlation technique at different blocks of frame no 3869 of bl-14 video is shown in Fig. 2. No motion is represented in block (4,4) with only a single highest pick (Fig. 2(b)). Single (block (10,14)) and complex motions (block (5,8)) are showed in Fig. 2(c) and (d) respectively. In contrast, frequency based motion estimation approach lacks of localization problem [24]. Therefore, motions obtained in both spatial and frequency domains are combined with foreground objects for video summarization.

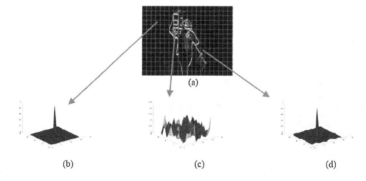

**Fig. 2.** An example of motion generated in each block of frame no 3869 of bl-14 video; (a) frame difference between 3868 and 3869 (multiplied by 6 for better visualization), phase correlation pick with no motion, complex motion and single motion are represented in (b), (c) and (d) respectively.

### 3.4 Fusion of Foreground and Motion Information

In order to select more accurate frame sequences, both area of foreground object and motion information are combined. In this approach, a weighted linear fusion is applied to combine the features for ranking each frame according to their representativeness in a video. Before applying fusion method, each feature is converted into z-score normalization using the following equation

$$Z(t) = (X(t) - \mu_f)/\sigma_f, \tag{9}$$

where $X(t)$ is a feature value at time $t$, $mu_f$ is the mean and $sigma_f$ is standard deviation of the feature values. Z-score, $Z(t)$ is a normalized form of $X(t)$. In this scheme, z-score normalization is the preferred method because it produces meaningful information about each data point, and provides better results in the presence of outliers than min-max based normalization [27]. The weighted linear fusion is obtained as follows

$$A(t) = W_1 \times Z_G(t) + W_2 \times Z_G(t) + W_3 \times Z_G(t), \tag{10}$$

where $A(t)$ is fusion value; $Z_G(t)$, $Z_S(t)$ and $Z_F(t)$ are z-score normalization of foreground feature ($G(t)$), spatial motion feature ($S(t)$), and motion information in frequency domain ($F(t)$) respectively at time $t$. Empirically, it is evaluated that if the values of weights $W_1$, $W_2$, and $W_3$ are set to 15, 60, and 25 respectively, it provides better results for all videos in BL-7F dataset. The rationality to provide higher weight to motion feature compared to the foreground area is that according to the psychological theories of human attention, motion information is more significant than the static attention clues [2]. After that, $A(1), A(2), A(3)$, ... ... $A(T)$ is sorted based on descending order where $T$ is total number of frames in a video.

### 3.5   Video Summary Generation

The proposed method summarizes a video based on the threshold ($Thr_{kf}$) provided by a user. From the sorted list of $A(1), A(2), A(3)$, ... ... $A(T)$, $Thr_{kf}$ number of frames are selected. A summary of video is generated from the selected frames by maintaining their chronological sequence.

## 4   Results and Discussion

The proposed method is applied on the publicly available BL-7F dataset [1] which contains 19 surveillance videos. A complete list of ground truth key frames for each video is also provided in BL-7F dataset. The foreground object, spatial and frequency domain motion information are extracted by the proposed method are shown in Fig. 3(d), (e), and (f) respectively.

In Fig. 4, a number of ground truth frames of bl-11 video of BL-7F dataset [1] and the results obtained by GMM based method, as well as the proposed method are shown. GMM based method fails to select frame number 9963 and 12523 even if they contain significant contents. In contrast, the proposed method can select these frames successfully. The main reason of this success is that the proposed method combines area of foreground objects as well as frequency and spatial motion information.

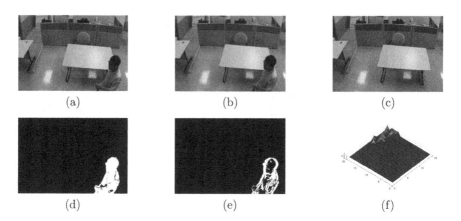

**Fig. 3.** An example of foreground and motion information extracted by the proposed method; (a) and (b) are frame no 740 and 741 of bl-0 video, (c) is the background image of (b), (d) is the foreground image of (b), (e) is the object motion between two frames and (f) is the motion obtained by phase correlation technique on frame no 741.

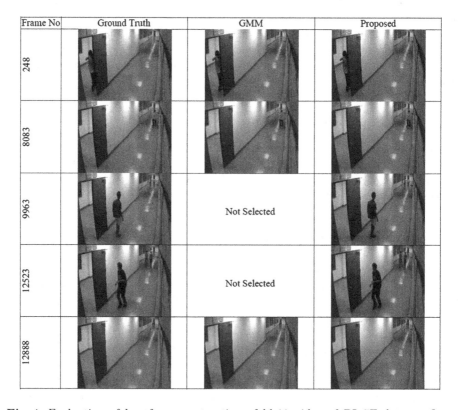

**Fig. 4.** Evaluation of key frames extraction of bl-11 video of BL-7F dataset; first, second, third, and forth columns indicate frame no, ground truth, results obtained by GMM based method and the proposed method respectively.

In this experiment, the quality of the summarized video is estimated by precision, recall, and F1-measure obtained using the following equations

$$Precision = T_p/(T_p + F_p), \qquad (11)$$

$$Recall = T_p/(T_p + F_n), \qquad (12)$$

$$F_1 - measure = 2 \times \frac{Recall \times Precision}{Recall + Precision}, \qquad (13)$$

where $T_p$, $F_p$, and $F_n$ indicates true positive, false positive, and false negative respectively.

The proposed approach is compared with the single-view video summarization results provided by GMM based method [1]. The GMM method is the most relevant and the state-of-the-art method to compare with because both techniques use GMM for the training purpose. However, there are two key differences between GMM based method [1] and Gaussian mixture-based parametric BGM [4]. Firstly, GMM based method works at frame level whereas Gaussian mixture-based BGM works in pixel level. Secondly, GMM based method utilizes color descriptor as feature while Gaussian mixture-based parametric BGM uses pixel intensity. Another reason to compare with GMM based method is that both techniques use BL-7F standard dataset to verify the performance.

In this proposed method, the summarization threshold $Thrkf$ is set to the total number of key frames suggested by the ground truth for each video. It is evaluated that the introduced scheme generates more accurate results if $Thrkf \times$ 1.35 frames are selected from the ranked sorted list of $A(1), A(2), A(3), \ldots \ldots A(T)$

**Table 1.** Precision, recall, and F1-measure of GMM [1] and the proposed method

| Video | GMM [1] | | | Proposed Method | | |
|---|---|---|---|---|---|---|
| | Precision | Recall | $F_1$-measure | Precision | Recall | $F_1$-measure |
| bl-0 | 70.30 | 91.83 | 0.80 | 87.97 | 90.79 | 0.89 |
| bl-1 | 28.90 | 78.99 | 0.42 | 62.26 | 72.79 | 0.67 |
| bl-2 | 77.80 | 64.21 | 0.70 | 72.89 | 83.09 | 0.78 |
| bl-3 | 27.40 | 98.53 | 0.43 | 71.89 | 96.38 | 0.82 |
| bl-4 | 62.40 | 88.11 | 0.73 | 74.16 | 93.15 | 0.83 |
| bl-5 | 26.10 | 97.62 | 0.41 | 68.98 | 89.63 | 0.78 |
| bl-6 | 2.10 | 100.00 | 0.04 | 77.78 | 100 | 0.88 |
| bl-7 | 63.90 | 80.88 | 0.71 | 80.45 | 100 | 0.89 |
| bl-8 | 83.60 | 100.00 | 0.91 | 88.94 | 100 | 0.94 |
| bl-9 | 97.50 | 60.22 | 0.75 | 99.06 | 82.25 | 0.90 |
| bl-10 | 61.40 | 78.60 | 0.69 | 86.61 | 99.85 | 0.93 |
| bl-11 | 98.30 | 62.71 | 0.77 | 95.47 | 81.91 | 0.88 |
| bl-12 | 88.30 | 97.97 | 0.93 | 83.45 | 91.48 | 0.87 |
| bl-13 | 0.00 | 0.00 | 0.00 | 100 | 100 | 1.00 |
| bl-14 | 76.90 | 97.67 | 0.86 | 84.29 | 95.6 | 0.90 |
| bl-15 | 92.40 | 96.51 | 0.94 | 98.6 | 99.09 | 0.99 |
| bl-16 | 55.60 | 96.98 | 0.71 | 91.15 | 96.04 | 0.94 |
| bl-17 | 88.10 | 81.92 | 0.85 | 87.28 | 94.74 | 0.91 |
| bl-18 | 21.30 | 89.20 | 0.34 | 81.88 | 98.72 | 0.90 |
| Mean | 59.1 | 82.2 | 0.63 | 83.85 | 92.92 | 0.88 |
| STD | 32.01 | 23.81 | 0.28 | 10.69 | 7.84 | 0.08 |

where $T$ is total number of frames in a video. The results of precision, recall, and F1-measure of GMM based method and the proposed method are shown in Table 1. It is observed from Table 1 that the mean values of the precision, recall, and F1-measure of GMM based method are 59.1, 82.2, and 0.63 respectively. On the other hand, the proposed method shows enhanced performance compared to GMM based method with mean precision (83.6), recall (94.2), and F1-measure (0.88). In addition to this, standard deviations (STDs) of precision, recall, and F1-measure of the proposed method are much lower compared to the GMM based method (see Table 1). This indicates that the proposed method not only performs in higher accuracy but also variance of the performance is more consistent in the different videos compared to the GMM based method [1].

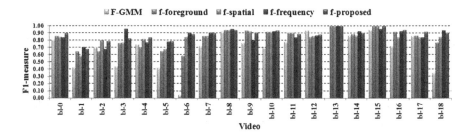

**Fig. 5.** F1-measure of the proposed and GMM based approach.

The graphical representations of F1-measure of GMM based method (F-GMM), the proposed method using only foreground objects (f-foreground), spatial motion (f-spatial), motion in frequency domain (f-frequency), and combining all these features (f-proposed) are shown in Fig. 5. After examining this graph, it is obvious that the proposed using only foreground objects shows less performance in bl-2, bl-4, and bl-12 videos compared to GMM based method. If only spatial motion is considered, it fails to outperform in bl-12 and bl-17 videos. Again, the proposed method applying only phase correlation technique shows poor result in bl-2, bl-12, and bl-17 videos. Therefore, the proposed approach combines all these features and performs superior to GMM based method in 18 videos. However, the proposed technique fails to perform better for bl-12 video compared to the GMM based method [1]. After observing the key frames extracted by the proposed method for bl-12 video, the reasons of failure have been explored. In bl-12 video, there are some frames with significant object, and motion, however, they are not selected as ground truth frames by [1]. Although there is no foreground object and/or motion, in some frames, they are considered as ground truth. For example, frame no 4083, 4120, and 4563 contain sufficient amount of object, and motion as shown in first row of Fig. 6. In these frames, it is clearly visible that a person is working near the door. However, these frames are not selected as ground truth (key frames). On the other hand, there is no object, and significant motion exist in frame no 12615, 12675 and 12750 (see the second row of Fig. 6). Nonetheless, they are selected as key frames (ground truth). There is no explanation found about this incident in [1]. After evaluating the proposed method quantitatively

| Frame no 4083 | Frame no 4120 | Frame no 4563 |
| Frame no 12615 | Frame no 12675 | Frame no 12750 |

**Fig. 6.** Sample frames of bl-12 are not selected as ground truth (first row) and considered as key frame (second row).

and qualitatively, it is revealed that the proposed method based on foreground objects, and motion in spatial and frequency perform superior to the state-of-the-art GMM based method [1].

## 5 Conclusion

In this paper, a novel framework is proposed to summarize surveillance video combining foreground object along with motion information in spatial and frequency domain. According to [1], foreground objects usually contain details information of the video contents. Moreover, human being naturally gives more attention to object motion in a video [2]. Therefore, there two important properties of a video are included in this approach. To include motion information in frequency domain, phase correlation technique [8] is applied. To the best of our knowledge, phase correlation technique is applied for the first time for video summarization. Extensive experimental results reveal that the proposed method outperforms the state-of-the-art method.

## References

1. Ou, S., Lee, C., Somayazulu, V., Chen, Y., Chien, S.: On-line multi-view video summarization for wireless video sensor network. IEEE J. Sel. Top Sig. Process. **9**, 165–179 (2015)
2. Gao, D., Mahadevan, V., Vasconcelos, N.: On the plausibility of the discriminant center-surround hypothesis for visual saliency. J. Vis. **8**, 118 (2008)
3. Paul, M., Lin, W., Lau, C., Lee, B.: Explore and model better I-frames for video coding. IEEE Trans. Circuits Syst. Video Technol. **21**, 1242–1254 (2011)
4. Haque, M., Murshed, M., Paul, M.: A hybrid object detection technique from dynamic background using Gaussian mixture models. In: IEEE 10th Workshop on Multimedia Signal Processing, pp. 915–920 (2008)
5. Chakraborty, S., Paul, M.: A novel video coding scheme using a scene adaptive non-parametric background model. In: IEEE 16th International Workshop on Multimedia Signal Processing, pp. 1–6 (2014)

6. Paul, M., Evans, C.J., Murshed, M.: Disparity-adjusted 3D multi-view video coding with dynamic background modelling. In: IEEE International Conference on Image Processing, pp. 1719–1723 (2013)
7. Paul, M.: Efficient video coding using optimal compression plane and background modelling. IET Image Process. **6**, 1311–1318 (2012)
8. Paul, M., Lin, W., Lau, C.T., Lee, B.-S.: Direct intermode selection for H.264 video coding using phase correlation. IEEE Trans. Image Process. **20**, 461–473 (2011)
9. Paul, M., Sorwar, G.: An efficient video coding using phase-matched error from phase correlation information. In: IEEE 10th Work on Multimedia Signal Processing, pp. 378–382 (2008)
10. Lee, Y.J., Ghosh, J., Grauman, K.: Discovering important people and objects for egocentric video summarization. In: IEEE Conference on Computer Vision and Pattern Recognition, pp. 1346–1353 (2012)
11. Lu, Z., Grauman, K.: Story-driven summarization for egocentric video. In: IEEE Conference on Computer Vision and Pattern Recognition, pp. 2714–2721 (2013)
12. Xu, J., Mukherjee, L., Li, Y., Warner, J., Rehg, J.M., Singh, V.: Gaze-enabled egocentric video summarization via constrained submodular maximization. In: IEEE Conference Computer Vision Pattern Recognition, pp. 2235–2244 (2015)
13. Gygli, M., Grabner, H., Van Gool, L.: Video summarization by learning submodular mixtures of objectives. In: IEEE Cconference Computer Vision Pattern Recognit, pp. 3090–3098 (2015)
14. Liu, Y., Liu, H., Sun, F.: Outlier-attenuating summarization for user-generated-video. In: IEEE International Conference on Multimedia and Expo, pp. 1–6 (2014)
15. Khosla, A., Hamid, R.: Large-scale video summarization using web-image priors. In: IEEE Conference on Computer Vision and Pattern Recognition, pp. 2698–2705 (2013)
16. Evangelopoulos, G.: Multimodal saliency and fusion for movie summarization based on aural, visual, and textual attention. IEEE Trans. Multimed. **15**, 1553–1568 (2013)
17. Tsai, C., Kang, L.: Scene-based movie summarization via role-community networks. IIEEE Trans. Circuits Syst. Video Technol. **23**, 1927–1940 (2013)
18. Sawada, T., Toyoura, M., Mao, X.: Film comic generation with eye tracking. In: Wang, M., Mei, T., Sebe, N., Yan, S., Hong, R., Gurrin, C., Li, S., Saddik, A. (eds.) MMM 2013, Part I. LNCS, vol. 7732, pp. 467–478. Springer, Heidelberg (2013)
19. Fu, W., Wang, J., Zhao, C., Lu, H., Ma, S.: Object-centered narratives for video surveillance. In: IEEE International Conference on Image Processing, pp. 29–32 (2012)
20. Sun, L., Ai, H., Lao, S.: The dynamic VideoBook: A hierarchical summarization for surveillance video. In: IEEE International Conference on Image Processing, pp. 3963–3966 (2013)
21. Wang, Y., Kato, J.: A distance metric learning based summarization system for nursery school surveillance video. In: IEEE International Conference on Image Processing, pp. 37–40 (2012)
22. Mehmood, I., Sajjad, M., Ejaz, W., Wook, S.: Saliency-directed prioritization of visual data in wireless surveillance networks. Inf. Fusion. **24**, 16–30 (2015)
23. Huang, C., Chung, P.J.: Maximum a posteriori probability estimation for online surveillance video synopsis. IEEE Trans. Circuits Syst. Video Technol. **24**, 1417–1429 (2014)
24. Ahuja, N., Briassouli, A.: Joint spatial and frequency domain motion analysis. In: International Conference on Automation Face Gesture Recognition, pp. 203–208 (2006)

25. Briassouli, A., Ahuja, N.: Integration of frequency and space for multiple motion estimation and shape-independent object segmentation. IEEE Trans. Circuits Syst. Video Technol. **18**(5), 657–669 (2008)

26. Paul, M., Frater, M.R., Arnold, J.F.: An efficient mode selection prior to the actual encoding for H.264/AVC Encoder. IEEE Trans. Multimed. **11**, 581–588 (2009)

27. Han, J., Kamber, M., Pei, J.: Data Mining, Southeast Asia Edition: Concepts andTechniques. Morgan Kaufmann, San Francisco (2006)

# Network Intrusion Detection Based on Neural Networks and D-S Evidence

Chunlin Lu[1,2], Lidong Zhai[2(✉)], Tao Liu[1], and Na Li[3]

[1] North China Electric Power University, Beijing 071000, China
[2] Institute of Computing Technology,
Chinese Academy of Sciences, Beijing 100190, China
zhailidong@iie.ac.cn
[3] Institute of China Mobile Communication Company Limited,
Beijing 100053, China

**Abstract.** Network traffic data is an important source of data to establish a network intrusion detection system (NIDS). The explosive growth of the network traffic data brings a huge challenge to network intrusion detection, and video traffic packet has been an important part of the network traffic. In recent years, more and more researches have been applied Artificial Neural Networks (ANNs), especially back-propagation (BP) neural network, to improve the performance of intrusion detection systems. However, in view of the current network intrusion detection methods, the detection precision, especially for low-frequent attacks, detection stability and training time are still needed to be enhanced. In this paper, a new model which based on BP neural network that is optimized by genetic algorithm and Dempster-Shafer (D-S) theory to solve the above problems and help NIDS to achieve higher detection rate, less false positive rate and stronger stability. The general process of our model is as follows: firstly dividing the main extracted feature into several different feature subsets. Then, based on different feature subsets, different ANN models are trained to build the detection engine. Finally, the D-S evidence theory is employed to integration these results,and obtain the final result. The effectiveness of this method is verified by experimental simulation utilizing KDD Cup1999 dataset.

**Keywords:** Network intrusion detection · BP neural network · Dempster shafer · Anomaly detection

## 1 Introduction

Network intrusion detection has played a central role to discover the process of abnormal behavior characteristics and provide early warning, to achieve the purpose of monitoring network behavior and network intrusion defense. With the development of network technology, network attacks become more and more complex and hidden. Detection precision and stability are two crucial indicators to evaluate the IDSs [1]. The traditional method, such as rule-based expert systems and statistical approaches [2] are difficult to deal with those problems such

© Springer International Publishing Switzerland 2016
F. Huang and A. Sugimoto (Eds.): PSIVT 2015 Workshops, LNCS 9555, pp. 332–343, 2016.
DOI: 10.1007/978-3-319-30285-0_27

as huge network traffic volumes in high-speed network environment, especially a large number of video traffic data, imbalanced network data distribution, and the difficulty to provide continuous adaptation.

In addition of that, artificial intelligence and machine learning have shown limitations in achieving high detection accuracy and fast processing times when confronted with these requirements. More and more researches explore new methods (such as artificial neural network) to solve the problems. Among the researchers who use neural network to work on IDS, BPNN is the first choice due to its ability of accurate prediction and better persistence over the other ANN techniques. However, BP neural network itself has some drawbacks,such as easy to fall into local minimum, slow convergence, weaker detection stability, network instability, high training time, etc. [3,4]. In order to solve the above problems, in this paper, we propose a novel anomaly detection model based on optimized BP neural network and D-S theory to enhance the detection precision for low-frequent attacks, detection stability and reduce the training time. To illustrate the applicability and capability of the new approach, the results of experiments on KDD Cup1999 dataset demonstrated better performance in terms of detection precision, detection stability and training time.

The rest of this paper is organized as follows. We discuss the related work on IDS in Sect. 2. In Sect. 3, we elaborate the framework of our model, and explain its principles and working procedures. To evaluate the model, Sect. 4 illustrates the results and discussions of experiments. Finally, Sect. 5 draws the conclusions.

## 2   Related Work

As mentioned above, more and more researches use artificial neural network to improve the performance of IDS. According to the number of the ANN techniques used, ANN based IDS can be categorized as: Simple ANN Based IDS and Hybrid ANN Based IDS.

Simple ANN applied to IDS mainly includes: Back Propagation neural network (BPNN). Wei Z et al. [5] used Back Propagation neural network (BPNN) to detect intrusion behavior, due to its ability of accurate prediction and better persistence. Authors of this paper illustrate BPNN is good in detection of the known and unknown attack. But, to train the BPNN, number of the epochs required was very high which lead to very high training time. If network is over trained then it can decrease the performance, and to overcome, one has to define the early stopping condition. Some researchers have compared the effectiveness of the simple ANN based IDS with other methods such as Support Vector Machines (SVM) and neural network [6], intrusion IDS using self-organizing maps (SOM) [7], simulated annealing neural network (SANN) [8]. Simple ANN based IDS had been shown to have lower detection performance and long training time, especially in dealing with a large amount of data at a high speed.

Hybrid ANN Based IDS is hybrid ANN which combines more than one ANN techniques. The motivation for using the hybrid ANN is to overcome the limitations of individual ANN. Horeis et al. [9] used a combination of SOM and Radial

Basis Function (RBF) networks. The system offers generally better results than IDS based on RBF networks alone. Paulo M et al. [10] propose two layers app- roach,called Octopus-IIDS, based on KNN and SVM, to provide an Intelligent Intrusion Detection System (IIDS) that is flexible, accurate, tolerant to varia- tions of attacks, adaptive to changes in the network, modular and that operates in real time. Chen et al. [11] proposed hybrid flexible neural-tree-based IDS based on flexible neural tree, evolutionary algorithm and Particle Swarm Optimization (PSO). Experimental results indicated that the proposed method is efficient. Song Guangjun et al. [12] proposed hybrid flexible dynamic change learning rate in BPNN and simulated annealing algorithm. Experiment results indicated that the proposed method is efficient to reduce the training steps. Wang G et al. [13] proposed a new approach, called FC-ANN, based on ANN and fuzzy clus- tering, to solve the problem and help IDS achieve higher detection rate, less false positive rate and stronger stability. Results indicated that FC-ANN, out- performs BPNN and other well-known methods in terms of detection precision and detection stability.

As mentioned above, a single artificial neural network technology can not meet the needs of current intrusion detection system, hybrid artificial neural network has been the trend in intrusion detection system. In this article,we use hybrid ANN to carry out our work.

## 3    Framework of Proposed Model

In this section, we will elaborate our new approach. Firstly, we present the whole framework of the new approach. Then we discuss the details of our new approach.

### 3.1    Framework of IDS based on ANN and D-S fusion model

Our approach firstly preprocess the network data because neural network classi- fication uses only numerical data for training and testing. During the preprocess- ing, there are including mainly the conversion process and normalization process. Numerical conversion process is taking non-numeric features into numeric value. In the KDD Cup1999 data set, all features of the data set take numeric values except three, namely, protocol type, service, and flag. Those three features will be converted to numeric value (e.g. for protocol type: TCP=2, UDP=3, ICMP=1). Due to features of the KDD Cup1999 data set contains discrete features and continuous features,which leads to unfavorable to training the network conver- gence. In order to accelerate the training of network convergence, the features were normalized by using min-max normalization to map all the different values for each feature to [0, 1] range.

After data preprocessing, the main characteristic of network data can be obtained through the feature extraction module. Dividing the main features into several different feature subsets is necessary in this article. Subsequently trains the different ANN using different features subsets. Finally the results from the different ANN will via D-S fusion model to get the final results. The whole framework is illustrated in Fig. 1.

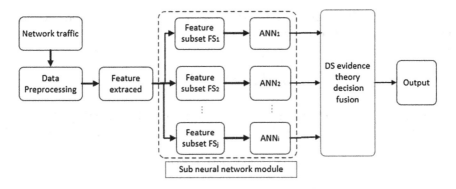

**Fig. 1.** Framework of IDS based on SANN and D-S fusion engine

## 3.2  ANN Module

ANN module aims to learn the pattern of every feature subset. It is composed of simple processing units, and connections between them. In this study, we will employ improved back-propagation neural networks trained with the Genetic algorithm to predict intrusion.

BPNN has an input layer, an output layer, with one or more hidden layers in between the input and output layer. In this work, we use only one hidden layer and due to this, efficiency of the system is good. The ANN functions as follows:

(i) in the input layer: each $i$ neuron has a signal $x_i$ as networks input

(ii) in the hidden layereach $j$neuron has a signal $HI(j)$ as input

$$HI(j) = b_j + \sum_{i=1}^{n} x_i w_{ij} \quad j = 1, 2, 3, \cdots, m \tag{1}$$

where $w_{ij}$ is the weight value between the input layer and the hidden layer, $b_j$ is the biases in the hidden layer.

The $HI(j)$ passed through the bipolar sigmoid activation function $f(x)$, and get $f(HI(j))$ as the input of the output layer.

$$f(x) = \frac{2}{1 + \exp^{-x}} - 1 \tag{2}$$

(iii) in the output layer: the input of the output layer as follow:

$$YI_k = b_k + \sum_{j=1}^{m} f(HI(j)) w_{jk} \quad k = 1, 2, 3, \cdots, K \tag{3}$$

where $w_{jk}$ is the weight value between the hidden layer and the output layer, $b_k$ is the biases in the output layer.

The output of the output layer as follow:

$$YO_k = f(YI_k) \quad k = 1, 2, 3, \cdots, K \tag{4}$$

The $YO(k)$ will be compared with the target value $T_k$; in this study, we used the mean square error as error function:

$$E(n) = \frac{1}{2n} \sum_{k=1}^{K} (T_k(n) - YO_k(n))^2 \tag{5}$$

where $n$ is the number of training patterns, the formula for adjusting the weight value is:

$$w_{jk}(n+1) = w_{jk}(n) + \eta \partial E(n) / \partial w(n) + \alpha \Delta w_{jk}(n) \tag{6}$$

where $\alpha$ is the momentum factor, and $\alpha \in (0,1)$.

In order to avoid falling into local optimal value, not the global optimal solution. In this paper, the genetic algorithm to optimize BP neural network [14,15]. The specific steps are as follows:

Step1: (Initial population) Using the binary coding method to encode the weights and threshold value of BPNN, weights and threshold of coding for the length of 10 bit binary number. For any one individual R, coding the individual as follow:

$$R = \{W^2, B^2, W^3, B^3\} \tag{7}$$

$$R(t) = (R_1(t), R_2(t), \cdots, R_i(t)) \tag{8}$$

where $W^2$ is the weight vector between the input layer and hidden layer, $B^2$ is threshold vector of the hidden layer; $W^3$ is the weight vector between the hidden layer and output layer; $B^3$ is threshold vector of the output layer. Randomly generate certain amount of individuals; is the $i$-th individual in the $t$ generation population during the process of evolution.

Step 2: (Fitness calculation) The Mean Square Error (MSE) value $E$ of the desired output and the actual output value as fitness function value of the vector/individuals in the population.

$$f(R_i(t)) = \frac{1}{N} \sum_{k=1}^{N} (y_k(t) - y'_k(t))^2 \tag{9}$$

where $N$ the number of training samples, $y_k(t)$ is the desired output value, $y'_k(t)$ is the actual output value.

Step 3: (Selection) Select a certain number of individuals from the population as a parent subsequent crossover operation. Roulette method is used to select individual, make fitness value $f$ high of individual is more likely to be selected, eliminate fitness values $f$ low of individuals at the same time.

Step 4: (Crossover) Ranking individual in the population according to the size of the fitness value $f$, then according to the row of good order, respectively from the head and tail of population pick out two individuals to crossover operation.

Step 5: (Mutation) Non-uniform Mutation is used to make a random perturbation with a changing probability. Replace genetic value with the result after perturbation. It amounts to a slight disturbance in the solution space for the whole solution vector. The changing probability means that, the range of random perturbation decreases with the evolution generations.

Step 6: (Terminal Condition) Determine whether the evolution come to an end. If not, return to the step 2, and turn into the next iteration. Otherwise, save and output the training result.

After the above six steps,we can get the best Initial weights and threshold value for BPNN train. Then every $ANN_i$ can complete training using different subsets $FS_j$.

### 3.3 D-S Fusion Model

The aim of D-S fusion module is to fusion different ANN's result. The module will utilize D-S evidence theory to merge and analyze these detection results from early ANN modules. That is to say, according to regression ability of sensors, we fuse these results by (11) and give decision results, that is, whether the attack or not.

D-S evidence theory [16,17] is considered as a general extension of the traditional classical probabilistic inference theory in limited areas. D-S evidence theory without a priori probability still can be used to deal with uncertainty and imprecision information. Therefore D-S evidence theory has greater flexibility.

D-S evidence theory is considered as theory built on a nonempty finite field $\Theta$ called the recognition framework, which includes a limited number of independent system state $\{A_1, A_2, \cdots, A_n\}$. An element in $p(\Theta)$ as a power set of system state $\Theta$ is called a system state hypothesis $H_i$. Through the observation results $E_1, E_2, \cdots, E_m$ for system state by each sensor, D-S evidence theory can merge these results and infer the former state of system.

Definition: Basic probability assignment function (BPA) is defined as a map from a power set of $\Theta$ to $[0, 1]$ interval. It is represented as $m: P(\Theta) \to [0,1]$, and satisfies:$m(\Phi) = 0$ and $\sum\limits_{A \in P(\Theta)} m(A) = 1$ , where $m(A)$ is called confidence value which means that current sensor decides hypothesis $A$ the degree of confidence according to the observation results.

When the same frame of discernment $\Theta$ has multiple data sources. For these data sources, according to their functions provide different evaluation value. Synthesis of these data sources all the rules of the information referred to as synthetic rules. one can achieve D-S general synthesis rules for the combination evidence from evidences as follows:

$$m_{1\cdots n}(A) = \frac{\sum\limits_{\cap_i E_i = A} m_1(E_1) m_2(E_2) \cdots m_n(E_n)}{\sum\limits_{\cap_i E_i \neq A} m_1(E_1) m_2(E_2) \cdots m_n(E_n)} \tag{10}$$

However, once there is a serious conflict between the basic probability distribution function of each proof, the results obtained after fusion is obviously unreasonable. And basic trust assigned focal element occurrence is extremely small, the change will bring dramatic changes their combined results. Therefore, the synthesis rule from formula (10) only applies to the case with the same precision in all sensors. To solve this serious issue, we apply a method to change with conventional D-S evidence theory. That is, combine weights with D-S evidence theory [18].

$$m_{1\cdots n}(A) = \frac{\sum\limits_{\cap_i E_i = A} \omega_1 m_1(E_1) \cdots \omega_n m_n(E_n)}{\sum\limits_{\cap_i E_i \neq A} \omega_1 m_1(E_1) \cdots \omega_n m_n(E_n)} \tag{11}$$

In this paper, we define the recognition framework $\Theta = (N, A)$, where $N$ represents normal status and $A$ represents abnormal status. We can see that status $N$ and $A$ are mutual exclusion, that is, $N \cap A = \emptyset$. Basic probability assignment function (BPA) is represented as $m: P(\{N.A\}) \rightarrow [0, 1]$, and satisfies: $m(\emptyset) = 0$ and $m(\{N, A\}) + m(N) + m(A) = 1$, where $m(N)$ represents the observation results of current feature by current sensor and considers that reliability of current status belongs to normal status. $m(A)$ represents the observation results of current feature by current sensor and considers that reliability of current status belongs to abnormal status. $m(\{N, A\})$ represents the observation results of current feature by current sensor and cannot decide reliability of current status belongs to normal or abnormal status. Then calculated $m(N)$, $m(A)$, $m(\{N, A\})$ for each $ANN_i$, select one of the maximum state for the final results.

## 4 Experiment and Result

In order to evaluate the performance of our approach, a series of experiments on KDD CUP 1999 dataset were conducted. In these experiments, we implemented and evaluated the proposed methods in Matlab 2010a.

The dataset contains approximately five million connection records as training data, about two million connection records as test data. In addition, it also provides 10% training subsets and the test subset. In this paper, we randomly select 18,285 records, similar to prior research [19]. Table 1 shows detailed information about the number of the data that used during the experiment.

**Table 1.** Number and distribution of training and testing dataset

| Connection type | Training dataset | Testing dataset |
|---|---|---|
| Normal | 3000 | 60,593 |
| DOS | 10000 | 29853 |
| Probe | 4107 | 4166 |
| U2R | 52 | 288 |
| R2L | 1126 | 16189 |

Features extracted from KDD Cup1999 are categorized into several groups. We use WEKA [20] to analyze the 41 features, and find that the 7, 8, 9, 11, 13, 14, 15, 16, 18, 19, 20, 21 have little influence on the result of the detection. So we will delete the above 12 characteristics. The above features are deleted from the feature data, and the remaining features are divided into three groups:

(1) Feature subset1 ($FS_1$): including TCP connection characteristics of the basic characteristics of data and content (1, 2, 3, 4, 5, 6, 10, 12, 17, 22).
(2) Feature subset2 ($FS_2$): including time-based features (23, 24, 25, 26, 27, 28, 29, 30, 31).
(3) Feature subset3 ($FS_3$): including host-based network traffic statistical characteristics (32, 33, 34, 35, 36, 37, 38, 39, 40, 41).
(4) $All = FS_1 + FS_2 + FS_3$

Then, the above feature subsets can be applied in $ANN_i$ training and testing experiments. The following measurements are proposed to evaluate the performance of the proposed intrusion detection approach: Precision, Recall and F-Measure which are defined as:

$$precision = \frac{TP}{TP + FP}$$

$$recall = \frac{TP}{TP + FN}$$

$$F - Measure = \frac{2 * precision * recall}{precision + recall}$$

Here, we define several parameters, respectively, as follows:

- TP: the actual class of the test instance is abnormal connection and the classifier correctly predicts the class as abnormal connection (abnormal connection itself);
- FN: the actual class of the test instance is abnormal connection but the classifier incorrectly predicts the class as normal connection (abnormal connection itself);
- FP: the actual class of the test instance is normal connection but the classifier incorrectly predicts the class as abnormal connection (normal connection itself);

In our experiment, the number of the input layer node is 9 or 10. The number of hidden node is determined by empirical formula $n = (a + b)^{\frac{1}{2}} + \alpha, 1 < \alpha < 10$, where $a$ is the number of input nodes, $b$ is the number of output nodes. The input and hidden nodes use the sigmoid transfer function and the output nodes use the linear transfer function. The Mean Square Error (MSE) in the training step is 0.001. The learning rate is set at 0.01, and a momentum factor of 0.9 is applied. The crossover probability of genetic algorithm is set as 0.7,

**Table 2.** Performance with different feaure sets of GABP (normal)

| Feature set | $FS_1$ | $FS_2$ | $FS_3$ | All |
|---|---|---|---|---|
| Precision | 0.834 | 0.703 | 0.789 | 0.859 |
| Recall | 0.936 | 0.968 | 0.972 | 0.976 |
| F-Measure | 0.882 | 0.815 | 0.871 | 0.914 |

**Table 3.** Performance with different feaure sets of GABP (PROBE)

| Feature set | $FS_1$ | $FS_2$ | $FS_3$ | All |
|---|---|---|---|---|
| Precision | 0.811 | 0.924 | 0.740 | 0.933 |
| Recall | 0.475 | 0.333 | 0.817 | 0.954 |
| F-Measure | 0.596 | 0.490 | 0.777 | 0.944 |

**Table 4.** Performance with different feaure sets of GABP (DOS)

| Feature set | $FS_1$ | $FS_2$ | $FS_3$ | All |
|---|---|---|---|---|
| Precision | 0.984 | 0.985 | 0.992 | 0.998 |
| Recall | 0,996 | 0.97 | 0.977 | 0.999 |
| F-Measure | 0.991 | 0.977 | 0.994 | 0.999 |

**Table 5.** Performance with different feaure sets of GABP (U2R)

| Feature set | $FS_1$ | $FS_2$ | $FS_3$ | All |
|---|---|---|---|---|
| Precision | 0.726 | 0.765 | 0.733 | 0.939 |
| Recall | 0.914 | 0.591 | 0.794 | 0.927 |
| F-Measure | 0.809 | 0.667 | 0.983 | 0.933 |

the mutation probability is 0.05, the evolution of the Genetic Algorithm (GA) algebra is 500. It is shown from Tables 2, 3, 4, 5 and 6 that the performance of GABP classifiers which using all features are similar to respectively using the $FS_1$, $FS_2$, $FS_3$ in terms of DOS and normal. But to PROBE, U2R and R2L, using all features have a higher Precision, Recall and F-Measure. That's to say, choosing multiple valuable properties will get better detection performance in the detection of low frequency attacks. Thus, the GABP-DS method can effectively perform intrusion detection in terms of detection precision, training time and detection stability.

For training time, as it is illustrated in Table 7, the GABP classifier which using all features has more training time than using a separate feature set. So applying the D-S evidence theory combined with GABP can make full use of all characteristics at the same time, also can effectively reduce the training time.

**Table 6.** Performance with different feaure sets of GABP (R2L)

| Feature set | $FS_1$ | $FS_2$ | $FS_3$ | All |
|---|---|---|---|---|
| Precision | 0.936 | 0.05 | 0.331 | 0.842 |
| Recall | 0.328 | 0.001 | 0.056 | 0.4 |
| F-Measure | 0.485 | 0.002 | 0.096 | 0.542 |

**Table 7.** Training time with different feaure sets of GABP

| Feature set | $FS_1$ | $FS_2$ | $FS_3$ | All |
|---|---|---|---|---|
| Train-time(s) | 637 | 26 | 32 | 1086 |

**Table 8.** Performance of GABP-DS

| Type | Normal | PROBE | DOS | U2R | R2L |
|---|---|---|---|---|---|
| Precision | 0.907 | 0.942 | 0.999 | 0.941 | 0.891 |
| Recall | 0.986 | 0.973 | 0.996 | 0.948 | 0.625 |
| F-Measure | 0.945 | 0.957 | 0.997 | 0.944 | 0.735 |
| Train-time(s) | | 680 | | | |

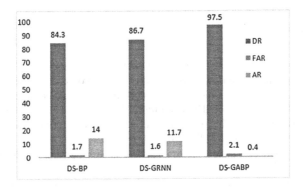

**Fig. 2.** Performance of comparison with [21]

The fusion results of intrusion evidence using DS-GABP method is given in Table 8. When compared to GABP method, the performance of DS-GABP method is improved significantly. Especially for low-frequent attacks such as U2R and R2L,our model can get higher detection precision, recall and stronger detection stability,and reduce the train time at the same time.

As shown in Fig. 2, when comparison with [21], the DS-GABP method has a higher detection rate (DR) and Lower levels of the unknown rate (AR). However, in contrast, the False Alarm Rate (FAR) is slightly higher than the other two methods, up 0.4% and 0.5%, respectively. The reason for this phenomenon may be due to different samples or choose to select different characteristics. However, this is just speculation, more rigorous rational theoretical analysis and experimental should be done in the future work.

## 5  Conclusion

Detecting new and evolution attacks is one of the challenges in the field of IDS. In recent years, more and more researches have applied Artificial Neural Networks (ANNs), especially back-propagation (BP) neural network,to improve the performance of intrusion detection systems (IDS). This paper has investigated a new approach for the network intrusion detection, which based on GABP and D-S theory to solve the problem and help IDS to achieve higher detection rate, less false positive rate and stronger stability. Simulation results have verified that the GABP-DS is an effective method for network intrusion detection. It can not only achieve higher detection rate, less false positive rate and stronger stability but also reduce the train time.

**Acknowledgment.** This work is partially supported by the Fundamental Research Funds for the Central Universities under Grants No. 2014MS99 and National Natural Science Foundation of China under Grants No. 61302105.

## References

1. de Silva, S.L., dos Santos, F., Mancilha, D.: Detecting attack signatures in the real network traffic with ANNIDA. Expert Syst. Appl. **34**(4), 2326–2333 (2008)
2. Manikopoulos, C., Papavassiliou, S.: Network intrusion and fault detection: a statistical anomaly approach. IEEE Commun. Mag. **40**(10), 76–82 (2002)
3. Shah, B., Trivedi, B.: Artificial neural network based intrusion detection system: a survey. Int. J. Comput. Appl. **39**(6), 13–18 (2012)
4. Beghdad, R.: Critical study of neural networks in detecting intrusions. Comput. Secur. **27**(5), 168–175 (2008)
5. Wei, Z., Hao-yu, W., Xu, Z.: Intrusive detection systems design based on BP neural network. In: IEEE International Symposium on Distributed Computing and Applications to Business Engineering and Science (DCABES), pp. 462–465 (2010)
6. Mukkamala, S., Janoski, G., Sung, A.: Intrusion detection: support vector machines and neural networks. In: IEEE International Joint Conference on Neural Networks (ANNIE), pp. 1702–1707 (2002)
7. Pachghare, K., Kulkarni, P., Nikam, M.: Intrusion detection system using self organizing maps. In: IEEE International Conference on Intelligent Agent & Multi-Agent Systems, pp. 1–5 (2009)
8. Gao, M., Tian, J.: Network intrusion detection method based on improved simulated annealing neural network. In: IEEE International Conference on Measuring Technology and Mechatronics Automation, vol. 3, pp. 261–264 (2009)
9. Horeis, T. Intrusion detection with neural networks-combination of self-organizing maps and radial basis function networks for human expert integration. In: Computational Intelligence Society Student Research Grants (2003)

10. Mafra, M., Moll, V., da Silva Fraga, J.: Octopus-IIDS: An anomaly based intelligent intrusion detection system. In: IEEE Symposium on Computers and Communications, pp. 405–410 (IEEE)
11. Chen, Y., Abraham, A., Yang, B.: Hybrid flexible neural tree based intrusion detection systems. Int. J. Intell. Syst. **22**(4), 337–352 (2007)
12. Guangjun, S., Jialin, Z., Zhenlong, S.: The research of dynamic change learning rate strategy in BP neural network and application in network intrusion detection. In: International Conference on Innovative Computing Information and Control, p. 513 (2008)
13. Wang, G., Hao, J., Ma, J.: A new approach to intrusion detection using artificial neural networks and fuzzy clustering. expert syst. appl. **37**(9), 6225–6232 (2010)
14. Montana, J., Davis, L.: Training feedforward neural networks using genetic algorithms. IJCAI **89**, 762–767 (1989)
15. Prasad, S., Babu, V., Rao, B.: An intrusion detection system architecture based on neural networks and genetic algorithms. Int. J. Comput. Sci. Manage. Res. **2**, 1344–1361 (2013)
16. Lin, L., Xie, X., Zhong, S.: A multiple classification method based on the DS evidence theory. In: Proceedings of the 9th International Symposium on Linear Drives for Industry Applications, pp. 587–596 (2014)
17. Hu, W., Li, J., Gao, Q.: Intrusion detection engine based on Dempster-Shafer's theory of evidence. In: International Conference on Communications, Circuits and Systems Proceedings, pp. 3, pp. 1627–1631 (2006)
18. Liu, Y., Wang, X., Liu, K.: Network anomaly detection system with optimized DS evidence theory. The Sci. World J. **2014**, 13 (2014)
19. Beghdad, R.: Critical study of neural networks in detecting intrusions. Comput. Secur. **27**(5), 168–175 (2008)
20. Weka. Weka Program (2011). www.cs.waikato.ac.nz/ml/weka
21. Yuan, Y., Shang, S., Li, L.: Network intrusion detection using DS evidence combination with generalized regression neural network. J. Comput. Inf. Syst. **7**(5), 1802–1809 (2011)

# A Secure Lightweight Texture Encryption Scheme

Alireza Jolfaei[1(✉)], Xin-Wen Wu[1], and Vallipuram Muthukkumarasamy[1]

School of Information and Communication Technology,
Griffith University, Gold Coast, QLD 4222, Australia
alireza.jolfaei@griffithuni.edu.au,
{x.wu,v.muthu}@griffith.edu.au

**Abstract.** Due to the widespread application of augmented and virtual environments, the research into 3D content protection is fundamentally important. To maintain confidentiality, encryption of 3D content, including the 3D objects and texture images, is essential. In this paper, a novel texture encryption scheme is proposed which complements the existing 3D object encryption methods. The proposed method encrypts texture images by bit masking and a permutation procedure using the Salsa20/12 stream cipher. The method is lightweight and satisfies the security requirement. It also prevents the partial disclosure of the encrypted 3D surface geometry by protecting the texture patterns from being partially leaked. The scheme has a better speed-security profile than the full encryption and the selective (4 most significant bit-plane) encryption by 128-bit AES. The encryption schemes are implemented and tested with 500 sample texture images. The experimental results show that the scheme has a better encryption performance compared to the full/selective encryption by 128-bit AES.

**Keywords:** Texture image · 3D object · Encryption · Salsa Dance · Permutation · Lightweightedness · Security

## 1 Introduction

Virtual reality and augmented reality are about to become explosive growth markets. Over the past decade, a substantial investment and a wide range of exciting prototypes have been made from the tech heavyweights such as Microsoft and Google. It is anticipated that the market for virtual reality and augmented reality will reach \$1.06 billion by 2018 at a Compound Annual Growth Rate (CAGR) of 15.18 % from 2013 to 2018 [1]. The growing applicability of 3D content and its potential revenue suggest the necessity for protecting such assets. The privacy-sensitive content in 3D environments, such as Second Life, are in risk of being recorded or monitored by malicious entities [2]. This allows manufacturing and selling real (counterfeit) objects, which is a great loss for their owner. A solution to this problem is encryption. Since the 1970s, a large number of encryption schemes have been proposed, some of which have been standardized and adopted

© Springer International Publishing Switzerland 2016
F. Huang and A. Sugimoto (Eds.): PSIVT 2015 Workshops, LNCS 9555, pp. 344–356, 2016.
DOI: 10.1007/978-3-319-30285-0_28

worldwide, such as Data Encryption Standard (DES) [3] and Advanced Encryption Standard (AES) [4]. However, the problem of 3D content encryption is beyond the simple application of established and well-known encryption algorithms. This is primarily due to the constraints imposed by the data structure and the application requirements, such as content usability, format compliance, real-time performance, complexity, and the security level. To address these concerns, several attempts have been made to develop robust encryption schemes for 3D content [5–9]. However, all these efforts are mainly focused on the encryption of 3D models rather than texture images.

Texture images are fundamental drawing primitives that add realism to computer graphics by improving surface details. Notionally, a texture image is a 2D image that is wrapped onto the geometry of a 3D model, to give the illusion of a specified pattern to the complex object [10]. Texture images contain intelligible information due to the strong correlation among adjacent elements. As each element is assigned to a particular vertex, texture patterns provide strong cues to the surface orientation, curvature and 3D surface geometry. Therefore, there is a strong correlation between the geodesic distance between pairs of points on the surface and the distance between corresponding pairs of points in the texture image [11]. This relationship provides a lot of information about the 3D geometry. Also, texture leakage may lead to a disclosure of the 3D surface geometry. It is therefore necessary to confuse this relationship by encrypting the texture image.

Texture encryption is a subclass of image encryption in which maintaining the real-time rendering performance, and preventing the partial disclosure of the 3D surface geometry by the texture pattern, are principally important in addition to providing confidentiality for texture images. These requirements may not be an issue in many image or video applications, but they are vital for most 3D applications. To meet these requirements, it is more important to obfuscate the coarse pattern rather than the detail of the texture image. This can reduce the capability of a competent adversary to reconstruct 3D objects exploiting the texture images. Also, it is necessary to keep encryption complexity as low as possible to save resources, such as computation, memory and bandwidth. One potential solution to the problem of texture encryption is in the use of a lightweight encryption scheme with a high level of security, tailored for maintaining the real-time performances. Using this idea, this paper proposes a novel texture encryption scheme that satisfies the need for both lightweightedness and security. The proposed cipher uses Salsa20/12 [12] as its core encryption primitive. Salsa20 is one of the finalists of the eSTREAM project [13] and is constructed by a simple and scalable design, which is appropriate for software implementations. Although Salsa20 has not received its deserved attention compared to AES, it has good potential for being used in multimedia applications, in which high-speed encryption is required. It is shown that in comparison with full encryption methods using the 128-bit AES, the proposed texture encryption method provides comparable level of security but with much faster performance. Also, compared to selective encryption methods [14], in which only a subset of the input bitstream is encrypted using the 128-bit AES, the proposed texture encryption method is much faster and more secure because it protects the entire input bitstream. Furthermore, it is shown that Salsa Dance conceals the shape and boundaries of underlying 3D objects, while the full and selective encryption using AES cannot protect such information.

This is the first paper that proposes a technical solution for the confidentiality problem of texture images. Although many image encryption methods have been proposed in the literature, they are not designed primarily for addressing the technical requirements of 3D applications. In this paper, the proposed encryption scheme is compared with AES, because AES is currently the main industrial encryption standard used in many multimedia applications. AES is a well-studied cipher and no practical attack has been found against it to date. In addition, AES is fast and on a Core 2 architecture, for example, runs around 12 cycles/byte for long streams. This speed is quite fast compared to other multimedia operations such as compression (For instance, Lempel-Zev and ZLIB Compressions). However, it is shown that AES cannot sufficiently address the confidentiality requirements of texture images, and therefore texture images encrypted by AES may leak crucial information about the protected 3D models. It is also shown that in comparison with AES, the proposed encryption scheme not only maintains the confidentiality of texture images but also maintains the security of protected 3D models from surface reconstruction attacks.

The remainder of this paper is organised as follows. Section 2 describes the encryption and decryption procedures. In Sect. 3, the performance of the proposed cipher is evaluated. Section 4 evaluates the security of the cipher from the data level and the semantic level. Finally, Sect. 5 concludes that the proposed texture encryption method is secure, relatively lightweight and prevents the partial disclosure of the protected 3D surface geometry by the texture pattern.

## 2  Proposed Texture Encryption Scheme

In a true color (24-bit) representation, 94.125 % of the total information is stored in the upper nibbles (4 bit-planes) of the texture image. This suggests employing a strict strategy to encrypt the upper nibbles and a lenient scheme for the encryption of lower nibbles. This approach improves the encryption performance and reduces the memory usage. The proposed scheme encrypts the upper nibble-image using a fast stream cipher, that is, Salsa20/12 [12], and scrambles the bit stream of the lower nibble-image by a zigzag pattern permutation. This mechanism is consistent with the movement performed in the (Latin American) Salsa dance. We therefore call our encryption mechanism 'Salsa Dance'.

To elaborate the steps of the encryption algorithm, denote by $P$ the plain-image, $N$ the nibble-image, and $C$ the cipher-image. In a 24-bit true color representation, each plain-image, nibble-image or cipher-image is represented by three $M \times N$ matrices, namely, $R$, $G$, and $B$ color layers. In any color layer of RGB, for any $x$ ($1 \leqslant x \leqslant M$), and $y$ ($1 \leqslant y \leqslant N$), let $p(x, y)$, $n(x, y)$

and $c(x,y)$, be the entry value at the position $(x,y)$ of the plain-image, nibble-image and cipher-image, respectively. $p(x,y)$ and $c(x,y) \in \{0,1,\cdots,255\}$, and $n(x,y) \in \{0,1,\cdots,15\}$.

The encryption procedure is described as follows, for one color layer of a 24-bit texture image. The encryption procedure is the same for the other color layers. Firstly, the plain-image is divided into two nibble-images, which are $N_1$ and $N_2$, by splitting every entry into upper and lower nibbles. For any $x$ $(1 \leqslant x \leqslant M)$ and $y$ $(1 \leqslant y \leqslant N)$, $n_1(x,y)$ and $n_2(x,y)$ are defined as follows:

$$n_1(x,y) = p(x,y) \bmod 2^4, \tag{1}$$

$$n_2(x,y) = (p(x,y) - n_1(x,y)) \cdot 2^{-4}. \tag{2}$$

In the upper nibble-image encryption, the binary stream of the upper-nibble images with size $M \times 4N$ is masked with a binary stream of the same size generated by the Salsa20/12 stream cipher. This procedure not only protects the coarse shape (major information) of the texture images from being leaked, but also prevents the disclosure of the 3D surface geometry. In the lower nibble-image encryption, the lower nibble-image is first extended to a bit-plane image with size $M \times 4N$, which is constructed by expanding every column of the lower nibble-image into 4 bit-plane columns. The bit-plane image then undergoes a bit-level zigzag pattern permutation process Perm($\cdot$). Displacement of the bit locations not only annihilates the high correlation among the nibbles but also increases the security level of the encrypted texture images. This process is as follows:

Assume that the entries of the bit-plane image are scanned in a raster order and they are enumerated by positive integers. Let $R$ denote the matrix of the entry (bit) locations, that is,

$$R = \begin{bmatrix} 0 & M & \cdots & 4MN-M \\ 1 & M+1 & \cdots & 4MN-M+1 \\ \vdots & \vdots & \vdots & \vdots \\ M-1 & 2M-1 & \cdots & 4MN-1 \end{bmatrix}. \tag{3}$$

An additional binary sequence of length $\lceil \log_2(4MN) \rceil$ with value $s$ is iterated by Salsa20/12. Then, mod $(s,MN)$ is used to select an entry in the bit-plane image, which determines the starting point for the zigzag-pattern permutation of the entries. To clarify further, Fig. 1 shows a zigzag path for the scanning of entries in a bit-plane image with size $3 \times 4$. In Fig. 1a, if mod $(s,12) = 7$, then the entry scanning commences from the 7-th entry, and stops at the 9-th entry which is previous to the initial one, that is 7. During the scanning process, bits encountered in the path are arranged sequentially, column by column in the same matrix. On completion of the permutation process, not only is every bit dislocated (diffusion), but also nibble values are modified (confusion) within the bit-plane image. For mod $(s,12) = 7$, the permutation result of the test bit-plane image is depicted in Fig. 1b. Following the permutation process, the encrypted lower nibble-image with size $M \times N$ is reconstructed by combining

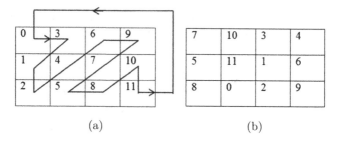

(a)                          (b)

**Fig. 1.** (a) A zigzag path to scramble bits of a bit-plane image, (b) Permutation result of the bit-plane image for mod $(s, 12) = 7$.

every 4 consecutive columns of the scrambled bit-plane image. Finally, the cipher-image is constructed by the radix $2^4$ combination of the encrypted upper and lower nibble-images.

In summary, the whole encryption process $E\left(\cdot\right)$ is as follows:

$$P = 2^4 \cdot N_2 + N_1,  \tag{4}$$

$$C = E\left(P\right) = 2^4 \cdot E_2\left(N_2\right) + E_1\left(N_1\right),  \tag{5}$$

where

$$E_2\left(N_2\right) = \text{Salsa20/12}\left(N_2\right),  \tag{6}$$

$$E_1\left(N_1\right) = \text{Perm}\left(N_1\right).  \tag{7}$$

$P$, $N_1$, $N_2$, and $C$ denote the plain-image, lower nibble-image, upper nibble-image and the cipher-image, respectively. In decryption, the cipher-image is divided into lower and upper nibble-images. The upper nibble-image is decrypted by the same key stream used in encryption, and the lower nibble-image is decrypted by the inverse permutation procedure. Note that in 24-bit texture images there is a strong correlation among different color layers of the image. Therefore, encryption of different color layers using the same key may reveal the underlying pattern. To address this issue, Salsa20/12 has a 64-bit nonce which changes after each color layer encryption. This ensures that whenever the same message is encrypted twice, the ciphertext is always different. If the same nonce and key are used to encrypt two different plaintexts, then the keystream can be cancelled out by masking the two different ciphertexts together.

## 3   Performance Analysis

To evaluate the performance of the proposed cipher, we implemented: (i) the full encryption by 128-bit AES, (ii) selective encryption of the 4 most significant bit-planes using 128-bit AES, and (iii) Salsa Dance, on a machine with Intel Core 2 2.4 GHz processor and 4 GB of installed memory. In this paper, the ECB mode of AES algorithm has been chosen to encrypt the texture images. AES supports several modes of operation, among which ECB allows parallelised

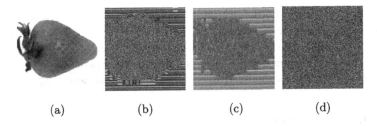

(a)                 (b)                 (c)                 (d)

**Fig. 2.** Encryption results of a sample texture image: (a) Original image, (b) encrypted image using full AES, (c) encrypted image using selective AES, (d) encrypted image using Salsa Dance.

**Table 1.** Comparison of the relative CPU time

| Encryption schemes | Relative CPU time |
| --- | --- |
| Selective AES | 2.47 |
| Full AES | 4.95 |
| Proposed (Salsa Dance) | 1.00 |

encryption/decryption and achieves better performance with trivial sequential message scheduling [15]. It is also suitable for applications that require random read/write to encrypted data. We tested the encryption performance using 500 sample texture images from CGTextures [16]. Figure 2 shows one test texture image with its corresponding encryption results. It is observed that Salsa Dance dissipates the correlation among the entries of the texture image while the full and selective encryption using AES cannot annihilate the coarse pattern of the texture image.

In the proposed encryption method, 24-bit texture images with size $MN$ (that is, 24 $MN$ bits in total) are encrypted by a pseudorandom binary sequence with size $12MN + 3\lceil \log_2 (4MN) \rceil$. In other words, the proposed cipher encrypts the input data by generating a pseudorandom sequence with the size of almost 50 % of the data. This means that compared to conventional full encryption methods, the proposed method reduces the computational cost to approximately half. This reduction in the computational cost can therefore save computational power, storage space, processing time, and transmission bandwidth; and, therefore, it would allow more processes to be executed in parallel.

Compared to the 10 rounds 128-bit AES, Salsa20/12 is considerably faster. On a Core 2 architecture, for example, Salsa20/12 runs at 2.54 cycles/byte for long streams, while the fastest speed reported for 128-AES is 12.59 cycles/byte [17]. This implies that Salsa20/12 is almost 5 times faster than the 10 rounds 128-bit AES. Therefore, Salsa20 provides a much better speed-security profile than AES. To evaluate the encryption speed of the proposed cipher, numerous encryption timing tests were performed. In addition, to have an accurate benchmark result, each timing test was executed 10 times and the average time was recorded. The results of timing tests demonstrated that the 4 bit-planes selective encryption methods have speed overheads of 247 % on average compared to Salsa Dance. Also, the full AES schemes have 495 % speed overheads compared to Salsa Dance. Table 1 compares the execution time of the encryption methods. Hence, the experimental results indicate that Salsa Dance has a better encryption performance than the full and selective encryption using AES.

## 4    Security Analysis

From the data level point of view, the security of encryption, including the upper nibble method and the lower nibble method, relies on the security of the encryption primitive, that is, Salsa20/12. To the best of the authors' knowledge, the best cryptanalysis breaks 8 out of 20 rounds of Salsa20 to recover the 256-bit secret key in $2^{251}$ operations, using $2^{31}$ keystream pairs [18]. Also, it is conjectured that Salsa20 and AES reach security with about the same number of rounds [12]. This means that the upper nibble encryption method offers a high confidentiality level. In addition, the lower nibble encryption method, that is, the permutation procedure, is secure as well, because the pseudorandom key stream controlling the permutation is generated by Salsa20/12. The generated key stream is different even for the same color layer encrypted at different sessions. This makes the permutation scheme robust to known/chosen plaintext attacks. Hence, the only attack model applicable to the permutation method is the ciphertext-only attack [19], in which the attacker can only access the lower nibble-image of the cipher-image and attempts to recover the lower nibble-image of the original image by trying all possible permutations ($4MN$ possible arrangements in each color layer). This attack becomes cumbersome and even impractical by increasing the input size $MN$ (This increases the data complexity of the attack).

However, from the semantic level point of view, encrypted texture images may contain redundant information which may be employed to not only retrieve the original texture images but also to reconstruct 3D objects. To evaluate the security of encryption to redundancy based attacks, several measurements were performed, including a correlation analysis, a key sensitivity analysis, and an edge detection analysis. Each of these measurements is described in detail in the following subsections.

### 4.1    Correlation Analysis

In the texture images, each pixel is highly correlated with its adjacent pixels. Therefore, the adversary may study the correlation among the pixels to determine a meaningful pattern inside the encrypted texture image. An ideal encryption algorithm should completely dissipate such relationship and produce cipher-images with no correlation in the adjacent pixels. A correlation of a pixel with its neighbouring pixel is then given by a 2-tuple $(x_i, y_i)$ where $y_i$ is the adjacent pixel of $x_i$. The following equation is used to study the correlation between two adjacent pixels in horizontal, vertical and diagonal orientations.

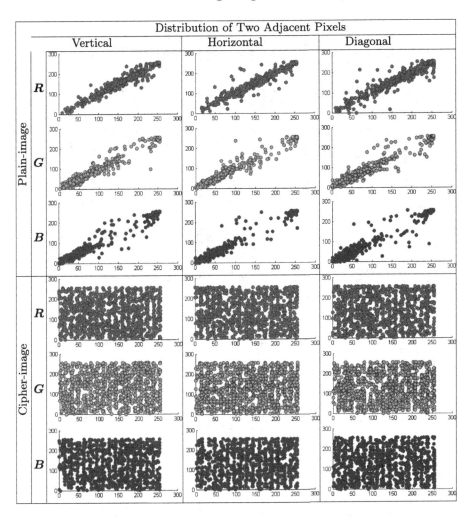

**Fig. 3.** Correlation analysis and distribution of two adjacent pixels in the plain-image and cipher-image.

$$corr_{(x,y)} = \frac{1}{n-1} \sum_{i=0}^{n} \left( \frac{x_i - \overline{x_i}}{\sigma_x} \right) \left( \frac{y_i - \overline{y_i}}{\sigma_y} \right), \tag{8}$$

where, $x$ and $y$ are intensity values of two neighbouring pixels in the image, $n$ represents the total number of 2-tuples $(x_i, y_i)$, and $\sigma_x$ and $\sigma_y$ represent the local standard deviation, respectively. To test the impact of encryption by Salsa Dance on the correlation among the adjacent pixels, we performed several correlation tests. Figure 3 shows the correlation distribution of two adjacent pixels in the plain-image shown in Fig. 2a and its corresponding cipher-image. It is observed that neighbouring pixels in the plain-image are highly correlated, while the neighbouring pixels in the encrypted image are almost uncorrelated.

**Table 2.** Correlation coefficients of two adjacent pixels in plain-image and cipher-image

| File name | Size | Channel | Plain-image | | | Cipher-image | | | | | | | | |
|---|---|---|---|---|---|---|---|---|---|---|---|---|---|---|
| | | | | | | Selective AES | | | Full AES | | | Proposed (Salsa Dance) | | |
| | | | Vertical | Horizontal | Diagonal | Vertical | Horizontal | Diagonal | Vertical | Horizontal | Diagonal | Vertical | Horizontal | Diagonal |
| Fruit 0056 | 2800 × 2656 | R | 0.9879 | 0.9882 | 0.9741 | 0.0542 | 0.0279 | 0.0541 | 0.0138 | 0.0179 | 0.0078 | 0.0164 | 0.0280 | 0.0756 |
| | | G | 0.9875 | 0.9868 | 0.9771 | 0.0122 | 0.0726 | 0.0564 | 0.0133 | 0.0317 | 0.0360 | 0.0267 | 0.0910 | 0.0032 |
| | | B | 0.9818 | 0.9856 | 0.9748 | 0.0134 | 0.0455 | 0.0042 | 0.0332 | 0.0006 | 0.0170 | 0.0306 | 0.0191 | 0.0402 |
| Buildings 0004 | 5000 × 3464 | R | 0.9863 | 0.9874 | 0.9777 | 0.0133 | 0.1278 | 0.0126 | 0.0238 | 0.0126 | 0.0041 | 0.0287 | 0.0493 | 0.0059 |
| | | G | 0.9866 | 0.9876 | 0.9764 | 0.0687 | 0.0957 | 0.0065 | 0.0018 | 0.0216 | 0.0311 | 0.0393 | 0.0217 | 0.0278 |
| | | B | 0.9866 | 0.9846 | 0.9732 | 0.0076 | 0.0693 | 0.0180 | 0.0085 | 0.0323 | 0.0058 | 0.0216 | 0.0226 | 0.0175 |
| Buildings Industrial 0088 | 1600 × 1024 | R | 0.9359 | 0.9325 | 0.8701 | 0.0953 | 0.1019 | 0.0538 | 0.0286 | 0.0360 | 0.0527 | 0.0297 | 0.0114 | 0.0204 |
| | | G | 0.9394 | 0.9374 | 0.8793 | 0.0321 | 0.1480 | 0.0303 | 0.0185 | 0.0235 | 0.0134 | 0.0267 | 0.0090 | 0.0212 |
| | | B | 0.9309 | 0.9259 | 0.8650 | 0.0175 | 0.1222 | 0.0054 | 0.0151 | 0.0517 | 0.0077 | 0.0015 | 0.0338 | 0.0099 |
| Bones 0009 | 936 × 1024 | R | 0.9793 | 0.9706 | 0.9521 | 0.0129 | 0.0159 | 0.0061 | 0.0159 | 0.0445 | 0.0409 | 0.0118 | 0.0321 | 0.0114 |
| | | G | 0.9739 | 0.9657 | 0.9521 | 0.0509 | 0.0442 | 0.0553 | 0.0344 | 0.0030 | 0.0190 | 0.0232 | 0.0229 | 0.0247 |
| | | B | 0.9747 | 0.9665 | 0.9487 | 0.0256 | 0.0128 | 0.0167 | 0.0064 | 0.0017 | 0.0400 | 0.0082 | 0.0188 | 0.0535 |
| Bones 0008 | 1192 × 1600 | R | 0.9753 | 0.9666 | 0.9435 | 0.0107 | 0.0211 | 0.0045 | 0.0075 | 0.0071 | 0.0121 | 0.0334 | 0.0008 | 0.0529 |
| | | G | 0.9788 | 0.9644 | 0.9475 | 0.0685 | 0.0033 | 0.0217 | 0.0514 | 0.0349 | 0.0573 | 0.0145 | 0.0182 | 0.0606 |
| | | B | 0.9753 | 0.9592 | 0.9564 | 0.0147 | 0.0358 | 0.0205 | 0.0082 | 0.0109 | 0.0139 | 0.0706 | 0.0445 | 0.0162 |
| Gobos 0125 | 3000 × 2000 | R | 0.8258 | 0.9066 | 0.8298 | 0.0688 | 0.3088 | 0.0624 | 0.0586 | 0.3155 | 0.0270 | 0.0061 | 0.0118 | 0.0223 |
| | | G | 0.8640 | 0.8892 | 0.8207 | 0.0483 | 0.2777 | 0.0468 | 0.0507 | 0.2483 | 0.0289 | 0.0157 | 0.0455 | 0.0210 |
| | | B | 0.8741 | 0.9140 | 0.8467 | 0.0069 | 0.2933 | 0.0143 | 0.0241 | 0.2480 | 0.0138 | 0.0011 | 0.0314 | 0.0618 |
| Gobos 0122 | 1600 × 1184 | R | 0.8638 | 0.9034 | 0.8177 | 0.0700 | 0.2376 | 0.0457 | 0.0189 | 0.2532 | 0.0336 | 0.0078 | 0.0192 | 0.0066 |
| | | G | 0.8534 | 0.9081 | 0.8307 | 0.0519 | 0.2654 | 0.0480 | 0.0373 | 0.2624 | 0.0043 | 0.0120 | 0.0006 | 0.0189 |
| | | B | 0.8459 | 0.9027 | 0.8327 | 0.0033 | 0.2749 | 0.0479 | 0.0097 | 0.2187 | 0.0002 | 0.0133 | 0.0743 | 0.0455 |
| BookSide 0027 | 1232 × 3000 | R | 0.9547 | 0.9992 | 0.9624 | 0.0504 | 0.4226 | 0.0038 | 0.0075 | 0.0552 | 0.0015 | 0.0049 | 0.0173 | 0.0056 |
| | | G | 0.9063 | 0.9985 | 0.9752 | 0.0084 | 0.4775 | 0.0560 | 0.0114 | 0.0755 | 0.0246 | 0.0257 | 0.0378 | 0.0620 |
| | | B | 0.9633 | 0.9983 | 0.9026 | 0.0012 | 0.4500 | 0.0371 | 0.0881 | 0.0667 | 0.0110 | 0.0417 | 0.0071 | 0.0054 |
| BookSide 0031 | 1600 × 648 | R | 0.9703 | 0.9981 | 0.9547 | 0.0330 | 0.4261 | 0.0185 | 0.0042 | 0.0563 | 0.0481 | 0.0723 | 0.0424 | 0.0069 |
| | | G | 0.9682 | 0.9960 | 0.9547 | 0.0026 | 0.4881 | 0.0041 | 0.0068 | 0.0789 | 0.0009 | 0.0045 | 0.0042 | 0.0250 |
| | | B | 0.9535 | 0.9981 | 0.9375 | 0.0248 | 0.4829 | 0.0530 | 0.0140 | 0.0247 | 0.0145 | 0.0198 | 0.0596 | 0.0309 |
| Windows Shutters 0114 | 5184 × 3456 | R | 0.8373 | 0.9898 | 0.8334 | 0.0383 | 0.5307 | 0.0013 | 0.0229 | 0.1393 | 0.0238 | 0.0536 | 0.0335 | 0.0086 |
| | | G | 0.8639 | 0.9848 | 0.8359 | 0.0262 | 0.4681 | 0.0430 | 0.0490 | 0.0704 | 0.0180 | 0.0057 | 0.0024 | 0.0193 |
| | | B | 0.8394 | 0.9843 | 0.8152 | 0.0019 | 0.4662 | 0.0243 | 0.0077 | 0.1228 | 0.0528 | 0.0649 | 0.0179 | 0.0296 |
| Windows Shutters 0096 | 1600 × 1048 | R | 0.8730 | 0.9866 | 0.8526 | 0.0087 | 0.5528 | 0.0158 | 0.0029 | 0.1292 | 0.0138 | 0.0249 | 0.0131 | 0.0485 |
| | | G | 0.8363 | 0.9839 | 0.8419 | 0.0065 | 0.5483 | 0.0068 | 0.0832 | 0.0783 | 0.0401 | 0.0232 | 0.0069 | 0.0198 |
| | | B | 0.8377 | 0.9832 | 0.8261 | 0.0371 | 0.4541 | 0.0102 | 0.0217 | 0.0516 | 0.0503 | 0.0233 | 0.0331 | 0.0299 |

Table 2 shows the results for correlation coefficients of the ciphers under study. The numerical results indicate that the correlation coefficients of plain-images are far apart from cipher-images. Also, results show that the selective/full AES and Salsa Dance efficiently dissipate the correlation among pixels within each color layer. Furthermore, we computed the 2D correlation coefficients between every two color layers of the encrypted images. Table 3 shows the correlation coefficients between different color layers of the cipher-images produced by the AES encryption and Salsa dance. It is observed that Salsa Dance can reduce the strong correlation between the color layers much better than the encryption using 128-bit AES. Hence, the results of the correlation analysis indicate that compared to the full and selective encryption using 128-bit AES, Salsa Dance has a better encryption performance and is more robust to redundancy based attacks.

### 4.2   Key Sensitivity Analysis

It is possible for an adversary to induce modifications in the secret key via tampering or fault injection [20]. This helps the adversary to observe the redundancy under different encryption keys and deduce a relationship between the used keys. To resist such kinds of analyses, a texture image encryption scheme should be sensitive to changes to the secret key. In other words, a change in a single bit of the secret key should produce a completely different cipher-image. The more the visual data is sensitive toward the secret key, the higher would be the amount of data randomness. To test the key sensitivity of the proposed algorithm, a number of texture images were encrypted using the selective/full AES and Salsa Dance with an original secret key ($K = 0$, $IV = 0$) and a slightly modified secret key ($K' = 1$, $IV = 0$). Numerical results show that the proposed technique is highly sensitive toward the small alterations of the secret key, that is, a different cipher-image is produced when the secret key is slightly changed. For comparison purposes, we used the PSNR measure. The higher the PSNR, the closer the images are. Table 4 provides the PSNR values of the encrypted images for the test image shown in Fig. 2a. It is observed that given the test image shown in Fig. 2a, encryption by slightly different secret keys creates different cipher-images by the selective/full AES and Salsa Dance. However, Table 4 shows that compared to the encryption by selective/full AES, Salsa Dance produces more dissimilar cipher-images with only 1-bit of change in the secret key. This indicates the high sensitivity of the proposed method to changes of the key, which makes the analysis of Salsa Dance even harder for the adversary in respect to finding any relationship between the used keys.

### 4.3   Edge Detection Analysis

From the semantic point of view, the coarse pattern of the visual data (that is, the shape information) carries more information than the details. Disclosure of the shape information not only may help a competent adversary in retrieving the texture image but also may facilitate the reconstruction of underlying

**Table 3.** 2D correlation coefficients between the RGB color layers of the cipher-images

| Encryption schemes | Selective AES | Full AES | Proposed (Salsa Dance) |
|---|---|---|---|
| Between R and G | 0.3639 | 0.3237 | 0.0016 |
| Between R and B | 0.3484 | 0.3041 | 0.0050 |
| Between G and B | 0.3834 | 0.3041 | 0.0018 |

**Table 4.** Comparison of the PSNR values

| Encryption schemes | Selective AES | Full AES | Proposed (Salsa Dance) |
|---|---|---|---|
| Between the original and encrypted image with original key | 6.0403dB | 6.0345dB | 6.0839dB |
| Between the original and encrypted image with 1-bit different key | 6.2709dB | 6.1846dB | 6.0821dB |
| Between the encrypted images using the original and modified keys | 8.5122dB | 8.3964dB | 7.7680dB |

3D objects. Therefore, the adversary would attempt to identify and locate the boundaries of the protected object within the encrypted texture images. The object boundaries, as well as sharp variations in surface structure, are typically manifested by sharp changes in pixel intensities. However, the randomness of encrypted images makes the edge detection hard. To this end, the adversary may use nonlinear operations, such as median filtering, to reduce the noise while maintaining the edges. He/she may then employ gradient and Laplacian operators for the edge-detection. This information is essential for the correct reconstruction of 3D surfaces [21]. To evaluate the resistance of the proposed texture encryption scheme to this kind of analysis, we examined the cipher-images using different edge detection methods [22], including the Canny method. Figure 4 shows the results of the edge detection analysis on the cipher-images of Fig. 2 using the Canny method. It is observed that Salsa Dance discloses no information about the shape and boundaries of the underlying 3D object, while the full and selective encryption using AES cannot resist the edge detection analysis.

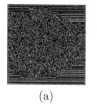
(a)

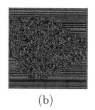
(b)

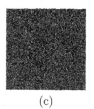
(c)

**Fig. 4.** Results of edge detection by median and Canny filtering on the encrypted image of (a) full AES, (b) selective AES, and (c) Salsa Dance.

# 5 Conclusion

To overcome the limitations of the current techniques in addressing the confidentiality requirement of texture images, this paper proposes a technical solution that meets the constraints imposed by the structure of texture images, such as large data volume, and the application requirements, such as real-time performance, complexity, and the security level. The proposed cipher encrypts texture images by bit masking and a permutation procedure using the Salsa20/12 stream cipher. Compared to the full/selective encryption using 128-bit AES, the proposed cipher is relatively lightweight and provides a better encryption performance. Salsa Dance also considerably dissipates the correlation among the entries of the texture image. This annihilates the coarse pattern of the plain-image and prohibits the data leakage from texture images. The key sensitivity analysis showed that even a single bit change in the secret key will result in an entirely different cipher-image. Thus, the original texture image cannot be recovered even though there is a slight difference between the encryption and decryption keys. Furthermore, Salsa Dance conceals the shape and boundaries of the underlying 3D object, while the full and selective encryption using AES is not secure from the edge detection analysis. Therefore, texture encryption by Salsa Dance not only maintains the confidentiality of texture images but also maintains the security of protected 3D models from surface reconstruction attacks using the data provided by the texture images. Due to space limitation, some preliminary results related to the security of Salsa Dance have been presented in this paper. Detailed results backed by theory and cryptanalysis will be presented in the extended version of this paper.

# References

1. Markets and Markets: Augmented reality & virtual reality market by technology types, sensors, components, applications & by geography, global forecast and analysis to 2013–2018 (2014)
2. Chen, Y., Kim, T.-K., Cipolla, R.: Inferring 3D shapes and deformations from single views. In: Daniilidis, K., Maragos, P., Paragios, N. (eds.) Computer Vision – ECCV 2010. LNCS, vol. 6313, pp. 300–313. Springer, Heidelberg (2010)
3. United States National Institute of Standards and Technology (NIST): Announcing the Data Encryption Standard (DES). Federal Information Processing Standards, Publication 46–3 (1999)
4. United States National Institute of Standards and Technology (NIST): Announcing the Advanced Encryption Standard (AES). Federal Information Processing Standards, Publication 197 (2001)
5. Koller, D., Turitzin, M., Levoy, M., Tarini, M., Croccia, G., Cignoni, P.: Protected interactive 3D graphics via remote rendering. ACM Trans. Graph. 23(3), 695–703 (2004)
6. Phelps, N.: Method for exchanging a 3D view between a first and a second user. US patent 2008/0022408 A1 (2008)
7. Éluard, M., Maetz, Y., Dorr, G.: Geometry-preserving encryption for 3D meshes. In: Actes de COmpression et REprsentation des Signaux Audiovisuels, pp. 7–12 (2013)

8. Éluard, M., Maetz, Y., Lelievre, S.: Method and device for 3D object protection by transformation of its points, US Patent 8869292 (2014)

9. Jolfaei, A., Wu, X.-W., Muthukkumarasamy, V.: A 3D object encryption scheme which maintains dimensional and spatial stability. IEEE Trans. Info. Forens. Secur. **10**(2), 409–422 (2015)

10. Garcia, E., Dugelay, J.-L.: Texture-based watermarking of 3D video objects. IEEE Trans. Cir. Syst. Video Tech. **13**(8), 853–866 (2003)

11. Zigelman, G., Kimmel, R., Kiryati, N.: Texture mapping using surface flattening via multidimensional scaling. IEEE Trans. Vis. Comput. Graph. **8**, 198–207 (2002)

12. Bernstein, D.J.: Salsa20 security. (2005). http://cr.yp.to/snuffle/security.pdf

13. Babbage, S., Canniere, C.D., Canteaut, A., Cid, C., Gilbert, H., Johansson, T., Parker, M., Preneel, B., Rijmen, V., Robshaw, M.: The eSTREAM portfolio, eSTREAM, ECRYPT Stream Cipher project (2008)

14. Podesser, M., Schmidt, H.P., Uhl, A.: Selective bitplane encryption for secure transmission of image data in mobile environments. In: The 5th Nordic Signal Processing Symposium, pp. 1–6 (2002)

15. Bogdanov, A., Lauridsen, M.M., Tischhauser, E.: Comb to pipeline: Fast software encryption revisited. In: Leander, G. (ed.) FSE 2015. LNCS, vol. 9054, pp. 150–171. Springer, Heidelberg (2015)

16. http://www.cgtextures.com/, September 2015

17. Bernstein, D.J.: Which phase-3 eSTREAM ciphers provide the best software speeds (2008). http://cr.yp.to/streamciphers/phase3speed-20080331.pdf

18. Aumasson, J.-P., Fischer, S., Khazaei, S., Meier, W., Rechberger, C.: New features of latin dances: analysis of Salsa, Chacha, and Rumba. In: Nyberg, K. (ed.) FSE 2008. LNCS, vol. 5086, pp. 470–488. Springer, Heidelberg (2008)

19. Stinson, D.: Cryptography: Theory and Practice. CRC Press, Boca Raton (2006)

20. Bellare, M., Cash, D.: Pseudorandom functions and permutations provably secure against related-key attacks. In: Rabin, T. (ed.) CRYPTO 2010. LNCS, vol. 6223, pp. 666–684. Springer, Heidelberg (2010)

21. Saxena, A., Sun, M., Ng, A.Y.: Make3D: learning 3D scene structure from a single still image. IEEE Trans. Pattern Anal. Mach. Intell. **31**(5), 824–840 (2009)

22. Parker, J.R.: Algorithms for Image Processing and Computer Vision, 2nd edn. Wiley, New York (2010)

# Event Analogy Based Privacy Preservation in Visual Surveillance

Wei Qi Yan[1,2(✉)] and Feng Liu[2]

[1] Auckland University of Technology, Auckland, New Zealand
weiqi.yan@aut.ac.nz
[2] Chinese Academy of Sciences, Beijing, China

**Abstract.** Privacy preservation as a thorny problem in surveillance has been arisen because of its relevance to human right, however it has not been completely solved yet today. In this paper, we investigate this existing problem and expect to get ride of those intuitive methods such as pixelization, blurring or mosaicking on human face regions through object tracking. We detail privacy preservation at event level and thereafter choose suitable events represented by motion pictures in virtual reality to replace those events of surveillance in real reality. The advantage of taking use of this approach is to leverage the utility and privacy of surveillance events. The outcome will not affect visual effects and surveillance security much however it is able to achieve the objectives of privacy preservation.

**Keywords:** Event analogy · Surveillance event · Privacy preservation · Real reality · Virtual reality

## 1 Introduction

Surveillance has been accepted as an effective way to protect our community especially after the September 11 attacks. Nowadays digital cameras are being networked at every corner of a metropolitan and monitoring our actions and behaviours in real time. This has made our ordinary lives too secure to have our own privacy. At anytime from anywhere we feel that a hidden eye is looking at the earth dwellers. Therefore, the emerging problem is how to protect our privacy especially in the era when it has high risk that surveillance data is abusively utilized.

The traditional ways to preserve privacy in visual surveillance are mosaicking, pixelization or scrambling human face regions [18] shown as Fig. 1. But apparently this is not enough since from the acquired clothes, behaviours or gait, even from a contour, silhouette or blob, several dots, we still are able to discern who this person is as shown in Fig. 2. Even if a face is not clearly seen from very far distance, such as a basketball or soccer player, we are still able to infer who the person is. Particularly from those processed images, photos or cartoon motion pictures, the similarity is still existential. This rolls out the motivation

© Springer International Publishing Switzerland 2016
F. Huang and A. Sugimoto (Eds.): PSIVT 2015 Workshops, LNCS 9555, pp. 357–368, 2016.
DOI: 10.1007/978-3-319-30285-0_29

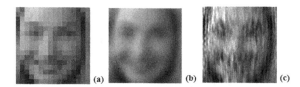

**Fig. 1.** Privacy preservation using: (a) mosaicking (b) Gaussian blurring (c) scrambling

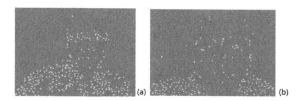

**Fig. 2.** An example of a perceptual human face in dots

that the best solution of privacy preservation is to completely remove the privacy information from the video frames. However the commitment will undoubtedly diminish the utility and visibility of surveillance videos.

Utility refers to video usage for various purposes. When an incident happens, we need track back and search for the persons and objects related to the incident. While the conventional ways of privacy protection such as image mosaicking, blurring and pixelization easily provoke the content damaging, if the surveillance video frames have been completely obstructed, that is equivalent to acclaim that this video has to be casted aside. Thus, the situation requires us find a way to leverage the utility, visibility and privacy of surveillance videos. Our goal of this paper is to resolve this tough problem.

In this paper, our idea is to replace a surveillance event in real reality using a resembling event presented by motion pictures in virtual reality, the two picture sequences carry similar semantic events however the privacy information in one of them has gone. Therefore, we segment our surveillance events into several states. For each state, we find the pictures which could be modelled and replaced by motion pictures. Aftermaths we still could understand the event content, however we have thrown away the annoying human privacy information.

We justify our idea as an effective way for preserving privacy. For an instance, in a typically monitored corridor, we use a walking Mickey Mouse to substitute a man for displaying purpose who is walking through from left to right or from right to left, the man may perambulate to pass this site, thereafter the mouse will be viewed in the correspondingly sluggish way such as entering, walking, standing, existing, alarming etc. If it indeed has an incident, namely the alarming state is activated, only the authorized security staff has the privilege to review the surveillance events, but normally this analogy based replacement for the purpose of privacy preservation is much reasonable for catering to unauthorized viewers.

The challenge of this research work is to seek the matching between two events presented by two groups of motion pictures using analogy. We therefore call this analogy at event level as event analogy. We have successfully developed a concept of video analogy based on image analogy [5,20], however event analogy gets out of the box at physical or object level and aims at semantics. In this paper, we will select suitable events in virtual reality to replace the surveillance events in real reality for the sake of privacy preservation.

Our idea was inspired by a movie pertained to bus surveillance. In the 1994 Hollywood movie "The Speed", a young cop must prevent a bomb exploding aboard a city bus by keeping its speed above 50 mph. The LAPD interrupted the live broadcasting connected to the on-board bus video surveillance system for the public and replayed a pre-recorded cassette video only having a few frames shown as Fig. 3, however the rival could not make out this minor change timely so that the bus passengers have ample time to alight and get rescued successfully. This story implies that event analogy could save human lives including privacy in very exigent time.

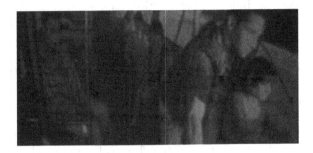

**Fig. 3.** The replaced picture of 1994 movie: The Speed

Event is defined as a semantic unit which bridges the gap between semantic world and cyberspace [19]. An event has the basic components such as who(object), when(time stamp), where(site), what(description), and why(reasoning). As a fundamental structure, discrete events could be stored in computers as logs for the purposes of analysis and archiving.

Our goal in this paper is to leverage the utility and security of surveillance videos so as to preserve human privacy in surveillance. The rest of this paper is organized as follow. The related work will be introduced in Sect. 2, our contributions will be presented in Sect. 3, Sect. 4 will provide the experimental results and analysis, conclusion and future work will be addressed in Sect. 5.

## 2   Related Work

Analogy as said is "The art of the metaphor" [8,9]. Metaphor is a rhetoric which has often been applied to our oral and writing presentations. It's believable that we always explain a profound and abstractive theory using an akin easy-understanding story to feed our audience. The concept analogy was from cognition science [8] and have been digitalized as a reasoning or inference method in Artificial Intelligence(AI).

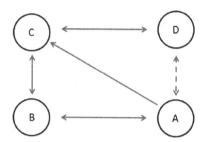

**Fig. 4.** The mechanism of event analogy

Figure 4 shows the fundamental relationships amongst participants of an analogy. Suppose we have similar events $A$ and $B$ as our start point, $C$ and $B$ are similar but $C$ has its outperforming attribute such as with visibility without privacy. We envision transferring the unique attribute of $C$ to the event $D$, where $D$ resembles from $A$. Therefore, we see the analogy operation as a kind of fundamental reasoning based on the facts at hand to get the unknown knowledge. The intuitive explanation of an analogy is that if event $A$ could remove its privacy, then the privacy in event $B$ also could be removed. However the visibility of two events is still preserved. In a nutshell, we denote an analogy mathematically as: if $A \Leftrightarrow B$, $B \propto C$ and $A \propto D$, then $C \Leftrightarrow D$.

Analogy has been applied to curves and geometry objects initially [6,7]. The concept image analogy is a metaphor between two digital images [5] which has been applied to render a gray scale image using another color image. Albeit we do not exactly affirm the colors of the photo, we still could map the colors of this scene of today to the gray scale image using color transferring technologies based on texture synthesis [1,3].

Video analogy was derived from image analogy [4,19]. Assume we have two similar videos at hand, we therefore create a relationship and bridge the gap between two videos. Thus, we could transfer some attributes of one video to the other which is lack of this attribute such as color, motion, contrast, etc. Based on the merit of video analogy, the media aesthetics could be transferred to amateur's craft work which has the longing to be forged as an art masterpiece, etc [10–14].

In multimedia analysis, the concept event analogy is created at semantic level which differs from object analogy, e.g. image analogy and video analogy both are manipulated at physical level. A semantic event could be presented in both real reality and visual reality, therefore a semantic event could have or have not privacy. Thereafter through attribute transferring of event analogy, we have the opportunity to add or remove privacy information from one event by analogizing the other event meanwhile keeping the semantic meaning. In this paper, we will work for the theory and implementation of event analogy.

Privacy of surveillance video [17] has been modelled by the parameters 'who', 'when' and 'where' due to the applications of events. The detected pedestrian face and head in a surveillance video usually are obscured by encrypting for the purpose of privacy preservation [18]. A privacy preservation method adopts data transformation involving the use of selective obfuscation and global operations to provide robust privacy [15].

Conventional privacy protection methods directly consider explicit privacy losing (such as facial information) and ignore other implicit channels. A privacy model [16] consolidates the identity leakage through both implicit and explicit channels. The computational model using a combination of quantisation and blurring also provides the best tradeoff between privacy and utility.

Unlike those existing work, the focus of this paper is on preserving privacy existing in surveillance events. The novelty of this paper is that it is the first time to create the concept event analogy in which we adopt the event in virtual reality to replace the surveillance event happened in real reality while conveying the same semantics. The replacement will remove privacy information in a surveillance event so as to leverage the utility and security of surveillance events.

## 3   Our Contributions

To the best of our knowledge, privacy preservation using event analogy is a brand-new approach. However, the main challenge is how to find the resembling event presented by motion pictures to replace the surveillance events in real reality. Therefore the first problem is how to optimize the motion pictures and remove the privacy information to match the surveillance video in real reality. Thus time line from the surveillance video has to be followed, correspondingly the motion pictures should be put on the time line flexibly, this is similar to achieve the results of synthesizing a multimedia message [21].

### 3.1   Surveillance Events

In surveillance environment, usually cameras will be deployed at a fixed site, motion pictures captured by a camera will show the events having steady patterns though the cameras have the functionalities such as panning, tilting and zooming. After thoroughly observed these events, we find in indoor environment a walker usually toddles from left to right or from right to left within a framed route such as corridor or walkway. While in outdoor environment the cameras are usually operating from morning to night under all weather conditions, the objects encapsulate moving vehicles and pedestrians restrained in their own track rigorously.

In this paper, we capture surveillance events using Finite State Machine (FSM) shown in Fig. 5. In the scenarios of walking through a corridor,

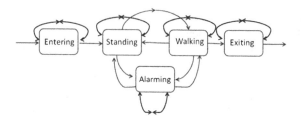

**Fig. 5.** Surveillance event capturing using FSM

we set 5 states including alarming. Our surveillance event capturing is based on the state changes [19]. The pseudo code for FSM based event capturing is shown as below algorithm.

*Algorithm. FSM based surveillance event capturing*

```
Input: Image sequence
Output: Captured events: e = {W(Walking), A(Alarming), S(Standing)}
Line 1. Initialization: set flags f := 0 and t := 0;
Line 2. while (True){
Line 3. Detect state: t;
Line 4. If (t == 0) && (f == 0) return;
Line 5. If (t == W|A|S) && (f == 0) {f := t;}
Line 6. If (t == W|A|S) && (f == t) return;
Line 7. If (t == W|A|S) && (f != t) {e := f; f := t; output: e;}
Line 8. If (t == 0) && (f != 0 ) {e := f; f := t; output: e;}
Line 9. }
```

In the event of detection of surveillance events, state changes are usually detected based on local intensity histogram $(N_x^l, N_y^l, N_t^l)$ from spatial-temporal viewpoint, motion changes $\triangle I = (I_x, I_y, I_t) = (\frac{\partial I}{\partial x}, \frac{\partial I}{\partial y}, \frac{\partial I}{\partial t})$ will be normalized so as to feed the distance calculator based on $\chi^2$-divergence [23–25],

$$d(H_1, H_2) = \sqrt{\frac{1}{3L} \sum_{l,i,k} \frac{|h_{1k}^l(i) - h_{2k}^l(i)|^2}{h_{1k}^l(i) + h_{2k}^l(i)}} \tag{1}$$

where an action is represented by a set of nine one-dimensional histograms: $\{h_x^1, h_y^1, h_t^1, h_x^2, h_y^2, h_t^2, h_x^3, h_y^3, h_t^3\}$, $B$ is the histogram bin numbers of each video frame, $L$ is total frame number of an image sequence.

From our observations, we find that surveillance events calculated by Eq. (1) have their own patterns owning the merits such as discriminative and covering. We therefore have the opportunity to seek the typical motion pictures with a specific pattern, such as the cartoon GIF pictures which could be played iteratively and are suitable for presenting these surveillance events. Therefore, adjustment of these motion pictures is entailed to match the necessity of surveillance events.

## 3.2    Event Analogy

Event analogy is derived from cognition sciences in AI which has been digitalized in curve analogy of geometry [6], image analogy in computer graphics [5] and video analogy in multimedia analysis and synthesis [20]. In visual surveillance, event analogy is reckoned to be applied to privacy preservation in Fig. 4. Hence we define event analogy as the below Definition 1.

**Definition 1 (Event Analogy).**  *If* $\forall\, e \in \{e_A, e_B, e_C, e_D\}$, $e_A \Leftrightarrow e_B$, $e_A \propto e_D$, $e_B \propto e_C$, *then* $e_C \Leftrightarrow e_D$.

Following Definition 1, the probability which event $e_D$ may happen could be predicted by using Dynamic Bayesian Network (DBN) as a directed graph in Eq. (2),

$$p(e_D) = p(e_D|e_C) \cdot p(e_D|e_A) = p(e_C|e_B) \cdot p(e_B)p(e_C|e_A) \cdot p(e_A) \cdot p(e_D|e_A) \quad (2)$$

Since $p(e_B) = 1$, $p(e_A) = 1$, thus,

$$p(e_D) = p(e_C|e_B) \cdot p(e_C|e_A) \cdot p(e_D|e_A) \quad (3)$$

This simplification reveals that whether the event $e_D$ will be happened or not, it is mostly decided by the relationship between $e_C$ and $e_B$, $e_D$ and $e_A$ since $e_A$ and $e_B$ have been given as the known condition.

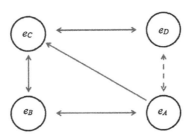

**Fig. 6.** Event analogy

Equation (3) reflects the ground truth of event analogy. We presume that event $e_C$ has the state set $S_C = \{s_C^1, s_C^2, \cdots, s_C^n\} \subseteq S_B$ meanwhile for the event $e_A$ and event $e_D$ we have the relationship $S_D = \{s_D^1, s_D^2, \cdots, s_D^n\} \subseteq S_A$.

In this paper, we anticipate the overlapping could correctly reflect visibility of the event however its privacy will be removed. Figure 7 is an example of event analogy, we used the video provided in the surveillance data set: CAVIAR to demonstrate a walker passing through a shop in a mall. The state diagram with video frames depicts the typical events of a walker when passing through a monitored corridor: *entering, standing, passing, alarming,* and *exiting.* The states could be switched between each other due to changes of the guard condition and actions. In order to analogize the event and remove the privacy information, we find an animal cartoon from online GIF picture store which has the similar state changes. Namely, we detect the state changes, we find cartoon pictures presenting the similar states, finally the privacy region on the surveillance video frames has been overlapped and the privacy of the event has been removed (Fig. 6).

State diagram in Fig. 7 illustrates the connections between the events, states and surveillance video frames. This example epulides how we could leverage human privacy in a surveillance event using event analogy.

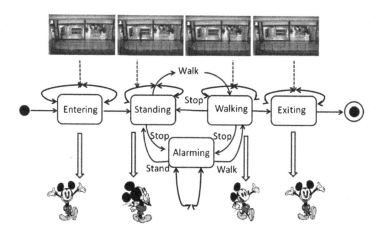

**Fig. 7.** A state diagram and video frames show an instance of event analogy for privacy preservation in visual surveillance

## 4    Analysis

We implement our privacy preservation of surveillance events using event analogy. Shown as Figs. 8, 10, 11 and 12, we detect moving object, track the object and find the state changes of an event in a surveillance scenario. In Figs. 8 and 11, we detect the 'entering', 'standing still' and 'exit' states of the surveillance event, therefore we could cover the moving object using cartoon characters.

In Fig. 9, we find the cartoon pictures from public web sites with swinging the right-hand, swinging the left-hand and standing still in virtual reality, the six cartoons represent the states of two opposite walking directions: left to right and right to left through the corridor, the actions of cartoon characters could represent the states of surveillance events in real reality.

The differences of surveillance videos before and after moving object overlapping by cartoon characters are measured by histogram based image entropy. In another word, the differences between them are approaching to the privacy difference.

Entering                    Standing Still                    Exit

**Fig. 8.** Object tracking from left to right with standing state

**Fig. 9.** The Donald Duck's actions in virtual reality for representing surveillance events in reality reality

**Fig. 10.** Overlapping moving object from left to right

**Fig. 11.** Moving object tracking from right to left

**Fig. 12.** Overlapping moving object from right to left

From the two results shown as Figs. 13 and 14, we see that the videos overlapped by cartoon characters have much entropy than that of original ones. This is due to the image region overlapped by cartoon characters has much information than the original. However after the overlapping operation, the privacy intensity of the surveillance video has gone. The viewers could not find any privacy information related to the moving object from the processed videos. Thus it achieves our goal of privacy preservation of this paper.

Therefore, we have the opportunity to choose the best event presented by motion pictures in virtual reality. Using event analogy, we could find the

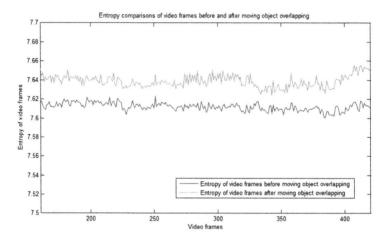

**Fig. 13.** Entropy comparisons of surveillance video 1 before and after moving object overlapping by cartoon characters

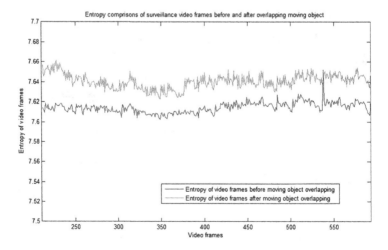

**Fig. 14.** Entropy comparisons of surveillance video 2 before and after moving object overlapping by cartoon characters

pertinent cartoon pictures in virtual reality to replace the events in real reality. Therefore we have to acquire event first, then preserve privacy, this is much different from those privacy preservation directly using blurring, mosaicking and blurring, thus the technical advance requirement is very high.

## 5  Conclusion

In this paper, we leverage utility and privacy of surveillance videos using event analogy. Our core idea is to overlap human privacy region of surveillance motion pictures using selected animated cartoons so as to preserve human privacy. It's the first time that we are in use of this concept: event analogy to seek the similarity in virtual reality and real reality of surveillance events. In future, we will embark on privacy preservation of visual surveillance and seek the best form in presenting surveillance events.

## References

1. Reinhard, E., Ashikhmin, M., Gooch, B., Shirley, P.: Color transfer between images. IEEE Comput. Graph. Appl. **21**(5), 34–41 (2001)
2. Klette, R.: Concise Computer Vision. Springer, London (2014)
3. Welsh, T., Ashikhmin, M., Mueller, K.: Transferring color to greyscale images. In: Computer graphics and interactive techniques, pp. 277–280, USA (2002)
4. Yan, W., Kankanhalli, M.: Colorizing infrared home videos. In: IEEE ICME 2003, pp. 97–100, USA (2003)
5. Hertzmann, A., Jacobs, C., Oliver, N., Curless, B., Salesin, D.: Image analogies. In: Computer graphics and interactive techniques, pp. 327–340, USA (2001)
6. Evans, T.: A program for the solution of geometric analogy intelligence test questions. In: Semantic Information Processing. MIT Press, New York (1968)
7. Hertzmann, A., Oliver, N., Curless, B., Seitz, S.: Curve analogies. In: Eurographics workshop on Rendering, Italy (2002)
8. Winston, P.: Learning and reasoning by analogy. Commun. ACM **23**(12), 689–703 (1980)
9. Gentner, D.: Structure mapping: a theoretical framework for analogy. Cogn. Sci. **7**(2), 155–170 (1983)
10. Dorai, C., Venkatesh, S.: Bridging the semantic gap with computational media aesthetics. IEEE MultiMed. **10**(2), 15–17 (2003)
11. William, T., Touis, R., Egon, C.: Example-based super-resolution. IEEE Comput. Graph. Appl. **22**, 56–65 (2002)
12. Adams, B., Dorai, C., Venkatesh, S.: Automated film rhythm extraction for scene analysis. In: Proceedings of the IEEE ICME 2001, pp. 1192–1195, Japan (2001)
13. Adams, B., Venkatesh, S., Dorai, C.: Finding the beat: an analysis of the rhythmic elements of motion pictures. Int. J. Image Graph. **2**(2), 215–245 (2002)
14. Herbert, Z.: Sight, Sound, Motion: Applied Media Aesthetics. Wadsworth Publishing Company, Belmont (1999)
15. Saini, M., Atrey, P., Mehrotra, S.: Adaptive transformation for robust privacy protection in video surveillance. Int. J. Adv. Multimed. **2012**, 4 (2012)
16. Saini, M., Atrey, P., Mehrotra, S., Kankanhalli, M.: Privacy aware publication of surveillance video. Int. J. Trust Manage. Comput. Commun. **1**(1), 23–51 (2012)

17. Saini, M., Atrey, P., Mehrotra, S., Emmanuel, S., Kankanhalli, M.: Privacy modeling for video data publication. In: IEEE ICME 2010, Singapore (2010)
18. Zhang, P., Thomas, T., Emmanuel, S., Kankanhalli, M.: Privacy preserving video surveillance using pedestrian tracking mechanism. In: ACM Workshop on Multimedia in Forensics, Security and Intelligence (2010)
19. Yan, W., Kieran, D., Rafatirad, S., Jain, R.: A comprehensive study of visual event computing. Multimed. Tools Appl. **55**(3), 443–481 (2011)
20. Yan, W., Kankanhalli, M.: Analogies based video editing. Multimed. Syst. **11**(1), 3–18 (2005)
21. Yan, W., Kankanhalli, M.: Multimedia simplification for optimized MMS synthesis. ACM Trans. Multimed. Comput. Commun. Appl. **3**(1) (2007)
22. Rogez, G., Rihan, J., Orrite, C., Torr, P.: Fast human pose detection using randomized hierarchical cascades of rejectors. Int. J. Comput. Vis. **99**(1), 25–52 (2012)
23. Prest, A., Ferrari, V., Schmid, C.: Explicit modeling of human-object interactions in realistic videos. IEEE Trans. Pattern Anal. Mach. Intell. **35**(4), 835–848 (2013)
24. Zelnik-Manor, L., Irani, M.: Event-Based Video Analysis. In: IEEE CVPR (2001)
25. Zelnik-Manor, L., Irani, M.: Statistical analysis of dynamic actions. IEEE PAMI **28**(9), 1530–1535 (2006)

# Author Index

Printed in the United States
By Bookmasters